Price, 50 Cents; or $5 per dozen.

CITIZENSHIP

SOVEREIGNTY.

BY

J. S. WRIGHT,

ASSISTED BY

Prof. J. HOLMES AGNEW, D.D.,

CITIZENSHIP.—We call him a CITIZEN, who has the privilege of sharing with others in Government, deliberative or judicial: and a City [or Commonwealth] is the number [the associated body] of such, self-sufficient for life.—*Aristotle, Politics*, Book III, c. 1.

SOVEREIGNTY.—A Nation, is a State, ... a body politic, or a society of men united together to promote their mutual safety and advantage, by means of their union.

From the very design that induces a number of men to form a Society that has its common interests, and ought to act in concert, it is necessary that there should be established a public Authority, to order and direct what ought to be done by each in relation to the end of the association. This Political Authority is the *Sovereignty*, and he or they who are possessed of it are the *Sovereign*.

It is evident, from the very act of the Civil or Political Association, that each Citizen subjects himself to the Authority of the entire Body, in everything that relates to the common welfare. The Right of all over each member, therefore, essentially belongs to the Body Politic, to the State; but the exercise of that Right may be placed in different hands, according as the Society shall have ordained.

If the Body of the Nation keeps in its own hands the Empire, or the RIGHT OF COMMAND [*le Droit de commander*], it is a Popular Government, a *Democracy;* if it refers it to a certain number of Citizens, to a Senate, it establishes a Republic, an *Aristocracy;* in short, if it confides the Empire to a single person, the State becomes a *Monarchy*.—*Vattel, Law of Nations*, Book I, c. 1, § 1-3.

CHICAGO:

PUBLISHED FOR AMERICAN CITIZENS,

THE TRUE MAINTAINERS OF STATE SOVEREIGNTY.

1863.

☞ The first volume of the work or compilation, of which this publication is a compend, to be entitled

OUR FŒDERAL UNION STATE RIGHTS AND WRONGS,

will be published about 15th November. The volumes will contain 500 to 550 pages each, similar to this in type and arrangement. One is to be published each six or eight weeks, and sold in muslin binding at $2.50.

Five volumes will probably suffice for the compilation, which is designed to furnish an epitome of governmental principles, historical facts, documents (each of which will be given entire), the substance of important debates, and of influential opinions in private and published letters, tracts, and other publications, and also a short examination of other Governments, to discover the right of our Revolution, and the superior excellences, and confused but not complicated systems, of our State and Federal Governments. Every family in the land needs this information, which is now scattered through hundreds of volumes, many expensive and inaccessible, in order to enable each Citizen, and the young lad who is soon to be a Citizen, to understand his individual rights, exalted privileges, responsible duties; and also the rights and wrongs of these Sovereign States. The wonder is not that we are in civil war, but that, with our ignorance of principles, and mistakes in *theory*, our *practice* has been so nearly correct.

To the statesman and politician, the compilation, if at all a success, will be particularly valuable; bringing together for the first time documents, opinions, and principles, to which every one needs to refer more or less often The marginal notes, with the thorough index which shall be supplied, will make reference quite convenient; and until superseded by something better, it will be the American statesman's manual. In such a work some would like room to record notes and comments; and should the demand justify, an edition will be printed on superior paper, with wide margin for writing, and in strong binding. Subscribers will please intimate their wish, and should an extra edition be printed, the volumes of this edition will be received in exchange, if uninjured, the party paying the difference in price.

The terms are already low, considering the present high cost of materials and the amount of reading supplied, but it is proposed to still further reduce them. The kind patron in New York and those in Chicago, who have thus far advanced the funds for publication, will not permit delay for the lack of means. But not to encroach unnecessarily on their liberality, it is proposed to supply the five volumes for $11 paid in advance.

Remittances can be made to the subscriber, either at Chicago, or directed to *Station D*, New York City, where most of his time must necessarily be spent until the publication is finished.

J. S. WRIGHT.

☞ Copies of this pamphlet are distributed immediately upon its publication to a few leading minds of our country, irrespective of their politics, religion, or occupation. An independent, unbiassed expression of opinion, is desired from each recipient, either *pro* or *con.* Should he be decidedly favorable, he would doubtless like to aid in extending the circulation of this Compend, and a short letter to a paper or two in his city or neighborhood, or to some editor at a distance with whom he may be acquainted, calling attention to it, would be very influential. He may also be willing to write to two or three prominent persons, enclosing a copy of the accompanying prospectus; and upon being furnished with the address, we shall be happy to forward those parties a copy each of the Compend.

It is hoped the recipient will be able soon to make the examination, and that it will not be partial or prejudiced. And experience already proves the propriety of a caution to the reader, not to make up his judgment from detached parts. If he will just glance his eye over the marginal notes from beginning to end, he will have a general idea of the views, and can then better judge of the several portions. Having sent a copy of only the first 80 pages to one of the most eminent scholars of our country, an old and valued friend, he thus remarks:

. . . Your present line of labor is one that I had not thought of in connection with you, but your object is so important, and you are performing it with so much ability, that I wish you all success. . . . My studies have not been much in the line of International Law, and I have accepted the doctrine commonly received, that there is such a thing as a United States *Government.* This I understand you to deny. [Not at all. So far from it, my main object is to prove that we have the grandest, most perfect systems of *Government*, both State and *Federal*, ever instituted. My friend says in another place, "I have only had time to run over" the pages, and probably a further examination of even the first eighty pages changed his opinion, as would surely a perusal of the remainder.] Where there is Government, there must be the *Right to Command*, and the obligation to *obey*, in regard to *some things;* and that, I suppose, would constitute a Government, as no Government, except that of God, extends to all things. [Very true; and when by the usurpations of Parliament, and the violation of his oath by our King, the *Right of Command*, the Sovereignty, of George III over these Colonies was forfeited by him, we took it into the keeping of each individual Colony, each of these Peoples becoming a Sovereign State, or nation. But as these Peoples are too widely distributed, even in the smallest State, to *exercise* directly their *Right of Command*, they have made use of *Republicanism* or *Representation*, to preserve to themselves their Sovereignty, and to govern their faithful or unfaithful subjects. And in great wisdom have they joined together, and delegated the *exercise* of some important *parts* of their *Rights of Command* to certain parties which constitute the Government of the United States.] If the apparatus at Washington is simply a Federal Agency, then very much of what has been done from the first, has been usurpation. [Most certainly "the apparatus at Washington is simply a Federal Agency," for the tenth amendment to the Constitution establishes the truth beyond peradventure, that the powers are not *granted*, but "*delegated.*" A *delegate* is ever an agent, restricted to the authority delegated; and whatever has been done by an agent beyond his authority, is surely usurpation, which circumstances may or may not justify.] I should wish it settled, first, whether we have a *Government;* and then that its powers might be defined. Any thing that will throw light on these points is most desirable, and you write with so much of research, and candor, and ability, that your labor cannot fail to be useful. [It shall be the constant aim of the writer to merit the encouraging encomiums of his partial friend, and he promises indefatigable "research," sincerest "candor," and unwearying, patient industry to supply in part his deficiency in "ability," to aid in determining that "we *have* a Government," which we ought by all means to preserve, or reconstruct another similar; and we shall find abundant occasion for wishing "that its powers might be defined;" and not only "be defined," but that each department of the agency be kept strictly within its defined limits.]

It would be a great thing to have all the authorities and debates bearing on these points *fairly* brought together. It has occurred to me whether, starting as you do with the avowed intention of making out a case, you could bring everything together in such a way that it would be accepted as done fairly. You will need care on that point. [The writer is deeply sensible of the importance of this friendly caution, which will be constantly heeded; and whatever else may be said against his performance, he trusts that the merit of fairness shall at least be accorded it. The writer acknowledges "the avowed intention of making out a case," and he cannot conceive it possible for any one to study the subject as he has done, without becoming settled in his convictions; without having the "case" thoroughly established in his own mind. But it happens, that "starting . . . with the avowed intention of making out a case" against the South, proving the heresy of State Sovereignty, and that this one People of the United States were a nation, and as such indissoluble as any other nation; the examination resulted in producing the directly opposite conclusion. The writer thinks he can make the "case" clear also to the reader, and carefully endeavoring to be fair and candid, he will bring together principles of International Law, the debates of the fathers, the documents, historical facts, &c., in such a manner that the reader can adjudge the "case" for himself. If the writer is disingenuous and unfair, his work will be to him a most disgraceful failure, and he would not only merit, but surely receive, the contempt of his fellow Citizens, for daring to tamper with their momentous concerns in this their period of imminent peril. But he believes with this most competent judge, that "it would be a great thing to have all the authorities and debates bearing on these points *fairly* brought together," and that there is to be an immense and growing demand for this important reading, which is now inaccessible to the masses, being scattered through hundreds of volumes. What he does shall at all events be done "fairly."]

If I could do anything to aid you, I should be glad, but it is plain I cannot. What you do is well executed in a literary point of view [thanks to Dr. Agnew], and in research you are far in advance of me.

Do you propose a large work for the few, or something for the many? If the former, I fear you would publish at a pecuniary loss. I should be glad to take a copy. [As the reader will see by the prospectus on the cover, and in the "Explanatory" remarks, the work is designed "for the many."]

But the writer expects not commendation alone. Already has he experienced the contrary. Another sincere friend and kinsman, of good repute in the world of letters, raps him severely, and is "amazed" that

"A man not conversant with such studies, should undertake to pronounce so confidently as you do, upon such subjects, and upon all the great publicists who have written upon them.

"Strike, but hear!" The writer yields to no man in respect and veneration for the wise men of the past, who have established the principles upon which all rightful authority is instituted, based upon the Bible; those who have created the code known by the name of International Law. Yet fallibility, imperfection is stamped upon their works, as upon all things human, and other great and good men have corrected errors preceding, to be in turn corrected by equally authoritative successors. In the main, however, they have agreed upon the chief points, and every Christian Government is based upon their solid foundation.

The more one studies those standard works, the profounder will be his admiration of their genius and excellence, notwithstanding the perception of errors.

And respect and veneration generated by these studies, is intensified with sincerest filial devotion, strengthened by loftiest pride in our fathers, who came nearer than any men of modern ages to a proper comprehension of those great principles of Government, and who put them more successfully into practice, in these our State and Federal systems, than had ever before been done by man, of which any record is left to us. Yet even our wise and honored fathers were not absolutely perfect in their knowledge, and made some errors which have led their sons astray, and many of "the great publicists" have been confusing *theories* until we have been led into essential errors in *practice.* Stands it not to reason, that, if there be established principles of Government, there cannot be such fundamental differences of opinion as to the nature of our Governments, the location of the *Right of Command,* and the rights and wrongs of these States touching slavery and every other question, without one party or the other being violators of those principles? There *must be* wrong, fundamental wrong, that the gradual divergence of opinions and plans of these Christians, these Christian Peoples, in the South and in the North, these sovereign States, should have at length culminated in the most terrible of all civil wars. The writer *does* dare "to pronounce [most] confidently," that many of "the great publicists who have written" since the days of Vattel, have not followed the teachings of that "elegant" author of the Law of Nations, and of his illustrious predecessors, but have issued vagaries and contradictions that have led us entirely astray.

It requires no great amount of legal knowledge to discern, that if there be any such thing as International Law, Hooker, Grotius, Pufendorf, Montesquieu, and Vattel, are the chief founders; and if they have established any one principle, it is that Sovereignty, the *Right of Command,* is one and indivisible; and if so, it follows as a necessary consequence, that Madison was mistaken in affirming that we were "partly national and partly Federal." But it has been taken for granted that Madison was correct, and the absurdity has grown and strengthened, until very many of our best men teach the nonsense that we are subjects of two Sovereignties, State and Federal. It is "amazing" that those learned in the law should have permitted such errors of *theory* to go on for so many years; and it betokens no great perspicacity in the writer, only a little common sense and independent judgment, that he should be able to point out the inconsistency of these teachings with the established principles of International Law. Either the old or modern writers are in error, for they surely are in conflict; which is right, the writer assumes not to judge. This the reader will please constantly remember, that the writer arrogates to himself nothing of the teacher. It is not his own thoughts and views that are to be presented in his forthcoming work, but those of unquestionable authorities; and surely our lamentable circumstances justify the humblest Citizen in doing what he can to restore our beloved country to peace and reunion. May he not also expect, that in the midst of present calamities, in the perils which threaten our free institutions, his humble but earnest effort to call the attention of his fellow Citizens, the business men in particular, to old truths and teachings which will serve to lead us out of this labyrinth of confusion, will be received and examined in all fairness and candor? From a certain class, the writer expects little else than derision and contempt. Unable to meet the views and arguments he will draw from eminent, unquestionable authorities, they will endeavor by ridicule to destroy their effect, because at this time presented by a Citizen unknown to fame, and unskilled in the mysteries of legal lore. Not so with the candid, reasonable, intelligent reader. With him will the truths themselves have weight, irrespective of the medium by which they are presented, and according to the power and influence of their eminent authors.

In the "Explanatory" pages, which it is hoped will not be unread, the writer shows that his views are concurred in by those competent to judge, and he deems it proper to add, that soon after he began this examination, nearly two years ago, he wrote some newspaper articles (which however were not published, as the subject expanded beyond a reasonable size for a newspaper,) calling attention to existing errors of opinion concerning our Federal Government. Being at variance with all the books treating upon our Government he had then examined, and not liking to trust his own judgment, he took his MS. to Hon. Charles O'Conor, who very kindly heard them read, approved the views in the main, and said that as to the law, they were unquestionably correct. The leading ideas of this Compend, and of the forthcoming work, were embodied in that MS., and two years of constant study has not materially altered one of those ideas, but strengthened and confirmed them. The writer therefore feels that he may claim a hearing, even from lawyers.

Nor does the writer desire commendation merely. He will be obliged to the reader for his opinion of the plan proposed, of its desirableness, and of its execution thus far, which it will be taken for granted may be used wholly or partially in a circular with the author's name, unless requested to the contrary. Friendly suggestions and advice as to the plan, or any of the details, will be gratefully received, though the writer cannot engage to answer letters, his time being constantly occupied with the work.

Copies will not be distributed to the newspapers for ten to twenty days, within which time it is hoped individuals will be able to examine the Compend, and give their independent judgment concerning it. Purchasers, too, or other readers of copies of this small edition first issued, are respectfully solicited to give their opinions as early as practicable, directed to

J. S. WRIGHT, *Chicago.*

P. S.—The postal regulations prohibit the writing on the cover, even the name of the party addressed. The writer will therefore avail himself of this opportunity to remark that this copy is sent "with the respects," or "the regards of the author," requesting attention to the first and concluding paragraphs of the foregoing. J. S. W.

CITIZENSHIP

SOVEREIGNTY.

BY

J. S. WRIGHT,

ASSISTED BY

Prof. J. HOLMES AGNEW, D. D.,

CITIZENSHIP.—We call him a CITIZEN, who has the privilege of sharing with others in Government, deliberative or judicial: and a City [or Commonwealth] is the number [the associated body] of such, self-sufficient for life.—*Aristotle, Politics*, Book III, c. 1.

SOVEREIGNTY.—A Nation, is a State, ... a body politic, or a society of men united together to promote their mutual safety and advantage, by means of their union.

From the very design that induces a number of men to form a Society that has its common interests, and ought to act in concert, it is necessary that there should be established a public Authority, to order and direct what ought to be done by each in relation to the end of the association. This Political Authority is the *Sovereignty*, and he or they who are possessed of it are the *Sovereign*.

It is evident, from the very act of the Civil or Political Association, that each Citizen subjects himself to the Authority of the entire Body, in everything that relates to the common welfare. The Right of all over each member, therefore, essentially belongs to the Body Politic, to the State; but the exercise of that Right may be placed in different hands, according as the Society shall have ordained.

If the Body of the Nation keeps in its own hands the Empire, or the RIGHT OF COMMAND [*le Droit de commander*], it is a Popular Government, a *Democracy;* if it refers it to a certain number of Citizens, to a Senate, it establishes a Republic, an *Aristocracy;* in short, if it confides the Empire to a single person, the State becomes a *Monarchy.*—*Vattel, Law of Nations*, Book I, c. 1, § 1–3.

CHICAGO:
PUBLISHED FOR AMERICAN CITIZENS,
THE TRUE MAINTAINERS OF STATE SOVEREIGNTY.
1863.

Old Letters, Pamphlets, Books, &c.—*The attention of parties possessed of valuable documents bearing upon our political history, or those knowing where there are such, is called to the foot-note on page* 81, *and it is earnestly hoped the request will be granted.*

☞ *Parties who would like to aid in disseminating these views by giving or sending their neighbors copies of this Compend, can be supplied at* $5 *per dozen.*

If a dozen or two could be sent to each regiment, some of the leisure of the camp would be well employed in considering the views, and help to make nearly every citizen-soldier a true Federal Republican.

Orders and remittances can be sent to the subscriber, as may be most convenient, either at Chicago, or at Station D, *New York City.*

J. S. WRIGHT.

EXPLANATORY.

OVER two years ago, the writer began to examine the principles and history of our Governments. Having full confidence in Clay and Webster, he had never imagined that they and others of our great statesmen, could have committed any serious error in Governmental science, or that there could be any important point in it which they, or any of our leading statesmen, did not thoroughly comprehend. Yet a pretty careful study of the Madison Papers, and of the Federalist, with which his examination began, seemed to show that our Government was purely Federal, Madison's judgment to the contrary notwithstanding, and that bewildering errors and inconsistencies existed. The study of works in the Astor, Mercantile, and Historical Libraries of New York for two years, to be duly acknowledged in a forthcoming preface, convinced the writer that we were wide astray in *theories* as to Government, while correctly following in *practice*, the teachings of Hooker, Grotius, Vattel, &c. We are in civil war from confusion of *theories*.

Over a year since, the preparation of the accompanying Compend was begun. But the study of one point led to another, and that to another, and caused delay; for, finding his conclusions at variance with the teachings of nearly all our great men, and also those of Europe since the days of Vattel, it behooved the writer to be cautious.

The translations of the ancient classics had been somewhat studied, and such use had been made of some of their important passages by distinguished authorities, that it became necessary to refer to the originals, and thirty years' devotion to business, had almost obliterated the acquaintance of boyhood with Latin and Greek. But comparing several translations with the originals, and with the aid of the numerous lexicons of the Astor Library, the writer was enabled to discover, as he thought, that the translators had not altogether apprehended the thoughts of the writers of the free States of antiquity upon Government and history, and that with the imperfection of the English language to convey correct and definite ideas in the science of Government, particularly as contrasted with the Greek, the clear and fundamental distinctions between Free States and Monarchies, which the ancients so well understood, had not been preserved in modern translations. But being a very incompetent judge on this important subject, he applied in February last to Prof. S. F. B. Morse, who has constantly aided these labors with judicious counsel, and encouraged with affectionate interest, to recommend some competent scholar to assist in the work. Being referred to Prof. J. Holmes Agnew, D. D., a most valuable and efficient co-laborer has been obtained. Entering with equal zeal and enthusiasm into the great work of examining Governmental principles, and finding translations defective, he has kindly undertaken the important task of a new version of the extracts required in this compilation. The translations of Grotius and Pufendorf from the original Latin, are also imperfect; and the extracts for this work will be carefully revised, and be, indeed, a new translation.

Professor Agnew is so impressed with the importance of our Citizens having a correct knowledge of the teachings of the greatest, most practical of all philosophers of antiquity, that he will, at an early day, publish a new translation of Aristotle's Ethics and Politics, with notes. He intends also translations of Grotius and Pufendorf, with appropriate notes from the Republican stand-point. A more patriotic, useful labor, can hardly be performed.

The writer's obligations are immense to this accomplished scholar for his indispensable aid; and as elsewhere observed, his concurrence in the views and plan, afford strong confirmation of their probable correctness. Not only has Dr. Agnew carefully corrected the errors of style in the MS., but he has also advised in respect to the ideas themselves; and were his counsel always heeded, it might be better. But Western men have their peculiarities, both of thought and of expression; and sometimes, no doubt, there will be too much obstinacy in adhering to what is written. So that Professor Agnew is not to be held responsible for all the views, nor for blunt, unpolished expressions.

Many of the ideas in this Compend, and also in the work, will be so novel to many readers, that the writer deems it suitable also to remark, that they are almost wholly concurred in, both as to governmental principles, and as to historic facts, by Mr. Henry B. Dawson, who being in a similar line of research, we have frequently had occasion to compare notes. The chief point of difference between us is, that he considers the word "nation" should never be used in connection with the United States, each State being the only "nation;" whereas it appears to the writer, that with clear conceptions that each State is the real nation, the United States may properly be entitled a "nation" of nations.

Mr. Dawson's edition of the *Federalist* has been alluded to, and his valuable notes will be found coincident with the views herein taken, and will be followed with the publication of other debates connected with the adoption of our Constitution, most opportune, and furnishing important information, of which few have knowledge.

It will be easily discovered from this Compend that the writer is not unfriendly to slavery; and lest anti-slavery men should conceive these views to be unfair, and a base cheat in order to strengthen the institution they abhor, it is deemed proper to state, that Mr. Dawson has for years been a thorough and consistent anti-slavery man,[1] and he advocates Federalism as the true and only means to eradicate slavery. His extensive historical explorations, convinced him years ago, that we were all wrong about the *theory* of our Governments. Both of us may be entirely led astray; but from opposite stand-points, pro and anti-slavery, our examinations have led to precisely the same conclusions, with the single exception above noted.

The views taken by Mr. Dawson as to the nature of our existing Government, and which are herein also presented, *are surely to be adopted by ninety-nine hundredths in the North;* but with such unanimity as to principles, established and practised in the present Federal Union, no doubt there is to be a tremendous conflict as to their application, and the changes that must be made in the new Union, which some will wish should be consolidated instead of Federal.

---

[1] Mr. Dawson very properly desires to have it added, that he has never favored any interference by Congress in the slavery question, which would be wholly inconsistent with his understanding of the Federal nature of our Government.

In presenting these views for the consideration of the North, the natural division into East and West has not been, is not to be, disregarded. The fear is that, as the war and the adjudication of our differences with the South progress, the different characteristics, and the diverse interests of the two sections, will become more and more prominent. We in the West hope the States occupying a middle position, geographically and characteristically, will be with us wherein we are right; yet quite possible is it, that the burthen of reconstructing a Union, to which all the thirty-four States will have liberty of accession, will, on the part of the North, rest chiefly on the West. We are the most deeply interested; and with God's blessing, we shall yet have a Federal Union to which every one of these States, that is willing to live up to the "Laws of Nature and of Nature's God," can cheerfully accede.

Should the opinions herein advanced be found correct, that these Sovereign States have become possessed of common rights in their common territory, as in the Louisiana purchase, which they have never relinquished; the South, true maintainers of State rights, will not endeavor unjustly, and by force of arms, to dispossess these States, particularly the Northwest, of what is rightly theirs. Yet, should they conceive that circumstances justify them in compelling us to relinquishment, putting our trust in God, we must continue to try our powers to defend our rights.

When the party which began the war, whichever it may be, shall have become satisfied with the use of force, it is to be hoped it will propose some other means. No peace can be expected, at least not if the West can prevent it, until we know what is to become of our rights, if rights these Sovereign States have in the seceded States. If International Law entitles us in the North to free-trade, fellow-Citizenship in what has been, or now is, the common territory, the common property of these Sovereign States, we in the Northwest will in any event fight for those rights, until they are acknowledged and protected, or we are subjugated. No peace can be made until we know, either that we have no rights in the seceded States, or that they are to be safely assured to us. But an armistice would be welcomed, especially by the Northwest, that we might confer with the South, ascertain definitely our mutual rights and wrongs, and discover if either party is indisposed to do the other justice. To that issue must the question come at last, for we can surely endure this war as long as can the South, and never by force are we to be dispossessed of our rights; and, if the South began this war unnecessarily, as we believe, it is their place to propose an armistice.

When the parties, these Sovereign States, especially those of them which are most deeply concerned in the questions at issue, can listen to reason, and have a conference by their delegates, it will not be so very difficult for the South and West to agree upon an arrangement that will be satisfactory to all States which are willing to confederate on just terms, and thereby shut out all possibility of again disagreeing concerning slavery, or any similar question. The only point with the West will be, that the Negro shall not be thrust upon us. Illinois has, by its Constitution, for many years prohibited Negroes from coming into the State, and though the provision is not rigidly enforced, it has the effect to make the State undesirable to them; and we have very few, and mean to have fewer. In the midst of this present excitement, more favorable than ever to the proscribed class, in voting last summer (1862) upon a new Constitution, three distinct propositions against the admission and the rights of Negroes were separately voted upon, and were adopted by about *four votes out of five*, notwithstanding the Constitution itself was defeated. Indiana, too, excludes the Negro, and aversion to him is the prevalent sentiment of the West. The South and West will have no difficulty in agreeing about the Negro.

The West, too, are strong asserters of State rights, coinciding on this important point also with the South. The significant motto of Illinois, "State Sovereignty, National Union," unmistakably bespeaks Western sentiments on this fundamental question of Federalism. The western States and New York and Pennsylvania, are abundantly large for Commonwealths; if the little States are dissatisfied with their insignificance, let them amend their difficulties by consolidating several of them together. Try that sort of consolidation, before attempting to consolidate all these States.

Probably, this very calamity is to exhibit more strikingly than ever, the wisdom of Providence in bringing about this division into moderate-sized States, with the important divergence of sectional characteristics. The West in this juncture may be the means of preventing permanent rupture. Making a new Union with the South on fair and satisfactory terms, it is quite possible that all the States may not at once accede; but they will almost certainly do so ultimately; and the wisdom of the fathers, particularly they of the South, who so liberally promoted and desired to see the rapid expansion of the West, will become very apparent. The sons of those fathers, when an opportunity for calm reflection returns, will not seek to destroy a connection made by nature, and indispensable to both South and West.

Therefore, while this Compend, and the volumes following, are prepared for Citizens of all these thirty-four States, more confidence is felt in the views influencing the West, than the extreme East. The Citizens of the West are mainly Farmers, and the writer knows them. While he does not enjoy the extensive personal acquaintance with new-comers, which he had with the old stock some twenty years ago, when, year after year, he travelled through all these States, to make the Farmers write for their paper, the *Prairie Farmer*, and to interest them in common schools; yet he knows the leaven of the good old stock has leavened the entire mass.

A kind Providence has wonderfully spared those valued friends to labor now in a more important field; nothing less than to save our imperilled institutions. Here and there is a bright name left only to treasuring memory; but the writer could by hundreds mention names whose joint will is yet omnipotent in the great Northwest; and their will is to be almost unanimous in the coming struggle. Some of them, misled by Madison's error, that we were "partly National" as well as "partly Federal," have imagined they had responsibility for slavery, at least in the District of Columbia and in the Territories. They will learn it is not so; and bearing now the honored, excellent name *Republican*, they will find they are true Federal Republicans, as was Jefferson, when they understand the term. We who style ourselves *Democrats*, as we study into principles, will find we, too, are true *Jeffersonian Republicans*, Federal Republicans. The West will be almost a unit in the contest to be waged against consolidation.

As month after month the writer has patiently prosecuted his studies, his strongest incentive to perseverance has been, the remembrance of those old and valued *Prairie Farmer* friends. For them chiefly is this work prepared, and for *auld lang syne* will it be welcomed and have a candid examination. The earnest coöperators in agricultural and educational progress, who witness such glorious results from well-bestowed efforts in laying proper foundations in our first settlement, have great encouragement to labor to preserve the free institutions for which the former efforts were chiefly valuable. Our whole grand system of free Government is in jeopardy, and must be saved by the Farmers of the West. Foundations are not now to be laid, but "that foundation" of Hooker's, the Supreme Power, Sovereignty—the *Right of Command* of Vattel—which, God be praised, is in these free Peoples, these Sovereign States, needs to be understood. As we survey this wide landscape, stretching from the Lakes to the Gulf, from the Atlantic to the Pacific, "the stateliness of houses the goodliness of trees when we behold them, delighteth the eye; but that foundation which beareth up the one, that root which ministereth unto the other nourishment and life, is in the bosom of the earth concealed; and if there be at any time occasion to search into it," surely has it now arrived to these great Peoples. We must know our rights and privileges as Citizens of these free States, fellow-Citizens of this Republic of States, and our duties as liege subjects of our respective Sovereign States; we must know also the rights and wrongs of these States, to stand manfully by the one, properly to correct the other.

Let the Farmers of the West, realize the responsibility resting upon them in this day of peril. Let them study into principles, and be prepared to make their omnipotence rightfully felt through the palladium of our institutions, the ballot box. In their hands is the power to save or to destroy. What they will, their States will do; what the Western States determine to have done, the North will do; and any who like not their doings may for themselves do better.

No nobler Aristocracy, none more intelligent, more high-toned, more honorable, than the farming population of the West, exists in equal proportion elsewhere on the globe. No gathering of Caucasians has ever been made, excelling in numbers and in worth that of the West; none which exhibits more of "the image of God." They can, they will understand this science of Government. They will know their rights according to those "Laws of Nature and of Nature's God," which our fathers affirmed to be their rule, and with manly heroism, Christian trust, will they maintain their rights; they will gladly investigate to learn their wrongs, and as Christians, Christian Peoples, will they do all in their power to right their wrongs.

When the West shall have made due investigation and given utterance to its voice in favor of State rights, and of a true Federal Union to perpetuate those rights; how much longer is it probable their brother Farmers, the worthy Aristocrats of the South, will wish to wage this war? Surely will it not be long before the Farmers of the South and of the West, will find some means of reconciliation and peace.

Another word to the Farmers of the West. Citizens! appreciate your high dignity of possessing Citizenship in these free States, *fellow*-Citizenship in this Republic of States. Most painful has been the sight, that even here in the West, even among the Farmers themselves, have there been those who have dared to raise the hand of violence against the laws, against the administrators of the laws. No matter how enormous the wrong done by the Administration, either with or without the forms of law; no matter what the usurpation or tyranny committed, let not the advantage be given the tyrants, of violent resistance to authority. That is only requisite in States under Aristocratic or Monarchic sway; not in free States, where the *Right of Command* is possessed by the Citizens themselves in the aggregate. The beauty of our system is, its chief excellence consists, in the ease and quiet with which, by the periodical revolution of power to the Peoples, they change their rulers who shall have perverted their authority. For the sake of our glorious institutions in peril, for the honor of our King, Jehovah, let these Christian Citizens, these Christian Peoples, sufficiently investigate the principles of their Government, to understand the sure and proper means they possess to protect their rights and liberties. If necessary to endure these wrongs for eighteen or twenty long and weary months, for God's sake let us summon our patriotism and fortitude to the manly, heroic work. Citizens! Christian Citizens! oh, let us avail ourselves of this grandest opportunity of centuries, which the hand of Providence has accorded us, of proving the adaptation of these Peoples to self-Government; of the wisdom and excellence of this compound system of State and Federal authorities!

Especially to fellow-Citizens who style themselves Democrats, is the appeal made to ever maintain law and order. Of all men in the land, should we Democrats, as we are called, truest *Federal Republicans* as we are, those of us especially who are sons of poverty and toil, be most earnest conservators of our institutions as they are.

Much is said of the necessity of a stronger Government, and every outbreak of passion on the part of the subjects of these free States, is joyfully welcomed, nay, promoted, by the infernal schemers who would change our Heaven-sanctioned form, for one which could be turned more to foster their selfish purposes. Are the mass of these Citizens to be benefitted by any change? If we are to have a change of Government, a privileged class, a Nobility, is to be created. Who will more likely have those honors, than the harpies, the scavengers, that have been gorging themselves with the spoils? the vile cheats, who by all sorts of trickery and corruption, have basely plundered the public coffers? Will any Citizen, any sincere *Federal Republican*, whether called Democrat or Republican, do aught to further the schemes of those scoundrels, who would now like next to secure their plunder by overthrowing our Government, and introducing a Nobility, with its rights of primogeniture and entail? Will any real Democrat, or true Republican, make himself an abettor of the conspiracies of those hellish traitors, who would avail themselves of this calamitous condition of our country to overthrow the People's liberties?

These Citizens want no other form of Government; they will have no other, if they will only investigate the excellences of this Federal system, which was given by God to his favored People of old, and which that same God and our God, has led us by His providences to adopt, with improvements adapted to the advance of this Caucasian race. Talk of a stronger Government? The equal of it to protect the right, guard against wrong, the world never had. What other system could bring such armies into the field as these Federal systems of the South and of the North? And had our Administration realized the magnitude of this contest as did the Citizens, and only permitted the free volunteering of our Citizen soldiery, the first twelve months would have given us armies that ere now would have brought honorable peace, and with no conquest of the South. And only let us bide our time patiently, and we shall discover new and unappreciated excellences in Federalism, in righting the wrongs of rulers, which only such events as these could properly develop. Not unless military usurpers should dare to interfere with the just and impartial verdict of the ballot box, allowing voters of one party to return home in sufficient numbers to control the election, and refusing others, as has been charged upon them in the late contest in Connecticut, will the People be justified in rising against their tyrants. I do not say the charge is true, but I do say, that if any such infamous attempt be made, let the Citizens rise in their might, and hurl the minions from their places of power, before they shall have a chance to fasten upon freemen the chains they will have forged. When the palladium of our rights and liberties, the ballot box, is interfered with, will it be time for these Citizens to take laws and authorities into their own keeping.

INTRODUCTORY COMPEND.

§ 1. Whether of the Image of God or Beast.

Whosoever sheds man's blood, by man shall his blood be shed, for in the image of God made he man. If this Rule holds as well in shedding the blood of a *Turk* as of a *Christian*, then *that wherein man is the Image of God is* REASON. Of all Controversys those of the Pen are the most honorable: for in those of Force, there is more of the Image of the Beast, but in those of the Pen, there is more of the Image of God. In the Controversys of the Sword, there is but too often no other Reason than Force; but the Controversy of the Pen has never any Force but Reason. Of all Controversys of the Pen next those of Religion, those of Government are the most honorable and the most useful; the true end of each, tho' in a different way, being that the Will of God may be *don in Earth as it is in Heaven.* Of all Controversys of Government, those in the vindication of Popular Government are the most noble, as being that Constitution alone, from whence all that we have that is good is descended to us; which, if it had not existed, Mankind at this day had bin but a Herd of Beasts. The Prerogative of Popular Government must either be in an ill hand, or else it is a game against which there is not a card in the whole pack; for we have the Books of Moses, those of the *Greecs* and of the *Romans*, not to omit Machiavel, all for it.

Harrington, *Prerogative of Popular Government,* 1656.

Reason and Force—Pen and Sword.

Governmental controversies honorable—popular most so.

Thus wrote Harrington, in his preliminary epistle to *The Prerogative of Popular Government*, published in London, 1656. A timely suggestion for the Christian English People in the troublous period of the seventeenth century, much more so is it for us, their children, in this most peaceful era of the world; for these most prosperous of nations; for us, who, among the most enlightened, most Christian Peoples, have, in this nineteenth century, had the hardihood to desert "reason" as the arbitrator of our differences, and resort to "force;" have exhibited the folly and the wickedness of choosing that which has "more of the image of the beast," to redress our wrongs, rather than that which has "more of the image of God."

Suggestions two centuries old, still timely.

§ 2.—Our Difficulties, and their Causes.

The struggle for supremacy in the days of Harrington, was between Monarchy and Republicanism; but we, in our madness, are on both sides fighting for one and the same purpose, the maintenance of popular

South and North fighting to maintain popular rights.

§ 2. Our difficulties and their causes.

rights. The South began the war, as we shall see, having been led, by circumstances too numerous, to believe that the North were for consolidation, and for administering the Federal Government on that basis; and we in the North are fighting chiefly to sustain our Government, unjustly attacked, and to preserve our Union and our institutions as they were established by the joint wisdom of the fathers of the South and of the North.

A few ultraists in the South have, no doubt, desired disunion *per se*, and also a few abolitionists in the North; but ninety-nine hundredths of the people in each section were and are anxious to maintain our Union and our institutions on the basis of our fathers; and on both sides are they fighting for that very and sole object. The South, it is true, make their first purpose the maintenance of State rights, the fundamental principle in a Federal Republic; but they only wish to establish State rights in order to make more secure a true Federal Union. We in the North are fighting for the Union directly; the South, having clearer, more correct conceptions of the nature of our Union, and that it must exist solely on the federal basis, guarding securely against the ever-dreaded evil of consolidation, are fighting first for State rights, which we in the North would ourselves fight for as quickly as they, under like circumstances.

The war will prevent consolidation.

An inscrutable Providence, but for wise and good purposes in due time no doubt to be discovered, has permitted the little handful of fanatics in the two sections to avail themselves of wrongs done on both sides, to engender animosity and strife, and, through errors and misconceptions, to lead these brethren, bound together by so many cords of interest and affection, into civil war. Perhaps Infinite Wisdom, seeing the dangers of consolidation into which we were fast drifting, gave us war as a less evil. To teach us the nature of our Union, to make it well understood by ourselves and all nations, and to perpetuate it for all time, perhaps the GOD of battles thought it best we should fight for it; and the probabilities are, that the lesson will be deeply impressed, and never effaced.

The war *just* if necessary to prevent consolidation.

I go further. If we in the North will not adhere to the views of the fathers as to our Federal Government and its administration, the South will be justified before the nations, and the GOD of nations, in separating themselves from Peoples who deliberately and knowingly violate the principles of Union; will be justified in this war, however unjustly begun, as a means necessary to separate themselves from false, perfidious Peoples. The West, at all events, will not put herself in that situation; neither will the Eastern States, particularly New England, when they learn the importance of perpetuating the truths ever inculcated by their early fathers, and most vigorously during the last war with Great Britain.

Elementary principles of government not understood.

The currents of our difficulties, swollen into torrents and bearing us to destruction, traced to their source, will be found to spring from ignorance and misconception of the elementary principles of Government.

On the part of the North, the error is the misplacement of Sovereignty, and misapprehension of its nature and powers; on the part of the South, it is misconception of the rights of individual States, the nature of compact, and the necessity of war. § 2. Our difficulties and their causes.

Both extremes are wrong; and their advocacy by fiery zealots, and oversight of the remedies our system itself provides, have led us to civil war. The first is to be deprecated, as tending to consolidation, which is at once unnecessary, inexpedient, and dangerous; the latter, as undermining, destroying the very basis of all social fabrics, the obligation of pact and faith; and both are alike opposed to the established principles of the Law of Nations. The North errs in imagining that a sovereign State should or can be governed by any earthly power; the South, in affirming that a sovereign State is not and cannot be bound, but may annul its compact at will. Notwithstanding the apparent paradox of a bound supreme power, the study of International Jurisprudence makes it clear and right, and the magnificent system of our Republic of Nations is firmly established upon that solid foundation. Resulting wrongs.

§ 3.—The Science of Government.

At any and all times is the science of Government worthy of our most earnest consideration. But situated as are we, fighting solely for its principles, and to establish and perpetuate our priceless liberty, with its rights and institutions as bequeathed to us by a common ancestry, it behooves us thoroughly to investigate the points in dispute. We may fight on and on for years, but the period must come when we shall leave the "beast" and take to "reason." Then shall we study the Law of Nations, to learn our mutual rights and wrongs; and if Christian nations, as we profess to be; if we properly realize our duties and obligations to the God of nations, to each other, to the whole family of nations; if we duly appreciate the influence of our example, the importance of this Federal experiment to all humanity, how long will it take us to understand our duty, and do it? how long is it necessary and best to continue the war, in order to prepare us for negotiation, and for the enjoyment of the blessings of peace? Importance of understanding its principles.

The science of Government is the grandest, most ennobling, that can engage man's attention; and in practical importance is it exceeded by none. What else affects the comfort, prosperity, happiness, safety of individuals, of families, of towns, of States, of the world, equally with Government? Transcending all other sciences, even in the judgment of Deity, this alone is singled out as worthy the Infinite Father's aid to unfold to His children its mysteries. Grandeur of governmental science. God teaches us this science.

There are good reasons for this, in a measure comprehensible by us. Jehovah, as the crowning work of His creation, said: Man's creation.

> Let us make man in our image, after our likeness: and let them have dominion over the fish of the sea, and over the fowl of the air, and over the cattle, and over all the earth, and over every creeping thing that creepeth upon the earth. *Gen.* i, 26.

§ 3. Science of Government.

Heb. ii, 7, 8.

He made man a little lower than the angels, crowned him with glory and honor, and set him over the works of His hands, putting all things in subjection under his feet. Thus was given to man dominion, proprietary right in all things of earth; and, had he continued holy, just, and good, he would probably have exercised joint dominion, using all things in common. These "sons of God," however, were not to be mere machines, but independent moral agents, capable of choosing for themselves between good and evil, right and wrong. Our first parents, the representatives of our race, when the choice was placed before them, deliberately took the evil, and violated the first command given them by God. Man then became a rebel against the Divine authority, and a system of Government must be framed suited to his fallen condition. His character was changed; and, instead of being governed by the law of God, seeking in all things the highest glory of God, the best good of his fellow, selfishness became the predominant trait.

Man's dominion.

Man's fall.

The judicious Hooker remarks:

Hooker's Works, i, 239.

Nature teaches law.

Man obliged in a state of nature.

States established that man could attain his highest dignity.

States must have government.

A State's foundation, and form of government.

Laws made for man as sinful.

> That which hitherto we have set down is (I hope) sufficient to shew their brutishness, which imagine that religion and virtue are only as men will account of them; that we might make as much account, if we would, of the contrary, without any harm unto ourselves, and that in nature they are as indifferent one as the other. We see then how nature itself teacheth laws and statutes to live by. The laws which have been hitherto mentioned do bind men absolutely even as they are men, although they have never any settled fellowship, never any solemn agreement amongst themselves what to do or not to do. But forasmuch as we are not by ourselves sufficient to furnish ourselves with competent store of things needful for such a life as our nature doth desire, a life fit for the dignity of man; therefore, to supply those defects and imperfections which are in us, living single and solely by ourselves, we are naturally induced to seek communion and fellowship with others.[1] This was the cause of men's uniting themselves at the first in politic societies, which societies could not be without government, nor government without a distinct kind of law from that which hath been already declared. Two foundations there are which bear up public societies; the one, a natural inclination, whereby all men desire sociable life and fellowship; the other, an order expressly or secretly agreed upon touching the manner of their union in living together. The latter is that which we call the Law of a Commonweal, the very soul of a politic body, the parts whereof are by law animated, held together, and set on work in such actions as the common good requireth. Laws politic, ordained for external order and regiment amongst men, are never framed as they should be, unless presuming the will of man to be inwardly obstinate, rebellious, and averse from all obedience unto the sacred laws of his nature; in a word, unless presuming man to be in regard of his depraved mind little better than a wild beast, they do accordingly provide notwithstanding so to frame his outward actions, that they be no hindrance unto the common good for which societies are instituted; unless they do this, they are not perfect. It resteth, therefore, that we consider how nature findeth out such laws of government as serve to direct even nature depraved to a right end.

Knowledge of the fall necessary to properly understand man's government.

Government of man over man would have been unnecessary, had he continued holy; so that the knowledge of man's creation, temptation and fall, was necessary to his understanding the end and purpose of Government, not less that relating to time than to eternity. We must know

[1] How perfectly this accords with Aristotle's sentiment, beautifully illuminated by the light of Revelation, as the reader will see in extracts following.

how it is "the heart of the sons of men is full of evil, and madness is in their heart while they live"—why "the heart *is* deceitful above all *things*, and desperately wicked," to understand the necessity of man's control by law and authority. We had lost all knowledge of this, and hence a Divine revelation became necessary. This we have in the BIBLE, which incidentally instructs in various subjects, but is replete with advice, direction, and laws for man's Government. The primary object is to inform us of our relations to the Ruler of the universe, and to His eternal Government; but it also teaches self-government, and how to govern each other. Indeed, the Creator has so interwoven the duties and obligations of man to himself and to his fellow with those to Deity, that they are not to be dissevered.

§ 3. Science of Government.

The Bible gives this. *Eccl.* ix, 3. *Jer.* xvii, 9.

With what deep concern should we regard a science that takes hold of every interest of time and of eternity, and in which we have all requisite instruction from the mouth of Infinite Wisdom! With what profound reverence does it become us to receive and examine those instructions, given not only by precept, but by example! To the Christian especially does this subject strongly commend itself. Investigating and applying to human government, which is more within the compass of our faculties, the principles GOD has communicated, we are led along step by step toward the great Fountain of all authority; and the study of man's finite works, unfolding the reasons upon which Sovereignty, *the Right of Command*, is based, helps us to comprehend more and more the propriety, wisdom, and excellence of the sway of the LORD of lords, the KING of kings, which rests not only upon His proprietary right as Creator, but upon the same principle of beneficence which justifies human Government.

Importance of governmental science.

But the Framer of man understood his frailties and imperfections. Knowing that precept would have less power over us than example, we are taught also by the latter; and a record is given of early nations in the Bible, nowhere else to be found, and the value of which, in the science of International Law, we little appreciate.

The Bible teaches by example as well as precept.

Of the antediluvian world, the account is short; and if any form of government existed, it must have become vicious, corrupt, worthless.

No Government before the flood.

And GOD saw that the wickedness of man was great in the earth, and that every imagination of the thoughts of his heart was only evil continually. The earth also was corrupt before GOD, and the earth was filled with violence. And GOD looked upon the earth, and, behold, it was corrupt; for all flesh had corrupted his way upon the earth. And GOD said unto Noah, The end of all flesh is come before me; for the earth is filled with violence through them; and, behold, I will destroy them with the earth.

Gen. vi, 5.

Ib. 11–13.

They had no proper systems of Government, or the earth would not have been filled with violence and corruption. Possibly that is the warning example to all sentient beings existing in the myriads of worlds throughout space, of creatures left by their Creator to their own management. But whether of value to other worlds or not, it teaches us the practical lesson, that, without strong and sufficient Government to control

Man goes to destruction without Government.

§ 3. Science of Government.

erring man, he goes to destruction; and though the bright bow in the summer's cloud bespeaks GOD's promise never more to bring a flood, we know destruction to man unrestrained, is none the less certain and irremediable.

The Hebrews a Federal Republic.

The tenth generation from Noah, and two hundred and ninety-two years after the flood, Abram was born. His descendants GOD chose to take under His special care, and He taught them the science of government. The Old Testament abounds with instruction given this favorite people; and, considering the circumstances, we may infer that, both as to the form and as to the details, GOD designed it to be a lasting example to the world, of what He deemed the best Government for man. As we shall see in the sequel, the Confederacies of ancient Greece, and this of the United States, appear to be more like it than any other, till that wicked people chose to rebel against GOD, consolidate their States, and have a king.[1]

The Jews subjected to the Romans.

The Jews became corrupt, and were enslaved to the Romans. About the same period, too, the Grecian Confederacies, torn to pieces by dissensions and wars among themselves, one after another became also subject to the empire of Rome.

Our Saviour's birth.

Amid the subjection of the Jews to the Romans, our blessed SAVIOUR was born. Although His errand was chiefly to fulfil the plans of Deity, with reference to the spiritual Government of our race, yet the interests of time and of eternity are so identified; the influences of this hand's-breadth of existence are so ineradicable from man's nature throughout eternal ages, that a large part of His teachings have direct reference to our duties toward each other, and particularly those relating to government. Both by precept and example did He teach entire subjection to the constituted authorities, notwithstanding His own people, and He with them, were enslaved to a foreign power; and He himself was, under Roman law, unjustly tried, condemned, and crucified, after a wicked, false, malicious trial and condemnation by the Jewish Sanhedrim.

His teachings concerning Government. His crucifixion— —not under Democracy, but Monarchy.

Further should we observe, that this iniquity was perpetrated, not under the form of free Government—*the Right of Command* in the people—as instituted by GOD for His favorite Israel, and under which Rome had risen to its great power, but, when, after seventy years of usurpation and tyranny, the Commonwealth had been changed into an Empire. In accordance with the plan of the Sovereign of the universe in the salvation of fallen man, the Son of GOD must be crucified; but Democracy, the form most nearly approaching, in its hidden mystery, that of the august

[1] This is not the generally received opinion. Sidney, Lowman, and others, styled the ancient government an aristocracy, and I supposed they knew. But a careful study of the Old Testament satisfied me that each tribe was a State, and that they were united in a Federal Republic till Saul was made king. Harrington treats them as a Commonwealth, Lewis as a Republic; but calling upon Dr. Raphall, an eminent Jewish rabbi in New York, he read to me from a work of his, confirming my opinion that each tribe was an independent Democracy, the twelve constituting a Federal Republic, and he has kindly promised his aid in the interesting examination of the government of his ancient people. Chancellor Matthews, too, I find, has issued a work, in which he takes the same ground with others.

majesty of Heaven, is saved from the commission of this awful crime, and Monarchy is made the instrument.

§ 4. Rise of Modern International Law.

Influence of the Bible not effective.

The Dark Ages.

The Reformation.

The Bible the basis of the new law of nations.

Our Saviour's teachings, and those of the apostles under Divine inspiration, have given new beauty, efficacy, and strength to Government; and had the principles of the Old Testament, with the meliorating influences of the New, been properly operative on man, we should have no record like that of the Dark Ages, succeeding the fall of the Roman empire. But a mysterious Providence allowed the mind and heart of mankind to grow darker and darker for many centuries, till, in the sixteenth, the light of the Reformation broke upon the world. All departments of knowledge felt the genial influences, and none more so than Government. The world was blessed with the beneficent rule of Elizabeth and Henry IV, though not unmixed with wrong. Toward the close of that century, the great Bacon taught the world new principles of philosophy, based upon the eternal truths of the Christian religion. Barbeyrac, in his able paper prefaced to Pufendorf, observes:

Barbeyrac's opinion of Bacon—*Preface to Pufendorf*, p. 79.

—of Grotius

—father of the science.

His qualifications.

His chief work, the *Law of War and Peace*, published in 1625.

'Posterity will be eternally obliged to him [Bacon] for the great Light and noble Projects he has furnished the World with; towards the general restoration and advancement of the Sciences. We have reason to believe, that it was the reading of the works of this great man, that inspired *Hugo Grotius* with the thoughts of attempting the first to compose a system of the Law of Nature; which he afterward undertook, at the solicitation of the celebrated *Nicholas de Pieresc*, Judge of the High Court of Parliament for Provence. 'Its pretended that *Melancthon* had already given a sketch of something of this kind in his *Ethicks;* and they tell us too of one *Benedict Winckler*, who published in 1615 a book entitled, *Principia Juris;* wherein he entirely departs from the method of the Schoolmen, and maintains against them, amongst other things, that the Will of *God* is the very Fountain and Foundation of all Justice. But 'its acknowledged, that the latter of these two often confounds the Law of Nature with that which is positive; and that neither the one nor the other has afforded any more than a small gleam of light; not sufficient to dissipate those thick clouds of darkness, in which the world had been so long invelop'd. Besides, *Melancthon* was too much prepossessed in favor of the Peripatetick Philosophy, ever to make any great progress in the knowledge of the true fundamental principles of the Law of Nature, and the right method of explaining that Science. *Grotius* therefore ought to be regarded as the first who broke the ice; and most certain it is, that no man could be better qualified for such an enterprise. Extraordinary clearness of understanding, exquisite judgment, profound meditation, universal knowledge, prodigious reading, continual application to study in the midst of a great many vexatious obstacles, and the necessary duties of several considerable employments, with a sincere love for truth, qualifications which no one can deny properly to belong to that great man, without wronging his own judgment, and bringing his character in danger of the imputation either of base envy or gross ignorance. If (as has been very rightly observed) [in *Parrhasiana*, vol. i, p. 346] he was not thoroughly acquainted with the art of thinking justly; the Philosophy of his time being still very dark and obscure; he has supplied, in a great measure, that defect, by the force of his good sense. If without the help of art, he has shown so much delicacy of taste, and true discernment, what would he not have done had he been entire master of the art of reasoning justly and of rightly methodizing his thoughts, which is now and has been for some time, to be had? His work was first published at Paris in 1625, and dedicated to Louis XIII. It is said he at first designed to have entitled it, *The Law of Nature and Nations*, but he chose after-

§ 4. Rise of Modern International Law.

Grotius' objects.

wards to give it the title it now bears of *The Law of War and Peace.* What he had chiefly in view was, to set forth those duties which the several nations of the world, in their sovereign powers that govern them, owe one to another; and how the differences arising between them might be justly terminated. For which purpose he takes into his work the principal subject matters of natural jurisprudence and politics, and lays down also principles sufficient to establish the most considerable duties of private men. He himself owns that he is far from having exhausted so copious a subject; and wishes that others may supply what is wanting; to the end that mankind may one day be furnished with a complete system of this science. Never had book a more universal approbation.

He applies the Bible to the Law of Nations.

Hugh Grotius (Hugo de Groot) was born at Delft, in 1583, and died in 1645. Not only is he the father of the modern system of governmental science, but to him is generally conceded the distinguished honor of being the first to apply to it the truths and principles of the Bible, though his great work is also supported by the wisdom of Greece and Rome, and of the early Christian writers. In his preface he observes:

Grotius' prolegomena to *Rights of War and Peace*, p. xviii.

His use of the Bible.

Of the authority of such books as holy men, by the afflate of God's Spirit, have written or approved, we often make use, yet with some difference between the Old and New Testament. The former is by some quoted for the very law of nature, but without doubt erroneously, for many things therein do proceed from the free will and pleasure of God, which notwithstanding is no whit repugnant to the truth of the law of nature; and so far arguments may be drawn from thence, so that we carefully distinguish that law of God, which God by men doth sometimes execute, and that which men execute among themselves. We have, as nearly as we could, avoided both this error and another contrary unto it, which is, that after the times of the New Covenant, there is no use at all to be made of the Old. As to this, we are of a contrary judgment, as well for what we have already said, as because such is the nature of the New Law, that whatsoever is commanded in the Old, appertaining to virtue and good manners, the same, or much greater, is commanded in the New, and after this manner do the ancient Christian writers make use of the testimonies drawn from the Old Testament. But to the right understanding of the sense of the Books of the Old Testament, we have no small help from the *Hebrew* writers, especially those who were thoroughly instructed in the language and manners of their own country. The New Testament I do also make use of, to instruct Christians in what is lawful for them to do, which cannot be elsewhere learned; which notwithstanding (contrary to what some have done) I have distinguished from the Law of Nature: Being most assured that, in that most holy Law, a greater sanctity is commanded than that which the Law of Nature doth of itself require. Neither have I omitted to observe, what is rather commended unto us than commanded, that so we may understand that to do the contrary to that which is commanded, is impiety, and renders us lyable to punishment; but eagerly to aspire to that which is most excellent, as it argues a noble and generous mind, so shall it not want its due reward.

Earlier authorities.

Nothing new under the sun.

Eccles. i, 10.

The honor due to Grotius is not to be diminished by admitting what is fairly due to others. Constantly, as these investigations have been prosecuted, has the force of Solomon's query been impressed: "Is there *any* thing whereof it may be said, See, this is new? It hath been already of old time, which was before us."

Aristotle and Cicero.

Imperfectly as have the writings of Aristotle and Cicero been preserved, they yet give quite completely the fundamental principles of Government, and are in remarkable harmony with the older, more perfect, better grounded teachings of the Bible. Nor was Grotius the only one, or the most ancient of his cotemporaries, to draw forth things old, if not new, from the rich treasure-house of governmental science.

§ 4. Rise of Modern International Law.

Hooker's *Ecclesiastical Politie*, 1592–1600.

Richard Hooker, who died in 1600, had published five books of his *Ecclesiastical Politie*, and the other three appeared soon after his decease. It abounds with solid truths relating to Government of State as well as Church; and the term *judicious*, which Izaak Walton says, in his interesting memoir, was used in his epitaph by Sir William Cooper, has by common consent been applied to him. The judicious Hooker developed so clearly and forcibly the principles of Government, that it is unaccountable Grotius and Pufendorf should not have referred to him, particularly as their views so well coincide. Locke quotes him as eminent authority, though their teachings on some important points, it seems to me, are not easily to be harmonized. He begins his great work with such remarkably judicious observations to the reader entering upon such an examination, that, although nearly three centuries old, they are precisely adapted to us. May they deeply impress us, as we seek for "that foundation which . . . is in the bosom of the earth concealed"—the Sovereignty of these Peoples by States. "What may seem dark at the first, will afterward be found more plain;" not made so by the glimmering rays of my feeble intellect, but by the strong and steady light of those burning suns of wisdom. Says Hooker:

Hooker, *Works*, i, 198.

Disorganizers never want hearers—

—being supposed special friends of the people—

—and people inclined to listen.

Friends of order supposed to be selfish.

He that goeth about to persuade a multitude that they are not so well governed as they ought to be, shall never want attentive and favourable hearers, because they know the manifold defects whereunto every kind of regiment is subject, but the secret lets and difficulties, which in public proceedings are innumerable and inevitable, they have not ordinarily the judgment to consider. And because such as openly reprove supposed disorders of state are taken for principal friends to the common benefit of all, and for men that carry singular freedom of mind; under this fair and plausible color whatsoever they utter passeth for good and current. That which wanteth in the weight of their speech, is supplied by the aptness of men's minds to accept and believe it. Whereas on the other side, if we maintain things that are established, we have not only to strive with a number of heavy prejudices, deeply rooted in the hearts of men, who think that herein we serve the time, and speak in favour of the present state, because thereby we either hold or seek preferment; but also to bear such exceptions as minds so averted beforehand usually take against that which they are loth should be poured into them.

Science of Government difficult.

Albeit therefore, much of that we are to speak in this present cause may seem to a number perhaps tedious, perhaps obscure, dark, and intricate (for many talk of the truth, which never sounded the depth from whence it springeth; and, therefore, when they are led thereunto, they are soon weary, as men drawn from those beaten paths wherewith they have been inured); yet this may not so far prevail as to cut off that which the matter itself requireth, howsoever the nice humour of some be therewith pleased or no. They unto whom we shall seem tedious are in no wise injured by us, because it is in their own hands to spare that labour which they are not willing to endure. And if any complain of obscurity, they must consider that in these matters it cometh no otherwise to pass than in sundry the works both of art and also of nature, where that which hath greatest force in the very things we see, is, notwithstanding, itself oftentimes not seen. The stateliness of houses, the goodliness of trees, when we behold them, delighteth the eye; but that foundation which beareth up the one, that root which ministereth unto the other nourishment and life, is in the bosom of the earth concealed; and if there be at any time occasion to search into it, such labour is

Examination voluntary.

Important to examine foundations—

§ 4. Rise of Modern International Law.

—when obedience to law is refused.

This difficult, the subject being dark, &c.

Authors' endeavor to make first principles clear.

Readers not to judge prematurely.

Though dark at first, at last plain.

then more necessary than pleasant, both to them which undertake it and for the lookers-on. In like manner, the use and benefit of good laws, all that live under them may enjoy with delight and comfort, albeit the grounds and first original causes from whence they have sprung be unknown as to the greatest part of men they are. But when they who withdraw their obedience pretend that the laws which they should obey are corrupt and vicious; for better examination of their quality, it behoveth the very foundation and root, the highest well-spring and fountain of them, to be discovered. Which, because we are not oftentimes accustomed to do, when we do it, the pains we take are more needful a great deal than acceptable, and the matters which we handle seem by reason of newness (till the mind grow better acquainted with them), dark, intricate, and unfamiliar. For as much help whereof as may be in this case, I have endeavoured throughout the body of this whole discourse, that every former part might give strength unto all that follow, and every later bring some light unto all before. So that if the judgments of men do but hold themselves in suspense as touching these first more general meditations, till in order they have perused the rest that ensue, what may seem dark at the first will afterwards be found more plain, even as the later particular decisions will appear, I doubt not, more strong when the other have been read before.

Raleigh, about 1610.

The renowned Sir Walter Raleigh, too, wrote a most interesting tract, which is preserved in the Somers' collection. When visiting the cell in the Tower of London in which that great soldier, civilian, and scholar was for fourteen years incarcerated, I trod with awe in the footsteps of the man who had the eminence of first planting Anglo-Saxon colonies in America, leading an enterprise that must be more influential upon all humanity, than any event since the discovery of the New World. I did not then know he had written a work on Government, antedating Grotius, well, though very succinctly, unfolding the same principles. The reader will be pleased to see the short tract and accompanying letter to Prince Henry, and learn on what a solid foundation of the *Right of Command* our colonial rights began to exist under our sovereigns, Elizabeth and James I.

Ridley, about 1620.

A volume by Sir Thomas Ridley has also come under note, entitled, *A View of the Civile and Ecclesiastical Law*, fourth edition, with the notes of J. Gregory, Oxford, 1676. It is dedicated to James I; and *Rose's Biographical Dictionary* says the author was

Rose's *Biographical Dictionary.*

An eminent civilian, descended of a family of that name in Northumberland, was born at Ely, and became master of Eton School, afterwards one of the Masters in Chancery, Chancellor to the Bishop of Winchester, and Vicar-general to Archbishop Abbott. He also received the honour of knighthood. He died in 1629. He published a view of the Civil and Ecclesiastical Law, which was much admired by James I., and was afterwards reprinted by the learned Gregory, chaplain to the Bishop Duppa.

Conflicting jurisdiction.

Ridley wrote, to clear up the controversy then existing between civil and ecclesiastical jurisdiction. The authority in both courts proceeded from one and the same fountain, the Sovereignty—*Right of Command*—of King James. Yet were there conflicts in the exercise of this authority, from not properly understanding fundamental principles. He remarks, in his address to the "Gentle Reader":

Ridley's *Preface.*

Besides, seeing how frequent prohibitions are in these dayes, in causes of either cognisance more than have been in former time, I thought it not unworthy my labour

§ 4. Rise of Modern International Law.

RIDLEY, *Civile and Ecclesiastical Law.*

Search the ground of interpretation.

to inquire and see upon what just grounds they are raised up in this multitude; not of any humour I have, to gainsay the lawful proceedings of my Court (which I reverence, and most readily acknowledge their authoritie in all things belonging to their place), but to know and search out the truth of those suggestions that give cause unto these prohibitions. For when as such Lawes as are written of these businesses, are written indifferently, as well for the one Jurisdiction as the other, no man is to be offended if the one Jurisdiction, finding itself pressed by the partial interpretation (as it supposeth) of the other, inquire the ground of such interpretation, and labour to redress it if it may be, by the right interpretation thereof: To the end, that either Jurisdiction may retain their own right, and not the one be overtopt by the other, as it seemeth to be at this day: And that in such matters (as they conceive) of their own right, as depend of no other authoritie but of the Prince alone: which is the thing onely that is sought in this little Treatise. And therefore the Reverend Judges of this Land are to be intreated, that they will vouchsafe an equall interpretation of these matters, as well to the one Jurisdiction as the other, for so it is comely for them to do; and if they do it not, the other are not so dull-sensed but they can perceive it, nor so daunted, but that they can flie for succour unto him, to whose high place and wisdome the deciding of these differences doth of right appertain. PENELOPE is said to have had many woers comely in person and eloquent in speech, but shee respected none but her own ULYSSES: Such should be the mind of a Judge, that whatsoever other appearance or show of truth be offered, one saying, This is the true sense of the law, and another that; yet the Judge should respect none but the very true germane and genuine sense thereof indeed. Which if it were religiously or indifferently observed in every Court, then needed not this complaint that now is, but every Jurisdiction should peaceably hold his own right, such as the Prince, Law, or Custome hath afforded unto it.

Conflict of our jurisdictions, State and Federal.

As a conflict of jurisdiction then existed from ignorance and misconception, so one now prevails in these States of ours, and for the same cause. Our Sovereignties, it is true, have wisely forborne to exercise their authority in ecclesiastical affairs, but have made an important division in their civil affairs, having given jurisdiction to one set of officials in their home concerns, and to another set of officials, jointly with their sister Sovereignties, in a few of their most important concerns, which could best be managed by a Union; and we have run into perfect confusion, both in the juridical practice, and as to the source of authority. The learned author begins his lucid exposition of the subject by observations concerning law, which are desirable for the uninformed reader, particularly those relating to *feuds*, in order to understand feudal rights; and the epitome, even cut short, as it must be, will prove the honor due to Rome for its high attainments in law, and afford a justification for Grotius, in particular, for having drawn precedents so largely from Roman authorities in establishing his principles. He has been criticized for this; but, while modern Christian nations afford the best precedents for International Law based upon the Bible, the most civilized and correct nation of antiquity is worthy of close observation, and was preëminently so in the age of Grotius.

Hobbes, *De Cive*, 1642; *Leviathan*, 1651.

BARBEYRAC, *Preface to Pufendorf*, p. 80.

In 1642, Thomas Hobbes, "a great mathematician, and one of the most penetrating geniuses of his age," published his *De Cive*, and, in 1651, his *Leviathan*. He agrees with Grotius as to the mode of existence and powers of States and of Sovereignty, and as to the forms of

§ 4. Rise of Modern International Law.

BARBEYRAC, *Preface to Pufendorf*, p. 80.

government, but is a strenuous advocate of Monarchy, and believes war to be the natural state of man, and that all obligation is the mere creation of civil authority. Barbeyrac says, "he passed for an atheist; and perhaps they were not very much out in their judgments who thought him so; for he admitted none but corporeal substances."

Harrington, *Oceana*, 1646.

James Harrington published his *Oceana*, in 1646, advocating Republicanism, and dedicating it to Cromwell, though opposed to his usurpations. He also published other works favorable to popular rights, that will be quoted herein.

Cumberland, *The Laws of Nature*, 1672.

In 1672, the valuable work of that eminent scholar and Christian, Richard Cumberland, Bishop of Peterborough, appeared, entitled, *The Laws of Nature.* I pretend not to have mastered this mass of profundity, which is nearly as hard to read as Butler's Analogy, but have studied it sufficiently to see that the argument is irresistible. By what logicians style the analytic mode—that from cause to effect, the opposite of that of Grotius and Pufendorf—the same conclusions are reached. Pufendorf highly estimated Bishop Cumberland's writings, and quotes him several times in the last edition of his great work. The original was in Latin, and is translated by Dr. Towers, who has added interesting notes and an appendix. To give a little insight into his method and style, a few sections are here presented from his prolegomena:

CUMBERLAND, Laws of Nature the foundation of morality and civil polity.

The Laws of Nature are the only solid Foundations of all Morality and Civil Polity; which we fully demonstrate in the following pages.

Mode of Demonstration.

These Laws (like most other conclusions discoverable by the light of Nature,) are investigated, traced out, and demonstrated, by the one or the other of these two ways, either,

1. Causes by their effects.
2. Effects from causes.

First, By such manifest effects as follow from these Laws themselves, which, in other words, is the demonstration of *causes by their effects.* Or, *Secondly*, By those evident causes from whence these Laws themselves originally take their source and rise; and this is no other than demonstrating effects from their causes.

The second method is Cumberland's,—the first is Grotius'.

According to the first method, the *Laws of Nature* are considered as causes necessarily producing effects. According to the second method, the *Laws of Nature* are looked upon as necessary effects resulting from such and such natural causes.*

TOWERS. Two methods of reasoning:

* There are two general methods of reasoning: 1st, the Synthetic, and 2d, the Analytic. The Synthetic method is called the *argumentum a priori.* The Analytic method is called the *argumentum a posteriori.*

1. Synthetic.

The Synthetic method, or the *argumentum a priori*, lays down some evident principles, and then deduces the several consequences necessarily resulting from them.

2. Analytic.

2. The Analytic method, or the *argumentum a posteriori*, begins with the phenomena themselves, and traces them up to their original; and, from the known properties of these phenomena, arrives at the nature of their cause. Now, the former of these two methods is evidently preferable, where it can be had (and I think it may be had almost everywhere but in the First Cause), since the latter must depend upon a large induction of particulars, any of which, when failing, invalidates the whole argument, and quite spoils a demonstration.

DR. CLARK.

"It is very true," says Doctor John Clarke, on natural evil, "that this is not a strict demonstration of the general conclusion; because that can be had no other way than by trying all the experiments that can possibly be made everywhere, which is infinite and endless; but it is the best that the nature of the thing is capable of." (Law's preface to Archbishop King's *Essay on the Origin of Evil*, page 5.)

Analogy differs both from synthetic and analytic methods.

The proofs drawn from analogy cannot be called either the Synthetic or the Analytic method of reasoning; it is rather arguing by illustration, from similitude or comparison, than from the direct principles of reason strictly so called; it neither proves the cause from the effect, nor the effect from the cause.

It is comparing together things which we are certainly sure have already a determined existence, and carry certain habitudes to each other, either of fitness or unfitness, but it never proves, neither is it brought to prove, the existence of the things themselves which are compared.

§ 4. Rise of Modern International Law.

The foundation of our enquiry is laid in the second method of reasoning.

The reality and force of these Laws themselves; the demonstration of them according to the first method of reasoning; their actual existence, and the binding obligation of them, are points well pursued and handled by *Hugh Grotius*, and by his brother, *William Grotius*, in that posthumous treatise of his, intitled, *De Principiis Juris Naturalis Enchiridion*, as also by our countryman, Dr. Robert Sharrock, in his Υποθεσις Ηθικη, in his *Book of Offices*, who all prove these Laws from the confirmed and well-established opinions of several authors in different ages and countries: As also by the corresponding testimony and concurring agreement of all nations, especially those of the more polished and civilized, in their customs and laws. The same method is likewise pursued by *John Selden*, Esq., in that learned work of his *De Jure Naturali Gentium juxta Disciplinam Ebræorum*.

Sharrock, *Book of Offices.*

Selden, *Natural Law of Nations according to the Hebrew code.*

And, indeed, in my opinion, all these authors have deserved very well from mankind, but in an especial degree that work of *Hugh Grotius*, *De Jure Belli et Pacis*, *&c.*: A work the first in its kind: A work truly worthy of its author, and as truly worthy of immortality. Some few errors (but such they are, wherein the customs of his native country have headlong carried away this great man) will easily obtain pardon from a good-natured reader.

Grotius commended.

§ 2. There is not, indeed, so much weight in those objections which are generally produced against this method of demonstrating the Laws of Nature, as to prove it either sophistical or trifling; and yet I must frankly own, that these objections have carried so much force over some ingenious minds, as to represent them very useful, and to be the securest way of searching after a more pregnant proof from an investigation of these causes, by whose operation a knowledge of the Laws of Nature might spring up in the human mind: but this will appear more evident, if we briefly state those objections, and produce likewise the sum and substance briefly of arguments in answer to them.

The synthetic method applicable to the Laws of Nature.

It is objected, first, *that such reasoning is weak, whose conclusions are drawn from the sentiments and customs of either a few men, or of small numbers of civil societies concerning the universal opinion and judgment of all mankind, since there is not any one man who perfectly understands the laws and customs even of that civil government under which he lives, to say nothing of all societies and governments; much less can he understand the inward sentiments of all individuals, so as that he can form fair comparisons and judgments, and to collect all those points wherein all agree.*

1st Objection: No one can know all laws and customs—

—or individual sentiments.

To which I answer, that the judgments, opinions, sentiments and [these two words are probably transposed] of different nations, concerning any one point which is obvious from daily experience (such as religion, or the worship of a Deity, in some mode or other, as generally understood; an humanity of some sort or other, sufficient to prohibit murder, theft, and adultery) may be easily formed by every man, every where, without such a knowledge of Law as is acquired by long study and application; because such sentiments sufficiently declare their universal agreement in these points, even from the very Laws of Nature themselves; which consent, we find, is acknowledged by many nations as a natural good; from whence we may presume that the same consent is also acknowledged by all other nations, from that similitude and likeness, and which universally holds in all human nature, especially since our adversaries cannot produce any instance confirmed by full experience which evinces that any nation entertains a contrary sentiment. Those relations seem to me very doubtful, nay, very little to be credited, which are told of some barbarous *Americans* and *Hottentots*, as paying no manner of worship to a deity, for such negative assertions can scarcely admit of any proof. For this reason, *Acosta* and some other authors seem to pass a very rash judgment on those people whose language, custom, and sentiments they could not possibly understand to any degree of perfection in so short a time, since their stay amongst those nations was so very transitory.

Answer—Concordant sentiments among men, establish rules.

Exceptions.

Nay, we read, indeed, that even the *Jews* and *Christians*, whose religious discipline was much more holy than the religion of any other nations, were (notwithstanding the Divinity of their worship and discipline at some certain times) falsely accused of the highest impieties.

§ 4. Rise of Modern International Law.

Entire unanimity not necessary.

Laws of Nature oblige all.

Let this matter stand as it will, manifest it is, that these truths are clearly enough discovered to all mankind, which have been without difficulty acknowledged by all, although that these very same truths have been either overlooked by some or opposed by others. For it will appear, in the consequence, a matter most significant and of the highest moment (since this argument is evident from other proofs, as well as from such testimony and customs) that those propositions (in which the Laws of Nature are contained) lay down the true means for attaining the best end, and that all mankind are indispensably obliged, by the help of these very means, to pursue that very end, *i. e.*, the *best end.*

2d Objection—An authority to enforce, requisite to a law—

—supported by Hobbes and Selden.

§ 3. Secondly, it is objected, *That although, as well by the force of our own understandings, as from the behaviour of many other persons quite separate and distinct from us, some certain dictates of reason may be allowed; yet that the authority of some public lawgiver, established by civil authority, is wanting, to enforce the universal obligation of these Laws; for otherwise (say these objectors) it is lawful for any one man that pleases to disobey them; i. e., he may, by the same parity of reason, reject the judgment of all others, by which all others may, both in word and deed, reject the judgment of any one man.* Not only the ancients, but also our own countrymen, at this very day, Mr. *Hobbes* and *John Selden*, Esq., put their objection in this light, but yet with a quite different view.

Hobbes destroys all obligation antecedent to civil society—

For Mr. Hobbes's objection is framed with this sinister view, that no one should think himself obliged, as to any acts of outward behaviour, by the dictates of reason, antecedent to the instituted authority of a civil magistrate, because that all the institutions of such a magistrate must be construed so many dictates of right reason, indispensably binding and obligatory, as we set forth in the following discourse.

—makes Natural Law not obligatory.

And to this proposition of his must be referred what he says in his book *De Cive*, chap. 14, sect. 15, "That Natural Laws, although set forth in the writings of philosophers, cannot, for that reason, be deemed written Laws, the supreme authority of the civil magistrate being wanting."

Hobbes disagrees with himself.

It was not, to be sure, in Mr. *Hobbes's* intention to take away from the Laws of Nature the title of *Laws;* because he has vouchsafed to honour these Laws with that title (altho' in a very improper acceptation of the word *Laws*, as he elsewhere acknowledges;) but he gives us to understand, that these Laws are not published by a sufficient authority; notwithstanding that the Philosophers have learned them from the *Nature of Things*, and which, from the *Nature of Things*, they have transcribed into their own writings. Manifest, however, it is, that these *Laws of Nature*, if they once become genuine, true Laws, as established upon the authority of Nature, don't require any new Authority, when they are copied and transcribed into Books, and become written Laws.

Selden's object—impotency of human authority.

God's authority necessary—

—gives virtue to Natural Law.

Selden, then, for the same reason, supposes so mighty a defect of authority in the Laws of human reason, in themselves considered, abstracted from all other considerations of authority, as to judge it necessary for us to have immediate recourse to the legislative power of Almighty God, and to tell us, that their dictates from thence only take their essential virtue, as the whole knowledge of them is communicated by Almighty God to mankind, who, at the same time that he communicates these Laws, in reality promulgates them to us; and this truly (if I be not out in my judgment,) *Selden* with a very prudent caution hinted to the Moral Philosophers, who, generally speaking, consider the dictates of Reason itself as so many laws, passing over, at the same time, every argument which proves the essential reality of such laws, without considering that these Laws are established by Almighty God himself.

Selden proposes two methods of Divine dispensation:

But here our author, since he finds the Dispensation must be shewn by the which God reveals these moral dictates to be his Laws, he proposes two methods of Divine Dispensation:

1. By revelation to Adam and Noah.

1. That God revealed them to *Adam* and *Noah* by his own most holy voice; whence, by tradition only, the precepts of the *Noachidæ* (*i. e.* Noah's posterity) were delivered down to future generations.

2. By creating a human faculty to judge.

2. That God endowed human nature with such a clear faculty, which faculty (by the help of that agent's understanding who explains those precepts or Laws) might open

and reveal these precepts or Laws to us, so as to distinguish them, when opened and explained, from every positive law whatsoever.

§ 4. Rise of Modern International Law.

Selden's method examined.

This second method he delivers under such loose and general terms only, that, in my opinion, it stands in need of much explication and proof.

The strength in first method.

The whole strength of Mr. *Selden's* reasoning depends upon the first method; and (according to the tradition of some *Jewish* doctors) he labours to prove, that God gave seven precepts to the sons of *Noah*, under which precepts, if obeyed, the whole Law of Justice is comprehended.

Jews imagined all nations bound to observe the laws of the Noachidæ.

Beyond all dispute, what Mr. *Selden* has said, in that treatise of his, entitled, *De Jure Gentium*, &c., fully proves that the *Jews* imagined all nations over the whole face of the earth, altho' they should not receive the Laws of *Moses*, tied down to the observance of some certain Laws of God; the principal heads of which Divine Laws they imagined to be contained in the *Laws of the Noachidæ.** What he has now said, at least serves to prove thus much, and upon the testimony of a nation neither insignificant nor unlearned, that the whole race of mankind are obliged by Laws which are not instituted by civil authority.

Man obliged by law, not instituted by civil authority.

Use of Selden's views in Christian theology.

It must, moreover, be confessed that this truly learned man had one chief design in view, which he executed to very good purpose, and the knowledge of this matter has several excellent uses in the Christian theology. At the same time, however, *Selden* has not been so fortunate as to solve that objection, which we have now raised against his opinion; for, notwithstanding that he himself was perfectly well acquainted with these *Jewish* traditions, and perhaps heartily believed them all, yet they are not equally clear and evident to all mankind.

Objection as to traditions.

Some traditions despised.

Nay,—that even several of these very traditions, which contain the highest and most solemn mysteries of their religion, are held by many in contempt and ridicule; nay, it appears to me a point even self-evident, that an oral tradition of the learned men in one nation is not so sufficient a publication of a natural Law, as to oblige and bind all mankind.

Cumberland to seek a Divine authority for the Laws of Nature—

—by a philosophical inquiry into their causes.

§ 4. That therefore some authority, and that a Divine one too, may more evidently appear (and by which authority these moral dictates become Laws), we resolve to make a *philosophical enquiry* into their causes, both internal and external, near and remote. For, by such a series of reasoning, we shall at length be led to the First Author, or efficient Cause, of them, from whose inherent perfections, and their inseparable sanctions of rewards and punishments, we demonstrate the authority of these Laws to arise.

Other writers content that nature dictates—

—must know more of their nature and power.

Almost all other writers content themselves with general terms, that these dictates, or the actions conformable to them, are taught by nature. But, to me, it seems necessary (especially considering the age in which we live) more distinctly and minutely to investigate after what manner the energy and power of such things, as both are and are not within our own influence, may contribute to impress and enforce the sanctions of these Laws.

Bacon thought so.

Something of this kind my Lord *Verulam*, our countryman, told us was wanting, *De Augm. Scientiarum*, lib. 8, cap. 3.

Success would instruct concerning laws—

—also afford a test of laws.

If so solid a foundation as this were laid, it would, upon this very account, be the most useful; because, from hence we might trace, both in what manner the human understanding might be instructed naturally in the knowledge of the Divine Will, or Laws; and also, according to what rule the instituted Laws of every civil society are to be tried and proved, whether they be just and right, or even whether they are capable of correction and amendment, by the supreme, civil authority; supposing that they have at any time deviated from the best and noblest end.

Further, demonstrate that duties of morality are not an imposition.

Upon this foundation can also be demonstrated, that there is something in the nature of God, and of mankind, distinct from ourselves; as also, that there is something within our own power which, upon an upright behaviour, administers immediate comfort

* The seven precepts given to the sons of *Noah* were as follows, viz.: 1. To abstain from idolatry. 2. To bless the name of God; or (as others express it), to abstain from malediction of the Divine name. 3. To abstain from murther. 4. To abstain from adultery, or from the pollution of impure mixtures. 5. To abstain from theft. 6. To appoint judges to be guardians of these precepts; or, in general, to preserve public justice. 7. To abstain from the limb of a living creature.

TOWER, *Laws of the Noachidæ.*

§ 4. Rise of Modern International Law.

and joy, as also substantial presages of future rewards; and, on the other hand, that there are natural causes of the bitterest anguish and apprehension, upon gross misbehaviour, from whence the decisions of conscience, which is armed (if we may so express it) with whips and scorpions against iniquity, may appear; and from hence clearly conclude, that mankind, in the duties of morality, are not imposed upon by cunning ecclesiastics or designing politicians.

The whole of this deeply interesting introduction should be given, but space cannot be taken. With the power of a giant, and with almost superhuman skill, is his great plan accomplished.

Milton.

The great poet, John Milton, was far more famous during his life for his political, than for his poetic writings. He can hardly be classed among the founders of International Law, though he has uttered many important truths in a very forcible manner. He was a true-hearted Republican, alike opposed to Monarchy and to Cromwell's usurpation, and his opponents are hacked, hewed, and pounded into mince-meat.

Pufendorf, *Law of Nature and Nations*, 1672.

Samuel Pufendorf was born in 1632, near Chemnitz, in Saxony. He died in 1689. The first edition of his *Law of Nature and Nations* appeared in 1672, and Barbeyrac says, "in 1684 he reprinted it at Frankfort-on-the-Main, augmented above a fourth part." Though adopting the same mode of argument with Grotius, his improvement is immense. Beginning with man as a sentient, moral being, he discusses the elements of his character and obligations, and traces out the various relations of life.

Summary of his great work.

In Book I, he discusses man's faculties, and the elements of right and wrong; in Book II, "that it is not agreeable to the nature of man to live without laws," and his duties to himself; in Book III, that he owes duties to his fellows; in Book IV, that rights of property, or dominion, may be acquired; in Book V, the mode of transferring these rights; in Book VI, that family relations are instituted; in Book VII, that man could not maintain his rights individually, and therefore created States, each of which is possessed of absolute Sovereignty; and he concludes, in Book VIII, with the rights, duties, and obligations of Sovereigns, which in free States apply to the Sovereign Peoples. So finished and complete is this great work, that no similar attempt has been made by later writers, that has come under my observation.

Filmer, *Patriarcha*, 1680.

Sir Robert Filmer, in 1680, published his *Patriarcha*, a work more ultra than Hobbes', in defence of the divine right of kings, which is completely overthrown by Locke and Sidney.

Locke, *Two Treatises on Government*, 1690.

John Locke published his *Two Treatises on Government* in 1690. It has been one of the most influential works upon International Law, and though, upon many important points, coincident with Grotius, Pufendorf, &c., he endeavors to establish two "supremes"—the "legislative" and the "people." Quotations will be found in our third chapter.

Sidney, *Discourses on Government*, 1683-1698.

No work has been read with more interest than Algernon Sidney's; *Discourses on Government*; not only because of the excellence of the views and argument, but as having been the ostensible cause of his condemnation and death in 1683 by the minions of Charles II, a part of the

MS. being produced on his trial. The work was first published in 1698. The third edition (1751) is prefaced with his memoirs, and the touching "apology" of this great and good man, written a few days before his death on the block. He was a strong Republican, and opposed to Cromwell's protectorate.

§ 4. Rise of Modern International Law.

Various other writers.

Other works appeared from Suarez, Zouche, Selden, Gentilis, Wicquefort, Temple, Textor, Coccejus, Loefler, &c., not differing from those herein quoted, so far as I can discover, on the points chief in this investigation.

Writers in the 18th century.

The wonderful progress in governmental science did not end with the seventeenth century. Though equal advance was not possible in subsequent as in the first discoveries, considerable improvements continued to be made. Early in the eighteenth century appeared the works of Wolf (Baron de Wolfius), Bynkershoek, and Heineccius, neither of which have I studied.

Barbeyrac, Notes on Pufendorf, 1706.

John Barbeyrac was born at Beziers, France, in 1674, and died in 1747. In 1706 he published an edition of Pufendorf with copious and valuable notes. Occasionally disagreeing with his author, he gives good reasons for his views, and his corrections generally commend themselves to the understanding and heart. As his annotations show, he was very careful and critical, referring to all the authorities, frequently adding those from which he ascertained Pufendorf had obtained his ideas, and enriching the views and arguments with quotations from Locke, Sidney, and other great writers subsequent to Pufendorf. I quote from the fourth edition, London, 1729. In 1724 he published an edition of Grotius, with judicious notes.

Grotius, 1724.

Burlamaqui, *Natural Law*, about 1730.

The pious John James Burlamaqui, born at Genoa, 1694, published his deeply interesting work on *Natural Law* about 1730. Christian statesmen must highly estimate this convincing argument in favor of the right, wisdom, and excellence of Government, both Divine and human.

Montesquieu, *Spirit of Laws*, 1748.

Charles de Secondat, Baron de Montesquieu, was born near Bordeaux, France, in 1689, and died in 1755. His *Spirit of Laws*, published in 1748, has been highly applauded, and never unduly, as I have seen; while by other writers, who should be competent judges, it has been more or less criticized, by some ridiculed. It does not become me to say that these authors failed for lack of genius in themselves to understand this work, but the parts which I have the capacity to comprehend, are so preëminently wise and excellent, that I am inclined to think the fault is in myself that other portions do not appear equally so. The learned Ferguson could say:

Ferguson, *Civil Government*, p. 108.

> When I recollect what the President Montesquieu has written, I am at a loss to tell why I should treat of human affairs; but I, too, am instigated by my reflections and my sentiments; and I may utter them more to the comprehension of ordinary capacities, because I am more in the line of ordinary men.

Criticisms of Montesquieu.

It has been amusing, though ludicrous, to witness the attempts of essayists and others, having a smattering of everything, knowing nothing

§ 4. Rise of Modern International Law.

profoundly, to pass judgment upon a work so far beyond their powers, either natural or acquired. This labor of twenty years, as century after century rolls by, will attain to higher and higher rank, have more and more weighty influence, when most of the efforts to criticize it will have passed into oblivion. Federal Republicans can, better than Monarchists, appreciate this great work, and an American edition must be published, with suitable notes.

Rutherforth, *Institutes of Natural Law*, 1754.

Dr. Rutherforth's *Institutes of Natural Law*, published in 1754 at Cambridge, is an able Anglicising of Grotius, which it would be well for some American, properly imbued with the genius of our institutions—the Sovereignty of the People—to imitate, and at the same time develope some of the fallacies of Dr. R. (This was written prior to my acquaintance with Dr. Agnew. He is abundantly competent for the task, which, as elsewhere observed, he is about to undertake.)

Vattel, *Law of Nations*, 1758.

Emmerich Vattel was born in Neufchatel, Switzerland, in 1714, and published his *Law of Nations* in 1758. His preface gives credit to Wolf for originating it, but, whatever that distinguished author may have produced, the principles established by Pufendorf in his first six books, and applied in the seventh and eighth to his greatest moral persons, are the basis of this immortal work. Most writers speak of it as "elegant," an adjective richly merited. Vattel was a Christian, a gentleman, and a scholar. My quotations are taken from a London 4to edition, 1759, though, comparing with another translation, I have taken the liberty to correct some typographical errors.

Coincidence of these authorities—

These writers agree in the main, except that Hobbes and Filmer unduly exalt *jure divino* of kings. They have differed about some metaphysical points, and as to whether the Law of Nature was identical with that of Nations, which Vattel seems to have set straight in his preface; but as to the chief points, the object of creating States, and their nature, rights, and obligations; the existence of Sovereignty in every State, and its indivisibility; that the location of and mode of exercising the Sovereignty—the *Right of Command*—determines the form of Government, whether it be Democratic, Aristocratic, or Monarchic; that these States may be more or less closely united by league without impairing Sovereignty—all these writers agree upon these fundamental points, so far as each discusses them. Neither did the knowledge of these governmental truths originate with Grotius; the same are taught by Aristotle, Cicero, Polybius, and others of the ancients, as our extracts will show.

—on chief points.

—and with ancient writers.

Does Locke differ from the rest as to Sovereignty?

Where differences of opinion are discoverable, they are not material to this investigation, except as to Locke's idea of Supreme Power, which appears to me irreconcilable with the others; although unquestionably if it be so, and has been the cause of our separation from Britain, and of this civil war, it is unaccountable that the difference should not have been earlier discovered.[1] The misjudgment of Pufendorf as to Federal

[1] With much reluctance do I venture to suggest what appears to have been an important oversight in discussing topics connected with Government. It seems folly to question the soundness

Republics, an important topic to us, arises not from difference with Grotius and Montesquieu as to *theories* concerning States, but from the misapplication of those theories to *practice* in framing a Federal Union or System. These great authors harmonize on the fundamental points, and one after another has corrected the immaterial errors preceding, till the Law of Nations has become an established science, founded on the Law of Nature, the principles and the statutes of the Law of Nature being derived mainly from the deep fountain of governmental instruction, the revealed will of Nature's Divine Author and Teacher. Other writers might be mentioned and quoted with profit, but these are the chief teachers, and all Christian nations recognize the binding obligations of the International Code they have framed.

§ 4. Rise of Modern International Law.

Pufendorf's mistake as to Federal Republics.

That the uninformed reader may properly appreciate the authority of the writers from whom we chiefly quote, extracts are taken from Robert Ward's *History of the Law of Nations*, published at Dublin, 1795. It is a standard authority, and the learned writer himself well discusses governmental principles. Having described the "jumble" into which the subject of Government had been brought in the sixteenth century, he thus continues:

Ward's opinion of these authorities. *History of the Law of Nations*, 1795.

It was in the midst of this uncertainty about true principles, and this dearth of proper authorities, that the philosopher of *Delft* rose like a star amid the surrounding darkness, and with an ability and happiness peculiar to himself, had at once the honour of inventing and bringing his system to perfection: For he gave to the world a Treatise which has stood the test of time.

WARD'S *History of the Law of Nations*, ii, p. 370.

---

of such authorities as Locke and Blackstone, and senseless impudence to intimate that the scores of able intellects which have learnedly discussed the writings of these great teachers, have not comprehended their subject, and have failed to discover a fundamental difference actually existing between them and other equally eminent authorities. Bentham, for instance, in his *Fragment on Government*, shows the absurdities of Blackstone, who follows Locke, and locates Sovereignty in the legislative or parliament. One would suppose at that period (1776), with Britain at war with the Colonies upon this very question, that such a keen discriminator would have perceived whether or not the dispute was simply about the proper location of Sovereignty—the *Right of Command*—in the British State. Any important difference between Blackstone and Locke, and other teachers of governmental science, would have certainly been pointed out, did it exist. He well exhibits the nonsense of Blackstone's teachings, but makes no effort to show the correctness of another school of Sovereignty, which would have led him to consider Grotius, Pufendorf, &c. Carried off with his utilitarian principles, sceptical as to religion, and thereby rendered incapable of comprehending the propriety and necessity of a Supreme Power, which is equally required over every earthly State as over the state of nature—the universe, he seems to have sought a basis for Government other than the *Right of Command;* and so that he could toss over the cob-house castle of Blackstone, it was immaterial what became of Sovereignty. So excellent as he is, however, in many of his views, in *Principles of the Civil Code*, a *Plea for the Constitution*, *Anarchical Fallacies*, *Principles of International Law*, &c., it leaves small reason to hope that I can see any mistake in Blackstone that he failed to perceive. Yet nevertheless, I *do* see that Locke and Blackstone make the *legislative* supreme. I *do* see that Pufendorf makes the legislative only *one of the parts* of the Supreme Power, and therefore not itself supreme. If any one has shown this difference of opinion, I have not discovered it, much less seen it explained, or one or the other shown to be wrong. Am I so bewildered by examining, as that a mole-hill has become a mountain? Is the difficulty only real to myself, having gone beyond my capacity, floundering in truth's deep waters? Is there anything in the difference or not?

Bentham's criticism of Blackstone—

—should discover existing difference.

Bentham's ability.

Did Bentham fail to see an existing error.

Indiscreet as it may be, very presumptuous, I freely admit, candor and truth require the point to be raised, whether the excellent Whigs of Britain, Guizot and all of that school in France, Dr. Lieber and his worthy coadjutors in our own country, in their earnest, noblest, heaven-blessed endeavors to restrict Administration of authority to its proper and legitimate sphere, have not too much disregarded the ground-work or basis, the source or fountain, of all Administration, of all Government—the *Right of Command*—Sovereignty. Pufendorf, still extant, throws much light upon this interesting, but confused, mystified subject, which our wise men must reinvestigate and see if it cannot be made more comprehensible.

Our wise men must examine.

§ 4. Rise of Modern International Law.

Grotius. Motives to his work.

During the life of this great man, a civil war had desolated the finest provinces of his country, and like other civil wars which are continued to any length, had degenerated into the most horrible licentiousness and personal hatred. He had besides this, observed throughout the Christian world, a cruelty and injustice of which, to use his own words, even barbarians might be ashamed. War was denounced upon the slightest, or without any cause at all, and arms once taken, all reverence for law human or divine was laid aside; "as if," says he, "an edict had been published for the commission of every sort of crime." With many philosophers, this threw things into the other extreme, and the amiable and learned *Erasmus*, a man who is described as "Pacis Ecclesiasticæ et civilis amantissimus," endeavoured to prove that all wars whatsoever, were illegal under the Christian Dispensation.

Grotius saw the disadvantages of the two extremes, and he had well discerned the total want of science both in ancient and modern times, in the methods pursued to obtain a knowledge of the duties of nations. He therefore resolved to give his labours to the improvement, or rather to the invention of a code of laws, which might go to the bottom of things, and supply authorities where authorities were wanting, to almost every case in the conduct of nations which could happen. And eminently qualified he was for this most noble and beneficial of all tasks. To the strongest mental powers, he added a learning which on almost every subject, and in every language was stupendous, and supported it by the most indefatigable industry, a virtue incorruptible, and the purest zeal for Christianity. . . .

His qualifications.

His method—

The method which he pursued in order to produce a work, which, although coming from a private man, should have the weight of a code of laws with Princes, he has himself expounded to us with great clearness in the preface. He found it necessary to get at some certain fixed principles which should be acknowledged to be such by all who read them. In order to do this, he was obliged to survey all the codes of morality and of general law which had ever been known: he penetrated into all the sciences between which and his own, he could discover any analogy; and he examined the opinions of all great men of whatsoever class, from which he could extract any thing like a community of sentiment. This, being properly arranged under its different heads, together with the vast additions of his own learning, and the support of all that could be drawn from history by way of precedent, he ventured, with very noble ambition to imagine might be received by the world as the rule for their duty in the most critical predicaments. The event answered all his expectations!

—researches.

Supports of his work.

The work of *Grotius*, therefore, has for its support, all that the Philosophers, the Poets, the Orators, and the Critics of antiquity or of modern times can furnish. It is aided by all the lights which can be drawn from the famous civil and canon laws, cleared from its defects and the false glosses which had been put upon it by corrupt or ignorant interpreters; above all, it is finally corrected and stampt with authority, by the indications of the divine will, as collected from the inspired writers of the old and new Testaments, from the comments of the Hebrew divines, and the authority of the fathers.

Its authority acknowledged

It is not surprising that a code thus supported, should have immediately advanced into celebrity, and put down in the end those various heterogeneous compositions which had till then formed the rule of conduct for nations, and occasioned many of those discordant arguments and cases which we have related. The Elector Palatine, Charles Lewis, was the first Prince who had the honour to be the real patron of the work; for although it came out dedicated to Lewis XIII. yet it was strangely neglected by that King, who gave no reward to the author. The Elector, however, struck with its utility, ordered it to be taught publicly in his University of *Heidelburg*, and founded a Professor's chair, for the express purpose of teaching the *Law* of Nature and of Nations. At the same time the envy of the Learned was almost equal to the merit of the writer. Parties were formed amongst them for the attack and the defence of the code, and those who defended it were stigmatized with the name of *Grotians*. All this was not uncommon; but what will be the ideas of those who are versed in this excellent Treatise, when they are told on the authority of *Barbeyrac*, that such was the prejudice against it, that it was supposed to be calculated to annihilate the three great principles

Its patrons.

Its opponents.

of the Roman law, "HONESTE VIVERE; NEMINEM LÆDERE; SUUM CUIQUE TRIBUERE." To such a height of error can prejudice and old habits carry us.

§ 4. Rise of Modern International Law.

Its merits.

The sound strength of GROTIUS, however, soon overcame such puny opposition, and he had the satisfaction of observing the progressive reputation of his code. It became very early the favourite study of the great GUSTAVUS, who is said to have found as much pleasure from it, as ALEXANDER found from reading the poems of HOMER, and who proved his admiration of the author, by ordering him to be called to the public employments of Sweden. In 1656, it was taught in the university of *Wittemburg* as public law; and in about sixty years from the time of publication, it was universally established in CHRISTENDOM as the true fountain-head of the EUROPEAN Law of Nations.

Its commentators.

We may suppose, however, that the minds of men being now called to new and important matters, did not let the subject pass off without adding their labours to its elucidation. Accordingly, innumerable commentaries were written upon it with various success, some of which have arisen to authority, although the most of them have died away, and are forgotten. Two great works, however, have been founded upon the Treatise, *De Jure Belli et Pacis*, which have deservedly attained to such celebrity and weight, that we cannot finish our subject without giving a place in it to their authors. The first is the famous work of PUFFENDORF; the second, of VATTEL.

Two other great works.

Pufendorf's *Laws of War and Peace.*

Although GROTIUS had taken a most extensive range, and endeavoured to search the duties of nations in war and peace to the bottom; yet the lovers of abstract reasoning, independent of particular application, found that there was something wanting to the perfection of his science. He had entitled his work, *The Laws of War and Peace*, in order, says *Barbeyrac*, to engage the attention of Statesmen and Generals, whom it most concerned to understand them. He was forced, therefore, to plunge at once into his subject; and although, as he goes along, he satisfies his readers as to the reasons for their duty, yet it is by arguments taken up as it were pro re nata, the elements of which are supposed to be already understood; or if elementary principles are necessary for the elucidation of the point before him, a long discussion branches out from the immediate subject, which we feel would be better disposed of somewhere else: in the same manner as if, in proving a proposition of *Euclid*, we had not gone over the preliminary propositions on which it was founded, but were obliged to stop in the middle of it, to prove the fundamental position.

Reasons for Grotius' imperfections.

These Pufendorf remedies

It was to remedy this defect *in method*, that *Puffendorf*, many years after *Grotius*, took up the subject anew; and, beginning with the system of human nature, endeavoured to analyze the heart and mind of man as independent of society, before he came to enquire into his duties as a citizen. The whole, therefore, of what is called MORAL PHILOSOPHY, was set forth in detail by this great writer, as a proper supplement to what was wanting in GROTIUS, and as the true foundation of the public duties of nations.

Moral Philosophy the basis.

The two works chief authority.

These two works together, formed for a long time, and form still, the sources to which all Statesmen and Moralists must look for the resolution of difficulties, and the direction of virtue. They are, however, not totally without objection, although the objection is applicable more to their manner than their matter; more to the accidents of time and place, than to their intrinsic worth. In the first place, they seem to labour too much under the heaviness of form, which characterizes most forensic treatises. Their speculations are, besides, loaded so much with quotations, that they are absolutely weighed down with them, and the progress of the reader to the end proposed, is inconceivably impeded. Not to mention that the work of *Puffendorf*, although it supplies the method which was wanting in *Grotius*, possesses not, perhaps, that brief perspicuity which in a long course of reasoning is so desirable. In addition to this, it has been supposed that the views which these two great men have taken of their subject, have not actually been so clear or so extensive as they might be. *Grotius* is imagined, in making the strong separation which he does between the Law of Nature and the Law of Nations, to have confined the latter too much to actual convention. *Puffendorf*, in affirming that the Law of Nations is *exactly* the same as the Law of Nature obeyed by individuals, only applied to states, instead of men; is thought not to have entered deeply enough into the matter. For it is contended, that the particular application of this Law to Nations, is susceptible of various modifications, according to

Objections to them.

§ 4. Rise of Modern International Law.

the different nature of the subjects on which it has to work, and which consequently renders the detail and minutiæ of it different from the mere Law of Nature as obeyed by individuals. Hence, therefore, something was still supposed to be wanting to the perfection of the science.

Another work wanted.

Vattel's *Law of Nations.*

It was this which gave rise to the Treatise of VATTEL, who, in his preface, has entered nicely into all these distinctions. Whether his objections to *Grotius* and *Puffendorf* were so weighty, as alone to render a new code necessary, it is perhaps needless to enquire. Certain it is, that the world is obliged to him for a very complete work, the model of which is more light and elegant than that of those heavy though magnificent structures which we have surveyed; for he has thoroughly cleared them from the cumbrous ornaments which were supposed to adorn them, and has rendered the way into the interior less difficult and obscure. His method is excellent: he marshals, in the outset, a series of preliminary principles, on which he professes to found all his future reasoning, and to which, in the course of it, he regularly refers. Whether his preliminaries, however, will always bear out his conclusions, it does not come within our intention to examine. At the same time one objection may, I think, fairly be made to him, which is, that he is too general, and often too slight, in his reasoning, and attends too little to its particular application; a mode for the most part unsatisfactory, and frequently dangerous. It is perhaps a consequence of this, or to avoid the opposite fault of his two predecessors, that his work, though stored with excellent argument, is not sufficiently supported by the authorities of cases, without which even the reasoning upon natural law will want much useful elucidation, but which forms the very essence and base of all that concerns what he calls the *positive* Law of Nations.

Complete—elegant.

Method excellent.

Query as to his preliminaries.

Criticisms, (are they merited?)

The Treatise of *Vattel*, therefore does not appear by any means to preclude the necessity of studying the works of his masters. Whoever, indeed, would understand his subject thoroughly, and become acquainted with the Law of Nations in all its nicety and extent, let what will be his own stores of knowledge, or the depth of his thought, can hardly arrive at the end he proposes, without giving all his mind to the Treatises of those wonderful men.

Vattel's masters to be studied.

Origin, right, &c., of International Law.

To understand how the Law of Nations has been created, why it has been instituted, upon whom it is obligatory, by what right and authority it operates, are important points, that are best set forth by Vattel in his preface, which every one in this Republic of Nations should study.

Vattel's preface.

Vattel's preliminaries.

This clear and forcible writer begins his great work by laying down preliminaries to which he subsequently refers as axioms. They are truths which Grotius and Pufendorf had fully demonstrated, the proof of which it was not necessary for him to reiterate; and though drawn directly from Wolf, as we learn from the preface, yet the remarkable coincidence with the earlier authorities proves the science of International Law, in its fundamentals, to be well established. To become familiar with them, will give point to the examination of other writers, and they will accordingly be found, with the preface, in chap. ii, on *Principles of Government.*

§ 5.—IMPORTANCE OF THE LAW OF NATIONS TO THE UNITED STATES.

International Law important to all States.

It is strikingly apparent from Vattel's preliminaries, that no member, however humble, of any Christian State, however small, is without interest in International Law. What affects the State, affects each individual of the State; and as the power and influence of the individual, of the State increases, so does the importance of the Law of Nations. All States, too, which recognize the International Code, are deeply concerned in its principles and construction, even though far removed from other nations, having little intercourse and few leagues. But to nations situated as are those of Europe, their borders joining, interests clashing, struggles arising, the code which all recognize as the measure of their rights and obligations, assumes vastly increased importance. Though disunited from each other, every State governing all its affairs independently, they yet find it necessary to make leagues concerning various subjects, the adherence to which tends strongly to peace and amity. The construction of these leagues is an important branch of International Jurisprudence, but each of the sovereignties of Europe claims the right to be its own judge of infractions, and of the proper means and measure of redress.

§5. Importance of Law of Nations to U. S.

Disconnected States interested—connected States more so.

Leagues formed under—

—construed by International Law.

It was a favorite project of those monarch minds, Elizabeth and Henry IV,[1] to unite the States of Europe in a republic, that their differences might be adjudicated by a competent tribunal. Had that been accomplished, a new and far deeper interest would have been imparted to the code by which their difficulties were to be tried and arbitrated. With what deep research, stringent scrutiny, might sovereigns, statesmen, all public men, even all private men, be led to examine the laws by which their States were to be governed, and see to it that their action should be such as the federal tribunal would not condemn! What a glorious project to check the wrongs of States, to promote peace and prosperity in the earth!

Plan of Elizabeth and Henry IV, to confederate.

What Europe in vain attempted, the providence of GOD has been openly accomplishing for America, and we have been too blind to perceive it. Britain, France, Russia, are not more independent nations, than are Massachusetts, Virginia, and Illinois. Each one of these Sovereignties is possessed of every prerogative that belongs to the Queen, the Emperor, the Czar, though these free Peoples, for the convenient exercise of their Sovereignty, have seen fit, as do other Sovereigns more or less, to delegate authority to subordinate agents. These States, too, have created a Federal Tribunal to adjudicate their differences, and yet stupidly have we lost sight of the chief object of its institution. We are precisely in the condition, in this respect, in which Europe would have been, could Elizabeth and Henry IV have realized their magnificent scheme; and if the importance of International Law would have been enhanced by a Federal Union in Europe, it is equally so with our own American States.

The effort that failed in Europe, being accomplished in America.

These States separate and independent.

Their Federal tribunal.

Importance to them of International Law.

But we have gone much farther in the principles of Confederation than those great geniuses of the sixteenth and seventeenth centuries ever

Our improvement in confederating.

[1] An eminent authority remarks concerning this: "During this period of our historical deduction was published the *Projet de Paix perpetuelle* [Project of Perpetual Peace] of the Abbe Saint-Pierre, which the benevolent author, by a kind of pious fraud, attributed to Henry IV. and his minister Sully, with the view of recommending it to the adoption of the sovereigns and ministers," &c.

Project of Henry IV to confederate Europe.

Though no confirmation of this statement has been observed, and the original report has been many times referred to by good authorities, Wheaton was probably correct. He would not have made this positive declaration without knowledge. But whether those great monarchs or Saint-Pierre were the author, the project was worthy of the mightiest intellects, the largest hearts of the world, and it is equally available for illustration.

WHEATON, *Law of Nations*, p. 261.

§5. Importance of Law of Nations to U. S.

To preserve liberty, small States best.

To obtain strength, unite them by league.

First attempt fails.

Improvements in second.

Rights dependent on International Law.

Deep interest of these States in that Law.

Our ignorance of it.

conceived. Resolved to preserve to the people their God-given liberty; knowing from all experience of the world, and from their own common sense, that for a free people a government over a moderate area was desirable, if not absolutely necessary; and at the same time knowing that these States would individually have little power and influence in the world, and perhaps become the prey of European despots, our fathers united these States by a league of closer alliance than any of which we have knowledge. That proving ineffectual to preserve the Union so dearly cherished, they made another closer still. It contains some well-known provisions, and some peculiar to itself, all of which have become to these Sovereignties their instituted Civil Law; but for the bulk of their code they are dependent on the Law of Nations. Therefore may it be affirmed, without fear of contradiction, that no Peoples have existed since the shining days of Grecian Confederacies, that were so deeply concerned as are these States in *jus gentium;* nor had even they, nor the Hebrews, by any means an equal interest with this much greater Union of over thirty millions of men; yet no people seem to be more ignorant of it; by none have its important and simple teachings been more mystified and confused.

Kent's advice to have a new text book.

These young nations to be pupils, not teachers.

Most heartily do I subscribe to the opinion of Chancellor Kent, that a new work on International Law is required, which shall embody the few modern improvements that have been made, and, what is more important, cut away the excrescences, monstrosities, which American teachers have added. These young Peoples must remember the sage advice of their great jurist, that "in cases where the principal jurists agree, the presumption will be very great in favor of the solidity of their maxims; and no civilized nation, that does not arrogantly set all ordinary law and justice at defiance, will venture to disregard the uniform sense of the established writers on International Law."

Who are the teachers.

What would be a gross assumption in us.

"The principal jurists," I am inclined to think, will in this case be allowed to be Grotius, Cumberland, Pufendorf, Montesquieu, Vattel, &c. These "established writers," it will be found, "agree" upon "their maxims;" and it would indeed appear to be a gross assumption for us, in the infancy of our Republic, in order to establish the theory of a double sovereignty, that is not less unnecessary and inexpedient than it is chimerical and absurd, to "arrogantly set all ordinary law and justice at defiance." Not only are we defying all Christendom, but are confusing the subject, and rendering it incomprehensible.

Confusion of terms.

See chap. iii.

State and *Sovereignty*, for instance, have clear and definite signification according to those old writers, and it is of fundamental importance that their precise meaning be preserved; yet Story's remarks quoted from his *Commentaries on the Constitution*, exhibit the utter confusion in the use of these chief words: A league is considered by these old authorities, and well established, too, to be the only means of binding sovereign States. Yet Mr. Webster, with his wonderful eloquence and power, intimates that we have found a means of subjecting supreme authority to the coercive control of government. At least, if it does not mean that, his great speech in reply to Calhoun means nothing.

§5. Importance of Law of Nations to U. S.

Kent's opinion of old authorities.

The most of our teachings are so directly at variance with these old authorities, as to imply their repudiation. To show that they are not rejected, and at the same time to indicate the erroneous method in which the received principles are handled by our ablest, most honored writers, I quote from Chancellor Kent's Commentaries:

The United States subject to International Law.

When the United States ceased to be a part of the British Empire, and assumed the character of an independent nation,[1] they became subject to that system of rules which reason, morality, and custom had established among the civilized nations of Europe, as their public law. During the war of the American Revolution, Congress claimed cognizance of all matters arising upon the law of nations,[2] and they professed obedience to that law, "according to the general usages of Europe." * By this law we are to understand that code of public instruction which defines the rights and prescribes the duties of nations in their intercourse with each other. The faithful observance of this law is essential to national character and to the happiness of mankind. According to the observations of Montesquieu (b. 1, c. 3), it is founded on the principle, that different nations ought to do each other as much good in peace, and as little harm in war, as possible, without injury to their true interests. But as the precepts of this code are not defined in every case with perfect precision, and as nations have no common civil tribunal to resort to for the interpretation and execution of this law, it is often very difficult to ascertain, to the satisfaction of the parties concerned, its precise injunctions and extent; and a still greater difficulty is the want of adequate pacific means to secure obedience to its dictates.[3]

KENT'S *Commentaries* i, 1.

Kent derives our right to International Law through English common law.

* Ordinance of the 4th December, 1781, relative to maritime captures, *Journals of Congress*, vol. vii, 185. The English judges have frequently declared that the law of nations was part of the common law of England. Triquet *v.* Bath, 3 *Burr*, 1478; Heathfield *v.* Chilton, 4 *ib.*, 2015; and it is well settled that the common law of England, so far as it may be consistent with the Constitution of this country, and remains unaltered by statute, is an essential part of American jurisprudence, *vide infra*, &c. [The Articles of Confederation having been ratified 1st March, 1781, Congress was duly authorized, under the International Code, to pass the ordinance, 4th Dec., . . . We need not look to "the Common Law of England" as the derivative channel of the right of these States, individually or united, to participate in the benefits of International Law. We have it by nature and the Law itself.]

Martens on such a nation.

[1] As observed by Martens (l. i, c. 3, § 2)—whom the learned jurist soon refers to as eminent authority, superior even to Pufendorf, "It is only in a very indefinite sense that these associations of states (the Seven United Provinces and the Helvetic Union) can be considered as *republics*" or nations, and he gives ample reason for it, as is elsewhere shown. The United States being another "association of States," can only, "in a very indefinite sense," be styled a "nation;" so that, to give the Law of Nations the definite application to which it is entitled, wherever acknowledged, the Chancellor should have spoken of these States as "independent nations," pluralizing that important word, for our fathers were very careful on this point, iterating and reiterating in their ever-memorable Declaration of Independence, that this "ONE people" were not to be a single State like Great Britain, but "free and independent STATES." This erroneous starting leads to the other principal errors in these Commentaries.

Nation should be pluralized—

—as in Declaration of Independence.

Assumption of power does not make Congress, Colonies, or States, a *nation*.

[2] Whatever "Congress claimed," whatever acquiescence emergencies compelled out of these States, during the revolutionary period, in the acts of the Colonial Congress, the last of which became the Continental Congress, gave *those* bodies no title to any position as a "nation." As the tacitly or explicitly authorized agent of the Colonies and afterwards of the nations comprising the United States, the Colonial Congresses, and afterwards the Continental Congress, may be said to have been governed by International Law, as Congress undoubtedly was under the Articles of Confederation, and now under the present Constitution. But that could never make a "nation" out of distinct colonies while they were constituent parts of another nation; nor could it, when these Colonies became sovereign Nations, destroy, consolidate, these States or Nations, and make a "nation" out of Congress, or out of these States united. In this land of written law, for such a change as that, written authority must be produced.

It is in no spirit of conceit or of carping criticism that these comments are made, but solely to call attention to these sources of error from which the others flow.

Judiciary to decide as to International Law.

[3] This difficulty was well apprehended by the framers of our Government, at least it would seem it should have been from their action. To provide a "common civil tribunal to resort to for the interpretation and execution of this [international] law" between these Sovereign States, as

§5. Importance of Law of Nations to U. S.

Natural and Positive Law of Nations.

There has been a difference of opinion among writers concerning the foundation of the law of nations. It has been considered by some as a mere system of positive institutions, founded upon consent and usage; while others have insisted that it was essentially the same as the law of nature, applied to the conduct of nations, in the character of moral persons, susceptible of obligations and laws. We are not to adopt either of these theories as exclusively true. The most useful and practical part of the law of nations is, no doubt, instituted or positive law, founded on usage, consent, and agreement. But it would be improper to separate this law entirely from natural jurisprudence, and not to consider it as deriving much of its force and dignity from the same principles of right reason, the same views of the nature and constitution of man, and the same sanction of Divine revelation, as those from which the science of morality is deduced. There is a natural and a positive law of nations. By the former, every state, in its relations with other states, is bound to conduct itself with justice, good faith, and benevolence; and this application of the law of nature has been called by Vattel the necessary law of nations, because nations are bound by the law of nature to observe it; and it is termed by others the internal law of nations, because it is obligatory upon them in point of conscience.*

Moral obligation of States.

We ought not, therefore, to separate the science of public law from that of ethics, nor encourage the dangerous suggestion, that governments are not so strictly bound by the obligations of truth, justice, and humanity, in relation to other powers, as they are in the management of their own local concerns. States, or bodies politic, are to be considered as moral persons, having a public will, capable and free to do right and wrong, inasmuch as they are collections of individuals, each of whom carries with him into the service of the community the same binding law of morality and religion which ought to control his conduct in private life.† The law of nations is a complex system, composed of various ingredients. It consists of general principles of right and justice, equally suitable to the government of individuals in a state of natural equality, and to the relations and conduct of nations; of a collection of usages, customs, and opinions, the growth of civilization and commerce; and of a code of conventional or positive law. In the absence of these latter regulations, the intercourse and conduct of nations are to be governed by principles fairly to be deduced from the rights and duties of nations, and the nature of moral obligation; and we have the authority of the lawyers of antiquity, and of some of the first masters in the modern school of public law for placing the moral obligation of nations and of individuals on similar grounds, and for considering individual and national morality as parts of one and the same science.

International Law in Europe and America.

The law of nations, so far as it is founded on the principles of Natural Law, is equally binding upon every age, and upon all mankind. But the Christian nations of Europe, and their descendants on this side of the Atlantic, by the vast superiority of their attainments in arts, and science, and commerce, as well as in policy and government; and above all, by the brighter light, the more certain truths, and the more definite sanction which Christianity has communicated to the ethical jurisprudence of the ancients, have established a Law of Nations peculiar to themselves. They form together a community of nations united by religion, manners, morals, humanity, and

---

Heineccius.

* Vattel Prelim. § 7. . . . Heineccius, in his "Elementa Juris Naturæ et Gentium," b. 1, c. 1 and 3 (and which is very excellent as to the first branch of the subject), and all the other great masters of ethical and national jurisprudence, place the foundation of the law of nature in the will of God, discoverable by right reason, and aided by divine revelation; and its principles, when applicable, apply with equal obligation to individuals and to nations. A recent French writer (M. Victor Foucher) divides the law of nature into two branches: (1) *Public* international law, which regulates the political relation of nation to nation; and (2) *Private* international law, which, though based upon the first, regulates the reciprocal and personal relations of the inhabitants of different states.

Foucher.

Lieber's *Political Ethics.*

† Dr. Francis Lieber, in his "Manual of Political Ethics," 2 vols., Boston, 1838, has shown with great force, and by the most striking and apposite illustrations, the original connection between right and morality, and the reason and necessity of the application of the principles of ethics to the science of politics and the administration of government. The work is excellent in its doctrines, and it is enriched with various and profound erudition.

---

well as of their Civil Law of the Constitution, would seem to have been the chief object of creating the Supreme Court.

science, and united also by the mutual advantages of commercial intercourse, by the habit of forming alliances and treaties with each other, of interchanging ambassadors, and of studying and recognizing the same writers and systems of public law.*

§5. Importance of Law of Nations to U. S.

After devoting the present lecture to a cursory view of the history of the law of nations, I shall enter upon the examination of the European and American code of international law, and endeavor to collect with accuracy, its leading principles, and to discuss its practical details.

Law of Nations in ancient Greece.

The law of nations, as understood by the European world, and by us, is the offspring of modern times. The most refined states among the ancients seem to have had no conception of the moral obligations of justice and humanity between nations, and there was no such thing in existence as the science of international law. They regarded strangers and enemies as nearly synonymous, and considered foreign persons and property as lawful prize. Their laws of war and peace were barbarous and deplorable. So little were mankind accustomed to regard the rights of persons or property, or to perceive the value and beauty of public order, that, in the most enlightened ages of the Grecian republics, piracy was regarded as an honorable employment There were powerful Grecian states that avowed the practice of piracy; and the fleets of Athens, the best disciplined and most respectable naval force in all antiquity, were exceedingly addicted to piratical excursions. It was the received opinion, that Greeks, even as between their own cities and states, were bound to no duties, nor by any moral law, without compact, and that prisoners taken in war had no rights, and might lawfully be put to death, or sold into perpetual slavery, with their wives and children.

The Amphictyons an international court.

There were, however, many feeble efforts, and some successful examples, to be met with in Grecian history, in favor of national justice. The object of the Amphictyonic Council was to institute a law of nations among the Greeks, and settle contests between Grecian states by a pacific adjustment.[1] It was also a law of nations among them, and one which was very religiously observed, to allow the vanquished the privilege of burying their own dead, and to grant the requisite truce for that purpose. Some of the states had public ministers resident at the courts of others, and there were some distinguished instances of great humanity shown to prisoners of war. During a cessation of arms in the course of the Peloponnesian War, Athens and Sparta agreed to an exchange or mutual surrender of prisoners. The sound judgment and profound reflections of Aristotle naturally raised his sense of right above the atrocious maxims and practices of his age, and he perceived the injustice of that doctrine of Grecian policy, that, by the laws of war, the vanquished became the absolute property of the victor. "Wise men," he observed, "entertained different opinions upon that subject. Some considered superiority as a proof of virtue, because it is its

MANNING'S *Commentaries on the Law of Nations.*

* The law of nature, by the obligations of which individuals and states are bound, is identical with the will of God, and that will is ascertained, says Mr. Manning, either by consulting Divine revelation, where that is declamatory, or by the application of human reason where revelation is silent. Christianity, in the words of Butler, "is an authoritative publication of natural religion," and it is from the sanction which revelation gives to natural law, that we must expect the gradual increase of the respect paid to justice between nations. Christianity reveals to us a general system of morality, but the application to the details of practice is left to be discovered by human reason. See *Commentaries on the Law of Nations*, by William Oke Manning, Esq., London, 1839, b. 2, ch. 1. This work is the first English treatise which I have seen, containing a regular and didactic discussion of the science, and it is a work of great excellence; and I beg leave to recommend it strongly to the attention of the American student.

International court of Greece— —our first attempt— —our second attempt. De Tocqueville.

1 It was; though Grote, Thirlwall and other authorities consider the Amphictyonic Union to have been chiefly for religious purposes. Our object was the same under the first Constitution, which signally failed. Having learned, by over a century of practice, the wisdom of dividing to different agents the exercise of Sovereignty, we applied it in the new Federal Constitution, by separating the legislative, executive, and judicial departments, and further dividing the legislative. The Amphictyonic Council, the Achean League, our first Congress, were liable to have their judgments warped by political and other considerations, and a tribunal must be devised that, rendered independent of all extraneous influences, would be able justly to decide every question of difference according to the laws instituted between the parties, and the immutable principles of right and justice, recognized and established in the code of International Law. De Tocqueville does not over-estimate the importance of the Federal Judiciary, in considering it in effect the key-stone of our governmental arch.

§5. Importance of Law of Nations to U. S.

natural effect, and they asserted it to be just that the victors should be masters of the vanquished; whilst others denied the force of the argument, and maintained that nothing could be truly just which was inconsistent with humanity." He then proceeded to weaken by argument the false foundations on which the law of slavery, by means of capture in war, was established; and though he does not write on the subject very distinctly or forcibly, it seems to be quite apparent that his convictions were against the law.

In like manner is the subject discussed as to Rome and the middle ages, but we pass over to page 10 of Kent.

Influence of Christianity.

Of all these causes of reformation, the most weight is to be attributed to the intimate alliance of the great powers as one Christian community. The influence of Christianity was very efficient towards the introduction of a better and more enlightened sense of right and justice among the governments of Europe. It taught the duty of benevolence to strangers, of humanity to the vanquished, of the obligation of good faith, and of the sin of murder, revenge, and rapacity. The history of Europe, during the early periods of modern history, abounds with interesting and strong cases, to show the authority of the church over turbulent princes and fierce warriors, and the effect of that authority in meliorating manners, checking violence, and introducing a system of morals, which inculcated peace, moderation, and justice. The church had its councils or convocations of the clergy, which formed the nations professing Christianity into a connection resembling a federal alliance, and those councils sometimes settled the titles and claims of princes, and regulated the temporal affairs of the Christian powers. The confederacy of the Christian nations was bound together by a sense of common duty and interest in respect to the rest of mankind. It became a general principle of belief and action, that it was not only a right, but a duty, to reduce to obedience, for the sake of conversion, every people who professed a religious faith different from their own. To make war upon infidels was, for many ages, a conspicuous part of European public law; but this gross perversion of the doctrines and spirit of Christianity had at least one propitious effect upon the Christian powers, inasmuch as it led to the cultivation of peace and union between them, and to a more free and civilized intercourse. The notion that it was lawful to invade and subdue Mahometan and Pagan countries, continued very long to sway the minds of men; and it was not till after the age of Grotius and Bacon, that this error was entirely eradicated. Lord Coke held that an alliance for mutual defence was unlawful between Christians and Turks; and Grotius was very cautious as to the admission of the lawfulness of alliances with infidels, and he had no doubt that all Christian nations were bound to assist one another against the attacks of infidels. Even Lord Bacon thought it a matter of so much doubt, as to propound it seriously as a question, whether a war with infidels was not first in order of dignity, and to be preferred to all other just temporal quarrels; and whether a war with infidels might not be undertaken merely for the propagation of the Christian faith, without other cause of hostility.[1]

Of Chivalry.

The influence of chivalry was beneficial upon the laws of war. It introduced declarations of war by heralds; and to attack an enemy by surprise was deemed cowardly and dishonourable. It dictated humane treatment to the vanquished, courtesy to enemies, and the virtues of fidelity, honor, and magnanimity in every species of warfare.

Of the Civil Law.

The introduction and study of the civil law must also have contributed largely to more correct and liberal views of the rights and duties of nations. It was impossible that such a refined and wise system of municipal and ethical jurisprudence as the Roman law, could have been taught in universities and schools, and illustrated by a succession of eminent civilians, who were worthy of being associated with the Roman

[1] These most Christian nations need to understand this important truth. It is *not* the duty of one sovereign State to correct the wrongs of another. Connecticut is not responsible for Maryland, and what is more, has no right to press her excellences upon the latter; no shadow of right to correct its errors.

sages without at the same time producing a great effect upon the public mind. This grand monument of the embodied wisdom of the ancients, when once known and examined, must have reflected a broad stream of light upon the feudal institutions and the public councils of the European nations. We accordingly find that the rules of the civil law were applied to the government of national rights, and they have contributed very materially to the erection of the modern international law of Europe. From the 13th to the 16th century, all controversies between nations were adjudged by the rules of the civil law.

§5. Importance of Law of Nations to U. S.

Treaties, conventions, and commercial associations, had a still more direct and visible influence in the formation of the great modern code of public law. They gave a new character to the law of nations, and rendered it more and more of a positive or instituted code. Commercial ordinances and conventions contributed greatly to improve and refine public law, and the intercourse of nations, by protecting the persons and property of merchants in cases of shipwreck, and against piracy, and against seizure and arrest, upon the breaking out of war, &c., &c.

Of treaties.

The learned jurist then discusses the law concerning shipwrecks, the treatment of prisoners, the admission of ambassadors, and reaches Grotius.

Thus stood the law of nations at the age of Grotius. It had been rescued, to a very considerable extent, from the cruel usages and practices of the barbarians. It had been restored to some degree of science and civility by the influence of Christianity, the study of the Roman law, and the spirit of commerce. It had grown in value and efficacy, from the intimate connection and constant intercourse of the modern nations of Europe, who were derived from a common origin, and were governed by similar institutions, manners, laws, and religion. But it was still in a state of extreme disorder, and its principles were little known and less observed. It consisted of a series of undigested precedents, without order or authority. Grotius has, therefore, been justly considered as the father of the law of nations. He arose like a splendid luminary, dispelling darkness and confusion, and imparting light and security to the intercourse of nations. It is said by Barbeyrac, that Lord Bacon's works first suggested to Grotius the idea of reducing the law of nations to the certainty and precision of a regular science. Grotius has himself fully explained the reasons which led him to undertake his necessary, and most useful and immortal work. He found the sentiment universally prevalent, not only among the vulgar, but among men of reputed wisdom and learning, that war was a stranger to all justice, and that no commonwealth could be governed without injustice. The saying of Euphemus in Thucydides, he perceived to be in almost every one's mouth, that nothing which was useful was unjust. Many persons, who were friends to justice in private life, made no account of it in a whole nation, and did not consider it as applicable to rulers. He perceived a horrible licentiousness and cruelty in war, throughout the Christian world, of which barbarians might be ashamed. When men took up arms, there was no longer any reverence for law, either human or divine; and it seemed as if some malignant fury was sent forth into the world, with a general license for the commission of all manner of wickedness and crime.

GROTIUS. Increased importance of International Law.

Its confusion.

Grotius father of the science.

His motives.

The object of Grotius was to correct these false theories and pernicious maxims, by showing a community of sentiment among the wise and learned of all nations and ages, in favour of the natural law of morality. He likewise undertook to show that justice was of perpetual obligation, and essential to the well-being of every society, and that the great commonwealth of nations stood in need of law, and the observance of faith, and the practice of justice. His object was, to digest, in one systematic code, the principles of public right, and to supply authorities for almost every case in the conduct of nations; and he had the honour of reducing the law of nations to a system, and of producing a work which has been resorted to as the standard of authority in every succeeding age. The more it is studied, the more will our admiration be excited at the consummate execution of the plan, and the genius and erudition of the

Grotius' objects.

Superior excellence of his work.

§5. Importance of Law of Nations to U. S.

Other works defective in illustration.

author. There was no system of the kind extant, that had been produced by the ancient philosophers of Greece, or by the primitive Christians. The work of Aristotle on the rights of war, and the writings of the Romans on their fecial law, had not survived the wreck of ancient literature; and the essays of some learned moderns on public law, were most imperfect, and exceedingly defective, in illustrations from history, and in omitting to place their decisions upon the true foundations of equity and justice. Grotius, therefore, went purposely into the details of history and the usages of nations, and he resorted to the works of philosophers, historians, orators, poets, civilians, and divines, for the materials out of which the science of public morality should be formed; proceeding on the principle, that when many men, at different times and places, unanimously affirmed the same thing for truth, it ought to be ascribed to some universal cause. His unsparing citation of authorities, in support of what the present age may consider very plain and undisputed truths, has been censured by many persons as detracting from the value of the work. On the other hand, the support that he gave to those truths, by the concurrent testimony of all nations and ages, has been justly supposed to contribute to that reverence for the principles of international justice which has since distinguished the European nations.

Pufendorf in first rank.

Too much ethics.

Among the disciples of Grotius, Puffendorf has always held the first rank. His work went more at large into the principles of natural law, and combined the science of ethics with what may be more strictly called the law of nations. It is copious in detail, but of very little practical value in teaching us what the law of nations is at this day. It is rather a treatise on moral philosophy than on international law;[1]

Kent & Ward.

See p. 21.

Moral philosophy and International Law.

[1] The similarity of thought and expression with the views of Ward concerning Grotius, Pufendorf, and Vattel, will be observed, and we are happy in having the concurrence of this eminent American authority with Ward, the learned historian, as to the fact that a code of International Law has been established, and that these three writers are the chief founders. On p. 9 the Chancellor refers to Ward by name in the text and in a note (not herein quoted), thus incidentally aiding to establish Ward's credit as an authority. But if Kent intended to follow Ward in his judgment of Pufendorf, it would seem quite a lapse was made. Referring to the extract, it will be seen credit is given by the historian to Pufendorf for applying the principles of moral philosophy to *jus gentium;* precisely what the Chancellor has well and properly commended in Grotius. Some of the ancients had attempted this, and Gillies, in his preface to Aristotle's Ethics and Politics remarks:

Gillies' *Preface to Aristotle's Ethics.*

The "Ethics to Nichomachus and the Politics" ought never to have been disjoined, since they are considered by Aristotle himself as forming essential parts of one and the same work; which, as it was the last and principal object of his studies, is of all his performances the longest, the best connected, and incomparably the most interesting. The two treatises combined constitute what he calls his *practical* philosophy; an epithet to which, in comparison with other works of the same kind, they will be found peculiarly entitled. In the Ethics the reader will see a full and satisfactory delineation of the moral nature of man, and of the discipline and exercise best adapted to its improvement. [This Christian writer meant, of course, that the work had been as well done as was possible for a heathen philosopher.] The philosopher speaks with commanding authority to the hearts and affections, through the irresistible conviction of the understanding. His morality is neither on the one hand too indulgent, nor on the other impracticable. His lessons are not cramped by the narrow, nor perverted by the wild, spirit of system; they are clear inductions, flowing naturally and spontaneously from a copious and pure source of well digested experience. [It appears to be the most perfect union of *theory* and *practice* in governmental science to be found outside of the Bible, and almost perfectly harmonizes with it. Oh, that we could have a *Christian* Aristotle to add the light of Revelation to the wisdom of this great intellect!]

Man a *Political* animal.

Laws for his government.

New discoveries are old.

Aristotle's *Politics* place government on a solid foundation.

According to the Stagirite [so called from being born at the city of Stagira, B. C. 384], men are, and always have been, not only moral and social, but also *political* animals; in a great measure dependent for their happiness and perfection on the public institutions of their respective countries. The grand inquiry, therefore, is, what are the different arrangements that have been found under given circumstances, practically most conducive to these main and ultimate purposes? This question the author endeavored to answer in his "Politics," by a careful examination of two hundred systems of legislation, many of which are not elsewhere described; and by proving how uniformly, even in political matters, the results of observation and experiment conspire with and confirm the deductions of an accurate and full theory. In this incomparable work the reader will perceive "the genuine spirit of laws" deduced from the specific and unalterable distinctions of governments; and with a small effort of attention, may discern not only those discoveries in science, unjustly claimed by the vanity of modern writers, [the principle of *representation* is one of the "discoveries" Dr. G. refers to, and *reciprocal control* another,] but many of those improvements in practice, erroneously ascribed to the fortunate events of time and chance in these latter and more enlightened ages. The same invaluable treatise discloses the pure and perennial spring of all legitimate authority; for in Aristotle's "Politics," and HIS *only*, government is placed on such a natural and solid foundation, as leaves neither its origin incomprehensible, nor its stability precarious; and his conclusions, had they been well weighed, must have surmounted or suppressed those erroneous and absurd doctrines, which long upheld despotism on the one hand, and those equally erroneous and still wilder suppositions of conventions and compacts, which have more recently armed popular fury on the other.

Yet neither Plato, his pupil Aristotle, nor Cicero, could properly ground the science of ethics and the same thing may be said of the works of Wolfius, Burlemaqui, and Rutherforth. The summary of the law of nations, by Professor Martens, is a treatise of greater practical utility, but it is only a very partial view of the system, being confined to the customary and conventional law of the modern nations of Europe. Bynkershoeck's treatise on the laws of war has been received as of great authority on that particular branch of the science of the law of nations, and the subject is by him ably and copiously discussed. The work is replete with practical illustration, though too exclusive in its references to the ordinances of his own country, to render his authority very unquestionable. The most popular, and the most elegant writer on the law of nations is Vattel, whose method has been greatly admired. He professed to have followed the voluminous work of Wolff on the Law of Nature and Nations, and to be enlightened and guided by his learning, with much improvement upon the doctrine and arrangement of his great master. He has been cited, for the last half century, more freely than any one of the public jurists; but he is very deficient in philosophical precision. His topics are loosely, and often tediously and diffusively discussed, and he is not sufficiently supported by the authority of precedents, which constitutes the foundation of the positive law of nations.[1]

§5. Importance of Law of Nations to U. S.

Martens more practical.

Bynkershoeck relates to war.

Vattel popular and elegant.

A high authority—

—unfair criticism.

---

either for man or States, being ignorant of the Bible, or not recognizing its Divine character. During the dark ages succeeding the enlightened days of Greece and Rome, ethics were little thought of; and though Bacon, Grotius, Cumberland, and others had started investigations, some wise man was wanted to complete the work, and especially to apply philosophical principles, as understood by the Christian world, to the science of Government. This great work, the grandest, most important the human mind had ever conceived, Pufendorf undertook and accomplished to admiration. It is true he did not begin with nations, but in the most natural, most effective way, he first establishes principles, which apply to man individually and in the family relations,—the first form of society, which was instituted directly, immediately by the Creator himself, for this social animal. He then shows why and how men unite and form a greater moral person, and applies these same principles to these States; and then as a Sovereignty—a *Right of Command*—had been generated by this union of men into States, or by direct gift from Deity, he applies these ethical principles to these sovereign States, whether under the rule of *one*, *the few*, or *the many*. And though the first six books are occupied in establishing the philosophic basis, every idea is with direct reference to the two concluding books, on the origin, nature, and duties of States and Sovereigns, and no thought dispensable; and it is therefore unaccountable that this great jurist should have so far detracted from the influence to which this work is entitled in the department of science for which it was designed, as to style it "rather a treatise on moral philosophy than on international law." The man who could devise and execute such a work, should certainly be able to give it a proper title, and he styles it the *Law of Nature and Nations*, which it merits more than any other book ever written. Probably if it did not, it would hardly have "always held the first rank" after Grotius, which Kent admits; and in method and thoroughness is it the superior. Martens' work is very excellent, and its "practical utility" is demonstrated in these pages, but it is not saying too much for Pufendorf, that of all the works since published concerning International Law, no ten could be named not better to be dispensed with than his; and even the whole of them would not supply the vacuum its loss would occasion.

The Bible the basis of ethics.

Pufendorf best applies it to International Law.

His method.

Kent's criticism unfair.

Pufendorf high authority.

[1] Our author here has the opinion of Ward to sustain him, and though my judgment is of small account against either, and as nothing against them jointly, I beg leave modestly to intimate, that unintentionally they perhaps do injustice to Vattel, and unnecessarily weaken his authority. As to his deficiency in "philosophical precision," I am not enough of a philosopher to discover it; but if his principles are not stated with "precision," his arguments not handled with "precision," his conclusions not reached with "precision," the world is greatly in error in admitting the weight his work has carried for three quarters of a century. If "his topics are loosely, and often tediously and diffusively discussed," I am so unfortunate as not to discover any less, at least, of these attributes in the composition and argument of these or any other of his detracting critics. Their works are excellent and "elegant," but scarcely equal that most perfect specimen of composition on this subject, as to precision both of thought and of expression—Vattel's immortal work upon the *Law of Nations*. He was a wonderful genius, a worthy cotemporary of Montesquieu's; and had essayists and others, who have attempted to show their profundity by fault-finding, as thoroughly mastered the science as had Vattel, they would, in my humble judgment, have found more to commend and less to criticize.

Ward & Kent unfair to Vattel—

—as to "precision"—

Neither is the objection just, that "he is not sufficiently supported by the authority of precedents;" at least they should have alluded to the reason given in his preface for not offering more of them. Had Grotius or Pufendorf never written, or had Barbeyrac not added to them his copious notes, this charge might be just. His predecessors have been styled heavy and cumbersome, overloaded with quotations and precedents, but they contain little or nothing the student does not need, and Kent judiciously commends Grotius on this account. Vattel undertook a different task, and well is it accomplished. His work is "elegant," the word exactly. The reader is supposed to be acquainted with Grotius and Pufendorf, and also with Wolf and others;

—as to "precedents."

§5. Importance of Law of Nations to U. S.

A new work required on the Law of Nations.

There is no work which combines, in just proportions, and with entire satisfaction, an accurate and comprehensive view of the necessary and of the instituted Law of Nations, and in which principles are sufficiently supported by argument, authority, and examples. Since the age of Grotius, the code of war has been vastly enlarged and improved, and its rights better defined, and its severities greatly mitigated. The rights of maritime capture, the principles of the law of prize, and the duties and privileges of neutrals, have grown into very important titles in the system of national law. We now appeal to more accurate, more authentic, more precise, and more commanding evidence of the rules of public law, by a reference to the decisions of those tribunals, to whom, in every country, the administration of that branch of jurisprudence is specially intrusted. We likewise appeal to the official documents and ordinances of particular states, which have professed to reduce into a systematic code, for the direction of their own tribunals, and for the information of foreign powers, the Law of Nations, on those points which relate particularly to the rights of commerce, and the duties of neutrality. But in the absence of higher and more authoritative sanctions, the ordinances of foreign states, the opinions of eminent statesmen, and the writings of distinguished jurists, are regarded as of great consideration on questions not settled by conventional law.[1] In cases where the principal jurists agree, the presumption will be very great in favor of the solidity of their maxims; and no civilized nation, that does not arrogantly set all ordinary law and justice at defiance, will venture to disregard the uniform sense of the established writers on international law. England and the United States have been equally disposed to acknowledge the authority of the works of jurists, writing professedly on public law, and the binding force of the general usage and practice of nations, and the still greater respect due to judicial decisions recognizing and enforcing the Law of Nations. In all our foreign negotiations and domestic discussions of questions of National Law, we have paid the most implicit respect to the practice of Europe, and the opinions of her most distinguished civilians.[2] In England, the report made in 1753 to the king, in answer to

Regard for legal decisions—

—official State papers—

—opinions of statesmen and jurists.

Force of these authorities.

---

and in beautiful, flowing language, so simple that any schoolboy can comprehend, the principles established by his predecessors, are applied to these States; and the precedents are to be found where the principles are found. His preliminaries, that are the ground-work of his arguments, are an admirable compend of truths established by Grotius and Pufendorf, though drawn directly from Wolf. To write Grotius and Pufendorf and Wolf all over, was unnecessary, and he remarks in his preface that he has sought to add modern precedents, which were necessarily few, for his work was published in 1758, and Barbeyrac had annotated Pufendorf in 1706, adding pretty much everything of importance. Barbeyrac also in 1724 published an edition of Grotius with notes, which probably gave the chief facts to that date, and some time or other published an edition of Cumberland, which Martens speaks of, but which I have been unable to find. Evidently Vattel could get but few precedents, unless he copied from preceding works with which the reader was supposed to be familiar.

"Distinguished jurists" must be careful.

[1] For that important reason should "distinguished jurists" be correct in their teachings. Their weight of responsibility is very great. Dealing with the affairs of nations, they should be much more careful than some of our American writers have been, lest, as Grotius observes, "they render that which, of itself, was not very easie, much more dark and obscure than it was before."

Who are the "most distinguished civilians"?

Have we followed them?

[2] The correctness of that remark is, I trust, at least questionable. It is to be hoped, either that we have *not* "paid the most implicit respect;" or that "the opinions" which we have respected and followed, are not those of Europe's "most distinguished civilians." There are other teachers in the science of Government besides those discussed by Kent, and who, it seems, have been most followed in our *theoretical* knowledge; while in our correct *practice*, in the main, of the teachings of these truly "most distinguished civilians," our success has wonderfully proved their consummate skill and wisdom. There has been, as I believe, from before our Revolution down, a direct conflict between our *theories* concerning Government, and our *practice*. The former have been lamentably wrong; the latter, almost uniformly correct. Particularly in our "domestic discussions of questions of International Law, we have paid the most implicit respect to the practice of Europe, and the opinions of her" Locke, Rousseau, and Blackstone—rather a strange concatenation, yet each a link in the chain that pulls to the downfall, it seems to me, of all genuine *Right of Command.* Had we in our *theories* followed Grotius, Vattel, and Montesquieu, as we have done in *practice*, we had never been led into this civil war: had Britain followed the "most distinguished civilians," we had never been separated from our mother-land.

If there is this conflict between theory and practice which is believed, and which it is the main purpose of this work to prove, it is quite time our wise, and good, and great statesmen in the South and in the North, were studying into the subject, to ascertain how the difficulties can be obviated. Never can the blessings of peace be again enjoyed by these States, till the Citizens of

§5. Importance of Law of Nations to U. S.

the Prussian memorial, is very satisfactory evidence of the obedience shown to the great standing authorities on the Law of Nations, to which I have alluded. And in a case which came before Lord Mansfield, in 1764, in the K. B., he referred to a decision of Lord Talbot, who had declared that the Law of Nations was to be collected from the practice of different nations, and the authority of writers; and who had argued from such authorities as Grotius, Barbeyrac, Bynkershoeck, Wiquefort, &c., in a case where British authority was silent. The most celebrated collections and codes of Maritime Law, such as the *Consolato del Mare*, the laws of Oleron, the laws of the Hanseatic League, and, above all, the marine ordinances of Louis XIV., are also referred to, as containing the most authentic evidence of the immemorial and customary law of Europe.

Dignity and importance of International Law.

The dignity and importance of this branch of jurisprudence cannot fail to recommend it to the deep attention of the student; and a thorough knowledge of its principles is necessary to lawyers and statesmen, and highly ornamental to every scholar who wishes to be adorned with the accomplishments of various learning. Many questions arise in the course of commercial transactions which require for their solution an accurate acquaintance with the conventional law of Europe, and the general doctrines of the prize tribunals. Though we may remain in peace, there is always war raging in some part of the globe, and we have at the present moment neutral rights to exact, and neutral duties to perform, in the course of our Mediterranean trade, and in the trade to the Brazils and along the shores of the Pacific. A comprehensive and scientific knowledge of International Law is highly necessary, not only to lawyers practising in our commercial ports, but to every gentleman who is animated by liberal views, and a generous ambition to assume stations of high public trust. It would be exceedingly to the discredit of any person who should be called to take a share in the councils of the nation, if he should be found deficient in the great leading principles of this law; and I think I cannot be mistaken in considering the elementary learning of the Law of Nations, as not only an essential part of the education of an American lawyer, but as proper to be academically taught. My object, therefore, in some succeeding lectures, will be, to discuss all the leading points arising upon the rights and duties of nations, in the several relations of peace, of war, and of neutrality.

Kent's high position.

He applies International Law to the U. States "nation"—

—not to these States.

Consequent failure.

We have no legal authority more eminent than the Commentaries of Chancellor Kent, and we shall have occasion to quote further. These extracts serve a double purpose: first, to prove who are the founders of International Law, and that this country recognizes the binding obligations of their code; and secondly, that these obligations are applied chiefly, if not solely, to the "nation" of the United States. These States of ours are nowhere recognized as the Sovereign Nations which, while they have instituted their Constitution as a civil law to direct them in part, are yet chiefly governed by International Law. Hence, throughout the work, there is no rising to the full dignity of the subject. To treat at length upon our Federal System, and never once allude to the grand idea that it was a new discovered plan—or, rather, an important improvement on an old plan—to conduct with harmony the affairs of sovereign States, is certainly to rear a work without its chief and proper basis. No one would infer from these Commentaries, that *State* and *nation* were precisely synonymous, interchangeable words; but the United States "nation" is raised to view as the peer of Sovereigns, and these States of ours are subordinated, degraded, and made to the Union

every grade become better informed than hitherto upon the subject of Government. When *theories* are understood, we can apprehend the rights, and correct the wrongs of these States; not before. Then, too, can we form a permanent Union.

§5. Importance of Law of Nations to U. S.

like counties and towns to a State. De Tocqueville, as we shall see, much more correctly apprehended the genius and dignity of our Government, than any of our northern authors.

De Tocqueville more correct.

Story's *Conflict of Laws.*

Story, another eminent authority, took for a subject, *Conflict of Laws, Foreign and Domestic,* which one would suppose might bring prominently to view the relations of these States to each other. In the dedication to Kent, the author remarks: "You have done for America, what Mr. Justice Blackstone, in his invaluable Commentaries, has done for England." Though neither Kent nor Story lived to see the striking manner in which this declaration is fulfilled, we do. The misconceptions of these great jurists, and others, have at length brought us to disunion, just as those of Blackstone caused the separation of these Colonies from the motherland. Is the separation to be alike permanent?

A prediction.

Its fulfilment.

Importance of International Law to U. S.

In the preface is this sensible observation: "The subject is one of great importance and interest; and from the increasing intercourse between foreign States, as well as between the different States of the American Union, it is daily brought home more and more to the ordinary business and pursuits of human life. The difficulty of treating such a subject in a manner suited to its importance and interest, can scarcely be exaggerated. The materials are loose and scattered, and are to be gathered from many sources, not only uninviting, but absolutely repulsive, to the mere student of the Common Law. There exists no treatise upon it in the English language; and not the slightest effort has been made, except by Mr. Chancellor Kent, to arrange in any general order even the more familiar maxims of the Common Law in regard to it," &c.

STORY'S *Preface.*

Lack of text books.

That such a statement could be made so lately as 1834, is good evidence of our ignorance of these State relations, and of the want of text books for the adjudication of their difficulties. Though the differences of laws and of decisions in several of these States are discussed, it is not the work it would have been, had the author realized that the "conflict" between these States was between sovereign nations.

General Importance of International Law.

With pleasure is a quotation made from the introductory remarks, giving Story's influential opinion as to the importance of International Law. Grotius is several times quoted, and also Vattel and Martens, Burlamaqui a few times, and Ward and Pufendorf, and other writers who are not in this work referred to, thus giving the influential sanction of Story to them as authorities in International Law.

Diversity of interests and views.

STORY'S *Conflict of Laws,* p. 1.

§ 1. The earth has long since been divided into distinct Nations, inhabiting different regions, speaking different languages, engaged in different pursuits, and attached to different forms of government. It is natural that, under such circumstances, there should be many variances in their institutions, customs, laws, and polity; and that these variances should result sometimes from accident, and sometimes from design, sometimes from superior skill, and knowledge of local interests, and sometimes from a choice founded in ignorance, and supported by the prejudices of imperfect civilization. Climate, and geographical position, and the physical adaptations springing from them, must at all times have had a powerful influence in the organization of each society, and have given a peculiar complexion and character to many of its arrangements

The bold, intrepid, and hardy natives of the North of Europe, whether civilized or barbarous, would scarcely desire, or tolerate, the indolent inactivity and luxurious indulgences of the Asiatics. Nations inhabiting the borders of the ocean, and accustomed to maritime intercourse with other nations, would naturally require institutions and Laws, adapted to their pursuits and enterprises, which would be wholly unfit for those who should be placed in the interior of a continent, and should maintain very different relations with their neighbours, both in peace and war. Accordingly, we find, that, from the earliest records of authentic history, there has been (as far at least as we can trace any) little uniformity in the laws, usages, policy, and institutions, either of contiguous or of distant nations. The Egyptians, the Medes, the Persians, the Greeks, and the Romans, differed not more in their characters and employments from each other, than in their institutions and laws. They had little desire to learn, or to borrow from each other; and indifference, if not contempt, was the habitual state of almost every ancient nation in regard to the internal polity of all others.

§5. Importance of Law of Nations to U. S.

§ 2. Yet even under such circumstances, from their intercourse with each other, questions must sometimes have arisen, as to the operation of the laws of one nation upon the rights and remedies of parties in the domestic tribunals, especially when they were in any measure dependent upon, or connected with foreign transactions. How these questions were disposed of, we do not know; but it is most probable that they were left to be decided by the analogies of the municipal code, or were abandoned to their fate, as belonging to that large class of imperfect rights, which rests wholly on personal confidence, and is left without any appeal to remedial justice. It is certain, that the nations of antiquity did not recognise the existence of any general or universal rights and obligations, such as among the moderns constitute what is now emphatically called the Law of Nations. Even among the Romans, whose jurisprudence has come down to us in a far more perfect and comprehensive shape than that of any other nation, there cannot be traced out any distinct system of principles applicable to international cases of mixed rights. This has in some measure been accounted for by Huberus upon the supposition, that at the time, to which the Roman jurisprudence relates, the Roman dominion extended over so great a portion of the habitable world, that frequent cases of contrariety or conflict of laws could scarcely occur. But this is a very inadequate account of the matter; since the antecedent jurisprudence of Rome must have embraced many such cases at earlier periods; and if there had been any rules, even traditionally known to govern them, they could scarcely have failed of being incorporated into the civil codes of Justinian. In many of the nations, over which the Romans extended their dominion, the inhabitants were left in possession of their local institutions, usages, and laws, to a large extent; and commercial, as well as political, intercourse must have brought many diversities of laws and usages in judgment before the tribunals of justice. We have the most abundant evidence on this head, in relation to the Jews, after they had submitted to the Roman yoke, who were still permitted to follow their own laws, in the times of our Saviour, and down to the destruction of Jerusalem.

Differences must be adjusted.

Ancients had no Law of Nations.

The Romans.

The Jews under the Romans.

§ 3. The truth is, that the Law of Nations, strictly so called, was in a great measure unknown to antiquity, and is the slow growth of modern times, under the combined influence of Christianity and Commerce. It is well known, that when the Roman Empire was destroyed, the Christian world was divided into many independent sovereignties, acknowledging no common head, and connected by no uniform civil polity. The invasions of the Barbarians of the North, the establishment of the feudal system in the middle ages, and the military spirit and enterprise cherished by the Crusades, struck down all regular commerce, and surrendered all private rights and contracts to mere despotic power. It was not until the revival of commerce on the shores of the Mediterranean, and the revival of Letters and the study of the Civil Law by the discovery of the Pandects, had given an increased enterprise to maritime navigation, and a consequent importance to maritime contracts, that anything like a system of international justice began to be developed. It first assumed the modest form of commercial usages; it was next promulgated under the more imposing authority of royal ordinances; and it finally became by silent adoption a generally connected sys-

Origin of the Law of Nations.

Influence of Christianity and commerce—

—of Roman law.

§5. Importance of Law of Nations to U. S.

The Law of Nations now established.

tem, founded in the natural convenience, and asserted by the general comity of the commercial nations of Europe. The system, thus introduced for the purposes of commerce, has gradually extended itself to other objects, as the intercourse of nations has become more free and frequent. New rules, resting on the basis of general convenience, and an enlarged sense of national duty, have been, from time to time, promulgated by jurists, and supported by courts of justice, by a course of juridical reasoning, which has commanded almost universal confidence, respect, and obedience, without the aid, either of municipal statutes, or royal ordinances, or international treaties.

Present necessity of International Law.

§ 4. Indeed in the present times, without some general rules of right and obligation, recognized by civilized nations, to govern their intercourse with each other, the most serious mischiefs and most injurious conflicts would arise. Commerce is now so absolutely universal among all countries; the inhabitants of all have such a free intercourse with each other; contracts, marriages, nuptial settlements, wills, and successions, are so common among persons, whose domicils are in different countries, having different and even opposite laws on the same subjects; that without some common principles adopted by all nations in this regard, there would be an utter confusion of all rights and remedies; and intolerable grievances would grow up to weaken all domestic relations, as well as to destroy the sanctity of contracts and the security of property.

Examples.

§ 5. A few simple cases will sufficiently illustrate the importance of some international principles in matters of mere private right and duty. Suppose a contract, valid by the laws of the country, where it is made, is sought to be enforced in another country, where such a contract is positively prohibited by its laws; or, *vice versa*, suppose a contract, invalid by the laws of the country where it is made, but valid by that of the country where it is sought to be enforced; it is plain, that unless some uniform rules are adopted to govern such cases, (which are not uncommon,) the grossest inequalities will arise in the administration of justice between the subjects of the different countries in regard to such contracts. Again; by the laws of some countries marriage cannot be contracted until the parties arrive at twenty-one years of age; in other countries not until they arrive at the age of twenty-five years. Suppose a marriage to be contracted between two persons in the same country, both of whom are over twenty-one years but less than twenty-five, and one of them is a subject of the latter country, is such a marriage valid, or not? If valid in the country where it is celebrated, is it valid also in the other country? Or the question may be propounded in a still more general form. Is a marriage, valid between the parties in the place where it is solemnized, equally valid in all other countries? Or is it obligatory only as a local regulation, and to be treated everywhere else as a mere nullity?

Different provinces of the same empire.

§ 6. Questions of this sort must be of frequent occurrence, not only in different countries wholly independent of each other; but also in provinces of the same empire, governed by different laws, as was the case in France before the Revolution; and also in countries acknowledging a common sovereign, but yet organized as distinct communities, as is still the case in regard to the communities composing the British Empire, the Germanic Confederacy, the States of Holland, and the domains of Austria and Russia. [Did the author class these States of ours, with French provinces and the States of Holland, now subject to a monarch, or with France, Spain, Russia, &c.? I discover nothing to indicate his view.] Innumerable suits must be litigated in the judicial forums of these countries and provinces, in which the decision must depend upon the point, whether the nature of a contract should be determined by the law of the place, where it is litigated; or by the law of the domicil of one or both of the parties; or by the law of the place, where the contract was made; whether the capacity to make a testament should be regulated by the law of the testator's domicil, or that of the location of his property; whether the form of his testament should be prescribed by the law of his domicil, or of that of the location of his property, or of that of the place where the testament is made; and in like manner, whether the law of the domicil, or what other laws should govern in cases of succession of intestate estates.

A query as to these States.

§ 7. It is plain that the laws of one country can have no intrinsic force, *propric vigore*, except within the territorial limits and jurisdiction of that country. They can bind only its own subjects and others who are within its jurisdictional limits, and the latter only while they remain there. No other nation, or its subjects, are bound to yield the slightest obedience to those laws. Whatever extra-territorial force they are to have, is the result, not of any original power to extend them abroad, but of that respect, which, from motives of public policy, other nations are disposed to yield to them, giving them effect, as the phrase is, *sub mutuæ vicissitudinis obtentu*, with a wise and liberal regard to common convenience and mutual necessities. Boullenois has laid down the same exposition as a part of his fundamental maxims. "Of strict right," says he, "all the laws made by a sovereign have no force or authority except within the limits of his domains. But the necessity of the public and general welfare has introduced some exceptions in regard to civil commerce."[1]

§5. Importance of Law of Nations to U. S.

Laws restricted to a country's limits.

§ 8. This is the natural principle flowing from the equality and independence of nations. It is an essential attribute of every sovereignty, that it has no admitted superior, and that it gives the supreme law within its own domains on all subjects appertaining to its sovereignty. What it yields, it is its own choice to yield; and it cannot be commanded by another to yield it as a matter of right. And accordingly it is laid down by all publicists and jurists, as an incontestable rule of public law, that one may with impunity disregard the law pronounced by a magistrate beyond his territory. *Extra territorium jus dicenti impune non paretur*, [*one may with impunity disobey a sovereign uttering law outside his territory*,] is the doctrine of the Digest, and it is equally as true in relation to nations, as the Roman law held it to be in relation to magistrates. Vattel has deduced a similar conclusion from the general independence and equality of nations, very properly holding that relative strength or weakness cannot produce any difference in regard to public rights and duties, and that whatever is lawful for one nation, is equally lawful for another; and whatever is unjustifiable in one is equally so in another. And he affirms, in the most positive manner (what indeed cannot well be denied), that sovereignty, united with domain, establishes the exclusive jurisdiction of a nation within its territories, as to controversies, crimes, and rights arising therein.

Only Sovereignty gives force to law.

A sovereign powerless out of his domain.

§ 9. The jurisprudence, then, arising from the conflict of the laws of different nations, in their actual application to modern commerce and intercourse, is a most interesting and important branch of public law. To no part of the world is it of more interest and importance than to the United States, since the union of a national government with that of twenty-four distinct, and in some respects independent states, necessarily creates very complicated relations and rights between the citizens of those states, which call for the constant administration of extra-municipal principles. This branch of public law may be fitly denominated private international law, since it is chiefly seen and felt in its application to the common business of private persons and rarely rises to the dignity of national negotiations or national controversies.[2]

Importance of International Law to the United States.

§ 10. The subject has never been systematically treated by writers on the common law of England; and, indeed, seems to be of very modern growth in that kingdom; and can hardly, as yet, be deemed to be there cultivated, as a science, built up and defined with entire accuracy and precision of principles. More has been done to give it form and symmetry within the last fifty years, than in all preceding time. But much

Not systematically treated in England.

---

[1] Here was an opportunity to present to the world the radical change we had made. Though usually, as Story says, "the laws of one country can have no intrinsic force except within [its] jurisdiction;" yet is it not entirely so with us. Thirty-four nations (before some seceded), the peers of any other nations, were "bound to yield [perfect] obedience to those laws" which no one of them had enacted, though, as Boullenois intimates, they have efficacy because "a Sovereign [who has] force or authority within the limits of his domains," has joined with other Sovereigns and authorized the enactment of laws upon certain questions that should be obligatory throughout their joint domains. Does not a change of commercial law, so important if not improving, merit notice in this first treatise in English upon this subject?

Story omitted to notice a change we made in commercial law.

[2] Had the learned jurist properly understood the question of Sovereignty, alluded to in § 8, preceding, would he not have had something to add to this § 9, concerning these sovereign States united?

Did Story understand sovereignty?

§5. Importance of Law of Nations to U. S.

yet remains to be done to make it, what it ought to be, in a country of such vast extent in its commerce, and such universal reach in its intercourse and polity.[1]

Every State has exclusive Sovereignty and jurisdiction.

§ 18. I. *General Maxims of International Jurisprudence.*—The first and most general maxim or proposition is that which has been already adverted to, that every nation possesses an exclusive sovereignty and jurisdiction within its own territory. The direct consequence of this rule is, that the laws of every state affect, and bind directly all property, whether real or personal, within its territory; and all persons, who are resident within it, whether natural born subjects, or aliens; and also all contracts made, and acts done within it. A state may, therefore, regulate the manner and circumstances, under which property, whether real or personal, or in action, within it, shall be held, transmitted, bequeathed, or transferred, or enforced; the condition, capacity, and state, of all persons within it; the validity of contracts, and other acts, done within it; the resulting rights and duties growing out of these contracts and acts; and the remedies, and modes of administering justice in all cases calling for the interposition of its tribunals to protect, vindicate, and secure the wholesome agency of its own laws within its own domains.

What it may do.

Boullenois as to the powers of a Sovereign State.

§ 19. Accordingly, Boullenois has laid down the following among his general principles (*principes généraux*). He says, (1.) He, or those, who have the sovereign authority, have the sole right to make laws; and these laws ought to be executed in all places within the sovereignty, where they are known, in the prescribed manner. (2.) The sovereign has power and authority over his subjects, and the goods, which they possess within his dominions. (3.) The sovereign has also authority to regulate the forms and solemnities of contracts, which his subjects make within the territories under his dominions; and to prescribe the rules for the administration of justice. (4.) The sovereign has also a right to make laws, to govern foreigners in many cases; for example, in relation to property, which they possess within the reach of his sovereignty; in relation to the formalities of contracts, which they make within his territories; and in relation to judiciary proceedings, if they institute suits before his tribunals. (5.) The sovereign may in like manner make laws for foreigners, who even pass through his territories; but these are commonly merely laws of police, made for the preservation of order within his dominions, whether they are perpetual or temporary. The same doctrine is either tacitly, or expressly conceded by every other jurist, who has discussed the subject at large, whether he has written upon municipal law, or upon public law.[2]

Restrictions of laws to their territory.

§ 20. II. Another maxim, or proposition, is, that no state or nation can, by its laws, directly affect, or bind property out of its own territory, or persons not resident therein, whether they are natural born subjects or others. This is a natural consequence of the first proposition; for it would be wholly incompatible with the equality and exclusiveness of the sovereignty of any nation, that other nations should be at liberty to regulate either persons or things within its territories. It would be equivalent to a declaration, that the sovereignty over a territory was never exclusive in any nation, but only concurrent with that of all nations; that each could legislate for all, and none for itself; and that all might establish rules, which none were bound to obey. The absurd result of such a state of things need not be dwelt upon. Accordingly Rodemburg has significantly said, that no sovereign has a right to give the law beyond his own dominions; and if he attempts it, he may be lawfully refused obedience; for wherever the foundation of laws fails, there their force and jurisdiction fail also. *Constat igitur extra territorium legem dicere licere nemini, idque si fecerit quis, impune ei non pareri, quippe ubi cesset statutorum fundamentum, robor, et jurisdictio.* P. Voet speaks to the same effect: *Nullum statutum sive in rem, sive in personam, si de ratione juris civilis sermo instituatur, sese extendit ultra statuentis territorium.*

Necessity of having American text books.

[1] If important to England, how much more so to this country! And if no text book has yet been issued properly treating this subject, quite time is it that some jurist who understands the A B C of State Sovereignty should engage in the work.

[2] These truths must be remembered. It takes sovereign power to enact a law, as will be more fully established, and when the Sovereign or Sovereigns delegate the power, as in the Federal agency, the letter of authority cannot be transcended.

[*Statute is of no effect either on person or property, beyond the territory of the enacting power.*] Boullenois, (as we have seen,) announces the same rule: *De droit étroit, toutes les loix, que fait un souverain, n'ont force et autorité que dans l'étendue de sa denomination;* and, indeed, it is the common language of jurists. Mr. Chief Justice Parker has recognised the doctrine in the fullest manner. "That the laws," says he, "of any state cannot by any inherent authority be entitled to respect extra-territorially, or beyond the jurisdiction of the state, which enacts them, is the necessary result of the independence of distinct sovereignties."

§5. Importance of Law of Nations to U. S.

§ 23. III. From these two maxims or propositions, there flows a third, and that is, that whatever force and obligation the laws of one country have in another, depends solely upon the laws, and municipal regulations of the latter, that is to say upon its own proper jurisprudence and polity, and upon its own express or tacit consent. A state may prohibit the operation of all foreign laws, and the rights growing out of them, within its own territories. It may prohibit some foreign laws, and admit the operation of others. It may recognise, and modify, and qualify some foreign laws; it may enlarge, or give universal effect to others. It may interdict the administration of some foreign laws; it may favour the introduction of others. When its code speaks positively on the subject, it must be obeyed by all persons, who are within the reach of its sovereignty. When its customary, unwritten, or common law speaks directly on the subject, it is equally to be obeyed; for it has an equal obligation with its positive code. When both are silent, then, and then only, can the question properly arise, what law is to govern in the absence of any clear declaration of the sovereign will? Is the rule to be promulgated by a legislative act of the sovereign power? Or is it to be promulgated by courts of law, according to the analogies which are furnished in the municipal jurisprudence? This question does not admit of any universal answer; or rather, it will be answered differently in different communities, according to the organization of the departments of each particular Government.[1]

A State may give authority to the laws of another State.

§ 24. Upon the continent of Europe some of the principal states have silently suffered their courts to draw this portion of their jurisprudence from the analogies furnished by the civil law, or by their own customary or positive code. France, for instance, composed, as it formerly was, of a great number of provinces, governed by different laws and customs, was early obliged to sanction such exertions of authority by its courts, in order to provide for the constantly occurring claims of its subjects, living and owning property in different provinces, in a conflict of the different provincial laws. In England and America the courts of justice have hitherto exercised the same authority in the most ample manner; and the legislatures have in no instance (it is believed) in either country interfered to provide any positive regulations. The common law of both countries has been expanded to meet the exigencies of the times, as they have arisen; and so far as the practice of nations, or the *jus gentium privatum*, has been supposed to furnish any general principle, it has been followed out with a wise and manly liberality.

European practice.

French provinces.

§ 26. The jurists of continental Europe have, with uncommon skill and acuteness, endeavoured to collect principles, which ought to regulate this subject among all nations. But it is very questionable whether their success has been at all proportionate to their labour; and whether their principles, if universally adopted, would be found either convenient or desirable under all circumstances. Their systems, indeed, have had mainly in view the juridical polity fit for the different provinces and states of a common empire, though they are by no means limited to them. It is easy to see, that in a nation, like France, before the Revolution, governed by different laws in its various provinces, some uniform rules might be adopted, which would not be equally fit for the adoption of independent nations possessing no such common interests, or such common basis of jurisprudence. The leading positions maintained by

The practice of Europe will never do for these Sovereign States—is what Story should have said.

[1] Why could not this *American* jurist, judge in the Federal Court, point to the advance we had made, and say that *our* "code [Constitution] speaks positively on the subject"? and though he could not say "it must be obeyed by all persons who are within the reach of *its* sovereignty," he could with correctness have said—of *their* Sovereignties.

§5. Importance of Law of Nations to U. S.

many of the French jurists are, that the laws of a country, which concern persons, who reside within, and are subject to its territorial jurisdiction, ought to be deemed of universal obligation in all other countries; that the laws, which concern the property of such persons, ought to be deemed purely local, and the laws of a mixed character, concerning such persons and property, ought to be deemed local, or universal, according to their predominant character.[1]

Wheaton's *Elements of International Law*, EDITOR'S introductory remarks, p. xiii.

Wheaton is another eminent authority in law, and probably, on the branch of International Law, would outrank any other American writer. The accomplished editor, Mr. Lawrence, says, in his introductory remarks to the sixth edition: "The rank, however, which is accorded to the 'Elements of International Law,' in the cabinets of Christendom, where it has replaced the elegant treatise of Vattel, whose summary long proved a substitute for the more elaborate works of Grotius and Wolff, and the consideration which it enjoys, not only among diplomatists, but in legislative assemblies, and in the tribunals administering the common jurisprudence of nations, seem to render it proper," &c. Whether this be strictly correct or not, Wheaton's works have a high authority at home and abroad, and he is more nearly in accord with Grotius and Vattel, in his allusions to our States and Union, than Kent and Story. Mr. Lawrence further observes: "Mr. Wheaton, whose nearest relatives were of the school of Jefferson, and whose republican sentiments were unavoidably strengthened by his European residence, was, during these years of comparative leisure, an efficient supporter, by his contributions to the periodical press, of the administrations of Jefferson and Madison." He was therefore inclined to view our Union as mostly Federal, has numerous judicious observations, and he generally considers these States free and independent, as are the various States of Europe. Still, he throws very little light upon the nature of our Union. He published another work in 1843, *History of the Law of Nations;* but nowhere, as I have observed, does he treat the subject as though our Federal League rested altogether on the principles of International Law. Neither Pufendorf nor Vattel is much authority with him, which might be expected of a writer who brings out a seemingly new division of Sovereignty, into Internal and External. Vattel remarks upon something from Grotius, concerning an Internal Law of Nations, but a division of Sovereignty is quite another matter. Some of Wheaton's teachings cannot stand, if Grotius, Pufendorf, and Vattel are to be sustained. Quotations from both works have been marked for this section, but space need not be taken. Hereafter, some of the points of this standard authority will find an appropriate place.

Vattel superseded.

Wheaton republican.

Ib. xxiii.

Did not well understand our Union.

Wheaton's *History of the Law of Nations.*

He divides Sovereignty.

Wheaton, Story, Kent, Paine, Rousseau, &c.

Some may regard it gross impertinence to class Wheaton and Story and Kent with Rousseau, Tom Paine, and the French school of infidelity, liberty, equality, and fraternity. Yet on important points, the governmental teachings of each and all have the same tendency.

[1] Nothing in this work that I can discover any more directly recognizes the individual existence and sovereignty of these States of ours, and for anything that appears, he would seem to consider a "conflict" of authority between them as equivalent to one between French provinces.

From Aristotle down, Government has been based upon a Supreme Power—Sovereignty—*Right of Command.* This Sovereignty has ever been, in every State, one and indivisible, possessed either by *one*, *the few*, or *the many;* never by the totality. Everybody within that State is a subject to its Sovereignty; and, even without the light of Revelation, the civilized States of Greece and Rome had ascertained abundant necessity for the Government of man under this sovereign *Right of Command.* But the Bible, and especially the New Testament, well explained what before was dark and uncertain, and its truths, properly applied, give a power and vigor to the Sovereign Authority, which make it truly efficacious in all Christian States. No wonder that a class of free-thinkers among us should have issued teachings, in the trying period of our Revolution, and of the foundation of a new Government, utterly subversive of all authority. They believed in man's actual, imprescriptible right to freedom; but they had the sense to see, that such an idea tallied neither with the Bible, nor the established views of Government, and endeavored to overthrow both. In close sympathy with France because of her kind and opportune aid, we became imbued with her philosophy. Says Paine, in his letter to Abbé Raynal:

§5. Importance of Law of Nations to U. S.

Sovereignty established from the days of Aristotle.

Its necessity

Infidels seek its destruction—

—to make man free.

Perhaps no two events ever united so intimately and forcibly to combat and expel prejudice, as the revolution of America, and the alliance with France. Their effects are felt, and their influence already extends as well to the old world as the new. Our style and manner of thinking have undergone a revolution, more extraordinary than the political revolution of the country. We see with other eyes; we hear with other ears; and think with other thoughts, than those we formerly used. We can look back on our own prejudices, as if they had been the prejudices of other people. We now see and know they were prejudices and nothing else; and relieved from their shackles, enjoy a freedom of mind we felt not before. It was not all the argument, however powerful, nor all the reasoning, however eloquent, that could have produced this change, so necessary to the extension of the mind and the cordiality of the world, without the two circumstances of the revolution and the alliance.

Had America dropped quietly from Britain, no material change in sentiment had taken place. The same notions, prejudices, and conceits would have governed in both countries, as governed them before, and, still the slaves of error and education, they would have travelled on in the beaten track of vulgar and habitual thinking. But brought about by the means it has been, both with regard to ourselves, to France and England, every corner of the mind is swept of its cobwebs, poison and dust, and made fit for the reception of generous happiness.

Sympathy between France and the United States.

PAINE'S *Works*, i, 338.

Our prejudices removed—

—and how.

Glorious results.

Yes; all such "vulgar and habitual thinking," as that we are subjects of Divine Government, was to be discarded; "the mind swept of its cobwebs, poison, and dust," derived from the Bible; and man was to "enjoy a freedom of mind, felt not before." And not only were they to be relieved from the "shackles" of "prejudice" as to the sovereign rule of GOD, but as to that of man also; and in his treatise on the *Rights of Man*, Paine remarks:

When men are spoken of as kings and subjects, or when government is mentioned under distinct or combined heads of monarchy, aristocracy, and democracy, what is it that *reasoning* man is to understand by the terms? If there really existed in the world two more distinct and separate *elements* of human power, we should then see the several

Science of Government opposed.

PAINE'S *Works*, ii, 200

Nothing in forms.

origins to which those terms would descriptively apply; but as there is but one species of man, there can be but one element of human power, and that element is man himself. Monarchy, aristocracy, and democracy are but creatures of imagination; and a thousand such may be contrived as well as three.

. . . .

Power of Revolutions.

From the revolutions of America and France, and the symptoms that have appeared in other countries, it is evident that the opinion of the world is changing with respect to systems of government, and that revolutions are not within the compass of political calculations. The progress of time and circumstances, which men assign to the accomplishment of great changes, is too mechanical to measure the force of the mind, and the rapidity of reflection, by which revolutions are generated; all the old governments have received a shock from those that already appear, and which were once more improbable, and are a greater subject of wonder, than a general revolution in Europe would be now.

Revolutions the panacea.

All those old absurdities of Aristotle, Grotius, Pufendorf, &c., as to a sovereign *Right of Command* existing in every State under the form of Monarchy, Aristocracy, and Democracy, those mere "creatures of the imagination," are to be dispelled. The glorious era of "revolutions," begun in America and France, is to break the chains of authority, and release man from thraldom and tyranny. No longer is he to be a subject, but a freeman. "The force of the mind, and the rapidity of reflection, by which revolutions are generated," is to be a sovereign panacea for the ills afflicting priest-ridden humanity, far superior to the sovereign *Right of Command* these false teachers have inculcated.

All opponents of Sovereignty are Paine's allies.

It matters not whether these subverting, hellish teachings come from Locke or Rousseau, from Paine or from Paley; they have the same direct tendency to overthrow all permanent authority. We must hold fast to this sheet anchor of the sovereign *Right of Command*, as taught by Grotius, Pufendorf, and Vattel, or these ships of State, in Europe and America, will be adrift upon a sea of anarchy.

Necessity of adhering to established principles.

We can better understand the importance of preserving the system of Aristotle, and of these founders of modern International Law, after examining the extracts from them in chapter ii, *Principles of Government.* They show what a State is, and how and why instituted; what its Sovereignty is, and how generated; what are the rights and powers of a sovereign State; what is a Republic; what is a Federal Republic. If we find a system defining all these important points—and, if not greatly mistaken, we shall see it clear as the light of day, and dating all the way back to Aristotle—we shall then be prepared to contrast with it some of our tortuous teachings. After examining some of the views of Marshall, Story, Rawle, Wheaton, Dane, Bradford, Chipman, Webster, Duer, President Lincoln, Messrs. Everett, Curtis, and Motley, it is believed the reader will admit that chapter iii is not misnamed—*Principles Confused.*[1] Finding that every one of the difficulties raised by these excellent men and pure patriots is easily solved by applying a little of the

Americans have not.

[1] The errors and misconceptions of the early fathers of our governmental system—or perhaps it should rather be said, the differences between their views and those of Pufendorf, Vattel, &c.—will be noticed in Part II upon *The Constitution*, in presenting their debates and writings concerning it.

common-sense principle from the vial of International Law, we shall also be pleased to see that they duly estimated the doctors who compounded the wonderful solvent. It is requisite that we have more testimony to establish the authority of the compilers of the International Code, which will not be neglected.

§6. Elementary principles applied to States.

§ 6.—Elementary Principles applied to these States.

Who in U. S. are subjects of International Law?

We have learned that the teachings of Grotius, Pufendorf, and Vattel, are the established Law of Nations, and that the United States recognize its obligations, and we shall have considerable more testimony confirmatory of Kent's judgment. But there is no slight difference of opinion, in this land of liberty, as to who are the parties bound to its observance. A few have an idea that these States, as the very word implies, have a good deal to do with it, and are possibly the sole parties in reality; whereas most in the North adopt the view of Kent, that the United States is at least the superior "nation;" and very many think a State has no more to do with International Law than has a county or a town.

Some think States—

—others the United States.

Our object to decide this.

The object of this work is to examine the principles of Government established for all Christendom by these recognized authorities, and then, by looking into our own records, to ascertain where, of what, and how American States are constituted, what our form of Government is, and what are the rights of the Federal Authority, of the States, of the People. And, strange as it may appear, this is the first attempt of the kind, to my knowledge, notwithstanding the immense fundamental differences of opinion among us, and which can only be harmonized and settled by such an examination. For many years we have had bitter altercations in Congress and elsewhere, as to what were affirmed to be State rights, and as to the wrongs of administration of authority, which was correctly affirmed to be merely delegated and strictly limited. But who has undertaken to prove it from the International Code? We wrangle and discuss the authority of officials, both in our Federal and State Governments, and the right of their acts, and our learned Congressmen are in sad perplexity as to whether they or the President has the Supreme Power; but who goes to the fundamentals of the subject, and brings International Law to bear upon the disputed points? Thus only can they ever be determined. These States are in war from ignorance and perversion of the teachings of these eminent authorities, and from not understanding our own short history. Who is examining and correcting these errors?—the only means possible of bringing peace.

First attempt of the kind.

Examination indispensable to a settlement of difficulties.

Facilities for the examination.

The examination should not be difficult. Having libraries rich in classic stores, ancient and modern, both in the originals and in our native language of England, and far beyond what our fathers enjoyed; having the accumulated wisdom and experience of more than seventy years, affording much and useful instruction, notwithstanding its imperfections,

§6. Elementary principles applied to States.

we ought now to be able to investigate and understand our systems of Government, much more perfectly than did our fathers. With exactness should we be able to discover the causes of their differences, the results of which Professor Fowler has most opportunely presented in his recent work, *Sectional Controversy;* and which, swelling in their onward progress till all barriers have been borne away, have engulfed us in civil war.

Prof. Fowler's *Sectional Controversy.*

Our history short—

Nor does the oblivion of antiquity interfere with the application of principles of International Law to our systems of Government, either in their beginning or progress. We are a people of recent origin. Not a century has elapsed since we were part and parcel of the State of Great Britain, and every important act since the separation has been printed and published, and is well authenticated. And not only so, but when these Colonies threw off allegiance to the British Crown, they resolved never more to have a Monarch over them, but that they would be free Peoples, and retain Sovereignty in themselves. They knew their ancestors had been formerly free, but that gradual encroachments had been made upon the people, until almost despotic power was claimed by the king, and the oppressed had to resist and overthrow the usurpations; and although *Magna Charta* and a few other acts had established some important popular rights, the Constitution of Great Britain was too indefinite, so much so that Bentham and others, with much show of reason, deny that Britons have a true Constitution.

—records complete.

English experience—

—indefiniteness of their Constitution.

Safety of written Constitutions.

The people of each State being possessed of all authority, of every prerogative of the *Right of Command*, to preserve it from the usurpation of their agents, to whom, of necessity, the exercise must be intrusted, and to guard against the inconveniences and doubts under which the motherland labored from the uncertainty of her Constitution, they wisely resolved to remedy the difficulty, by writing out their Constitutions in full. We live in a land of written law, and well know that no party, single or collective, has any right to exercise any power, for which the specific letter of authority is not produced in the Constitution. All else is reserved to the Sovereign People.

Authority not written is reserved.

A time of reflection to come—

Believing the time is not far distant when these Peoples will again seek "Reason" rather than "Force" to rule them; when they will discover that war can never settle our differences; when a desire will, on both sides, be manifested to study into the causes of our variance and strife; and above all, when, like Christians, we shall be willing to see and know our wrong, and right it; I have been led to prepare this work against the good time coming. My object, too, is to reach the fountain of authority, the suffragans themselves. Being one of "the plain people," and knowing what they need with regard to the science of Government, I have endeavored to arrange the information for them. Learned lawyers may deem it unnecessary to make these long quotations from musty old writers; but no more space is taken than is requisite to exhibit the clearness of the principles which have become confused and involved

—to study causes—

—return to Christian duty.

This work for business men.

Quotations from old writers.

The scarcity of the old works makes the extracts necessary; and in such a mass of wisdom, the difficulty has been to cut short the quotations. A reference to the originals will show that quite as good stock is left as is taken. Very probably the chief benefit of this publication will prove to have been the leading to an acquaintance with these most valuable authorities.

§ 7. Summary of the Examination.

§ 7.—Summary of the Examination.

An examination sought to be candid, has led me from being strongly anti-Jeffersonian, a thorough Henry-Clay Whig—an earnest follower and personal friend of Webster—to adopt the following opinions:

Colonies had no right of union.

Colonial Congress—

—conducts war of Revolution—

—advises the Colonies.

Colonies become States before and after 4th July.

Declaration of Independence.

Not a single, but thirteen States.

That though the colonies were prohibited all right of Union, and therefore could not legally combine themselves while under British allegiance, they made a *quasi* Union in sending delegates to a Colonial Congress in 1774, and to another in 1775, which, in accordance with their authority, made efforts to settle difficulties with the mother Government, but without avail, and on the 19th of April, 1775, the British began war, which caused the Congress to exercise the war power for the Colonies, till arrangements were completed to create a proper Confederate Congress; that, in addition to conducting the war, Congress also gave advice to the individual Colonies when desired, particularly as to the organization of separate governments independent of Great Britain; that, in accordance with that advice, some Colonies prior to the Declaration of Independence, others after, organized themselves into States and adopted their Constitutions; that on the 4th day of July, 1776, authority having been duly obtained from the States, and the other Peoples that were yet Colonies, Congress passed the ever-memorable Declaration, that these individual Peoples had become "*free and independent States*," not a single State like Great Britain, from which they separated; and, that their character should not be mistaken, they again declare explicitly, "that, as FREE AND INDEPENDENT STATES, they have full power to levy war, conclude peace, contract alliances, establish commerce, and to do all other acts and things which INDEPENDENT STATES may of right do;" and being enabled, by Divine aid and by Union, to maintain their Declaration, they thenceforth were entitled "to assume, among the powers of the earth, the SEPARATE AND EQUAL STATION to which *the Laws of Nature and of Nature's God entitle them;*" and by no means least among the privileges of their new and exalted station, was that of being governed by "*the Laws of Nature and of Nature's God*," the chief part of which is to be found in the International Code; that the States, in framing their Governments, were careful to adhere to the Law of Nations, and that some of them, particularly Massachusetts and New Hampshire, closely followed Pufendorf; that the war they were prosecuting taught them the necessity and benefits of Union, although not till 1781 could they agree on the terms, and adopt their first Federal Constitution, which declared that "each State retains

Their rights—

—to "the Laws of Nature"—

—to which they have adhered.

Union appreciated—

—not closed till 1781.

—care of State Sovereignty.

§ 7. Summary of the Examination.

its Sovereignty, freedom, and independence," &c.; that, owing to want of knowledge and experience concerning Federal Unions, the first Constitution proved defective; that a convention was called, in 1787, to revise the Constitution, when strenuous efforts were made by some to create a "national" instead of Federal Government; that the chief advocates of the former, Hamilton and Morris, acknowledged, what was self-evident, that they had been defeated in their efforts; that great alarm was created, the new Constitution being regarded as consolidating the States, and that if it did not, that it tended strongly thitherward; that in the Conventional debates, and elsewhere, the Constitution was clearly shown to be Federal; that, to guard against all possibility of consolidation, important amendments were urged at the time of ratification, the chief of which were adopted; that, according to principles of International Law, our Central Government is and can be nothing but a pure Federal Republic; that comparison with others, particularly the Hebrew and Grecian, shows it to be much the best of which we have knowledge, the chief improvement being the division of the Federal authority, as in their State Governments, into independent departments (independent of each other, not of the separate Sovereignties); that, thus delegating authority to two sets of agents, and subdividing their Federal and State Agencies into distinct departments, legislative, executive, and judicial, and further subdividing the legislature into two branches, they created the most perfect system of checks and balances ever devised for the preservation of liberty to free Peoples, each of the six departments watching all the others with jealous care lest powers should be exercised in an unauthorized manner, or further powers be stolen from the People, and each of the two systems being thoroughly organized and prepared to resist the usurpations of the other; that, though we have undoubtedly the best governmental system ever invented, yet that we live in a world of imperfection, from which even our Federal Republic is not exempt; that, though this division into States was an indispensable safeguard to liberty, and to the proper administration of Government by a free People, yet the individual Sovereignty, freedom, and independence of each, which could not be invaded but with the annihilation of the States, gave occasion for anxiety, and for the exercise of great prudence and moderation; that, understanding the liability of these greatest moral persons to err, and that, amid the constant intercourse which must exist between States united in a Federal Republic, differences important and strong might be expected to arise, which, unsettled, must end in war, the Supreme Court was instituted. A machinery had been arranged for this purpose under the Articles of Confederation; but a considerable improvement was made in the new Constitution, by creating an independent Judiciary, designed to be separated from all political influences, and supplying a tribunal of higher character than had ever been instituted, and suitable to adjudicate causes between these august parties. The Sovereign States could not be coerced to appear, but, under the obligations of right,

First Constitution fails. Convention of 1787—desires and fears of consolidation. New Constitution Federal. Its improvements— —division of authority— —its checks and balances. Imperfection even in our Federal Republic. State divisions cause difficulty. Supreme Court to adjust their difficulties. Improvement over old Constitution.

§ 7. Summary of the Examination.

States obligated by International Law

No right of coercion of a State, delegated.

and in fulfilment of their solemn compact, they were bound to appear when summoned; and though the Court had no authority to enforce its decree, each State was obliged by highest honor and good faith to submit. "The Laws of Nature and of Nature's GOD," which entitled them to their "separate and equal station" among nations, required this, and supplied the chief rules for their Government, and for the decision of disputed points; and at the same time, the Infinite Author of these laws, not having seen fit to delegate to any human agency the infliction of punishment for their breach, and no such agency having been created by mortals, or even attempted, GOD only has the legal right to punish these greatest moral persons, whatever may be their offence.

Court competent to adjudicate every question.

Va., in 1798—

—her wrongs.

Mass., wrong in 1814.

S. Carolina, wrong in 1833.

The investigation further shows, that no difficulty has arisen between these States, that probably none could occur, beyond the province of the Supreme Court of the United States, fairly and satisfactorily to investigate and decide. An agent of the Virginia Sovereignty, its legislature, believed correctly that the Federal Agency had exceeded its power in 1798, in enacting the Sedition Law, though in error, as I think will be shown, as to the Alien Law; but instead of properly bringing the case into Court, and having the wrong righted, as the Constitution had provided, that Agency threatened the secession of her Sovereignty from the Union. So, too, during the last war with Great Britain, the Agencies of Massachusetts and other northern Sovereignties, instead of applying to the Court for the redress of their grievances, as they had solemnly agreed, threatened to break away from the Federal Compact. And in 1833, the Sovereignty of South Carolina itself, not by its agent, but in solemn convention of delegates assembled for the express purpose, instead of applying to the Courts, as she had agreed, for the remedy of unconstitutional acts, attempted to violate its sacred compact, and annul a law of the Union, which by explicit agreement was to be to her "the supreme law of the land," and which therefore she had no right to annul while she continued to be a part of "the land" of the United States. Several State Agencies, too, in the North, in violation of honor and good faith, have endeavored to nullify the law of the Federal Congress, passed in pursuance of a necessary and proper provision of the Constitution, for the rendition of fugitive slaves. To take cognizance of precisely such acts as these, was the chief occasion of creating the Supreme Court, and yet not the first one of them has been directly presented. Even for South Carolina, after she seceded and became an independent State; for all the other States that in due form separated themselves; for even the Southern Confederacy immediately upon its becoming a power in the earth, was the Supreme Court of the United States a proper and authorized tribunal, to take cognizance of the questions at issue, and prevent a resort to arms. And no respectable person in the South will affirm, that even after the withdrawal of the Southern judges, the remainder would not have rendered a fair and honorable decision. Surely, should the South have tried this means before wielding the war power, and had she seen fit to resort

Other wrongs by Northern agencies.

Neglect to use courts in these cases.

Seceded States should have used the courts—

—not arms.

Justice sure.

§ 7. Summary of the Examination.

to the Court instead of the sword, she would have taught the North a valuable lesson, and had the honor of a proud and peaceful triumph.

Importance of having such a tribunal independent.

But such a Court, to have the confidence of all parties and all sections, must be put beyond the reach of a partisan Senate and President to disturb. Leaders of the party in power, threatened that the Judiciary should be remodelled to their will; and while the South have themselves to blame for withdrawing their votes, giving their adversaries an opportunity to accomplish their purposes, it must also be remembered, that such had been the progress of anti-slavery sentiment in the North, that the South knew not where it was to stop; and the threatening and apparent danger of the overthrow of this bulwark of their rights, is one of the strongest palliations of the South in rupturing our Union. At the same time, it is pleasant to point the South to the moderation of the Administration in availing themselves of the present opportunity to perform their threats, exhibiting a solitary, indeed, yet striking instance, in this Administration, of the tendency to conservatism of even strong partisans, where responsibility is incurred, and great interests are at hazard.

Threats to change it.

Moderation in present changes.

Webster concerning compact.

The investigation also shows that, notwithstanding Mr. Webster's eloquent argument to the contrary, no means exist, none can possibly be devised, to bind a sovereign State, except a compact or league; that the very object of creating a State with Sovereignty, is to have a power that should be unaccountable to all else than Deity, and whose right and duty it is to seek out and promote the highest good of its subjects, properly regarding the rights of others; that therefore a State has no right to make a compact adverse to the interests of its People, and one so made is void in its nature; that if a State should misjudge as to its interests in forming a compact, both right and duty require it to reconsider and revoke; and it is to be its own independent judge, and none but the Almighty Sovereign may question its acts.[1]

State Sovereignty.

Right of revoking compact.

Obligations of a compact.

But it also becomes manifest, that a State is bound by its compact, notwithstanding no superior authority is or can be created over a Sovereignty to call it to account.[2]

Not only is a State bound by its compact, but all the more bound because reliance is so largely upon its honor and faith. Cast away this sheet-anchor, and these ships of State, with all others, are indeed adrift

---

These States rightfully seceded in 1788, 1789.

[1] Upon this principle, and this only, were the eleven States justifiable in breaking away from the first Constitution, notwithstanding it was positively declared perpetual, "in order to form a more perfect Union" under the new Constitution, leaving two Confederates, North Carolina and Rhode Island, to shift for themselves. The number engaged in an act affects not the qualities of its ethics, and what the eleven could do conjointly, each Sovereignty had a right to do individ ually.

Calhoun on Secession and Nullification.

[2] I am aware of Mr. Calhoun's powerful argument that each Sovereignty must be allowed to judge for itself of means and measures affecting it. So it must unquestionably, from its very nature, but only as a last resort, and probably bringing war with it. The right of Secession is, indeed, and can be nothing more nor less than the right of Revolution. But his view blends Secession and Nullification together as one and the same right, in violation of the whole principle of compact, the binding obligation of which he admits, notwithstanding. A State may secede from a Federal Union, and has no right nor power to bind itself not to do so, if necessary; but it has no right nor power to set up its single opinion against a law enacted by the joint Sovereignties, which she has agreed "shall be the supreme law of the land." She may secede, but she cannot nullify, This will be discussed in its place, and space need not be here taken.

upon a dark ocean of doubts and perils. This truth, or we misjudge altogether, is the basis, the very foundation of the modern Law of Nations.

§ 7. Summary of the Examination.

The compact not violated by the North.

Wrongs were done by their agents—

The South cannot affirm that the compact had been violated by the North. Fortunately for us, in the midst of all our confusion of governmental principles, we have steered clear of that wrong. The agents of some of these Sovereignties, both legislative and executive, and possibly judicial also, have done wrong; but no more than was expected in forming the Federal Compact, perhaps not as much, and the Supreme Court was organized designedly to correct these wrongs. When has one of these States refused to obey the mandate of an aggrieved sister, and appear before the Federal Court to render an account of itself, and, if wrong, to rectify it? More should not be expected of these than of other earthly Sovereigns. A Sovereignty is of course responsible for the acts of its agents, and if a wrong be done, the aggrieved Sovereign, if actuated by proper and Christian motives, applies in a reasonable way to the Sovereign by whose agency the wrong has been done, that it may be acknowledged and redressed. One who would do differently, and at once resort to "force" and war, Harrington says has "more of the image of the Beast" than "of the image of GOD." And we have provided a clear and plain way for redressing all the wrongs of these Confederate States, through the Federal Court.

—to be corrected in proper manner.

Federal Government not responsible for State wrongs.

Much less still is the Federal Government to be held responsible for any of the acts of these States, or of their agents, no matter what they be, except in the guaranty to the States of a Republican form of Government. The restricted powers of the United States Agency, none have so well comprehended as they of the school of South Carolina. Solely by means of its Court, and that merely by its bare decision, without power of enforcing its decree, can it interfere in any shape or manner between the Sovereignties. It is true, as we shall learn from Pufendorf, that these Sovereign Parties to the compact of the Constitution, having themselves strictly fulfilled its terms, have a natural right to enforce fulfilment, if they can, from delinquents; but that is one of the most important rights, which, not being delegated to the direction of the Federal Agency, is reserved to the Sovereignties themselves. The right of coercion has not been delegated, but the right of defence has been delegated.

Federal Government has done no wrong not reparable under the Constitution.

Neither can a single act of the Federal Agency be named, which has been deemed oppressive or unjust to any section, which has not been remedied upon proper, and even improper application. Whatever mistakes the Federal Government has made, none have been beyond the province of the Federal Court to correct, and never has there been a refusal to hear an application or determine a cause; never has a decision of that Court been regarded violative of the Law of Nations or of the Constitutional Compact, though undoubtedly, in our confusion of principles, even that august tribunal has committed errors. There has therefore been no breach to justify the South in its present Secession.

No justifying cause for present Secession.

§ 7. Summary of the Examination.

As Webster affirmed, "a compact broken on one side, is broken on all sides;" and if the South can show a fracture anywhere, she is justifiable in its repudiation. And until she can show such a violation, she stands before the world, the first to break the sacred compact of the Constitution, though no doubt unwittingly, supposing it to have been already and repeatedly broken by the North.

The South too precipitate in war.

But the investigation will show further, that not only have the South unnecessarily and wrongfully seceded from the Union; have not only begun an unjust, offensive war, but were most unreasonably precipitate in their attack. This important question will be considered; and here we only remark, that the South have ever and rightfully contended, that the Federal authority was one of strictly limited powers. They believed that no authority had been delegated by the Constitution to authorize the President and Congress to treat with seceded States, and divide with them the joint property; for while the Confederate States adopted in the main the Constitution of the United States, they made a few important additions, one of which was in these words:

Federal Government had no authority to act upon Secession.

The South knew this.

Consequent addition to the Confederate Constitution.

"The Government hereby instituted shall take immediate steps for the settlement of all matters between the States forming it, and their late confederates of the United States, in relation to the public property and public debt at the time of their withdrawal from them, these States hereby declaring it to be their wish and earnest desire to adjust everything pertaining to the common property, common liabilities, and common obligations of that Union, upon principles of right, justice, equity, and good faith."

New powers required equally by the Federals as by the Confederates.

If the Confederate Government must be authorized to divide and *receive*, surely it was equally necessary for the United Government to have authority to divide and *surrender*. Secession involves many complicated questions. Take the Louisiana purchase, for instance. Not only is its cost to be apportioned, but other and far more important points are to be regarded. It was bought, not merely to add more States to the Union, but to give to existing States and new ones to be added, to which have been granted equal rights with the old in all the benefits and properties of the Union, additional conveniences and advantages, as the navigation of the Mississippi, free markets, &c. These and various other complications were to be arranged, and no power for that purpose, it was believed, had been constituted by these States united. The original authorities must be resorted to; else, why did the South, who, so much better than we, understand the nature of Federalism, make the addition to their Constitution above quoted?

The South knew this.

Ignorance of this in the North.

It is true, our Administration has never availed itself of this plea, and probably would deny its validity; for the President and Congress evidently conceive, that what one of them cannot do, the other can; and though they have not yet decided which is supreme, yet they act upon the full assurance that Sovereignty is in some of them, somehow or other. But the South knew better, and, to take the best view possible, it was seeking an unfair advantage of Northern ignorance, to ask Congress, or

The South seek unfair advantage.

the President, to act without authority. And if our Administration, in their misconception of governmental principles, would not have hesitated for lack of authority to comply with Southern demands, other causes indisposed them. The same ignorance led the North, almost to a man, to deny the right of Secession; and the President, in his inaugural, took that view of the subject. So that not only was the Government powerless, but, from errors and misconceptions, was indisposed to any action in the premises.

§ 7. Summary of the Examination.

Such was our situation. The North was altogether wrong in denying the abstract right of Secession; but as we shall see, some of the most eminent of Southern statesmen have aided to mislead us. In the most critical period of our history, owing to unfortunate divisions of the Democracy, for which the South is largely accountable, a partisan Administration comes into power, more deeply imbued with prevalent errors as to the nature of our Union, than any preceding one. Prudence and moderation in the highest degree are required; yet because the Federal Government would not at once change its fundamental views of our Union, and of the nature of the Federal Compact, which had become firmly rooted in the progress of more than half a century, and that, too, by the aid of some of the most eminent statesmen of the South as well as of the North; because we of the North would not at once change our opinions at the bidding of the South; and further, because President Lincoln would not usurp powers the South well knew he did not possess; in only five weeks from the advent of the new Administration, the South begin the war. It is not to be forgotten, that the South had excessive provocation in the infamous deception as to supplying Forts Sumter and Pickens, and in the defeat of the peace measures, to say nothing of previous wrongs, which are greater even than the South have known, and all these points will be impartially presented with accompanying documents; yet after all, the South cannot but see their great wrong in beginning this war.

The South unwisely precipitate.

In all probability, if the South had not taken the offensive, the North would soon have done so, owing to the utter misconception of the rights and powers of the Federal Agency. Had the South exercised a little prudence and discretion, and the attack been made by the Federal Government, she would have been in a *just* and *defensive* war, and might without doubt have had aid from European nations to accomplish our division. But we have to deal with facts, with things as they are, not as they might have been; and opportunely comes even now, as I write this part of my paper, Lord Russell's manifesto of the 28th July, in which he observes: "From the moment that intelligence first reached this country that nine States and several millions of inhabitants of the great American Union had seceded, and had made war on the Government of President Lincoln, down to the present time, her Majesty's Government have pursued a friendly, open, and consistent course. They have been neutral between the two parties to a civil war."

Had the South been less precipitate, the North might have taken the offensive.

The South now on the offensive.

Lord Russell's opinion, 28th July, 1862.

Thus incidentally but directly is the important truth recognized and

§ 7. Summary of the Examination.

proclaimed, that the South "*had made war on the Government of President Lincoln;*" and in that one fact, in these few words, is a sufficient reason why England, with all the desire of her nobility to see this Union torn asunder, dares not take part against the North. *The South has made the war;* it was without the *right* and the *necessity* the Law of Nations enjoins, and therefore is *unjust;* and neither Britain, nor any other nation, dares engage against the United States in this struggle, one of the most *just, defensive* wars which a people was ever called to wage.

The South in an *unjust* war.

The North in a *just* war.

Present compact broken—

—a new one to be made.

Another point developed is this: Though the Southern States had no right to secede as they did, and violated their compact in doing so, yet the wrong is done, and is without remedy except by subjugation, or by a renewal of the league.[1] In a proper form, by conventions of delegates elected by the Sovereignties for the purpose, did most or all of the Southern States secede, and resume the powers delegated to the United States. These Sovereign Powers each seceded State had unrestricted right to exercise individually; and when a part of them were again delegated to the Agency of the Confederate States, that new body politic became responsible to their Peoples collectively and individually for their acts. It is a properly constituted power in the earth *de facto*, though not *de jure*, has been so acknowledged by us in the exchange of captives, and foreign nations are at liberty to recognize it as such, when they please.

The Southern Confederacy duly constituted.

The damages and costs of war to be paid—

—or we acknowledge free institutions a failure.

Whatever obligations have been incurred, are quite as legal and binding on the Confederate States as upon the United States; and every dollar's worth of property destroyed, every slave absconded or stolen, all injuries and losses of every description, consequent on the action of Federal, Confederate, or State authority, has by some one of these authorities to be paid for, or injustice and wrong is done individuals, to guard against which civil society is instituted. The dignity and worth of popular institutions, I trust, are too truly appreciated in this land of liberty, to acknowledge that civil society is here a failure; and if not, the individual damages occasioned by all the civil authorities, are to be fairly estimated and paid. It was no slight encouragement to the prosecution of these investigations, to see it stated that Mr. Seward had informed Lord Lyons, that there would be a settlement of damages at the end of this war, such as was never before witnessed. Eminently desirable is this, as affording the best of evidence of the superior excellence of popular Government. And though the debt should reach five or six thousand millions, as it probably will, the money will have been well expended, and even the blood of our beloved friends on both sides well shed, if these immense sacrifices were necessary to save us from consolidation, to which we were blindly rushing.

Webster concerning a broken compact.

[1] Mr. Webster's declaration as to a compact broken, is solidly based upon the Law of Nations. We had to sever the Union when we last revolutionized the Government, because North Carolina and Rhode Island refused immediate ratification of the new Constitution. It remains to be seen whether the same desire of Union, the same spirit of accommodation, the same willingness to compromise our differences, will operate now as in 1787–'91. Then, indeed, the compact was rightfully broken, now wrongfully; yet still, alas! it is broken.

§ 7. Summary of the Examination.

The investigation also shows that, while the South is altogether wrong in beginning the war, they have had great provocation in our improper interference with slavery, and in the denial of their equal rights in the common territory, all originating in deserting the Federal principle; and that they were led into the war by misunderstanding the designs and purposes of the North, which misapprehension, instead of being corrected, has been strengthened by errors in the Administration.

Wrongs by the North.

Errors of Administration.

Though the North was engaged, from the beginning, in a just and defensive war, which the whole world saw must be one of the most important and terrific of all time, we had not the sense to perceive its existence, and for many months denied it, affirming it to be only a little "rebellion," that we would "squelch out in sixty days;" and since it began, there has been no time when within ninety days this "rebellion" was not to be ended. The naval officers and sailors were "pirates;" the civil and military officials, acting under oaths as sacred to their States and Confederacy as those to our own, were "traitors," and by summary justice and a short shrift, was this happy land soon to be freed from such ignominious wretches. We have at length discovered that we are really at war, and although we still exhibit the ignorance and the bad taste of calling them "rebels," we treat the Confederates as our equals in all respects, as they are; and the fact is so apparent from examining International Law, that on our part we are engaged in a *just, solemn,* and *defensive* war, that it is even questionable whether to apply the term *civil* be allowable.

Wrong ideas of the war.

Prisoners were pirates and traitors.

The President's usurpations.

President Lincoln, too, one of the most honest, straightforward patriots ever in the Executive chair, in his inexperience and bewilderment, jostled and pushed hither and thither by his fanatical partisans and greedy spoil-hunters, has usurped some of the most important powers, which a prudent and jealous care of liberty would not intrust to the Executive, and therefore delegated to Congress. This action has afforded the strongest possible testimony to the allegations, that we were what we claimed to be, a consolidated "nation," which President Davis used with skill and effect to perfectly unite the South. It is not too much to declare, that the proclamations of blockade of ports, increasing the army and navy, and the suspension of the writ of *habeas corpus,* the illegal arrests, and interference with the press, are the most infamous, outrageous usurpations of modern days; and the President, when he shall have time to study into governmental principles, will himself acknowledge them to be such, and lend his best efforts to guard these Peoples against the dangerous precedents he has unwittingly set.

Their effect in the South.

The President will correct his errors.

Wrong acts of Congress—dividing Virginia— —emancipation in D. C.— —confiscation law.

Then comes the ridiculous ignoring of States and their boundaries, with attempts to divide them, as in Virginia; the injudicious, unauthorized act of Congress, taking advantage of our calamitous condition, to pass the Emancipation Law in the District of Columbia; the inoperative confiscation law, acts and proclamations of freedom to slaves, and I hardly know what wrong, in our ignorance, has not been attempted, even

§ 7. Summary of the Examination.

to the exonerating of one department from its Constitutional liabilities for wrongs and usurpations, by another coördinate department of this mere Federal Agency.

Wrongs by both North and South.

They are palpable.

Mutual atonement honorable.

The North must correct its errors as to Federalism—

As usual, the investigation proves both parties to have been in fault. Each side will enjoy looking into the errors of the other, but let them examine their own also, and be considering their correction. Fortunately, they stand out with distinctness. Only when error is doubtful, ill-defined, obscure, is remedy difficult. Fortunately, too, the mutual wrongs stand in such relations, that each party can with honor and highest dignity make its atonement. The North must and will see and acknowledge its wrong, and declare the truth, that we have misunderstood the nature and principles of our Union, and the powers of the Federal Agency, and that we will have none other than a pure Federal Republic. It is due to truth and justice, in order that the world may know the excellence of our institutions, and the reasons of our prosperity, that we speedily and forcibly explain the character of our Government. That done, the occasion for the initiation of the war by the South is removed; and how long will she wish to prosecute it, when with honor she can propose a truce? How long before she will desire a convention to reconstruct the Union on the basis of our fathers, that of a pure Federal Republic, the desertion of the principles of which, caused her to fight?

—which allows the South to stop its war.

Long established laws.

The question is whether our system is Federal, not whether it is desirable.

The reader in the North and in the South will please bear in mind, that we are dealing with legal principles long established; with facts as they exist, not as we might wish, or as they might have been. One may consider a Federal Republic, with its inseparable State Sovereignty, a very loose, disjointed system; but its expediency or inexpediency, is not the first point. Is our Government Federal or consolidated? is the disputed question. If wrong as to the form actually existing, let us have the manliness to acknowledge it; what is desirable, is quite another question; though the more it is investigated, the more satisfied shall we be with the wisdom of the fathers in framing this Federal Republic.

South to learn about pact and faith, and the necessities of war.

And the South, too, will observe, that the principles of pact and faith are no new fangled teachings in order to entrap them; nor have we in the North declared the rights and necessities of war to meet the present juncture. Of old were the rules laid down and well defined; and applying them to the facts, as we shall endeavor to do in Part IV, is the South herself to judge whether she was right in breaking her sacred compact; whether or not she is in a *just* and *solemn* war.[1]

This war: its extent—

We are indeed in war. Other modern warfare was but a bagatelle to this of which we are victims. Even war is waged by us on the true American scale of grandeur. Befitting is it that this land of large lakes, large mountains, large rivers, large prairies, with their powerful influence

---

Southern documents wanted.

[1] All the documents that come to hand are preserved for use, and I have been so fortunate as to obtain a copy of Mr. Pollard's *Southern History of the War*. It shall be my endeavor to examine with candor and fairness every point connected with the present Secession and War, and it will be a favor if friends and others in the South will aid me with documents. I want particularly the legislative act of South Carolina, convening the delegates in December, 1860.

to expand the mind and the heart of man; very natural is it that these American Peoples, fighting on both sides, as we have seen, for the maintenance of our precious rights, our heaven-ordained institutions, should wage war, even civil war, on a scale commensurate with the sway of nature in which we live. We have demonstrated to the world, that, though a nation most inclined to peace, we can and will fight if we deem it necessary; that we are a nation of soldiers. No doubt this war, with all its horrors, is to bring us important benefits; but ere long we shall begin to think we have taken enough of these benefits, and be casting about for means of restoring peace. When that period arrives, which I fear is not yet, and may be two years distant, we need to be prepared for prompt and resolute action. No doubt many plans will be proposed, and I beg to offer my fellow-citizens of the North my humble opinion upon the query—*how to end this war.*

§ 7. Summary of the Examination.

—not without benefits—

—nor to last always.

§ 8.—Considerations for the North—How to End this War.

The North can never with honor make to the South propositions of peace. Instead of resorting to the Federal Court, the arbiter provided with wonderful skill and wisdom to adjudicate difficulties that might arise between these Sovereignties, those affecting State rights as well as every other, the South have chosen the sword and the cannon. These must the North use till the South tender other means.

The North cannot propose peace—

Were disparity in number and power greater between the two sections, we might propose means of adjudication; but the North being only about three to one of the Southern whites, and only two to one including the blacks (which are worth more to the South in this struggle than any four millions of laboring population in the North), we should simply expose ourselves to ridicule for assuming magnanimity to avoid a contest with a lesser but more plucky antagonist. We must fight on and on, and never speak of peace till the South say the word.

—not strong enough.

Neither can it be ended by foreign intervention. The Confederate States may be acknowledged a power in the earth, and probably soon will be, but that in no way changes the nature of the war, or affects its prosecution. That the South began this war, is a well-attested fact, incidentally admitted by Lord Russell, which admission has not received the attention it merits. Because the South "*had made war on the Government of Abraham Lincoln,*" is the sole reason why [in the language of Lord Russell], "*down to the present time, her Majesty's Government have pursued a friendly, open, and consistent course. They have been neutral between the two parties to a civil war.*" It has been seen by that power, that the South had not the "*necessity*" required by the Law of Nations to justify her in beginning war, and consequently, being engaged in an "*unjust, offensive war,*" no Christian nation dares so violate, outrage the International Code, as to take part openly against the North. The Queen is friendly, and probably the mass of the British people, but

Foreign intervention impossible.

See page 51.

Britain not to interfere—

—notwithstanding the hostility of the aristocracy.

§ 8. To the North: how to end this war.

the aristocracy, who have never ceased their efforts to disunite us since Colonial days, are having their plans again thwarted; the South, with its natural impulse and unnecessary haste, having begun an unjust war.

Had the North taken the offensive, Europe might have interfered.

In our ignorance of governmental principles, the Federal Administration would probably soon have commenced hostilities, reversing the character of the war, and giving the South the side of justice and defence. A happy day might that have been regarded by England's aristocracy, in which the sun of liberty would have been partially obscured by the dark and portentous clouds of disunion in America. But Providence seems to have directed, that we are now only to suffer the horrors of civil war, and by them are to be saved from the far greater evils both of disunion and of consolidation. Did England dare to interfere, the result of this contest might be doubtful; but judging from the course of events, it would appear we have only to fight, until, on one or both sides, we are satisfied with the use of force, and return to reason; believing the GOD of nations will prevent this grand experiment in free Government from being jeopardized either by permanent disunion or consolidation. The Law of Nations makes the right and duty of neutrals very clear,

Why England cannot.

and even England, with all her aristocratic malevolence and pretentious animosity to slavery, dares not transgress and take active part against

France not to interfere.

the North. Neither is it probable that Louis Napoleon will interfere. That sagacious monarch knows full well the obligations we are under to the house of Bourbon, for the timely support in money, as well as in war, which Louis XVI rendered us in our Revolutionary struggle. He would not see it for his interest to have the power of the North to join with the Bourbon prince for his overthrow; and let him take a hand in the game of Revolution here, and he will find two can play it at the same time.

Foreign intervention by force improbable.

The North neither seeks nor wants aid in its just defence. Foreign intervention by force, is therefore probably not to occur.

Peaceful intervention unavailable, either upon the South—

Neither is foreign intervention by reason and argument of much more avail. What use for the nation most friendly to the South, to urge them to stop the war and take steps to reunite with a Government, which they have come firmly to believe is established upon a false and dangerous basis, that of a consolidated instead of Federal Union? One might as well whistle down a hurricane, as attempt to stop the South in its frenzied course, until they are taught by the North itself that they are wholly mistaken as to Northern wishes and purposes.

—or upon the North.

And of what avail were it for any friendly nation to advise the North to make propositions of peace, coupled with disunion? Will the West ever listen to such mawkish sentiment? Never, never. With the great Northwest, the power on this continent, peace and reunion are inseparable. The waters of the Mississippi, from their source to the Gulf, must ever be free to the States along their banks.

Is the South to be destroyed?

Is peace to come by the destruction of the aggressor? There may still be a few in the North who believe this; but those who once thought that half or two thirds of the whites would be required at home to keep down the negroes, are beginning to open their eyes to the truth, that the slaves are a main support in this war. Neither can we reach that support to tear much of it away. We have overrun most of the South that we can approach very conveniently, and out of four millions have taken a few hundred thousand, that are costing an immense sum to support; and of what use are they? What is to become of them? If in two years, and in the most favorable section of the South to effect emancipation, this is all we can accomplish, how idle to rely upon it as a means of subjugation! The Administration has done all it could in this way, even to the issuing proclamations of freedom, and by ample time and effort has the President's prediction been proved correct, that such proclamations would be as inoperative as the Pope's bull against the comet.

§ 8. To the North: how to end this war.

Can slavery help us?

Are negroes to be made soldiers?

As for making soldiers of the negro, it cannot be done with any advantage. Few, in the first place, can be gotten; and the thousands, hundreds of thousands, of patriots that have volunteered to save their Government, instituted for white men, will nearly all throw down their arms, if they must fight alongside negroes to sustain the star-spangled banner. Argument upon the point is fruitless; it is a sentiment inbred in the Caucasian race, developing equally among Eastern troops as in the Western.

Is a servile war desired?

Few, very few, are the inhuman miscreants who would involve the South in a servile war. Such an event is hardly to be reckoned among possibilities, not at all among probabilities; yet it is well to remember we are engaged in a righteous, defensive war, and are about two to one against our aggressors, counting in their negroes, as we should. If we Americans, and the whole civilized world, could cry shame to Britain for inciting the merciless savage of the forest to wage war against us, far more would the North be disgraced, by the diabolical act of stimulating the slaves to insurrection and bloodshed.

The negro of little avail.

If we may not incite the negro to revolt and carnage; and we cannot if we would, and would not if we could; if we cannot use him as a soldier without losing more in white men; how in the name of reason is he to be made serviceable in our defence? A few could be used advantageously as laborers in camps while the war lasts, but what is to become of them afterward? They will prove an immensely expensive aid.

Subjugating the South impracticable.

As to subjugating and destroying the South, either with or without negro aid, few, I apprehend, really expect this. The latter, it will be admitted, will be necessary to the former; and being only three to one without their blacks, and two to one with, the task would be very difficult. The South altogether misconceive the character of the war they have begun, and believe they are fighting for their own liberty, for the safety of their own homes and families. Every man, woman, and child over ten years old, is engaged heart and soul in this struggle. Suppose we are numerically two or three to their one—though our two or three can never be brought to engage in this fight as do the South; is that

§ 8. To the North: how to end this war.

sufficient to insure their conquest and subjugation? *They are Americans* with whom we are fighting, bone of our bone, flesh of our flesh. Reverse the case. Suppose one third, or even one fourth; yes, even one tenth of any part of the North were at war with the other nine tenths; could the little fraction be subjugated? Never; they might be annihilated, but subjugated, never; and never could two thirds or three fourths destroy or subjugate the other portion. So it is with the South. They have grown stronger month by month since the war commenced, and are better able to-day to prosecute it, than when they attacked Sumter; the wearing out of their railroads probably excepted. We are making slow progress for a war of conquest, and for the subjection of "*rebels.*"

We are not in a war of subjugation, but of defence.

But fortunately for the credit of the North, we are not engaged in a war of subjugation. We are only defending our Government. The South, totally regardless of the wisdom of the fathers in creating a Federal tribunal of higher dignity than any before known, worthy to adjudicate differences even between sovereign States, and its special object being to protect their rights; the South, more clamorous than all the Union for State rights, the importance of which they by no means overestimate; the South, I say, regardless of all its duties, obligations, and interests, violating unnecessarily, but not causelessly, the sacred compact of the Constitution, instead of resorting to the Court in which, with right unquestionably on their side, they would by reason and argument have worsted the North, have chosen the battle field to decide the question. Instead of bringing a suit in the Supreme Court of the United States for the possession of Fort Sumter, to which South Carolina was still entitled, notwithstanding her Secession, and which even the Southern Confederacy could have instituted after its organization, and which would have developed all our errors, and given a grand triumph to the South; both South Carolina and the Confederate States have deliberately chosen to seize that fort, and hold it by force of arms. We must oppose force to force, so long as the South choose that means of arbitrament; and should have never a word to say of aught else than force, till the South itself proposes another means.

Can the South end the war?

Can the South, then, end this war? If the North can take no step toward peace; if foreign intervention be not available; if the South cannot be subjugated; it becomes a momentous question how the South can bring this war to an end. Though they are the aggressors, few of them expect to conquer us; and how can the South be brought to stop the war they have begun?

The South led to war by our deserting Federalism—

Though the South was wrong in its secession, still more wrong in beginning an unjust, offensive war, they had much excuse in the desertion of the Federal principle upon which our Government was established. The North have affirmed that we are consolidated; the South that we are a Federal Republic. Since the advent of the Republican party to power, the Government has been administered more than ever, both by the President and Congress, on the consolidated basis. Neither does the war justify usurpations of power and departures from the Constitution. That instrument will be found, upon examination, to be perfectly adequate to the best conduct of our Government, in even this critical emergency. So long as the spirit of consolidation continues, so long must the South continue their war, for they understand (or will) that it is of no use to talk of peace except with reunion. The South can never with honor consider the question of reunion except upon the Federal basis. So that it comes to this point. When the North can see its error as to our form of Government, and is willing to acknowledge it, the South can with honor end the war, and propose terms of reunion on the Federal basis of our fathers. Till then the war goes on, increasing in wretchedness and horror day by day. And the alternative being war or consolidation, which must bring Monarchy, I hope with all my heart the South will adhere to its course, though the war should last fifty years.

§ 8. To the North: how to end this war.

—can cease it on our return to Federalism.

The South is right on the Federal question, though wrong on other equally important points; and were it prepared to-day to reconstruct the Union upon the very same basis of our fathers, the large majority of the North would reject the proposition. Our systems, State and Federal, have worked so harmoniously and perfectly, that we have scarcely been aware that we had a Government, and have been so engrossed in the various pursuits of life enjoyed under its beneficent sway, as to be careless and indifferent to the supervising care, except as we could use it for selfish aggrandizement. We have become ignorant of the first principles of our Government.

The South right as to Federalism.

Prospering as no other Peoples ever did, and, as we have correctly conceived, because of Union, we had naturally come to regard disunion as our greatest evil; and ignorant of the objects, principles, advantages, and necessities of a Federal Union, the great mass of the North believe we are consolidated; that the words, "We, the people of the United States," in the preamble of the Constitution, mean consolidation, and nothing less. This unfortunate omission to use the word *Peoples* instead of *people*, when the plural was intended, as we shall see, has led to great mistakes and wrongs. And although the North is by no means responsible altogether for this misconception, it has caused grave errors, which should be understood and corrected.

How the North were led into errors as to Federalism.

We have eminent authority, Madison and others, for the belief that we are "partly Federal and partly national." To the extent that we are "national" as contradistinguished to Federal, are we consolidated; but if any one point in this work is successfully established, it is, that to be "partly Federal and partly national" is absolutely impossible. States cannot be partly consolidated, and partly not consolidated; partly with Sovereignty, the *Right of Command*, partly without it. The *Right of Command*, pertaining to any one State or domain, whether in earth or heaven, is in its nature indivisible, however much its *exercise* may be distributed to subordinate agents. Incidentally this idea of Madison's is noticed in this first volume, in connection with extracts from Pufendorf; but in Part

Madison's error that we were partly "national."

§ 9. To the North: Union and slave responsibility.

II of this work, upon *The Constitution*, it is analyzed with considerable care, and, I trust, successfully.

§ 9.—To the North: Federal Union and Slave Responsibility.

Madison's error misleads the North.

The idea just alluded to, that we were "partly national," as well as "partly Federal," appears to have been the chief cause of our errors and strifes, particularly concerning slavery and its concomitant, the Territories. When beginning this examination, over two years since, no language was adequate to express my detestation of the Abolition fanatics, who, seeming recreant to obligation and duty, instigated by malevolence, sought by any and all means to overthrow slavery, though it buried this temple of freedom in the ruins. No doubt some few have labored, and do still, sincerely and earnestly for this object; and if our Union is to be restored, our institutions preserved, it must be in spite of them. But most of even strong Republicans, as they style themselves, are very differently actuated. Taught by influential statesmen that we were "partly national," as the fathers of the Constitution have passed away, most of whom comprehended and practised the idea that we were Federal, though a little bewildered as to the theory of "nationality;" the sons, dreading disunion as the chief of evils, have come more and more to believe that we were chiefly "national," and a very large part of the North think we are so altogether. The North are eminently a practical people, and have correctly reasoned, that if we were "partly national," to that extent were they responsible for what was deemed the sin of slavery in this "nation" of the United States; and that at least in the District of Columbia, and in the Territories, the common property of this "nation," the evil should not be tolerated. Right or wrong as to slavery, such have been the prevalent sentiments; and being to a good degree conscientious and religious, our people will act out their principles. The South itself, which has even more religious sentiment than the North, would not wish it otherwise. And were we made "partly" a State or nation by Federal Union, as in the primary organization of society into a State, then every individual Citizen in this "nation" of the United States, would to that extent be responsible for the sin and evil of slavery, as he regarded it. "As a man thinketh in his heart, so is he." "To him that knoweth to do good and doeth it not, to him it is sin." There *is* a law higher than all human institutions, given us in the Bible, and written on our hearts, and woe to him who violates it unrepentant. But International Law is not counter to this; it is in perfect harmony with it, and based upon it, and no provision of our Federal Constitution conflicts with either. Being, however, imperfect men, knowledge limited, passions swaying, prejudices influencing, interests affecting, habits almost controlling our views, of law human and Divine, we have all sorts of notions as to what is expedient and inexpedient, right and wrong. What a wretched condition would be ours, were the conscientious slavery-hater of Massachusetts made either wholly or "partly" responsible for the Carolinian's holding men in cap-

If "partly national," "partly" responsible for slavery.

Prov. xxiii, 7. *James* iv, 17.

The higher law.

Advantage of State divisions in promoting morality.

tivity! But by our Providential division of territory into States of reasonable area, every man is able to live under a Government suited to his conscientious belief. If liquor dealing be to him a sin, he can find a State that prohibits it; if slavery be "the sum of all villanies" in his estimation, he need not go into the South.

§ 9. To the North: Union and slave responsibility.

Federal leagues give no responsibility for the management of each Confederate's affairs.

Neither does our Federal Union with slaveholding States, make us responsible in the slightest degree for any Confederate's mismanagement of its domestic concerns. These States, these citizens of States in the North, have no more to do with slavery in Kentucky than in Turkey. The States, by their Federal Agency, hold diplomatic intercourse with the latter, though she enslaves the beauteous Caucasian, our own race of GOD's image; but we thereby incur no legal nor moral obligation for any of her acts. Providence has so located these Peoples, and by nature, and a gradual progress in improvements, has so interwoven their interests, that it is desirable for us and for all humanity, the negro included, that these States should have between themselves more intimate relations than with all the world besides; and yet the channel of those relations, and the only channel, is the same Federal Agency by which more distant relations are held with Turkey.

The compact of Union prevents intermeddling in State affairs.

With jealous care, too, have we guarded, not only against undue responsibility, but that the compact of Union should not authorize interference in the individual concerns of these free and independent States, either by any Confederate itself, or by their joint Agency; and we violate the solemn compact of Union, all principles of International Law, and the sacred commands of Scripture, if otherwise than by friendly Christian counsel, one State intrudes upon another. Story has given us sound advice on this point, and we shall have more of the sort; for our States are equally as sovereign, free, and independent, as any other States, their Confederacy authorizing no interference with them on any subject not explicitly mentioned in the Federal League, in which slavery is not included. What we, as individuals or as States, may rightfully do in Cuba, in Turkey, in Britain, we may do in Delaware, Maryland, or Kentucky, and no more; and the Federal Agency can do no act not specifically authorized by these Sovereignties in their letter of attorney to it, the Constitution.

No State responsibility for slavery in the Territories.

Nor does our Union give us any responsibility for slavery in the Territories. As to the country east of the Mississippi and north of Florida, all was included in the bounds of one of the original thirteen States. In the Northwest were conflicting claims, but all the territory belonged to some one of the old States, and was a portion of its area. Kentucky was part of Virginia, Tennessee of North Carolina, Alabama and Mississippi of Georgia, and the Northwest of Virginia and of New York; equally as Vermont was part of New York, and Maine of Massachusetts. The Constitution and laws of each State extended to all parts of its territory, and there was no power on earth rightfully to make any change in the rights of property therein, till the territory and its inhab-

§ 9. To the North: Union and slave responsibility.

itants were transferred to some other Sovereignty, or was organized into a free and independent State. And we shall find, that the first Confederation to which the cessions of territory were made, constituted no such State, and, by a singular oversight, no authority had been given the old Congress even to dispose of, or in any way manage, the ceded territory. And we shall further discover, or I misjudge, that the much-vaunted Dane ordinance of '87, which has been supposed to have consecrated to freedom the great Northwest, was not only void as a gross usurpation, but also as violating positive and clear principles of International Law.

The new Constitution has not augmented State responsibility.

Neither does the new Constitution give any authority to Congress in any shape or manner to control *a Territory*, as we call our primary organizations of Peoples into States. The language of the Constitution is, "The Congress shall have power to dispose of and make all needful rules and regulations respecting *the territory or other property* belonging to the United States; and nothing in this Constitution shall be so construed as to *prejudice any claims* of the United States, *or of any particular State.*"

The territory east of the Mississippi.

"*The territory*" Congress was thereby authorized to manage with "OTHER PROPERTY," was made up of the western parts of several distinct and sovereign States, reaching the Mississippi, and together extending from near the Gulf to the Lakes. No title was ever gained to a rood of territory within these United States, except by and for these Sovereignties. The Constitution and laws of each State extended to its remotest boundary, as did those of Massachusetts to Maine before the latter became a State, and notwithstanding its disconnection from the mother-portion. Virginia had no right to cede the jurisdiction over that part of her State northwest of the Ohio, to the Federal Agency; and what is more, she never did so, either under the old or the new Constitution. It is not right, but is contrary to the whole genius of our institutions, to govern a people by an authority foreign to it. What else caused and justified our Revolution, but the usurpation of this right by the British Parliament? I care not that we have been all in confusion upon this subject; the touchstone of International Law we shall find sufficient to make it clear.

DUER's *Constitutional Jurisprudence*, p. 118.

On this subject President Duer remarks in his able *Lectures on Constitutional Jurisprudence:*

KENT's *Commentaries.*

Right of governing Oregon by Congress.

Same subordination as of these Colonies to Parliament.

Adverse to the genius of our institutions.

It was observed by the late Chancellor Kent, in his valuable "Commentaries," that "if the Government of the United States should carry into execution the project of colonizing the great valley of the Oregon west of the Rocky Mountains, it would afford a subject of grave consideration what would be the future civil and political destiny of that country. It would be a long time," he thought, "before it would be populous enough to be created into one or more independent States; and in the mean time, upon the doctrine taught by the Acts of Congress, and the judicial decisions of the Supreme Court, the Colonists would be in a state of complete subordination, and as dependent upon the will of Congress as the people of this country would have been upon the King and Parliament of Great Britain, if they could have enforced their claim to bind us in all cases whatsoever. Such a state," he continues, "of absolute sovereignty on the one hand, and of absolute dependence on the other, is not at all congenial with the free and independent spirit of our native institutions; and the establishment of distant Territorial Governments, ruled according to will and pleasure, would have a very natural tendency,—as all proconsular Governments have had,—to abuse and oppression."

§ 9. To the North: Union and slave responsibility.

The hand that traced these lines has long lain cold in death; but their learned and estimable author lived to see not only the "project" they refer to realized, in the organization of Oregon as a Territory, but the establishment of Territorial Governments in other and more remote portions of the continent, some of which had not as yet been acquired; and had his already lengthened life been prolonged for a few years more, his fears would have subsided as he witnessed the erection of some of those Territories into States. So rapid, indeed, has been the increase and settlement of the National domain, that our political geography becomes obsolete at home, before it is known abroad.

Duer discovers nothing wrong in Congress governing Territories.

It is a little singular that neither of these distinguished writers should have observed, that distance or contiguity affected not in the least the propriety of placing over a People a Government foreign to it; and what the Chancellor correctly deemed a wrong in Oregon, was wrong in Ohio, Mississippi, Iowa, California, and Arizona. Nothing has been discovered in the principles of International Law in this investigation, adverse to the sound, judicious views of Governor Cass and Senator Douglas, as to the right of each People to govern itself, and the doctrine of "Squatter Sovereignty" is far more in consonance with the genius of our institutions, than the usurping "Acts of Congress, and the Judicial decisions of the Supreme Court." It is the true solution of the whole slavery controversy, for the South were just as wrong in seeking unauthorized legislation by Congress for the protection of slavery, as the North were in its Missouri restriction and Wilmot proviso.

Right of Congress depends not on contiguity of Territory.

The "Squatter Sovereignty" doctrine accords with International Law, and with the genius of our institutions.

On reading the treaty with France for the Louisiana purchase, which with other documents will be given the reader, it will be found that slavery existed at the date of purchase all over that territory, from the Gulf to the head waters of the Mississippi; and we properly agreed in the treaty, that all rights of property should remain as they then were, till the people organized into States, should be admitted into the Union with equal rights with the old States. Yet, in direct violation of that agreement, was the Missouri restriction enacted in 1820, attempting to annul the rights of a master in his slave north of 36° 30′. Every acre of the Louisiana purchase, which has not been brought under a State Sovereignty, is to-day legally slaveholding territory, and the slaveholder is entitled to the protection of his rights by the whole force of the United States, according to the laws existing therein at the date of purchase. Failing to afford this protection, we violate important stipulations of the treaty, and France has just cause of war, for disregarding the rights of her former subjects and their inheritors, if, after due admonition, we refuse compliance with the treaty.

The Louisiana purchase controlled by treaty stipulations.

We shall ascertain, also, if I mistake not, that, irrespective of the treaty, Congress was impotent in the premises. Sovereign power is requisite to annihilate rights in property; and in this land of written law, our Agents, particularly the Federal, are restricted to the letter of authority. Taxation is a mode of exercising this prerogative, and with distinct limitations and strong safeguards has it been partially intrusted to

No authority in the premises delegated to Congress.

§ 9. To the North: Union and slave responsibility.

State Sovereignty can alone extinguish slavery.

Congress. Except upon this point, the right of eminent domain, of which taxation is a branch, is altogether withheld. But by the sovereign will of a State, can property in slaves, or in any other form, be taken for the public good; and if slavery ever comes to an end in America, it will be accomplished through this Providential division into States, whereby, as each State finds it unprofitable, or sinful, if you please, it can be made to cease. Have we not pursued this course, and made many States free that were slave? Is it not notorious, that efforts were in progress a quarter of a century ago, for gradual emancipation in several more slave States, and which would ere this have been successful in more or less of them, but for Northern interference? It is too great, too ramifying an interest to be suddenly uprooted, even were it the unmixed evil regarded by Abolitionists. By one of these States after another duly exercising its Sovereignty, its *Right of Command*, slavery may in time be brought to an end, though probably not to be expected, nor in my judgment desired, but in no other way. Anti-slavery men, of all in the land, should be most earnest advocates of pure, unadulterated Federalism.

Anti-slavery men must be Federalists.

§ 10.—To the North: Federalism Desirable.

Advantages of Federalism.

The more Federalism is understood, the more highly will it be estimated. The extracts from Aristotle will prove his judgment to have been, that diversity of interests, of pursuits, and of character, the greatest possible variety, is requisite to a perfect State, else it partakes too much of the family relation. That homogeneous condition, is desirable for man for certain purposes; but he needs something directly the opposite, for developing other parts of his nature, that he may reach the highest attainments of which he is susceptible. This the State supplies.

Free States must be small:

—to have diversity and strength, unite them in a Federal Republic.

Montesquieu, too, has shown us, and his wisdom accords with all experience, Rome only excepted and for very peculiar reasons, that a free State must be of moderate extent, so that to have the desirable diversity, is not practicable in a simple Republic, and he teaches that the end may be attained by a union of small States in a Federal Republic. Aristotle, too, teaches that a πολιτεια πολιτειων, a polity of polities, a Republic of Republics, is the highest condition of man.

Other writers, however, and some highly and justly esteemed, do not subscribe to this doctrine. Says Lord Brougham:

Advatages of the Representative principle.

Defect of Federal Union.

Small societies undesirable, as the inhabitants are regarded.

The first and most striking property of the Representative principle is that it enables a free or popular government to be established in an extensive and populous country. This we have already illustrated, by referring to the state of the ancient commonwealths, and the imperfect devices which became necessary for the purpose of enlarging the limits of the State without giving up Republican Government. Beside the other defects of the Federal Union, its manifest tendency to create mutual estrangement, and even hostility, between different parts of the same nation, is an insuperable objection to it. Small communities are exceedingly apt to conceive against their neighbors feelings of rivalry, jealousy, and mistrust; each individual bearing so considerable a proportion to the whole society that the worst personal prejudices and passions are nourished, and, the most ignorant and violent of the people being the most numerous, the tone of the whole takes the turn which these bad passions tend to give it. If any illustration of this truth were wanted, we have only to remind the reader of what we found in the history of the Italian republics. The government always is influenced by such feelings, most of all in a democracy, but in a great degree also in an aristocracy, and even in a petty principality. For the rulers themselves in such a narrow community partake of the general sentiment, even if the public opinion should not sway them. Whoever would see further proof of this position may be referred to the Ancient Commonwealths of Greece. As a Florentine hated a Siennese worse than a German or Spaniard, or even an infidel in modern times, so of old did an Athenian hate a Spartan or a Theban worse than a Persian. Now the Federal Union, by keeping up a line of separation among its members, gives the freest scope to these pernicious prejudices, feelings which it is the highest duty of all governments to eradicate, because they lead directly to confusion and war.

§ 10. To the North: Federalism desirable.

BROUGHAM'S *Political Philosophy.*

Federalism made responsible for these evils.

It may further be doubted if the existence of a small community is of itself desirable for the improvement of society. Undoubtedly great public spirit may be expected to prevail in such a nation, and the feelings of patriotism to be excited, or rather to be habitual with the people, each individual of whom feels his own weight and importance instead of being merged and lost in the countless multitude of a larger state. But this advantage is more than counterbalanced by the attendant evils of petty, contracted ideas, which such a narrow community engenders, and especially by the restlessness which arises among all the people, when each takes as much interest in the state's concerns as if they were his own. There is thus produced both an over zeal, a turbulent demeanor, a fierce and grasping disposition, hardly consistent with the peace of the community; and also a proportionate inattention to men's private affairs inconsistent with the dictates of prudence, as well as a disregard of the domestic ties, equally inconsistent with amiable character and with the charities of private life.

Evil of smallness upon the State itself.

It would further appear that limits may be much more easily set to the bounds within which a Federal Union can be established, than to those within which a representative system may conveniently exist. For the central government in a Federacy is of necessity feeble. It is more like a congress of ambassadors from many nations than the council of one nation. Each person is only animated with zeal for his own state, while none feel for the general welfare. But a representative government may extend over the largest dominions, and they who comprise it may exercise an authority at once vigorous and considerate, thinking for the advantage of each portion of the whole community, as well as consulting for the welfare of the whole.

Representation better employed in a large State than large Union.

Does not this learned and excellent Whig writer overthrow his argument against Federalism, by proving too much? Earnest patron as he has ever been of popular rights, zealous defender against governmental tyranny, he at the same time perceives, as shown in the above extract, and in other parts of his able work, the tendency of Democracies to anarchy and misrule. This he sees the principle of Representation aids effectively to counteract; yet not equally well in a Federal Union, he conceives, as in a single State. The same reason that would cause Aristotle to desire a large polity of polities, in order to have the greatest variety of character, interests, and influences, would lead Lord Brougham to reject it, in order to attain more homogeneity; for he says, "the Federal Union, by keeping up a line of separation among its members, gives the freest scope to these pernicious prejudices," &c.

Is not too much proved.

Representation saves Democracy from anarchy.

Brougham differs with Aristotle as to variety in a State.

No doubt at all, man's selfishness makes him antagonistic to his fellow, and the same trait predominates in every society of men. Adjacent school districts are rivals, adjacent towns are rivals, and so are adjacent counties and States. Rivalry has its evils, but not without countervail-

Rivalry natural to man.

This trait available in Government.

§ 10. To the North: Federalism desirable.

ing benefits; and it is the height of wisdom in governmental science, to make most available a trait immutable and incident to associated as well as individualized humanity.

The smaller bodies devoted to the larger.

While school districts are jealous of each other, they have, nevertheless, a common interest and pride in the advancement of their town, as have the towns in their county, the counties in their State, the States in their Federal Union. Did men all think alike on moral and religious subjects, the fundamental organization into States, might embrace continents, or even unite all mankind in a single State. But having all sorts of opinion in the world, and it being of the first moment that the laws and institutions of a people accord

Difficult in a large State to adapt laws to all characters.

with its conscientious convictions, it becomes exceedingly difficult for a Sovereignty to frame a system of Government that shall be just and give equal satisfaction to all classes and conditions of the subjects, in

In a monarchy inconveniences.

a widely extended empire. This is the chief inconvenience of a monarchy; that is, if Aristotle was right in considering the greatest variety the highest perfection of a State. Nor is it practicable nor expedient to have authority in a kingdom much divided. No doubt the incorpora-

An example in Britain.

tion of England and Scotland, and subsequently of Ireland, making a single State out of the three, was for the general good. But it renders much more difficult the enacting of suitable laws to govern, by one and the same, English, Scotch, and Irish, than if they had their separate parliaments. Yet with unity in the *Right of Command*, a division of the legislative power into separate parliaments, is perhaps impracticable, or at least has inconveniences. As Montesquieu says of single Republics, "the evil is in the very thing itself; and no form can redress it."

Kings disinclined to part with power.

Another disadvantage of Monarchy is, the natural disinclination of the possessor of power to part with its exercise. When the *Right of Command* comes into the possession of *one*, or even of the *few*, as in an Aristocracy, the possessor wants undividedly to exercise the whole power; and the contest in Britain has been for hundreds of years chiefly on this

The Sovereignty in a free State obliged to delegate.

point. But a free People, even in a simple Democracy like the ancient States of Greece, cannot, in most concerns, themselves exercise the *Right of Command*, but have to delegate it to subordinate agents; and in States like ours, simple Democracy is altogether out of the question, it being impracticable, even in the smallest, for the Citizens to meet *en masse.*

Representation advantageous.

The *Republican* feature, that of *Representation*, the worth of which is so well appreciated by Lord Brougham, must be altogether employed in the exercise of Sovereignty. As the sovereign People cannot themselves

General good the object in a free State.

exercise their *Right of Command*, as can a King, but must delegate it, proper considerations for the general good have a better chance to operate; and the best possible distribution of authority to control the wayward and rebellious, to protect the good and virtuous, becomes the highest aim, the strongest desire of every patriotic Citizen. In such a State, truly the good of one is the good of all.

Small societies a nuisance.

Lord Brougham also remarks, "It may further be doubted if the existence of a small community is of itself desirable for the improvement of society." In my humble judgment it is not to "be doubted." A small school district, or a small town, is very undesirable, for the excellent reasons given in his preceding paragraph; and equally undesirable is a small county, or an insignificant State. Free States must be small; yet, in the language of Montesquieu,

§ 10. To the North: Federalism desirable.

> If a Republic is small, it is destroyed by a foreign force; if it be large, it is ruined by an internal imperfection. To this twofold inconvenience both democracies and aristocracies are equally liable, and that whether they be good or bad. The evil is in the very thing itself; and no form can redress it. It is therefore very probable that mankind would have been at length obliged to live constantly under the government of a single person, had they not contrived a kind of constitution that has all the internal advantages of a republican, together with the external force of a monarchical government: I mean a *Confederate Republic*.

Small States made strong in a Federal Republic.

MONTESQUIEU. *Spirit of Laws*, l. ix, c.1.

Almighty GOD, too, taught this Caucasian race the same truths, ages before Montesquieu. Having chosen Democracy as the best form of Government for His favorite people of old, He divided them up into little tribes or States, and with the infinite love and wisdom of our Heavenly Father, did He teach the principle of Federal Union in the Government of His choice. Earnestly did He, by Samuel, remonstrate against the folly of His rebellious children, in deserting the free Government He had instituted, in order that they might "be like all the nations."

GOD teaches Federalism.

1 *Sam.* viii, 20.

Not believing that Montesquieu was a fool; that our own experience of seventy years is valueless; that JEHOVAH is incapable of judging of what is a desirable form of Government for His creatures; or that the only example He ever instituted should be radically defective, is the reason why the query was made, whether Lord Brougham did not prove too much for a sound argument.

Reasons for the query to Lord Brougham.

Nor is Lord Brougham's reason why "limits may be much more easily set to the bounds within which a Federal Union can be established, than to those within which a representative system may conveniently exist," at all satisfactory. He adds the reason, "For the central government in a Federacy is of necessity feeble." This was also De Tocqueville's judgment. But our experience proves the incorrectness of the opinions of these eminent philosophers, and perhaps this examination may show wherein they were mistaken. Notwithstanding the North has been divided up into factions, yet witness the power of the Government, despite the wrongs of Administration and the abhorrence of many of its leading acts, by at least two-thirds of our citizens. It is this grand principle of Representation, so justly estimated by this wise and excellent friend of true and proper Government, which enables these States to have something more than merely "a congress of ambassadors from many nations," by which we have the power here demonstrated, not only in the older Government of the United States, but in that of the Confederate Government, which has risen into being, and thoroughly established itself as a power in the earth, in spite of adverse surroundings and internal difficulties.

Lord Brougham misjudges of Representation in Federalism—he considers a Federacy weak.

De Tocqueville also, Part I, c. 8 and 18.

Our experience not corroborative.

Representation the means of strength.

Success in both Federal and Confederate Governments.

§ 10. To the North: Federalism desirable.

Federalism not understood.

Its foundation is State Sovereignty.

It is not surprising that Federalism should not have been well comprehended by Lord Brougham; we have not understood it ourselves. It is a most important, deeply interesting field of exploration, which, when our wise men shall again travel over, their paths illuminated with the lamps of truth of these old writers, will have new beauties; and "the stateliness of houses, the goodliness of trees, when we behold them" in this field of Federalism, will still more "delight the eye," when we shall have discovered "in the bosom of the earth concealed," "that foundation which beareth up the one, that root which ministereth unto the other nourishment and life." "That foundation," "that root," will be found to be none other than Sovereignty, the *Right of Command*, in the possession of free Peoples. No wonder is it our landscape is adorned with such "stateliness of houses," such "goodliness of trees."

Madison's error as to National—

Hamilton corrects it.

The occasion of error not developed.

Sovereignty not understood, as the basis of Government—

—of the State:

—also Federal.

Change in the Federal—

—drought to bear on the subjects.

Allusion has been made to Madison's misconception, considering our system "nationalized" by bringing the Government to bear upon individuals, which the great Hamilton first corrected in his effective speech in the Constitutional Convention, proving it not to be a "national" feature; as under the then existing Government, which was unquestionably a Confederacy, Congress had power to punish in certain cases. But the why and wherefore has never been developed, and when our wise men find "that foundation," "that root," they will enable us to understand the subject better. Quite probably they will teach us, that these free Peoples, in the proper exercise of their *Right of Command*, ruling their subjects with the most despotic sway, had the right and power to place over their subjects, any sort of Government they pleased. Each of them had its State Government, and every subject that owed allegiance to the Sovereignty which had instituted it, in consequence owed obedience to that Government. But these Sovereignties, for good and sufficient reasons, chose to join together and create a Government to manage some of their most important concerns. The first attempt was a failure, because they relied too much upon the machinery of their several States, and in the second attempt they made a further advance in the true application of the Federal principle, than had ever come down to them in history. They wisely and rightly, in the judicious exercise of their Sovereignty, subjected their faithful liege subjects, and their property for certain purposes and with guarded restrictions, directly to the authority of their Federal Government, without any intervention of their State Governments.

Checks in Federalism upon the exercise of Sovereignty.

Present errors no criterion.

Unless we altogether misjudge, our wise men will further investigate this subject of Federalism, and instead of being so abhorrent of absolute, despotic authority, they will teach us it is the very life and soul of all Government; and that, while Federalism exhibits its gigantic power, as demonstrated in our wars of the Revolution, of 1812, in Mexico, and now in this most tremendous of all modern wars, it also affords more and better checks upon the *exercise* of the sovereign *Right of Command*, than any system ever devised. Nor does the disregard of these checks in the present Administration of Government, exhibit weakness or imperfection in Federalism itself, in the slightest degree. Surely will this examination prove, in whatever else it may fail, that it is the abandonment of Federal principles, ignorance and misconception of most simple, self-evident truths, that every school-boy in the land should be perfectly familiar with, in order to his proper qualification to exercise the high and responsible duties of Citizenship; it is the desertion of Federalism that has not only led us into civil war, but into the usurpations and wrongs that have characterized this Administration, and which will be a warning to all future generations. The blackest, foulest spots of despotism that in modern years have defaced the historic page, may they be a perpetual memento, till all earthly Governments shall cease, of the evils of deserting Federalism! GOD grant that these free Peoples may never again be called to witness such violation of their Sovereignties, such usurpations of their sacred *Right of Command*, as in misconception and ignorance, not with malice prepense, our rulers have committed. A return to Federalism by rulers and ruled, is the first and most important step, not only to reunion, but to the preservation of our free institutions.

§ 10. To the North: Federalism desirable.

Federalism is abandoned.

Usurpations a warning example.

To be relieved by Federalism.

Nor does the lamentable lapse we have made, indicate undue confidence in Federalism, or presage a decline in the estimate of its worth. In this state of imperfection, everything human has its ups and downs. What other Government of earth can show for eighty years, any less wrong and misconduct? What other can show equal benefits, either to the Peoples themselves, or to the whole human family? And it must be remembered, that we started an experiment. The Dutch Confederacy, an incongruous mixture of Democratic and Aristocratic States, the Helvetic, another of the same sort, were of little practical benefit in giving shape and order to our Federal Union, particularly the last of '89; the examples in Greece, are and were too little known in the details, to be of much avail; and that of the Hebrews seems never to have been considered; at least in none of the debates pending the change of Constitutions, is it referred to, that we have observed. So that to us, this was a new experiment. Besides, after the days of Barbeyrac, Burlamaqui, Montesquieu and Vattel, the whole civilized world seems to have become impregnated with the delusive teachings of man's natural liberty. Instead of recognizing the grand truth, the fundamental idea, that lies at the foundation of all Government, Divine or human, that every man, woman, and child is a subject to a Supreme *Right of Command*, the contrary was taught and believed, that man is naturally a free-man, and can only be brought under authority by his consent; which consent, as a natural inalienable right, he may at his pleasure revoke, and overthrow the Government, provided he can have the aid of a sufficient number of discontents. Some of the wisest, best, most pious men of Europe, abhorring oppression and tyranny, properly desirous of keeping within reasonable bounds the *exercise* of authority, came to mistake the limiting of the *exercise*, for the limiting of the *Right of Command* itself, and they became abettors of the scheme of liberty, fraternity, equality, that culminated in

Worth of Federalism not disproved by these errors.

Other Governments imperfect.

Ours an experiment.

Evil of teachings of natural liberty.

Everybody a subject.

Errors on this point of good men.

French Revolution.

§10. To the North: Federalism desirable. — In that era our Government was established. — Providence saved us. — No teachers of the *Right of Command.* — Federalism saved us.

the French Revolutions of 1789–'95. It was in this dangerous era that our new Government was instituted; and let any one study our history, and he will find that Paine did not misrepresent the intimate relations between France and us, and truly wonderful is it that we escaped the vortex. The Christian will recognize in our deliverance, the hand of our Heavenly Father; and in Federalism, the Providential division of this country into States, the means Infinite Wisdom employed; and from that day to this, there is not a single writer upon Government, that we have seen, who grounds it on the Sovereignty, the *Right of Command,* of Grotius and Vattel. The wonder is that with our *theories* so wrong and confused, our *practice* should have been so nearly correct; and under Providence, it is nothing but genuine Federalism that has saved us, and that, too, in spite of the absurd dogma that we were "partly national."

POPE'S idea of forms of Government.

Federalism has not yet had a fair chance to have its excellences tested. We have seen a little how Paine endeavored to overthrow theories of Government, and the same idea had been inculcated by the excellent Pope in that often-quoted passage:

> For forms of Government let fools contest,
> Whate'er is best administered is best.

Such heresy to be abolished. — Theory important to practice.

Not until all such heretical teachings as that are banished, and we become indoctrinated anew with the solid and correct truths of the chief founders of International Law, can we form a true estimate of the intrinsic excellences of Federalism. In politics, as in religion, a man's faith must be right in the fundamental truths, or he will be liable to go astray. Sound *theories* are indispensable to sound *practice;* and not till at least a half century after we shall have been well schooled in this fundamental doctrine of Sovereignty, the *Right of Command,* shall we be able to demonstrate the superiority of its exercise by Free Peoples, united in a Federal Republic.

FREEMAN'S *History of Federal Government.* London, 1863. — Sovereignty not comprehended.

Since penning the above, a very interesting and able work, *History of Federal Government,* by Mr. Edward A. Freeman, has come under observation, which evidently is a very opportune publication, though the copy could only be kept in hand long enough to barely glance through it. But, notwithstanding its excellences, the introduction proves that the author did not well comprehend the fundamental idea in a Federal Union, as in all forms of Government, the *Right of Command,* State Sovereignty. He remarks:

Requisites of a Federal Government. — Manage some affairs, subject in others. — Correct view of State Sovereignty— —erroneous view.

> Two requisites seem necessary to constitute a Federal Government in this its most perfect form. On the one hand, each of the members of the Union must be wholly independent in those matters which concern each member only. On the other hand, all must be subject to a common power in those matters which concern the whole body of members collectively. Thus each member will fix for itself the laws of its criminal jurisprudence, and even the details of its political constitution. And it will do this, not as a matter of privilege or concession from any higher power, but as a matter of absolute right, by virtue of its inherent powers as an independent commonwealth. But in all matters which concern the general body, the sovereignty of the several members will cease. Each member is perfectly independent within its own

sphere; but there is another sphere in which its independence, or rather its separate existence, vanishes. It is invested with every right of sovereignty on one class of subjects, but there is another class of subjects on which it is incapable of separate political action, as any province or city of a monarchy or of an indivisible republic. The making of peace and war, the sending and receiving of ambassadors, generally all that comes within the department of International Law, will be reserved wholly to the central power. Indeed, the very existence of the several members of the Union will be diplomatically unknown to foreign nations, which will never be called upon to deal with any power except the Central Government. A Federal Union, in short, will form one State in relation to other powers, but many States as regards its internal administration. This complete division of sovereignty, we may look upon as essential to the absolute perfection of the Federal ideal. But that ideal is one so very refined and artificial, that it seems not to have been attained more than four or five times in the history of the world.

§ 10. To the North: Federalism desirable.

Independence vanishes.

A State not Sovereign on some subjects.

State existence unknown.

Sovereignty divided.

The chief "requisite" in "Federal Government" or any other is, that a State should possess absolutely, indivisibly, its *Right of Command.* Such a State is "on the one hand," "on the other hand," and on all hands, not only "wholly independent," but also perfectly free and *sovereign.* It *can never* "be subject to a common power," either in matters "which concern the whole body," or any other matters. Never can a sovereign be a "subject." True is it that, "not as a matter of privilege or concession from any higher power, but as a matter of absolute right, by virtue of its inherent powers as an independent commonwealth," "each member will fix for itself the laws of its criminal jurisprudence, and even the details of its political constitution." In every respect, in all the details of Government, does this "absolute right" of Sovereignty operate within the confines of the State; and if it shall have joined with sister Sovereignties to manage some of their affairs by a Federal League, the same Sovereign Authority imparts the power to operate the machinery within its boundaries. *Never* can it be said under any circumstances, "the Sovereignty of the several members will cease," till those "members" "cease" to be States. Neither on this planet or any other, is there "another sphere in which its independence, or rather its separate existence, vanishes," till it shall sleep the sleep that knows no waking. "Invested with every right of Sovereignty," not only on "one class of subjects," but on every class, a Sovereign State can never become "incapable of separate political action as any province or city of a monarchy, or of an indivisible Republic." It may delegate to subordinates jointly with other Sovereignties, "the making of peace and war," and other affairs that can be best conjointly conducted; but it is to be hoped it will never extend the delegation so far, as to include "generally all that comes within the department of International Law." The taking for granted that this has been done with these States, is the chief cause of complaint against our excellent Kent and Story, and others. That great "Central Power" is powerless, except as its limbs and muscles are operated by the souls of these greatest moral persons, these sovereign States; whereby, as one effect, they deputize some of their faithful liege subjects, to go and visit kings and queens, the ordinary monarchs of earth.

Requisite in Government, *Right of Command.*

A State never a subject.

A truth.

Sovereignty rules in a State—

—and in a league—

—never ceases.

A State's independence never vanishes—

—never as a province—

—should not give up right to International Law

Sovereignty the soul of a State.

The majesty of free States.

§ 10. To the North: Federalism desirable.

"Indeed, the very existence of the several members of the Union will be diplomatically unknown to foreign nations," not only because they "will never be called upon to deal with any power except the Central Government," but because of the august majesty of these Democratic States, which severs them from contact, not only "diplomatically," but every way, with common sovereigns. Mere kings and queens and emperors, admit ambassadors and subjects into their immediate presence and hold converse with them; but these Sovereignties of ours, like the Sovereignty of Heaven, withheld even from vision, only by delegates and humble subjects, condescend to hold intercourse even with emperors themselves. And though invisible as Deity, invisible as is the soul, yet does the Sovereignty, the *Right of Command*, operate within the realms of these States, as does Jehovah throughout the universe; as the soul of man moves his cords and muscles, his hands and feet, so do the souls of these greatest moral persons operate the legislative, judicial, executive, and other parts of their bodies politic.

Invisible, like that of Deity.

See Note, p, 162.

God's division of the *exercise* of the *Right of Command.*

God, too, has condescended to teach us, in what should be the standard authority in International Law, that even with Him, all-wise, all-perfect as He is, the *exercise* of His Sovereignty had best be divided; and without any explanation of a subject too far beyond our comprehension to be understood, as to how He exists, one in three, and three in one,—for, if with all our efforts, we cannot comprehend in any degree our own existence as a natural body, a spiritual body and a soul, three in one, and one in three, of what use to explain to our finite intellects the infinitely deeper mystery of Jehovah's existence—He merely declares the fact that he exists as one God in Three Persons, and that the *exercise* of His Sovereignty is divided, part being in the hands of the Father, part in the Son, part in the Holy Ghost, yet does the *Right of Command* belong absolutely, indivisibly, to the one Jehovah. When we come to consider Sovereignty, we shall see the excellent views of the judicious Hooker, on this interesting subject.

Suitable for the creature to follow the Creator.

Well may weak, finite man imitate Infinite Wisdom in Government, the most intricate and difficult of all sciences; but, as already observed, the selfishness of man disinclines him to divest himself of any power of which he becomes possessed. Hence arises a difficulty with Mr. Freeman's consideration of Federalism, apparently altogether overlooked, of its inadaptation to Monarchy. This prevails not in Heaven's chosen form of Government, a Democracy. Notwithstanding these free Peoples are possessed of majesty so august that no man can approach it, monarch though he be, yet are they compelled to delegate the whole *exercise* of their Sovereignty. The only question then is, as to a choice of parties to be employed; and this *exercise* of power, being one of the most self-aggrandizing things in nature, it becomes an interesting and important problem, how best to distribute the *exercise*, so as to establish a system of checks and balances to control every wheel and spring in the governmental machinery, and to keep it in its proper place and at its appro-

difficult in monarchy—

—not in Democracy—

—consequent benefits.

Checks and balances.

priate work. And, of all systems ever devised to accomplish this great desideratum, none will compare with Federalism. With an undivided and indivisible, unaccountable and uncontrollable Sovereignty, do these free Peoples require and appoint certain of their subjects to perform such and such duties. The Sovereignty must have its Agency to speak new bodies into existence, and also to legislate, and it instructs its subjects how the persons are to be designated to these important duties. Others must serve their Sovereignty as Judges of law, and of conduct infringing its prerogatives, and the subjects are commanded how to appoint these servants, most important safeguards of the People's Majesty. An Executive, too, must be chosen to see that the Sovereign will, expressed through these subordinate Agents, is duly performed; and the appointments of such other officials are provided for, as the Sovereignty of the People deems adequate for its protection and glory; "for the punishment of evil-doers, and for the praise of them that do well."

§ 10. To the North: Federalism desirable.

Sovereignties employ subjects for special duties.

1 *Peter* ii, 14.

Admirable, indeed, does this system appear to be for the accomplishment of its purposes, and all the Citizens being equally interested in protecting their *Right of Command*, keeping it inviolate, one would suppose that with moderate sense and skill, such a system would perpetuate itself. But power has a terrible tendency to self-aggrandizement, and circumstances favoring a selfish, adroit, able intriguer, not even the sacred *Right of Command* is secure against its usurpations. When in the sequel we come to look into the history of Rome, the grandest example of a Republic recorded in history, we shall see how easily Julius, and then Octavius Cæsar, transformed the *civitas*, the Commonwealth, the Republic, into an empire, which in only the fourth reign from the memorable (Octavius') Augustan era, became a tyranny under Nero. France, too, with its "Republic, one and indivisible," will show us, by example after example, how a Bonaparte can become possessed of the Sovereignty. Something else is wanted, effectively to preserve in a free People, its sovereign *Right of Command*, than the simple checks and balances afforded in a single Republic.

The apparent excellence of the system.

Still, dangers in single Republics.

Rome an example.

Also France.

This safety is secured more perfectly by Federalism, than by any other means yet discovered, and probably nothing equal to it for that important purpose can be devised. The danger in a true πολιτεια, polity, or Republic, a proper *civitas*, or Commonwealth, is, that some one man or set of men will become possessed of the whole authority. The *Right of Command* is mainly exercised by its Legislative part, and its Executive part; the other parts, as the Judiciary, the power of taxing, &c., being so far subordinate, as to be usually controlled by those possessing the two former. The chief excellence of a Commonwealth is in the People having a controlling power in enacting their laws, as in the glorious days when Rome was truly a *civitas*. But a Cæsar could suborn the Legislative, and controlling the two great powers of the Republic, he soon usurped the Sovereignty, came into full possession of the *Right of Command*, and changed the Republic into a Monarchy, though he and succeed-

Safety afforded by Federalism.

The difficulty in a single State.

Usurpation possible.

§ 10. To the North: Federalism desirable.

ing Emperors, to make the People think the change unimportant, still spoke of the *respublica* and *civitas*.

Federalism protects against usurpation— —in a State official.

Now Federalism appears to afford a perfect protection against this rascality. For a number of Commonwealths to divide the *exercise* of their *Right of Command* to two entirely different sets of deputies, seems to render it absolutely impossible for any one man or set of men to usurp the entire Sovereignty. If the Executive in one of these Republics could corrupt and control its Legislative, which only has power in regard to certain affairs of home concern, others of chief consequence being delegated to the Federal Legislature; and any usurper should dare to attempt to steal from the people their *Right of Command*, and control not only the parts of Sovereignty delegated to the State Agency, but those delegated to the Federal Agency also; the State has a sure safeguard in its Compact of Union with sister-Sovereignties, which declares that "The United States shall guarantee to every State in this Union a Republican Form of Government, and shall protect each of them against invasion, and on application of the Legislature, or of the Executive (when the Legislature cannot be convened) against domestic violence." So important was this regarded, that full, unrestricted power of coercion of a Sovereign State, is herein delegated to the Federal Agency, and it is the sole respect in which it has the least shadow of right to coerce. Should the time ever come, that one of these States reunited should reach such a depth of corruption as to attempt to change the GOD-sanctioned form of a true Republic into any other, we shall have a new opportunity to display the superior excellence of Federalism, and triumphantly will it be vindicated.

Rights of Confederate States to guard against usurpation.

Coercion sanctioned.

States a safeguard against Federal usurpation.

Then, too, suppose a Federal usurper should arise; how is he to become possessed of the entire *Right of Command* in these States of ours? Fortunately, at this most critical epoch in our history, we have in the Executive chair of the States confederated, and in that of the States united, incorruptible patriots, who, whatever their failings, would guard as jealously the liberties of their Peoples, as did our Father, WASHINGTON. But suppose it were otherwise, and taking advantage of the immense armies in the field, in either or both sections, an attempt were made to establish a military despotism. It has come too near to it in the North, nowithstanding the honesty and integrity of our President—far nearer than any other two years in our history will ever witness, I trust; yet has subversion of liberty not been intended, and any one acquainted with Abraham Lincoln as well as is the writer, knows that he does not mean to infringe a single right of a single Citizen; and when he has had time and opportunity to look into these rights, and sees how outrageously, unnecessarily they have been violated, in spite of the wise protections put about them, no one in the land will be more anxious to make atonement for the wrongs done; none will be more solicitous than he to take effective measures to protect against such lamentable, infamous attempts in future. But suppose, instead of President Lincoln, we had General ——— (I would like to write the name instead of the dash, but it is not

The present failure to protect.

The wrongs will be corrected when understood.

A real usurpation could not be successful.

expedient), what could he do, with even these immense armies of a million of men? Of whom are these armies composed? Not, as the South suppose, of foreigners, but, as the statistics show, in a large majority, of native-born Americans. They are possessed of the inestimable privilege of Citizenship, which we are soon to consider. Would it be easy to bring such men to consent to overthrow their free institutions, to establish a despotism? Suppose even this could be done; Federalism still has an abundant safeguard, in the existence of these thoroughly organized State Governments, with their full control of the militia, the People themselves; of those who are CITIZENS, or hope soon to be CITIZENS, of these free States, *fellow* CITIZENS of this Republic of States. The very prince of fiends himself in the shape of General ———, or any other general, could never become possessed of the *Right of Command* in these free States, till they should have become such sinks of corruption, as that even the most despotic tyranny would prove a blessing in removing the plague-spots from existence. § 10. To the North: Federalism desirable.

To develope the advantages of Federalism, is an almost endless task. It is the chief point in the whole of this work, and even to indicate them is impossible in this compend. The object has been in the foregoing remarks rather to show how little the subject has been and is comprehended; the difficulty lying, as it appears to me, in losing all knowledge of "that foundation," "that root," that bears up all "the stateliness," "the goodliness," that preëminently characterize Federalism—THE SOVEREIGNTY, the RIGHT OF COMMAND, wielded by free Peoples. And our judgment is sadly at fault, if these able and excellent writers, Lord Brougham and Mr. Freeman, do not become the most earnest and successful seekers of "that foundation," "that root," of which we have lost knowledge. None will more rejoice than they in discovering the true secret of Anglo-Saxon success in Government, on this side the Atlantic; which, in the event of another attempt by Britain's monarchs to overthrow the People's rights, as in the Stuart reigns, would result in the abolishing of Monarchy, the redivision into the old States, and their Union in a Federal Republic. The true principles of this *Right of Command* need only to be understood, as taught by Grotius down to Vattel, and that, if once forfeited by the Sovereign, from violating her or his sacred trust, it again reverts to the People, and will there be permanently kept; and then no Monarch of Britain will be so unwise as to endeavor to revoke powers delegated by the Crown to its faithful subjects, and the *exercise* of which, it is best for Monarch and People, should continue to be entrusted to subordinate agents, as by custom has been long established; the source of authority, the *Right of Command*, being nevertheless in the Monarch, according to the terms of the grant by the People, through their duly elected representatives, the Convention Parliament, in 1688, to William, Prince of Orange, and Mary, his wife, William being really the monarch. Impossible here fully to develop the excellences of Federalism. Misapprehension of it. Brougham and Freeman to aid to correct. Sympathy of Anglo-Saxons To examine may benefit Britons.

To Anglo-Saxons here and *at home*, the basis and excellences of

§ 10. To the North: Federalism desirable. — Important for Anglo-Saxons to understand Federalism.

Federalism is the most important and interesting of all earthly subjects. We shall find that European writers have correctly understood that we were no consolidated State, but a Federal Republic; and in proving this, and establishing the excellences of Federalism, we shall not only have the benefit of quotations from Lord Brougham and Mr. Freeman, but from M. Guizot, Lacroix, Necker, and others.

These States in a polity of polities could defy the world.

No other country on the globe affords such diversity of soil, of climate, of productions, as that of these thirty-four States. Could they be once again united in a polity of polities, we could, in the language of Aristotle, defy the world. But this very diversity in nature creates a

Advantage in morals.

diversity in interests and in character. To adapt our institutions and laws to this diversity, is of prime importance, that all Citizens may conscientiously and religiously stand by and uphold their Government. Only on a few subjects of Government should we so agree, that it would be de-

Dignity of their Federal Government.

sirable to commit them to the care of a joint Agency; but they happen to be so consequential and weighty, that their conduct has already given a character and dignity to the Government of these States united, that has made it honored and respected throughout the world. All other interests and concerns not specifically delegated to the joint Agency, are re-

One Confederate not responsible for another.

served to the separate Sovereignties. And we have no right, in any way, to interfere with a Confederate State, more than with Russia. So that by means of Federalism, we can have all the advantages of a Union with States affording this immense diversity of productions, of character, and of institutions, without the slightest responsibility for what may be deemed wrong in their individual management. Important as is the

No other system will suit the North.

Union of all these States to the North, condemning slavery as many of our Citizens will doubtless continue to do, we have no resource to secure the one and allow toleration of the other, but our Federal System. Most earnest Federalists should we all be in the North.

§ 11.—To the North: Importance of Union among ourselves.

Present divisions of the North.

We need to study into the principles of our Government, not only as an indispensable means to a new Federal Union with the South; equally important is it to obtain unanimity of sentiment in the North. Divided into war Democrats and peace Democrats, conservative Republicans and radical Republicans, and of various shades, we are not with proper vigor

We must support our Government.

supporting our Government, which we must do, despite the wrongs of Administration. The latter we can change as we deem necessary; the former must be maintained. To examine the nature of our Union, and

To examine principles will unite us.

the principles of its Government, thereby learning the rights and wrongs of these States, concerning which we are so at variance even among ourselves, will, it appears to me, unite us almost as one man.

Federalism has strong bands.

We know not the strength of bands that encircle this Union. The pledge of pact and faith is strong, yet may that be broken, and as Pufendorf shrewdly remarks:

§ 11. To the North: we must have Union.

Interest stronger than covenant.

Although the argument of Mr. Hobbes which we have here endeavored to refute, does not perform the service he intends it for; that is, does not take off the validity of *pacts* in a *natural state;* yet is in some measure capable of good use, inasmuch as we may draw from it the following rules of prudence; Never to depend much on a covenant, but when we know that the interest of the other party is concerned in the performance of it, as well as our own; and that upon default he is likely to suffer some greater evil or inconvenience, than he can incur by standing to the agreement.

PUFENDORF, *Laws of Nature and Nations*, iii, 6, § 9.

Common interest of these States in their common territory.

As we pursue this investigation, we shall discover that each one of these Sovereignties is one of the parties to the compact of the Constitution, whereby a Federal Agency has been created for the joint convenience of these sovereign States. One of the duties of this Agency, is to hold in trust for the Sovereigns some of their property. These British Colonies, which afterward became free States, had large areas, much too extensive for a single Republic, and with great generosity they severally ceded their proprietary right in their surplus territory to the United States. Whether the State Agencies, the Legislature and the Executive, could do more than this, will appear in the investigation; probably they could not. But this joint proprietary right created a strong ligament of Union between the Sovereignties, with regard to which Mr. Curtis with excellent judgment remarks:

Rights ceded by some States to all the States.

A ligament of Union.

A confederacy of States, which had become possessed of such a common property, was thus bound together by an interest, the magnitude and force of which cannot now be easily estimated. The Union might incur fresh dangers of dissolution, after the war had ceased; its frame of government and its legislative power might prove wholly inadequate to the national wants in time of peace; the public faith might be prostrated, and the national arm enfeebled; still, while the Confederacy stood as the great trustee of property large enough for the accommodation of an empire, a security existed against its total destruction. No State could withdraw from the Confederation, without forfeiting its interest in this grand public domain; and no human wisdom could devise a satisfactory distribution of property ceded as a common fund for the common benefit of sovereign States, without any fixed ratio of interest in the respective beneficiaries, and without any clear power in the government of the Confederation to deal with the trust itself.

CURTIS' *History of the Constitution*, i, 140.

States proprietors, not only of the land, but of navigation, &c.

The original thirteen States, by these cessions, became possessed in common, not only of the ownership of the land, the payment for which was to go into the common treasury, but to an equal share in all the privileges and benefits of that territory, as the navigation of its rivers, free trade with the inhabitants who were to settle it as the Indian title became extinguished, &c. Out of this common territory have all the new States east of the Mississippi (Florida excepted) been formed; but no one of the Peoples resident in any of the areas or Territories, as they are commonly called, has been recognized as having a free and independent State existence, except to be admitted into the Union, and then at once binding itself to the compact of the Constitution. And though each new State has been admitted to full equality in all the rights and benefits of the Union with the older Confederates, I discover nothing in the acts of admission implying any surrender of any one entire preëxisting right in that Territory to the State individually; and even had the attempt been

New States formed and admitted into the Union—

—with parity of rights.

All rights not thereby surrendered to it.

§ 11. To the North: we must have Union.

made by Congress, the act would be void for lack of authority, no delegation for that purpose being found in its power of attorney, the Constitution. The new State giving its assent to the Constitution, upon admission into the Union, is, indeed, a pledge to sustain the old rights of the Sovereignties, and discharge faithfully the obligations, new to it, incurred by coming into the Union.

Injustice to Virginia had Illinois seceded.

Had Virginia, for instance, remained in the Union, what a wrong and injustice would have been done her, had Ohio, or any of the five States formed out of her Northwest Territory, seceded from the Confederacy.

Rights of Virginia in the Northwest.

Not only was a large part of it hers by charter, but in the Revolutionary contest, properly exercising her Sovereign Power of peace and war (it not having then been delegated to the Federal Agency), she sent out an expedition under General George Rogers Clarke, which took Kaskaskia and Vincennes; so that her title by charter was strengthened by right of conquest, and in '78 she organized her entire area west and north of the Ohio into a county by the name of Illinois. How unjust the treatment toward Virginia, remaining in the Union, had Illinois attempted to secede, and unquestionably would our mother have had the right to prevent it if she could, even by war.

Virginia's rights ceded to all the States.

Yet Virginia, after her liberal cession, for which she cannot be too highly praised, had no right in that territory, not equally shared by every member of the Confederacy.

The Louisiana purchase—motives to it.

Let us again glance also at the Louisiana purchase, which will be more fully considered in Part III. The far-sighted Jefferson knew that ere long great States would arise within our domain east of the Father of Waters, to which the free navigation of the Mississippi would be of incalculable importance. We believed we had a natural right to it, though contested by Spain; but of that power we had no fear, and had she resisted our equality of rights, we could easily have enforced them. But Spain transferred this colony to France, whose greater power would have made a war to sustain our rights more calamitous. Besides, we specially deplored a contest with our kind and faithful ally in the Revolutionary war, and Bonaparte wanting money, and we the Louisiana

Rights in it shared wholly and equally between the States.

province, a trade was made, and these States united, became the joint proprietors through their Federal Agency of the tract between the Mississippi and the Pacific Ocean. And, whereas some antecedent rights might be imagined still to pertain to the original States that ceded the territory east of the Mississippi, none could be laid to the territory west. The rights of each of the States united, were precisely equal at the date of cession.

Also by new States.

Since that date, new States have been organized east of the Mississippi, and admitted into the Confederacy, and with parity of rights with the older members. And not only so, but in this very Louisiana purchase, the inhabitants of which, from the mouth to the head waters of the Mississippi, were united as one People, or colony or province, and had

And by new States formed out of the purchase.

common rights and interests in the whole territory, that have never been surrendered; out of this territory have numerous States been formed and admitted into our Union, which also have been granted equality in all the rights of the older Confederates. Are these States likely to relinquish their rights in the territory below them, if by any honorable means they can be preserved?

§ 11. To the North: we must have Union.

Are these rights to be surrendered?

From my knowledge of the West, I judge they will not surrender these important rights if they can avoid it. A residence here from boyhood, and an active participation in its business concerns, and a wide acquaintance, enable me to speak understandingly on this subject. Never will the States in the Mississippi Valley abandon their rights in the territory below them. Neither will the East. The rights of the Western States in the South are more prominent, and their loss would be a greater evil, yet are they no stronger than those belonging to Maine and New Jersey. These common rights are indeed a bond of Union; and let us investigate and understand them, and not only will the States East and West be even more firmly knit together in our struggle to preserve them, but all our Citizens, except the little nest of fanatical Abolitionists, will be united as one man for our defence. Let us know our rights, and, knowing, dare maintain.

Never will the West surrender them.

Nor will the East.

Let *Jeffersonian Democrats* study this great question of the rights of these sovereign States. Never, till the last two years, did I expect to be a friend and admirer of Jefferson. He was not immaculate, and made important mistakes, more, however, in theory than practice; but I find he was indeed one of our most valuable statesmen. On a scroll headed WASHINGTON, no name seems more worthy to follow next than JEFFERSON; and our highest obligations to this learned and excellent man, rest mainly upon his undying confidence in Republicanism, and his firm, unyielding determination to preserve the Federal Union of these States, and prevent consolidation. Properly did he and his party take the name of *Republican*, though they were as truly Federal as any in the land. And you! sons, grandsons, and great-grandsons, of the conquering host of patriots under the lead of Jefferson, in that critical period of our history; you! especially who bear the same political name, so honored and honorable in Jefferson, let me beg you to study into the principles of your revered apostle. Nothing there will you discover to justify the gross usurpations of your chosen leaders, precisely the dangers the fathers feared, and which caused the chief opposition to the present Constitution. Nor will the war be found a justifying cause of these wrongs. Every true Republican will be a *Federal* Republican, as was Jefferson, when he understands the term.

Jeffersonian Democrats to study his principles.

Jefferson next to Washington.

Was a true Republican.

You, Republicans! follow your leader in the path of Federalism.

Let us, too, sons, grandsons, and great-grandsons of the conquered host of *Federalists*, study into the history and principles of our Union and Government, and lay our equal claim to patriotic blood, with those who were successful, owing to the division between the great leaders, Adams and Hamilton. Most of them were true to the honorable name they bore, Federalists indeed and without guile, though a few were Consolidists, not having confidence in the binding nature of a Federal League,

We Federalists must stick to our Fathers' principles.

The Federalists true patriots.

§ 11. To the North: we must have Union.

and still less in Republican Democracy. But even the Consolidists were none the less sincere and patriotic, and we are immensely indebted to them for obtaining the requisite grants of authority to give vigor and power to the Federal arm; and the great majority of the Republican opponents, were in sentiment precisely what their name indicated, *Federal.* And though the differences in that day, as we shall see, were more in *theory* than *practice*, and owing in a good degree to the misuse of words, yet we have less knowledge, more errors in language, and have run so much farther astray in *theory*, that we have been led into fundamental errors in *practice.* Never would Samuel Adams, Parsons, Hancock, Sullivan, Ames, Dana, Sumner, Thacher, and the other patriots of Massachusetts, have ratified the Federal Constitution, could they have seen down the vista of many centuries, that such usurpations would be enacted, as have characterized this Administration, in the first century of our Government. The little majority of nineteen votes would never have been given by that Commonwealth, had these tyrannical acts been foreseen; nor would assent have been given in most of the other States.

Our desertion of Federal principles.

Had these wrongs been anticipated, Massachusetts had never been in the Union.

Necessary to know the views of the fathers.

We need to be better informed with regard to the views and motives of the fathers, and very agreeable will it be for the few who are familiar with the debates in the Constitutional Convention, preserved by Madison, and for which we owe him an immense debt of gratitude, and with the debates in the State conventions of ratification, to run over the important parts. To those who have never studied them, it is an imperative duty, in order to learn what Government we have, why it should be preserved, and by what means. These debates afford most important instruction, with which every Citizen should be familiar; and, however the work may be performed, one of the most important attempts in this compilation will be that of Part II, *The Constitution*, in which the chief parts of the debates, not only Madison's and those compiled by Elliott, but others that I may be able to obtain, will be arranged under their appropriate clause of the Constitution. For instance, in discussing, "We, the People of the United States, ... ordain and establish this Constitution," the remarks and the facts concerning it will be brought together, to see what was designed, and what was done. So the discussions and facts concerning the Senate, when brought in juxtaposition, will enable every reader to decide for himself, whether the desire was to make one State out of the Thirteen, or to keep the Thirteen States each sovereign, free, and independent. Then the frequent references to the Principles of Government in Part I, derived chiefly from Grotius, Pufendorf, Vattel, Burlamaqui, and Montesquieu, will enable every Citizen to judge for himself, what Government we have, and whether it is worth perpetuating. It will not be necessary to the present purpose, to discuss every point in the Constitution, and only the chief will be taken; but these will draw together the prominent thoughts in the Constitutional Convention, and also in the Conventions of ratification, and the contemporaneous discussions. The numerous memoirs, too, of the fathers, contain important letters and valu-

Their debates,

—to be compiled in Part II,

—according to subjects.

Comparing them with International Law, we can decide what is our form of Government.

Memoirs, letters, &c., of the fathers.

able information,[1] extracts from which will aid to elucidate difficult points, and supply information which everybody ought to have, yet which few ever see. The volumes will not only be found instructive and profitable, but deeply interesting, for, with the exception of my lucubrations, they will be filled to a great extent with choice extracts from hundreds of volumes of eminent literary merit.

§ 11. To the North: we must have Union.

Most of these volumes, choice extracts.

There is one invaluable work, however, *The Fœderalist*, which will be little quoted; or rather, it must nearly all be quoted. Says Hamilton, in the first paragraph of the introductory number:

The Federalist not much quoted.

AFTER an unequivocal experience of the inefficacy of the subsisting Fœderal Government, you are called upon to deliberate on a new Constitution for the United States of America. The subject speaks its own importance, comprehending in its consequences, nothing less than the existence of the UNION, the safety and the welfare of the parts of which it is composed, the fate of an empire, in many respects, the most interesting in the world. It has been frequently remarked, that it seems to have been reserved to the people of this country, by their conduct and example, to decide the important question, whether societies of men are really capable or not, of establishing good Government from reflection and choice, or whether they are forever destined to depend, for their political constitutions, on accident and force. If there be any truth in the remark, the crisis, at which we are arrived, may with propriety be regarded as the æra in which that decision is to be made; and a wrong election of the part we shall act, may, in this view, deserve to be considered as the general misfortune of mankind.

HAMILTON, *Fœderalist*, D. p. 1. H. p. 1.

The question in 1788, whether SOCIETIES OF MEN could establish Government.

The question in that day was undoubtedly, not whether this *one people* of the United States could institute a Government, but whether "*these Societies of men*," these sovereign States, could perform that great work. From that extract to the end of the volume, is it true in the main to the principles its title forcibly indicates. And it is because reference must be made to almost its every page, that it is not deemed best to occupy space in these volumes with many extracts, particularly as a new and corrected edition is now in press. Both the new and the Hallowell edition will be referred to by page or by chapter, so that each reader must get the *Federalist*, if he would understand these volumes; and if he will obtain it immediately, and study it thoroughly, it will be an excellent means of preparation to understand our governmental system. The chief point of dissent in these volumes from the teachings of the *Federalist* will be, concerning Madison's idea of "national" features in the Constitution, which, it will appear, Hamilton had shown in the Constitutional Convention, were truly Federal, as he does again in the *Federalist*; and which, more remarkable still, Madison himself admitted to be Federal, not only in the Constitutional Convention, but also in the *Federalist*.

The *Federalist* truly Federal.

Dawson's new edition.

A copy of the *Federalist* must be obtained.

These volumes, in accord, except as to Madison's "national" features.

[1] There are numerous letters bearing upon this examination, which have not been published. Also old tracts and old books that are scarce, which would be of invaluable service in this compilation. If parties having them will give me information, and allow the use of the originals, or the obtaining of copies, they will render an essential aid, for which due acknowledgments will be made. Any information relating to the organization of the State or Federal Governments, or important facts in the Administration of either, will be acceptable. Particularly is information desired touching the State Conventions of Ratification, and the Administrations of Washington, John Adams, and Jefferson, and the threatened Secession of New England. Early acquaintance with any documents giving such information, is desirable.

Copies of old letters, tracts, and books, wanted.

§ 11. To the North: we must have Union.

Deserting Federalism caused our troubles.

Having learned from unquestionable documents, precisely what Government we have; examined our wrongs both of the North and of the South, which will prove that it is not the principle of Federalism which has caused our difficulties, but our desertion of it in every instance; we must then in the sequel look a little into other Governments, in order to appreciate our own. Rome will speak strongly to us in behalf of the Federal principle, as we see how easily, in a single State, a Julius or Octavius Cæsar, under favoring circumstances, can become possessed of the Sovereignty; and in trumpet tones will "the Republic one and indivisible" of France, warn us of the rock of consolidation on which she split. The British Government will have been fully discussed, and its many and great excellences considered, and at the same time its utter inapplicability to us will be apparent. Then, when we shall have examined the Confederate examples of the Hebrews, the Greeks, the Dutch and Swiss, and observe the improvements we have made, and may yet make, we shall come to a determination, I trust, to maintain our institutions and our Union, so wisely established by our fathers under Providential direction.

Rome an example in favor of Federalism.

Also the French Republic.

The British Government.

Examples of Confederacies.

Our choice, Despotism or Federalism.

Certain it is, it seems to me, that no American patriot can understand these things, and not be a firm Federalist, whether he has confidence in free Governments or not. However earnestly we might desire a change, we must adhere to the system of our fathers, and LET WELL ENOUGH ALONE. Despotism or Federalism is our only alternative.

Another political party needed.

We are all Republicans.

We are mostly Federalists.

A new party of FEDERAL REPUBLICANS.

We must organize one more political party. The word *Democrat* does not express what we want. We never could endure simple Democracy, in which the People do all things themselves. We operate by Representatives, which is Republican. We are therefore all Republicans, and why not call ourselves what we are? Few wish that we should be a single Republic, a consolidated State. If not, and Union is desired, it must be a Federal Union. There is no other. We are therefore nearly all Federalists, and, being all Republicans, why not take to ourselves the appropriate party name of FEDERAL REPUBLICAN? Thus uniting the sons, grandsons, and great-grandsons of all the patriots in the North, who struggled for supremacy at the beginning of this century, under the rival names of Federalist and Republican; joining not only in name but in heart, inscribing upon our banner—OUR FEDERAL REPUBLIC, WITH ALL ITS RIGHTS AND INSTITUTIONS, shall we go forth to certain victory.

Errors as to the war.

It is not against "rebels."

TODD'S *Johnson*, SHERIDAN, RICHARDSON, &c.

How differently will this war be waged when we ascertain its true nature and object! Many suppose it to be, on the part of the North, a war to subdue "rebels"; a war of conquest and of subjugation. It is no such thing, as the examination will prove. The Confederates are no "rebels," according to the proper acceptation of the word. Rebellion is defined "insurrection against lawful authority," meaning, of course, within the boundaries of that authority, for we have learned from Story that laws have no power beyond. Had citizens of the Southern States begun war at Sumter prior to their ceasing to acknowledge the "lawful author-

§ 11. To the North: we must have Union.

The South not in "rebellion."

We are in war with the Confederate States.

ity" of the Government of the United States, it would have been rebellion. But they had cast off the authority of the United States, and assumed that of the Confederate States, and so far from their soldiers being rebels in fighting the United States, they would have been rebels against the Confederate States, had they not obeyed the mandate, and attacked that fort. We are at war with the Federal Republic of the Confederate States.

The war *defensive*—

—for State-rights.

Our wrong notions united the South—

—and divided us.

The people right in practice if not in theory—

—have nobly sustained their Government, notwithstanding its errors of Administration.

We are not in a war of conquest and subjugation.

We are in no war of aggression, as we shall see, but in one of defence. Our carrying it into the enemy's country, does not make it a war of conquest and of subjugation. We can take it where we have power, and still is it *just* and *defensive*, until we have secured our rights jeopardized by the attack. We are fighting for State rights, the rights of these Sovereignties, of which the South are endeavoring to despoil us by force of arms. Adopting the contrary and wrong idea, making us the attacking, aggressive party, has been the most effective means of consolidating the South, and no wonder is it they have united so heartily for the defence of their hearthstones and their every right, which from our own gasconading declarations they have believed endangered. And while the foolish bombast has united our opponents, it has divided ourselves. The people of the North rallied, in the beginning of this contest, almost as one man, to defend our Government, unjustly, unnecessarily assailed; to protect our rights in the Union. Though not well understanding the *theory*, the *practical* good sense of the people, as we shall frequently have occasion to observe, has kept them in the path of duty. Despite the mismanagement, the want of plan and purpose, the disgraceful folly, the iniquitous usurpations of the Federal Agency, the people have nobly stood by our Government and their State rights; and when some master hand shall portray this grand subject as it deserves, a stronger confidence than ever will be given, at home and abroad, in the adaptation of our Governments to these Peoples, and of these Peoples to self-Government. The victims of outrageous usurpation, of infernal tyranny, even in this land of strong safeguards to protect the people from oppression, their rights from trespass; neither the victims nor their sympathizing friends have precisely understood the *theory* of their wrongs, though they have learned full well the *practice* is most unbearable. Patiently or impatiently have wrongs been borne, which the fathers never anticipated would be possible, and which had they foreseen, this Government had never existed. In spite of their wrongs, have they generally sustained their Government. Notwithstanding the errors of Administration, endeavoring to change the character of the war from one of defence into one of conquest, have the people rallied for the support of their Government. At least two thirds, probably seven-eighths of the Northern people, have no desire to subdue the South, any further than is necessary to reëstablish the just rights of these sovereign States, yet have they had to fight in armies vauntingly and lyingly termed armies of conquest and of subjugation.

Precisely where the philosophic De Tocqueville thought was our chief

§ 11. To the North: we must have Union.

Government strong where De Tocqueville thought it weak.

danger of failing, have we proved ourselves strongest; in the power of the Federal Government to conduct a war. In the South has it been well demonstrated, amid all the difficulties and embarrassments of organizing a new Government; but under the circumstances, is it still more remarkable in the North. The repeated checkings of enlistment, the attempted change from a war of defence to one of conquest, and the many incidental follies, have checked the enthusiasm with which the people first rallied; yet has the sober judgment, the sound sense, the firm resolution, that should characterize free Peoples, kept them steady to their purpose and to duty.

All must study into principles.

No one wants dishonorable peace.

The North not to speak peace.

Vigorous war wanted.

Then study principles.

From the President down, must we all study into principles, and learn our rights and the character of this war, and thus we shall unite ourselves and divide the Confederates. There is not a copperhead Democrat in the North, as true Union men are derisively called, who wants peace on any other terms than those of honor and the maintenance of every State right. Not a word have any of us to say for peace, till the South want it. The first step toward peace and reunion, is the most vigorous prosecution of the war; and if half a million more troops were called at once into the field, it would be the best peace measure. This can be done, and the people will rally under their banners with the same hearty enthusiasm that characterized the beginning of the conflict, if rulers and people will study into and understand the principles of our Government.

A change necessary in the conduct of the war.

But to have this unanimity among ourselves, the war must be differently conducted. If in a *just, defensive* war, let us wage it accordingly. The destruction of private property has been immense and unnecessary, is contrary to every principle of International Law, and most disgraceful to us. Never will the South propose peace, until we reform in our mode of warfare. There seems not to be the least conception of private rights, and continually are such paragraphs published, as the following from the Richmond *Enquirer* of May 15, 1863:

The North waging uncivilized warfare.

RICHMOND ENQUIRER, *May 15th*, 1863.

There is evidently to be an active summer campaign. The plan of the enemy seems to be to keep our attention constantly excited at every point at once, so that no part of our whole wide frontier may be freed from the urgent immediate apprehension of an attack. Then they can strike where they think our line is weakest, or where our defenders are least prepared, and if repulsed they can retire and direct a blow at some other quarter. In the meantime they can bag much plunder and cause much sorrow, and heart-break our people by expeditions through thinly peopled regions destitute of troops. They can also force more and more of our people within their lines to take their hated oath for a quiet life and to save their property from confiscation. Thus they can both demoralize and rob us within our own borders, preparing all the while for serious assaults, and delivering them just when they are ready and where they choose.

Activity of the North.

It is hard to say at what point they are most active just now. If one looks Southwestward it would seem that the State of Mississippi is the region of most extensive operations. Immense armies are gathering in and around Vicksburg, and while preparations are in progress for a new assault upon that place, the back country is devastated and the people plundered by cavalry raids; but at the very same moment Charleston is kept on the *qui vive* by energetic preparations for another attack by sea or land, or both at once. The object may be only to prevent General Beauregard

§ 11. To the North: we must have Union.

What we steal.

from sending away any of the troops which now defend Charleston. At the same instant Burnside threatens East Tennessee; and Hooker, largely reinforced, is expected to cross the Rappahannock somewhere or anywhere from Culpepper to Port Royal, to keep some of our forces employed in the defence of Richmond. Reinforcements are sent to Fortress Monroe, and lest any part of the country should [not?] have to resist, the enemy's gunboats are harassing North Carolina. In the Raleigh *Progress*, of the 13th inst., we read "gunboats continue to prowl up and down the Chowan and Perquimans rivers." They steal negroes, silver ware, jewelry, and everything they can lay their hands on, and have broken up a number of fisheries. They stole some four thousand dollars' worth of jewelry from a man named Cook, breaking up his furniture and committing other depredations. In one instance they entered a soldier's house and broke up his crockery and furniture, &c. Five or six thousand Yankees are reported in Plymouth and several gunboats are in the Sound. There is no enemy at Edenton or Elizabeth City. They recently burned a mill on the Chowan river, the property of Mr. Haye, situated a mile below Winton. Some persons entertain the idea that the forces at Plymouth meditate an expedition up the Roanoke.

Our power admitted.

Our object, plunder.

In no hurry.

War our settled business.

We do not regard defeats.

The great numbers of the enemy's forces and the multitudes of their shipping make it easy for them to carry on simultaneously all these operations, and they do not care for delay, for it is our people who are suffering, not theirs. The longer this style of warfare lasts the greater will be the mass of plunder carried North. The more of our mills, machine shops and railroads they will have destroyed, the more of our national resources they will have ruined and wasted, and the better chance they will have for an irresistible advance at last. They are in no hurry. Last year, indeed, there was urgent haste to get the rebellion crushed in thirty days, or in ninety. Now we hear much less of that vehement urgency, and the whole Yankee nation seems to have laid out its accounts for war as the settled business of life rather than consent to peace and separation. They are perfectly willing to fight upon the present system for twenty years or forty. They are willing, during all that time, to go on submitting to such defeats as they have sustained at Fredericksburg and on the Rappahannock, because by these defeats they lose not a foot of ground—they lose nothing but men, and men are of less value to them than to us. To kill one thousand Southern soldiers they would be willing at any time to sacrifice five thousand Hessians to sustain a repulse, which they would, however, represent as "a mere retreat for strategic reasons," and rather honorable than otherwise, and they would regard the transaction as a rather paying one on the whole.

Our object to wear the South out by a long war.

One thousand gallant Southern lives lost to us, are ill balanced by the killing of five thousand of their base hirelings. Jackson alone is a dearer loss to us than Hooker and his whole one hundred and fifty thousand would be to them, and then they speculate that it may be Lee's turn next or Longstreet's, and that at any rate they are killing us slowly off, and they are, in the meantime, stealing much and ruining more; and their women and children are safe at home, many of them dressed better than ever before in the spoils of our homes, while Confederate women and children are routed out of house and home and chased like wild beasts. In short, if we can endure this war for the next half century they can, and they will wish us joy of our victories and our glory. We urge nothing, suggest nothing, hint nothing—only state the facts. Such is the policy of the enemy—such is his calculation—such is his interest and intent.

Our armies made to disgrace, instead of honoring the North.

Destruction of property—

No doubt the wrongs are often much exaggerated, but very many are, alas! too true. An infamous wrong to the whole North is it, that its armies should be made to bring us contumely and disgrace, instead of glory and renown. Were we in a war of conquest, the consequences of our misconduct would not be so deplorable. Rapine and burning of public libraries, State houses and private dwellings, might be necessary to subdue an obstinate foe; but not in such a war as this. No matter that recompense is to be made for the property destroyed; much of it, money can

§11. To the North: we must have Union.

—of valuable papers.

Wrongs done in ignorance.

never replace. The destruction of private papers, and of historical documents in the classic ground of Virginia and the Carolinas, has been immense, and the loss irreparable. It is one of the most lamentable occurrences of the war. Let this cease, and every effort be made to preserve and to return documents of value. These wrongs have been done by soldiers and by officers in ignorance. Never would they have disgraced their cause, and the stars and stripes, in these wrong acts, had they known them to be wrong. They were fighting their enemy, and supposed that war meant to do him all the harm they could. That is the warfare of brutes and savages, not of civilized and Christian Peoples. Let us wholly change our course, and wage this war according to the Law of Nations, as a *just*, *defensive* war.

We must change and wage a *just*, *defensive* war.

We can and will endure a *just* and *defensive* war, for fifty years, if necessary.

The above article is full of instruction and encouragement to us to put this war upon its proper basis, that of *justice* and *defence*. Let the South well understand that such is its character, and that it is to be waged accordingly; and they will soon see, that something else than arms must be employed to enforce their supposed rights of Secession. "We *can* endure this war for the next half century," and what is more, we *will*, if it be necessary to defend our just rights.

International Law applied to the Negro.

The rule of International Law is to be applied to another important question, that of the Negro, which materially affects Northern unanimity, and also our rights in the prosecution of this war.

Rights of slavery rest on the Law of Nations.

Necessity of instruction in the Law.

However unwelcome the truth may be to the few fanatics, whether truly philanthropic and sincerely loving the slave, or devilishly malignant and hating the master, the whole question concerning the negro in slavery, rests upon the solid foundation of International Law; and every true patriot in the land will be relieved in obtaining correct information, as to the relative rights and duties of Northern citizens, of Northern States, of the Federal Government; to Southern citizens, to Southern States, to the Confederate Government, according to the Law of Nations. It will not be expected of me, a mere novice in this deep science, to offer instruction on a subject so far exceeding my feeble comprehension, and with the anxious public, shall we wait on such competent instructors as Doctor Lieber and Professor Bowen, who in their *Political Ethics* and *Economy*, have shown so much correct conception of true principles, and only need to reach "that foundation," "that root," upon which their admirable superstructures really rest—STATE SOVEREIGNTY, *the Right of Command*, which, GOD be praised, in these free States, abides in the Peoples.

We shall have good teachers.

Sovereignty the foundation.

Was Grotius, and even GOD, mistaken as to Sovereignty?

Why the remonstrance with the Hebrews?

1 *Sam.* viii.

A caution as to the use of the Bible.

If it be the myth Doctor Lieber seems to make it, then Grotius and the great writers down to Vattel, were sadly mistaken in their fundamental basis; Aristotle was a fool; and even Almighty Wisdom seems to have not understood this *Right of Command*, for Samuel was instructed to remonstrate earnestly with the rebellious Hebrews, because they would have a king, in order to be like "all the nations." The Doctor has very judicious cautions against erroneous use of the Bible, which is made to prove all sorts of absurdities; yet it does seem in this case, as though GOD thought His people were about to *grant*, (I should say,) their Sovereignty to one man, creating a Monarchy. Yet Doctor Lieber says: "It appears then that Sovereignty is a power and energy naturally and necessarily inherent in society," &c. "Society never can *delegate* or *pledge away* Sovereignty, and, of course, never have done so." What was it then, the Hebrew tribes parted with? or parted they with nothing? In what did the change consist, which God Himself seemed to think so great and terrible?

§ 11. To the North: we must have Union.

LIEBER, *Political Ethics*, Part I, p. 250.

What did the Hebrews part with?

With all deference to the superior judgment of Doctor Lieber, "It does [*not*] appear then [at least not from the teachings of Aristotle, Grotius, and Vattel] that Sovereignty is a power and energy naturally and necessarily inherent in society." That was Locke's idea. Sovereignty has, to be sure, by Hobbes and Pufendorf, with great propriety, been likened to the human soul, as the source of the power and energy that move the limbs of the body politic; yet strictly and correctly speaking, Sovereignty is not the *power* itself, and Doctor Lieber himself in another passage discriminates with nice accuracy between Sovereignty and Supreme Power. Sovereignty is not the Power, it is not the Authority, it is not the Command, but it is the *Right* of Power, the *Right* of Authority, the *Right of Command*, as Vattel so beautifully and correctly declares. Supreme Power, Supreme Authority, Supreme Command, is the superstructure, resting upon "that foundation and root," the *Right* of it, which is SOVEREIGNTY.

Sovereignty distinguished from power and authority.

It is the *Right* of power, of authority, of Command.

Nor is this *Right* "naturally and necessarily inherent in society;" if, as it seems, the author means by "inherent," inalienable, untransferable. Like any other right, it may be granted away; not merely delegated, but actually, entirely parted with. There is no such thing in a civil State, as an inalienable right, however it may be in that fanciful state of nature, into which no man on earth can get. Our life, our liberty, our property, our everything, is alienated to the STATE of which we are the subjects; and by its Sovereignty, its *Right of Command*, does it take any of us to be a soldier, to be a legislator, to be a president; by its omnipotent Right, does it take whatever of our property it requires; and if we be not true and faithful liege subjects, it has the *Right*, clear and unquestionable, to take our very lives. Into such a STATE is every child born, and the instant he breathes the breath of life, he becomes a subject of that State and of its *Right of Command*, and must so continue till he chooses to change his allegiance, and become the subject of another State.

This Right may be granted.

We are under absolute subjection.

Everybody a subject.

This *Right* may be actually granted away. The Hebrews did this when they made Saul king, and they did it again when they made David king. Our ancestors of England, when their *Right of Command* reverted to them by the abdication of James II, granted it to William III, (not to William and Mary.) Usually this *Right* is inheritable like other Rights, but in some States, as formerly in Poland, it reverts to the people upon the death of the king, and is then again granted to another. Doctor Lieber seems to have been thinking about some other sort of Sovereignty

Sovereignty granted by the Hebrews—

—by the English.

It is inheritable.

It may be regranted.

Dr. Lieber correct.

§ 11. To the North: we must have Union.

Sovereignty never delegated.

from that of Grotius, when he says, "Society can never *delegate* or *pledge away* Sovereignty, and, of course, never have done so;" or more probably he intended a nice use of language, and has had his usual success, for it is literally the truth, that "society never can *delegate* or *pledge away* Sovereignty." It either keeps it altogether, or actually grants it—a distinction which it seems that John Adams, clear-headed patriot as he was, never comprehended.

Our wise men to examine for our "foundation."

It is to be hoped our wise men will again examine principles of International Law, and, if possible, come to some better understanding of this vexed subject of Sovereignty. Every right in these States rests upon it, and we must search "that foundation and root," before this war can be ended and a new Union formed. Doctor Lieber correctly estimates the value of Hooker's *Ecclesiastical Politie*, in establishing governmental principles, and as he particularly admires Book VIII, he will be pleased again to recur to it and observe the remarks in chapter ii, § 1, 2, &c., upon "Definition of Supreme Power," &c., which, if not in accord with Grotius and Vattel, is misunderstood by us. It is this Book which concludes his great work, to which he doubtless refers in the extract already made, where he advises to patient examination and says, "What may seem dark at the first will afterward be found more plain." He remarks, too, in the same extract, that "for better examination of their [the laws'] quality, it behoveth the very foundation and root, the highest well-spring and fountain of them to be discovered." And if it be not here done, and "that foundation and root" be not the *Right of Command* of Vattel, we are sadly out in our reckoning.

Dr. Lieber commends Hooker.

Hooker's Book VIII worth examining.

See p. 10.

It discovers "that foundation."

Discouragements in seeking "that foundation."

It is indeed discouraging when one reads such profound, excellent works as Doctor Lieber's *Political Ethics*, Lord Brougham's *Political Philosophy*, and M. Guizot's *History of Representative Government*, and sees such elegant superstructures reared, entirely ignoring "that foundation" upon which all just Government must rest, the *Right of Command;* it makes the task almost hopeless that "that foundation" is ever again "to be discovered." Surely it is not becoming in me to attempt to teach counter to these great and good men, and the folly will not be committed; but it will be a heavy disappointment, if these and other wise men do not decide, upon further consideration, that it is best to rest Government upon the *Right* of it—upon THE RIGHT OF COMMAND. That is Hooker's foundation as well as Grotius' and Vattel's; and, though the system has its imperfections, as have all things human, is it not the best to be found, all things considered?

Grotius and Vattel have Hooker's "foundation."

It is taken for granted our system rests on "that foundation."

Taking it for granted that no essential difference will be discovered between Hooker and Grotius, &c., and that their "foundations" will be taken as the basis on which the magnificent governmental superstructures of Britain and America have been established, we beg leave to intimate a few principles in International Law, which will be found to regulate and control the *exercise* of that *Right of Command;* not the *Right* itself, but its *exercise.*

§ 11. To the North: we must have Union.

Every State possessed of Sovereignty— —either in *one*, the *few*, or the *many*. Its *exercise* regulated— —not the *Right* itself. Everybody a subject. Sovereignty absolute. It fixes the status of the subjects— —creates inequality. The more inequality the better the State. What equality is desirable.

Every State is of its own nature possessed of Sovereignty, a *Right of Command*, absolute and uncontrollable, which is precisely what the word indicates. This right may be in the possession of the *many*, the *few*, or the *one*, never of the totality till a new sort of State is invented hitherto unknown in governmental science. In these three forms, Democracy, Aristocracy, and Monarchy, it is requisite that the *exercise* of that Sovereignty should be controlled by checks and balances, owing to the fallibility and imperfections of the parties to whom the *exercise* is intrusted; yet, nevertheless, the Right of Command itself is perfectly absolute within its own domain. Further, as already remarked, every man, woman, and child living on this planet, is a *bona fide*, complete subject, to some one of the Sovereignties. Over every one of its subjects, has each Sovereignty full and absolute authority, and not only does it require this subject to perform this duty, and another to do that, as before observed, but it also fixes the status of the different subjects, according to its sovereign will and pleasure. Equality in the subjects is never sought, but, on the contrary, inequality; the chief object of the best Sovereignties being to protect their faithful liege subjects to the utmost extent, in their acquisitions of good, whether intellectual or physical, whether in power or in property, or in whatever else man rightfully desires. The masses of mankind have never risen to high eminence, and the more the ambition of subjects can be stimulated, the loftier their attainments in the paths of true excellence, the more genuine aristocrats can be made; in short, the greater the inequalities that can be established between other orders and the lowest grade of subjects, the more perfect is the STATE, the more properly is its Sovereignty exercised. All the equality that is or should be sought for in a desirable State, is the equal privilege of equal subjects, by equal laws and equal justice, to preserve the inequalities that good fortune, genius, and industry enable them to establish.

Some States establish inequality. Our monarchs did this— —allowed some of their subjects to be slaves.

Some States, in order to institute permanent inequality, grant titles and privileges with primogeniture inheritance, and entailment of estates; and where the Sovereignty is granted by the People to *one*, the system of nobility unquestionably possesses great excellences, as our mother-land has well proved in its centuries of experience. Our Monarchs, the Kings and Queens of those of us who are Anglo-Saxons, made of some of their liege subjects, Princes, Dukes, Earls, and Barons; others they permitted to have a voice in the election of certain agents of the Sovereign; others they required should be simply subjects; and yet others they allowed to be brought in as slaves, who were as perfectly subject to their masters, as are the subjects to their king, or as are the subjects in a free State, to the State itself.

International Law creates no right, only regulates its exercise. The Bible regulates slavery.

International Law has not established this right of a State to create these distinctions and inequalities, it simply regulates the exercise of that right; and the BIBLE, the leading text book in the great Code of Nations, sets the example worthy of all imitation. Read in the twenty-first chapter of Exodus, the earliest laws recorded concerning master and slave.

§ 11. To the North: we must have Union.

Slavery and war necessary evils.

Rights of slavery not to be discussed.

The Bible is quite a practical, common-sense book, and instructs as to what is right and best for us in this fallen condition. We are liable to war, to robbery, to slavery, to oppression of every kind; but so far from war and slavery being reprobated as are robbery, adultery, oppression, and other heinous offences, even the Bible authorizes both of the former by giving instructions concerning them. They appear to have been regarded as a necessary evil, till of late years some excellent philanthropists, so super-excellent as to seem to be more loving of peace and of the slave, than were the Apostles, or even our blessed Saviour himself, have set to work to rid the world of this odious wickedness, which the Sovereign of the universe Himself has recognized by positive laws. But we do not propose to discuss these questions here or elsewhere; that of slavery, in particular, belongs exclusively to each State, and we shall confine ourselves strictly to points of International Law affecting Federal relations.

International Law prevents interference in fixing the status of subjects.

The Sultan a right to hold Caucasians in slavery.

A Christian State will not interfere with the Turk.

Nor does International Law permit any State to interfere in any shape or manner with the status of the subjects of another State. Each one does what it pleases within its own domain, and if the Sultan of Turkey sees fit to bow-string an innocent but offending vizier, other States must not interfere; and though the Sultan has no right to go to the Caucasus and by force of arms to steal and carry away the young maidens, yet if any are brought into his dominion as captives, no matter by what right or wrong they were enslaved, it is his privilege under the Law of Nations, to buy and keep those girls in slavery, though they are of our own race, and of the country which has the eminence to give the name to our race, the only one that we know was created in God's image. If States could ever rightfully interfere with another State in fixing the status of its subjects, it would be in this case of Turkey; but the Christian State, obedient to the principles of International Law, will not intervene even to correct the Turk's flagrant wrong.

Our British monarchs allowed the enslaving of Africans.

The master protected in his rights by his sovereign.

Right of slaveholding not the creature of Law.

The Law of Nations recognizes the right—

—the Civil Law aids i

Our English and British Monarchs, in fixing the status of their subjects here in America, by legitimate authority, allowed the bringing in of captive Africans. They had been stolen in unjust, outrageous wars, waged almost solely for the purpose of capturing the natives in order to sell them to the slave-buyer on the coast, to be transported to America; yet was the traffic legal under the International Code, and the king's liege subjects had the Royal protection and the aid of Royal laws which they aided their Sovereign to enact, to enjoy their rights as masters, and transfer them to others. The idea is prevalent that slavery can only exist where civil laws have been enacted, creating the right of slave-holding. This seems to be erroneous. "The Law of Nature and of Nature's God," has sanctioned it as a natural right of man; and then the Civil Law comes in to the aid of International Law, for the maintenance of that natural right, and for the more perfect regulation of its exercise.

A Sovereignty determines what is property.

Another prerogative of the Sovereignties, is to declare what shall be deemed property within the boundaries of that State. Some States recognize the rights of property in a dog, others do not; some in a full-blooded African Negro, others do not; some in a quadroon or octoroon, others do not. International Law leaves to each State to establish its own custom as to property, though it clearly recognizes what is generally regarded as property; and particularly concerning rights in slaves, Grotius and Pufendorf are thorough and explicit. Then comes in the prerogative of the Sovereignty to regulate the rights in property, and their mode of transfer. In all these respects our Sovereigns of England and Britain down to George III, seem to have conducted their Colonial affairs strictly in accordance with International Law, though some acts were no doubt inexpedient. So that at the time of our separation from the mother-country, our institutions had become well established, and every Colony recognized and protected property in slaves.

§ 11. To the North: we must have Union.

A slave recognized as property.

Laws regulate its transfer.

Our Colonial rights well established.

Slaveholding is included.

Nor was any change made by the Revolution in our rights according to the International Code, except to make the principles apply to each one of the bodies politic, which, from having been a Colony, had become a free and independent State. Our Declaration says, that being about "to assume, among the powers of the earth, the SEPARATE and EQUAL station to which the LAWS OF NATURE AND OF NATURE'S GOD entitle them," &c. Those "Laws" are this International Code, mainly as expounded by Grotius, Pufendorf, and Vattel, and these States having "*the separate and equal station*" among the nations, to which the Law of Nations entitles them, there is no more right nor power in Massachusetts, or Britain, or Russia, to interfere in the status of a subject of Virginia or California or Iowa, than they have in Turkey. These States, it is true, have created a Federal Agency, which in certain affairs is authorized to interfere with a State; and committing all foreign relations to that Agency, they wisely committed to it the right of naturalization, whereby a subject of a foreign Sovereignty, who desires to transfer his allegiance and become a subject of one of these Sovereignties, can do so. But there is no such nonsense in that oath, as to make the man swear allegiance to the Government of the United States. He simply swears to support the Constitution and laws, which, by the omnipotent will of some one of these Sovereignties, to which he is to be a subject, has been placed over him.

The Revolution did not change those rights.

Each State entitled to International Law.

No right in Massachusetts to interfere with Virginia.

The Federal Agency restricted in interfering.

Naturalization of foreign subjects.

No allegiance to the U. S. Government.

The privilege of fixing the status of subjects, is of highest moment in free States, because it involves the determination of who are to be admitted to the august privilege of Citizenship; and it appears, that for a strong State-rights man like Chief Justice Taney, his decision in the Dred Scott case, or rather the *obiter dicta*, has curious teachings. There surely is no limit in International Law to the power of a State to admit an infant, a woman, or a Hottentot, if it pleases, to Citizenship; nor is there a word of restriction in the Constitution. Whence, then, becomes it impossible for New York to say, that if a Guinea Negro is worth two hundred and fifty dollars, it so elevates him into aristocracy, as that his vote shall be equal to that of any other aristocrat; and if Massachusetts so loves the negro, as that at her polls he shall be allowed to vote even without the two hundred and fifty dollars, who shall say nay to her black-

The question of Citizenship.

Judge Taney in the Dred Scott case.

A State has full authority as to Citizenship.

New York can make a Negro a citizen—

—also Massachusetts.

§ 11. To the North: we must have Union.

International Law to be regarded.

diamond bestowed affection? Because the Constitution declares explicitly, that "The Citizens of each State shall be entitled to all Privileges and immunities of Citizens in the several States," and because New York and Massachusetts and other States are injudicious in making Citizens, shall the main, fundamental principle of International Law applied to Free States, be disregarded or destroyed?

The *obiter dicta* of the Supreme Court.

If our wise men in the reëxamination of International Law and our practice of it, should find Judge Taney was wrong in that case, and Judge Curtis right, it will only afford a striking example of the evils of *obiter dicta*, which, from my imperfect examination of the decisions of that august tribunal, our Supreme Court, affords the chief cause of complaint against it.

A query as to excluding all inferior races from Citizenship.

This subject will also suggest, whether we cannot make one farther advance in the excellences of Federalism, by providing that no inferior race, as Indian, Malay, Negro, &c., shall be admitted to Citizenship in one of these free States. Illinois and Indiana have set an example in this respect it would be well for other States to follow; and it is a point to be considered, whether an amendment of the present Constitution in that respect, may not be judicious, relieving individual States from a responsibility on this point, some of them might not like to assume. We in the West have no compunctions as to enforcing and living up to the doctrine of our lamented Douglas, that "this [Federal] Government was made on the white basis, by white men, for the benefit of white men and their posterity forever."

International Law to teach us what to do with captured slaves.

The slave is property.

If States have an indubitable right to fix the status of their every subject, which, it would seem, our wise men must surely teach us; and as we are coming in possession by the hundred thousand of those subjects whose status is that of slavery, it becomes us well to examine International Law, and see how it regulates the exercise of Sovereignty under such circumstances. The slave is known in slave States chiefly as property, and almost literally has he no rights the master is bound to respect. Almighty God himself teaches this, for He enacted this law:

Exod. xxi, 20, 21.

"And if a man smite his servant, or his maid, with a rod, and he die under his hand, he shall be surely punished. Notwithstanding, if he continue a day or two, he shall not be punished: for he *is* his money." That is the status of a subject in slave States that is a slave, and his status is not changed by getting out of his State, particularly against the will of his master; and if he is gotten back into his State, the Sovereignty has as full power and authority over him, as has the Sultan over his vizier.

His status not changed by running away.

The State may rightfully take the life of a rebel slave.

Many of them, too, have never left their State, and yet have dared to rise in arms against their master, and their sovereign State. If that Sovereignty shall have delegated to its State or Confederate agency, authority to take the life of that slave for daring to take up arms against his master and his sovereign State, it is well, and most righteous is it by the most condign punishment to restrain the slaves from such enormous guilt; and even if the power be not properly delegated, as it probably, almost certainly, is, yet is there no authority this side of Heaven, except the sovereign State itself, to call the conduct into question.

§ 11. To the North: we must have Union.

That appears to be the rights which we shall probably be taught the South have under the International Code. Now, what are we attempting to do with those slaves, in this *just*, *defensive* war? We are, to our disgrace, doing all that is in our power, to array the slave against his master, and we make all sorts of promises to induce him to engage in war, which will take him, if captured, to certain death; and if not captured, what is to become of the poor victim, which, for our selfish, contemptible purposes, we have enticed from his master? In ninety-nine cases in a hundred, is a short life of misery and wretchedness, if not of crime, to bring him to his grave; and the shorter the better, both for white man and slave.

Our wrongs toward the slaves.

As for colonizing the Negroes, we have enough uses for our Federal funds, without attempting any such chimerical scheme; and the day is not far distant when it will be found, that the Federal Agency was never instituted to embark in an enterprise, that, more than any other, would tend to involve us in foreign complications and war. We will not have the Negro in the West, in any considerable numbers, and the East will soon be following our example; and it is to be hoped that with our return to reason and to Federalism, we shall be willing to give the South good evidence of our sincerity, by the most stringent measures of capturing and returning to the South, all who have been slaves. Many will have become demoralized, and only the severe discipline of the cotton and sugar plantation will suffice to govern these; but even that will be preferable for them, both for time and for eternity, to the wretched life most of them will otherwise spend.

They are not to be colonized.

They cannot live in the West.

Best to return them to their masters.

Is it not time that in this *just*, *defensive* war, we white men should *require*—yes, *compel*—our Federal Administration to abandon its reliance on the Negro? We are abundantly able to protect ourselves and our every right, against the assaults of the South. We want no Negro aid in our defence, and we want to be saved the disgrace, at the end of this war, of having it said, that the North could do nothing except with the help of the slaves.

White men do not want Negro aid to defend their rights.

Abundant and pressing are the motives and necessities, of which a few have been named, for our wise and judicious men in the North, and for our Citizens, to examine thoroughly the principles of International Law, and apply them strictly and fairly to our Federal Government and its Administration. Under any circumstances, too, would it be sensible for these young Peoples, in the first century of our existence as States, to heed the advice of our great jurist, and not "disregard the uniform sense of the established writers on International Law," and thus "arrogantly set all ordinary law and justice at defiance." But in this terrible emergency, time must not be wasted in establishing new truths, however wise they may be. We must be content to examine and take the old Law and the facts as they exist, and thereby determine what is our form of

Abundant reasons for examining International Law.

Kent's advice to be regarded.

No time to create a new system—must take the old.

§ 11. To the North: we must have Union.

Government, and what are the rights and wrongs of its Administration, and what the rights and wrongs of these Sovereign States.

Our good men will teach us.

Nor will our great and good men be backward in their duty to their beloved country, in this its period of most imminent danger. Had not errors been made by the fathers, their sons would not have gone so far astray, and our teachers have only followed in the paths of their wise and

The examination to be of no injury.

excellent predecessors. Nor need we fear that the examination will injure the reputation and influence of our great and patriotic statesmen, either past or present. As a friend remarked of Webster, "You may strike out all there is in the least degree faulty, and yet is there more of wisdom and excellence, than any ten ordinary statesmen could produce." And though the wise and honored Madison shall be proved to have committed the error that has actually led us to this civil war, we shall love and revere him far more than ever before, when a candid examination shall show how much he has done for his beloved country.

Our statesmen will restore us to Federalism, and reconstruct our broken Union.

If our living statesmen find that serious misconceptions have led to our present calamities; if the mistakes that are fancied shall be found to have a real existence, they will rejoice in the opportunity afforded, and by magnanimously acknowledging and correcting the mistakes, they will become our noble leaders in measures soon to end this war, to take back these wandering Peoples to the blissful fields of Federalism, and speedily to reconstruct our broken Union.

§ 12.—To the South: Benefits of examining International Law.

All our States entitled to the Law of Nations.

See p. 45.

Mason and Dixon's line unknown.

As we have seen, the Declaration of Independence declared a never-dying truth, that the original Thirteen States were to have and enjoy "*the separate and equal station to which* THE LAWS OF NATURE AND OF NATURE'S GOD entitle them." There was never a word said about such a line as "Mason and Dixon's," and the States north as well as south, and south as well as north, are supposed to be entitled to all the benefits resulting from "THE LAWS OF NATURE AND OF NATURE'S GOD." If

Laws of value not only to punish but to restrain and instruct—

these laws are good and efficacious, their power will be seen, as in every other system of law, not only in punishing the subjects who do evil, but in praising them who do well; not only in preventing wrong by the forcible exercise of authority, but in the instructing of the law-abiding in the path of duty. The observance of law by the good and virtuous, is the

—especially the International, which gives no right of coercion.

rule; the punishment for its breach, is the exception. Preëminently is this the case in International Law, the parties subject to the Code being of such a nature, that no earthly authority can be instituted over them, with the right and power of punishment. The entire system rests on rectitude and honor, and on the principle, that what is for the best good of all States, is truly for the best good in the end of every State; and therefore that self-interest will lead every Christian State to careful observance, to faithful obedience of International Law. The right of punishment has very little potency in this Code, though, as we shall find, these greatest moral persons have a natural right to enforce compliance from delinquent parties, and so far to punish as to guard against like wrongs in future. The chief value, then, of International Law, is in its being correctly practised, and this depends chiefly upon the amount of knowledge of its provisions.

§ 12. To the South: Examining International Law.

Knowledge requisite to practice.

Having seen, in some measure, how sadly the North has failed, through ignorance and misconception, to avail itself of the immense benefits that should result from a perfect knowledge and thorough practice of "the Laws of Nature and of Nature's God;" seeing some of the States which declared the never-dying truth, actually in war with some of the very States who joined in making the Declaration, and only by whose joint efforts was it possible to maintain the momentous Declaration; and that this war is in direct violation of every principle of those "Laws of Nature and of Nature's God;" and the wrongs in a controversy being seldom altogether on one side, it would seem reasonable to examine a little, and measure the conduct of Southern Sovereignties by the Laws to which, in their beginning, they declared themselves entitled. A law is nothing but a rule, and "it is a poor rule that will not work both ways;" so that if these "Laws of Nature and of Nature's God," must govern us to their benefit, they should also govern them to our benefit.

The North has failed through ignorance.

States have disregarded the Law and gone to war.

Wrongs seldom on one side.

Examine the South by rule.

A Law a rule to work both ways.

While they have far better than we understood the nature of our Union, and the application to it of "the Laws of Nature and of Nature's God," some fundamental principles in those Laws, of special importance to States united by a league, seem not to have received due consideration. Their great teacher left, to be published after his death, one of the very best treatises on the Science of Government that has been written. Americans will be prouder than ever of the memory of their fellow countryman, whose philosophic mind has presented more clearly and concisely the right, the necessity, and the objects of Government, than any author I have examined. The extracts from this posthumous work of Calhoun, will be among the most interesting in these volumes, to Northern as well as Southern readers. So far as he goes in the presentation of principles, he is irresistible on almost every point, and puny would be the effort to put my feeble intellect against this giant to prove that he had not wholly comprehended his subject, and that there were points beyond his argument, fundamental and omnipotent, which he had not reached. But Cumberland will be found a match even for Calhoun, and he establishes the obligations of pact and faith as being sufficient to bind even Sovereign States, a little intimation of which is perceptible in the quotation already made.

The South seem to have disregarded some laws.

Calhoun's teaching.

Its excellence.

Correct as far as it goes.

Cumberland goes farther

See pp. 14–16.

The South will probably discover, on further examination, that States like these of ours, each perfectly sovereign, free and independent, and as such unaccountable to any human authority, are nevertheless bound by "the Laws of Nature and of Nature's God," to fulfil their every engagement rightly made; every one not contravening the end and objects for which States are instituted. Any promise that would tend to the destruc-

A Sovereign State bound by law to keep pact and faith.

A promise contrary to a State's true interest, is void.

§ 12. To the South: Examining International Law.

tion or injury of a State, it has no right to make, and any such is void in its origin upon first principles of International Law, that "Law of Nature and of Nature's God;" all others are obligatory, particularly those that are reciprocal.

The South wrong as to the Judiciary.

Another subject, concerning which the North has been equally ignorant with the South, and yet against which the South have manifested the more determined hostility, is the Federal Judiciary. These States, these greatest moral persons, composed of those same erring mortals, rulers and ruled continually going astray from ignorance or malice, have the same liability with their constituent members to error and wrong. The honorable, Christian Citizen, the main supporter of authority, law and order, wishes to live in a State whose blunders can be best corrected, its wrongs soonest righted. Such a State gives him best protection for himself, his property, his family, his every interest. But the wit of man has been insufficient to devise an efficacious means of State control. We, without being aware of the fact, have come nearer than any recorded example, to a peaceful mode of correcting the wrongs of Commonwealths. Our Federal Judiciary is a wonderful improvement in the science of Government, which in our theoretical confusion we have never appreciated. De Tocqueville better comprehended the dignity of our Supreme Court, and its importance to our Union, than any American writer that I have examined. He remarks:

States liable to error. Its correction desirable. We nearest in providing means without knowing it. Dignity of our Supreme Court.

De Tocqueville, *Democracy in America*, i, 160.

In the nations of Europe the courts of justice are only called upon to try the controversies of private individuals; but the Supreme Court of the United States summons sovereign powers to its bar. When the clerk of the court advances on the steps of the tribunal, and simply says, "The State of New York *vs.* the State of Ohio," it is impossible not to feel that the court which he addresses is no ordinary body; and when it is recollected that one of these parties represents one million [now two millions], and the other two millions of men [now over three millions], one is struck by the responsibility of the seven judges whose decision is about to satisfy or to disappoint so large a number of their fellow-citizens.

South Carolina agreed that the Constitution, &c., should be "the supreme law." The United States Court first to judge.

South Carolina in 1788 ratified the league between these States united; one provision of which, as previously observed, was, that the Constitution, and the laws and treaties "made under the authority of the United States, shall be the *supreme law of the land.*" The laws and treaties were, it is true, to be only those "which shall be made in pursuance thereof," i. e. of "this Constitution;" and had no common arbiter been appointed to decide whether they were in conformity with the Constitution, each State must of necessity have been its own judge. The impolicy of leaving each State to be its own judge in the first instance, was self-evident, and the Sovereign States therefore agreed further in the league, to institute an arbiter between them of higher dignity than any court ever established, as follows:

Constitution, *Art.* iii, § 2.

The judicial Power shall extend to all Cases, in Law and Equity, arising under this Constitution, the Laws of the United States, and Treaties made, or which shall be made, under their Authority;—to all Cases affecting Ambassadors, other public Ministers, and Consuls;—to all Cases of Admiralty and maritime Jurisdiction;—to Controversies to which the United States shall be a Party;—to Controversies between two or more States;—between a State and Citizens of another State;—between Citizens of different States;—between Citizens of the same State claiming Lands under Grants of different States, and between a State or the Citizens thereof, and foreign States, Citizens, or Subjects.

§ 12. To the South: Examining International Law.

So sweeping was this extent of authority, that individual Citizens brought suits against States, as in Georgia and Massachusetts, and on further consideration, it being regarded beneath the dignity of a Sovereignty to allow itself to be sued by individual subjects, the eleventh amendment of the Constitution was ratified by the States; but being only restrictive of "any suit in law or equity, commenced or prosecuted against *one of the United States*," it does not extend to the Federal Agency; and that may still be sued by any individual, as well as any State, which shall judge a law or treaty to be unauthorized by the Constitution, or any act of United States officials improper.[1] And so long as any State remained part of "the land" of the United States, so long as any Citizen of the United States remained subject to any one of the Sovereignties, by which the Constitution was ordained and established, the State or Citizen was bound by the compact, and by the principles of the International Code, to resort to the court of the States united, for the redress of any grievances. Failing there to get its wrongs righted, if the Confederates persisted in the wrong, and the best good of the State, according to its own free and independent judgment, required resistance to the wrong, the State would fail in its duty to itself and its subjects, if it did not offer that resistance. For this purpose, its first step is to cease to be a part of "the land" of the Confederacy. So long as it is part of "the land," the laws and treaties are to be "the supreme law," and it must adhere to its compact. It violates no compact in withdrawing, because the league is void for one of two reasons; either, 1st, that it has already

Individuals sued States. Constitution amended— —does not protect U. S. from suit. Each State to apply to Court for redress. Failing there, may resist. Must first secede. Such secession no violation of pact.

[1] I am aware that the opposite of this declaration is the general belief. It is supposed that somehow or other, a Sovereignty has been imparted to the United States, which exempts it from suit, for the same reason that the Monarch of Great Britain cannot be prosecuted. But a slight examination into principles will show, that the Sovereignty which in Britain abides in the Monarch, in these free States is in the People, the People by States; and it would be a remarkable anomaly, that Sovereign States should have subjected themselves to answer writs of their courts, and that their Federal Agency, this mere creature of the Sovereign wills of these States, should be so far exalted above its masters, as to be exempt from suit. We need to look no farther for evidence of the necessity of recurring to first principles in order to understand our governmental system, than this absurd notion that the United States cannot be sued, which is the prevalent belief of our statesmen, alike in the South and in the North, so far as I have examined, and that, too, against the clear and explicit provision of the Constitution itself.

It is supposed U. S. cannot be sued. A strange error.

It has been to me one of the most inexplicable points in this examination, how Southern statesmen, with their correct ideas of the Federal character of our Government, could have so misconceived this important question of the Judiciary. Jefferson and others well versed in ancient Governments, had fears of this branch overshadowing the Executive and Legislative; but apprehensions of danger should not have prevented a trial of any plain and palpable provisions. As before remarked, the Constitution is to be carried out as it is, till changes are properly made, without consulting hopes or fears.

Southern errors as to judiciary inexplicable.

It must be there are reasons not apparent on the surface, why the parties failed to put in full operation the Supreme Court, according to the extent of authority in the Constitution. Sure are we that nothing in International Law could have interfered with the operation of the courts as evidently designed, and which was much the most important improvement we made.

What are the reasons.

No doubt Southern statesmen have been led by our common calamities to study more thoroughly than we in the North, into principles of Government, and this interesting and important question of the Judiciary, has probably been by them already completely unfolded.

Southerners have no doubt examined.

§ 12. To the South: Examining International Law.

been violated by the Sovereignties in acquiescing in, or failing to correct, unjust, unauthorized acts of their Agencies, State or Federal; or, 2d, that the Compact has failed to promote the best good of the seceding State, to attain which object only had it the right to join the league.

South chief in error as to Judiciary.

The South, we shall find, more than any part of our country, have misapprehended, undervalued, this our greatest improvement in Federalism, the adjudication of wrongs done by these States or by their Federal Agency, in courts of law, as we shall endeavor to substantiate in Part IV, *Wrongs by the South.*

§ 13.—To the South: as to their Present Secession.

Secession, though right in the abstract, may be wrongly practised.

It also appears that the South need to look deeper into International Law and understand the doctrine of State-rights in all its bearings, in order to judge with correctness, whether due regard has been paid the "Laws of Nature and of Nature's God," in the present Secession. Although a Sovereign State must be possessed of an absolute right to revoke its compact and secede from a Federal Union, yet may it not wrongfully

No right to do wrong.

exercise that right. Even the absoluteness of Deity is insufficient to justify a wrong; and what a State might rightfully do under certain circumstances, it could not do under other circumstances. For instance, a

Difference between old and new States.

distinction seems quite possible to be made, between the rights of the old Thirteen, and the new States. As to the former, it may be doubtful whether they have not a right, at will, to withdraw from the Confederacy, forfeiting their rights therein by withdrawal, and if not forfeited, the

Natural right of States to enforce treaties.

questions become very complicated; although the other States have a natural and legal right to compel compliance with treaty obligations, if

Secession complicated, particularly as to new States.

they have the power, and have themselves fulfilled their covenants. The right of Secession, in either case, seems quite involved; but, as to the new States, the complication and difficulties are immensely enhanced, by the important rights acquired individually and equally by these Sovereignties in their common territory, and antecedent to States being formed within it.

The South has overlooked State rights in their common territory.

Strenuous advocates of State rights as are Southern statesmen, and no more earnest and determined than their transcendent importance requires, this weighty branch of the subject is not to be disregarded. Yet, if it has ever been examined by the South, it has been my misfortune not to have met with the treatise. Notwithstanding their inseparable connection with the doctrine of Secession, the pregnant and equal rights of these Sovereign States in all the territory that ever belonged to them jointly, seem never to have been deemed worthy of consideration.

Rights east of the Mississippi.

We have alluded to the common rights of the States in the territory ceded to the United States, by the original Thirteen States, and lying east of the Mississippi. It is, however, quite possible, that the Compact of Union failing to fulfil its purpose, of which in the last resort every free and independent State is its own judge, the rights in the Southern seceded States, have reverted to the original donors; that is, of Tennessee to North Carolina, and of Alabama and Mississippi to Georgia. Perhaps the right of eminent domain in the original States, which, with the new States, now constitute the body politic of the Confederate States, will give them an unquestionable title to Tennessee, Alabama and Mississippi. Upon the same principle, too, would the rights of Virginia in Kentucky, and in the Northwest, revert to her; but, having with her consent been formed into several sovereign, free and independent States, we, in exercising the prerogatives of Sovereignty, have the right of choice to follow our mother or not into the new Confederacy. We have not deserted her, but she has deserted us, and has no authority, it would seem, to control us.

§ 13. To the South: as to the present Secession.

Tennessee, Alabama, and Mississippi, legally transferred to the Confederate Government.

How Kentucky and the Northwest are excepted.

Altogether different from this, perhaps, are the rights of the Sovereignties constituting the body politic of the United States, in the Territories of Louisiana and Florida, purchased from France and Spain.

Louisiana and Florida territories a different case.

Sovereign States have the right and power to do whatever seems best to them to promote their highest good, paying due regard to the rights of other States, according to the International Code. One of the most important objects of a State is to increase its strength, and this may often be done by the annexation of territory, which is usually effected by purchase or conquest. When purchased, or when peace is proclaimed and rights determined, the treaty-making power is employed, which in these States united, has been delegated to the President and Senate. This appears not to have been well comprehended by Jefferson and his advisers, who supposed that, in making the Louisiana purchase, he transcended his authority. No necessity could justify an infraction of the Constitution, and, in my humble judgment, he was not guilty of this offence. Does not the Constitution delegate to the President and Senate the treaty-making power without restriction? Is not the settlement of a boundary within the province of a treaty? May not one State, by treaty, relinquish a portion of territory here and take another there? If inconvenient to adjust equally by land, may not money be used to settle the difference? Is it necessary that land be a part of the consideration? May not money alone be used? We had been in dispute with Spain as to the boundaries, as well as concerning the navigation of the Mississippi, and the same might have occasioned war with France. Strict construction of the Constitution was an excellent trait in Jefferson, but it is lamentable that he should have left such an example on record, and it is quite evident he little comprehended the doctrine of State Sovereignty, and the limited authority of Congress, when he conceived that the acquiescence of the two houses in the purchase, in their making the requisite appropriation, healed the breach of the Constitution.

States to seek their best good.

To gain strength, territory may be acquired.

This done by treaty.

President and Senate have power of treaty.

Jefferson misjudged.

Queries as to his mistake.

His example deprecated.

He did not comprehend Sovereignty.

The cession or acquisition of territory, depends on treaty with foreign nations, and the right of treaty has by these Sovereign Nations been absolutely, unconditionally delegated to the Federal Agency. If that Agency does wrong, and its wrongs cannot be redressed by the terms of

Power of treaty wholly in the Federal Agency.

§ 13. To the South: as to the present Secession.

If wrong is done a State, it may resist.

Must first secede.

Otherwise bound to its compact.

Calhoun's blending Nullification and Secession.

the compact, or in some other way, to the satisfaction of the aggrieved Sovereignty, as might have been the case with Maine in settling the northeastern boundary, it has the natural right of a Sovereign State, to resist the aggression. But it cannot do this, so long as it is a member of the body politic of the United States, for it has agreed that the Constitution, laws and *treaties* of the States united, made through their Federal Agency, shall be the supreme law of the land. So long as it is part of the land of the United States, a State is bound by its compact to observe its Constitution, laws and *treaties;* and it was by Calhoun's not properly regarding the sacred nature of pact and faith, the only means of obligation between Sovereign States, that he was led to confound the right of Nullification with that of Secession. The former is a violation of all principles of natural and International Law; the latter is an incontestable prerogative of Sovereignty.

The Louisiana purchase made for these Sovereign States.

THE TREATY WITH FRANCE for Louisiana, Art. iii.

This treaty for the purchase of Louisiana was made in 1802, by and for the States united, by their duly constituted agents, the President and the Senate. The third article of the treaty provides: "The inhabitants of the ceded territory shall be incorporated in the union of the United States, and admitted as soon as possible, according to the principles of the Federal Constitution, to the enjoyment of all the rights, advantages, and immunities of citizens of the United States; and in the mean time they shall be maintained and protected in the free enjoyment of their liberty, property, and the religion which they profess."

Slaves property in Louisiana territory.

No right anywhere to interfere.

Congress usurped the right in the Missouri restriction.

Each State should have resisted.

The South have not understood their rights—never brought a suit.

Slaves were property under the laws of Louisiana, and, according to this treaty and the International Code, there was no power on earth that could rightfully touch a master's rights to his slave anywhere in that territory, till an independent Sovereignty was created, which can do its will in annihilating property in a slave, or in a horse, or in land. Yet, right in the face of this truth, which will not be questioned by any one examining the subject, did Congress usurp this august prerogative of Sovereignty, and pretend to annihilate property in slaves north of 36° 30′. Nay, more. Whereas this purchase had been made for the joint Sovereignties, and each one of them was bound by honor and its natural obligations to protect such of its subjects with their property as chose to remove into this common territory, whether that property were cattle, dogs, or slaves, yet so little have the Southern States, which have been such strenuous asserters of State rights, understood their rights, and the admirable provisions for their maintenance, that never has a suit been brought in the Federal Courts to redress this weighty grievance, and very few have even known that the grievance existed.

Again wrong as to State rights.

The territory was the property of the States—

And now, suddenly arousing themselves to this doctrine of State-rights, they would over-ride all rights of pact and faith. The Louisiana purchase, I again repeat, was made by and for these joint Sovereignties, through their Federal Agency. The territory was bought for and became the joint property of these united Sovereignties, and the rights thereof inured to such as then constituted the body politic of the United

States, antecedent to the creation of a State in that territory. As a province had it been transferred to France by Spain; as a province was it transferred by "the Republic one and indivisible" of France, to this Federal Republic of the United States; and it was equally a province of and subject to the Sovereignties of these States united, as it had been to the Sovereignty of the French Republic, or to the Sovereignty of the Crown of Spain. These States, it is true, have yielded some of their rights and powers over large areas of that territory, and ceasing to regard those parts as subject provinces, have consented to allow their brethren to organize themselves into sovereign States, and as such have they been admitted into our Federal Union, and are possessed of entire equality of rights with the older Confederates. But surrendering a part of our rights and powers, and admitting a new State to an equal participation with us in our remaining rights and franchises, cannot be regarded as destroying our rights altogether. A distinct declaration must be shown, to make a valid transfer, which will be difficult to find. One of these rights in jeopardy, is the free navigation of the Mississippi. The South very properly proclaim that it shall be forever free, and no doubt they are sincere. But we in the West are a very practical, common-sense sort of people, though somewhat bewildered as to the theory of our rights; and we shall much prefer holding on to our franchises acquired by purchase and by possession, to relying on any treaty stipulations, with any party, however honorable and friendly. And we cannot help thinking, that there would be more or less danger of a rival Republic, more jealous of its neighbor than of all the world beside, refusing to adhere to a treaty when it should be judged for its interest to break it, particularly when the party contestant avows and acts upon the doctrine, that there is nothing that can bind a Sovereign State. If the sacred compact of the Constitution, with all its influences and powers, is inadequate to bind these States, any mere treaty stipulation will prove a wisp of straw.

§ 13. To the South: as to the present Secession.

—a subject province of these States.

Parts of the territory made into States, and admitted into the Union with equal rights.

All our rights not thereby surrendered.

Free navigation our right.

The West will prefer her rights by purchase, to a treaty.

A rival Republic might break its treaty—

—particularly if a State is not bound to observe pact and faith.

The right of a Sovereign State to unrestricted sway within its own domain; the prior and equally unquestionable rights of the older members of the Confederacy in the territory out of which the new States have been formed, particularly that acquired by joint purchase and conquest, make indeed a complicated question, but one not easily solved by disunion. So that if this doctrine of State rights has some tendency to disintegration, it seems to my feeble comprehension to possess also strong ligaments of Union; and the more it is understood, the firmer will be our determination to maintain it in the North as well as in the South.

State rights complicated—

—not solved by disunion—

—has strong bonds of Union.

Probably no one, even of the sea-board States, when they come to understand their Union rights, will assent to their surrender; but never will we in Wisconsin, Illinois, Indiana and Ohio, be driven from our rights in the Louisiana purchase; and Minnesota, Iowa, Missouri, and Kansas, and the other States to be soon formed, a part and parcel of this very purchase, and in which, from the sources of the Mississippi to the Gulf of Mexico, the scattered inhabitants had a common and equal interest, that

Eastern States will not part with their rights, certainly not the Western.

§ 13. To the South: as to the present Secession.

has descended to their heirs, and which they have never relinquished,—these Sovereign States west of the Mississippi, will be even less inclined to be dispossessed of their rights, than we on the eastern bank of the Father of Waters. If the South want our rights in the Louisiana purchase, let them show by those "LAWS OF NATURE AND OF NATURE'S GOD," to which they no doubt still adhere as they did in 1776, how we have become dispossessed of our rights; how our rights have legally and properly come to be possessed by others. The South are strong; manfully, heroically have they conducted this gigantic war under most terribly adverse circumstances, and we are proud of our fellow Americans; but they are not strong enough, however brave, to dispossess the Northwest, by force of arms, of what is rightfully hers.

The South must prove how we have lost our rights: —are not strong enough to take them by force.

Disunion no remedy for disagreement.

Besides, it is a great mistake to suppose that disunion will remove disagreements and clashing interests. A homogeneous State is imperfect, as the profound philosopher of antiquity has remarked. A diversity of character, interests, pursuits, is necessary, else the State partakes too much of the character of a family, and fails to accomplish the object of its institution. Pope truly remarks,

All Nature's difference keeps all Nature's peace.

A large area desirable for a Federal Republic.

As we are Republican Democracies, and necessarily restricted to a small area, the variety desirable to form the most perfect State, could not have been attained but for the discovery of a Federal State, whereby the greatest possible diversity is secured. Of course this diversity leads to more or less clashing, but that "evil," to again quote the apposite language of Montesquieu, "is in the very thing itself; and no form can redress it." Division, once begun, is not to cease with two Confederacies. In each Federal Union, will the individual members be more jealous of each other than in the old Union, as there is more bickering and strife in a small than in a large town; and while they could, and generally would, assent to measures adopted by the whole thirty-four States for the general good, they would refuse acquiescence in the very same measures enacted in the smaller Confederacy. We shall soon have Southern opinion on this very point, from a leading Southern journal, and see their efforts already begun, and boldly advocated, to divide the North.

Clashing unavoidable. One division brings others. This the South understand.

JEFFERSON'S opinion.

This was a subject well comprehended by the sagacious Jefferson. He had a friend, John Taylor of Caroline, an eminent statesman, and author of two works upon our Government, among the best written, though not without errors, and from which liberal quotations will be made in these volumes. In a letter to him in 1798, Jefferson remarks:

Works vi, 246.

Man's nature ensures discord.

> Be this as it may, in every free and deliberating society, there must, from the nature of man, be opposite parties, and violent dissensions and discords; and one of these, for the most part, must prevail over the other for a longer or shorter time. Perhaps this party division is necessary to induce each to watch and delate to the people the proceedings of the other. But if on a temporary superiority of the one party, the other is to resort to a scission of the Union, no federal government can ever exist. If to rid ourselves of the present rule of Massachusetts and Connecticut, we break the Union, will the evil stop there? Suppose the New England States alone cut

A party injury temporary. The South not made perfect by scission.

off, will our nature be changed? Are we not men still to the South of that, and with all the passions of men? Immediately we shall see a Pennsylvania and a Virginia party arise in the residuary confederacy, and the public mind will be distracted with the same party spirit. What a game too will the one party have in their hands, by eternally threatening the other, that unless they do so and so, they will join their northern neighbors. If we reduce our union to Virginia and North Carolina, immediately the conflict will be established between the representatives of those two States, and they will end by breaking into their simple units. Seeing, therefore, that an association of men who will not quarrel with one another is a thing which never yet existed, from the greatest confederacy of nations down to a town-meeting or a vestry; seeing that we must have somebody to quarrel with, I had rather keep our New England associates for that purpose, than to see our bickerings transferred to others. They are circumscribed within such narrow limits, and their population so full, that their numbers will ever be the minority, and they are marked, like the Jews, with such a perversity of character, as to constitute, from that circumstance, the natural division of our parties. A little patience, and we shall see the reign of witches pass over, their spells dissolved, and the people recovering their true sight, restoring their Government to its true principles. It is true, that in the meantime we are suffering deeply in spirit, and incurring the horrors of a war, and long oppressions of enormous public debt. But who can say what would be the evils of a scission, and when and where they would end? Better keep together as we are, haul off from Europe soon as we can, and from all attachments to any portions of it; and if they show their power just sufficiently to hoop us together, it will be the happiest situation in which we can exist. If the game runs sometime against us at home, we must have patience till luck turns, and then we shall have an opportunity of winning back the *principles* we have lost. For this is a game where principles are the stake. Better luck, therefore, to us all, and health, happiness and friendly salutations to yourself. Adieu.

§ 13. To the South: as to the present Secession.

New differences.

Confederates can threaten to join their rivals.

Discord being inseparable from man—

—the South had best keep New England to quarrel with.

Noble, proper confidence in the People.

Better to bear some ills than to try those of scission.

Principles will ultimately triumph.

§ 14.—To the South: as to the Nature of this War.

An examination of principles of International Law, is the only means to determine the character of this war, whether it be *just* or *unjust*, and which party is in the *offensive*, which *defensive*. As to the first, it will, perhaps, be difficult to decide, the South having had so much unjust provocation; and at such a very critical stage of the proceedings, having been subjected to infamous deception in the attempt to supply Forts Sumter and Pickens. Could the South have exercised patience a few weeks longer, the discovery of that deception might have been used to the permanent disgrace and discomfiture of the Federal Administration. With great propriety could the South then have proposed, that for a short time, say for three or for six months, supplies would be admitted to Fort Sumter under strict surveillance, to see that only provisions and clothing were introduced. Not for three weeks would that condition of affairs have been endured, and had the Federal Administration under these circumstances begun the attack, the South would have been placed on the side of *justice* and *defence*. Or had the North, contrary to all probabilities, exercised prudence and endured the insult of the surveillance, after waiting three or six months, and giving due notice that longer time would not be allowed for consideration, had the South then assumed the *offensive*, it might still have been a *just* war. Its *justice* would have been determined by the *necessity* that existed. Pufendorf is very thorough in examining

What character does International Law give this war.

Is it *just*?

Difficult to decide.

Deception of the South.

South could have taken advantage of it.

Would have caused the North to begin war.

If not, the South might still have been in a *just* war.

Justice determined by *necessity*.

§ 14. To the South: as to the Nature of this War.

necessity in the abstract, and Grotius is so full in its application to the rights of war, that it was not necessary for Pufendorf to add much as to the application of his principles of *necessity* to the case of war. Yet is it exceedingly difficult, and especially in this instance, to draw the line between *justice* and *injustice*. The provocations had been excessive, the threats had been strong and positive, that the South should not have its equal rights in the common Territories; that no more-slave States should be admitted into the Union; that the Supreme Court should be remodelled and made subservient to Abolitionists; and the Republican party had come into power on the distinct issue, that the Union could not exist with part of the States free, others slave. The peace measures had been defeated, the beautiful azure of our glorious Union had been overspread with heavy and murky clouds of disunion; lightning flashes of passion came from the dark background; and in the distance were already heard the threatening mutterings of the thunder of civil conflict that, once begun, must be the most terrific of all time. The utmost prudence and correct conduct were requisite to keep the excited and hostile parties from contact, and from the sight of blood, which, when it once began to flow, would still more madden and infuriate. It was under these circumstances that the Administration deemed it just and proper to deceive the South and violate its faith, in the attempt to supply Forts Sumter and Pickens.

Difficult to decide.

Provocations, &c., excessive.

Danger of collision.

Base deceit at this critical juncture.

Grotius on the duty of keeping faith.

Grotius takes several chapters to discuss Promises, Contracts, Leagues, and Sponsions, &c., all bearing upon this subject, from which we shall hereafter quote, and in a subsequent chapter, "Concerning Faith to be kept between Enemies," he discusses various points, as "That faith is to be kept with all sorts of Enemies," "The Opinion, That faith is not to be kept with Thieves and Tyrants, refuted," until, under the thirteenth head, "That faith is to be kept even with such as are perfidious," he observes:

Faith to be kept even with the perfidious.

GROTIUS, l. iii, c. 19, § 13.

Roman ideas of faith.

That faith ought to be kept with such as are notoriously perfidious, we have in a more general treatise already proved: Which also we may learn from St. Ambrose, which without doubt reacheth even unto such enemies as are altogether faithless. Such as the Carthaginians were unto the Romans, who notwithstanding kept their faith inviolably with them. For, as Valerius Maximus well observes, "the Roman Senate regarded not what the Carthaginians deserved, but what in honor became the people of Rome;" which is the testimony that Sallust gives of them: "In all the wars," saith he, "between Rome and Carthage, though the Carthaginians, as well in times of peace as during their truces, committed many outrages, yet would not the Romans upon any provocation permit that the like should be done unto them." And concerning that fact of Sergius Galba, who, in revenge upon the Portuguese for so often breaking their league with him, first deceived them with a new league, and then slew eight thousand of them; Appian gives this answer: *Perfidiâ perfidiam ultus, contra Romanam dignitatem, barbaros imitabatur;* "In revenging one treachery with another, he wounded the majesty of the people of Rome, imitating therein the barbarians." For which he was afterwards worthily accused by Labo, a tribune of the people, whereof Valerius Maximus gives his opinion thus: "It was not equity, but compassion, that pleaded in that cause; for that absolution which his own innocency could not challenge, was given to his innocent babes:" which is also confirmed by

Cato, "He had certainly died for his treachery, had not his own tears, and the innocency of his children, procured his pardon."

§ 14. To the South: as to the Nature of this war.

The South not perfidious.

Even with "the perfidious" is faith to be kept; but it cannot be charged upon the South that they were perfidious, treacherous. They have done wrong, as we believe, have unnecessarily violated their sacred compact of the Constitution, but it has been done boldly, openly, manfully. No enemy of the South can attribute to those States perfidy, treachery. Yet were they even perfidious, the sacred promise of the President of the United States had been given by his duly authorized agent, the Secretary of State, and that promise must be kept. It was not kept, but shamefully violated, and had the previous and chief causes of provocation come from the Federal Government, this deceit, under the circumstances, might have been a justifying cause of beginning hostilities.

The President's promise should have been kept.

It was broken.

Fear the only extenuation.

The "more general treatise" referred to, is probably the above-named chapters, and no extenuation of this deception is perceptible, except it be that of *fear*, on which point Grotius observes:

Grotius concerning *fear*, l. ii, c. 11, § 7.

Concerning those promises that are made through fear, questions do arise no less perplext. For herein they do usually distinguish of fears, which are either great and vehement, or light and slender: if great, then they consider whether it be so absolutely, or in respect only of the person fearing: then whether it be occasioned justly or unjustly; and whether by him to whom the promise was made, or by some other: as also they distinguish of the acts, whether free and generous, or grievous and burdensome; and according to this diversity, are some acts said to be void, others revocable at the pleasure of the promiser, and others to be wholly renewed. Concerning every one of these cases, there are great differences in opinions. But I do wholly incline to those who hold, that setting aside that authority of the civil law, which sometimes takes away, and sometimes moderates the binding power of such promises: he that promiseth any thing through fear, is obliged to perform what he hath so promised; because the consent he gave was not conditional, as in the case of error, but absolute. For as Aristotle well observes, he that, for fear of being shipwrecked, throws his goods overboard, would willingly preserve them on condition that he might not be wrecked; but upon a serious consideration of the present danger he is in, he absolutely resolves that his goods rather than himself, shall perish. But yet we must also crave this allowance, that if he to whom the promise was made, did occasion not a just, but an unjust fear, though but slight; and that thereupon the promise was so made, he is bound to discharge the promiser if he desire it; not that the promise is in itself void, but for the damage that he sustained who made it, by reason of the injury done him. But what exceptions the Law of Nations admits herein, shall in its proper place be hereafter explained.

Fear does not release from promise.

Aristotle in confirmation.

The promisee may be required to release the promisor.

Nor is any extenuating circumstance perceptible in the exceptions referred to by Grotius; and even if fear be admitted in palliation, it only adds to the disgrace of the North. We are no cowards; would never yield an iota of right through fear. There is nothing for us to do but to admit the wrong, and let the President find his excuse in his inexperience and the bewildering circumstances.

Fear only adds to the disgrace of the North.

But there is another subject of consideration as to the *justice* of this war, and that is, that the South were unreasonably precipitate in its commencement. South Carolina knew, the whole South knew, that the Constitution had failed to provide for an emergency like the present. The consequences of a State or States' seceding from a Union that had been

The war *unjust* because of precipitancy.

§ 14. To the South: as to the Nature of this War.

to the fathers the *summum bonum*, had not been contemplated; and the Federal Government, restricted to the letter of the Constitution, was in all its departments powerless to act in the premises. But it was the sworn duty of the Executive to enforce the laws and preserve and defend the property and officers and soldiers of the United States anywhere and everywhere; and as Commander-in-Chief of the army and navy, to bring every power to bear to defend the Government against domestic as well as foreign assailants. If South Carolina, having seceded, by virtue of eminent domain, could claim a fort of the United States within her boundaries, the President was unauthorized to recognize that right. In a proper and constitutional manner, had the body politic of the United States become possessed of the title to the site of that fort; by the Sovereignty of South Carolina, through its duly authorized Agencies, had consent been given to that purchase, and jurisdiction ceded over it to the Federal, jointly with the State Government; the money of all these sovereign Peoples had been expended in the purchase of the site and the erection of Fort Sumter, and the President was fully justified in his double office of Executive and Commander-in-Chief, in holding its possession. No matter what the proportion of value of the property belonging to the United States within that State, whether more or less than it would be entitled to in the division; the President was unauthorized to entertain the subject, could know and do nothing about it. The same views apply, of course, equally to the new Confederacy as to South Carolina.

The duty of the Executive. Unauthorized to recognize Secession. The rights of United States in Ft. Sumter.

Immediate possession of Fort Sumter unimportant to the South.

Besides, the reduction of Fort Sumter at that period, was of no considerable importance, either as a military or other necessity. Their nineteen batteries rendered forcible reënforcement almost an impossibility, and had the little garrison been allowed to receive or purchase its supplies a while longer, all occasion of war there might have been avoided by the withdrawal of the troops. This appears probable from all the circumstances; and although President Lincoln could with no propriety be forced to give up possession of a fort he was sworn to protect, yet could he rightfully have taken the responsibility of its abandonment, to save his country from civil war.

Might have been surrendered without war.

The South began the war to ensure disunion.

The South may at its pleasure insist that the United States would not have evacuated that fort, and assert that at best, the war would only have been delayed a few weeks, and that a little earlier or later attack makes no difference; they can give no adequate reason for the attack then, except that which is written with sunbeams all over that black transaction, that they intended to make sure the accomplishment of their long-cherished purposes, in the destruction of our Government, though it involved the country in all the wretchedness of fratricidal bloodshed. No further delay must be allowed; their schemes of disunion would surely and speedily be frustrated, unless the blow were then and there struck, which would at least retard the abhorred reunion.

The South attack the wrong Government:

Let another most important point be considered. This war is waged against the Government of the United States! The attack is not made upon the individual States, that have done or tolerated the tantalizing wrong to sister-Sovereignties. Not at all. It is our common Federal Government that is assailed, for evils it is powerless to remedy. No authority is to be found in the Constitution for the Executive or for Congress to interfere, in any way or manner, with the malignant assaults of which the South have just cause of complaint; and foremost and loudest as are the Southern Sovereignties in their acclaims to State rights, they should be ashamed in the same breath to clamor against the Federal authority for its non-interference. Clamor! did I say? Why, they have evoked all the horrors of civil war, because the Central Government would not exercise powers, the usurpation of which they themselves would have been first to condemn.

§ 14. To the South: as to the Nature of this War.

—one unauthorized to act—

—against their own correct ideas—

—because it would not usurp powers.

The South have little occasion of complaint even, much less of war, against our Federal Government. The Missouri restriction was undoubtedly the severest trial the South have been called to bear, and yet for many years it had its chief support in that section itself. As to the tariff, the early debates in Congress under the Constitution, show that South Carolina aided most effectively to establish the system, and may almost be considered its father. Can it be that the wise and good men of that day so erred in judgment, that a system then right and expedient, now adhered to, is adequate cause for destroying the Union they so loved and cherished? Did not the Pinckneys, Butler, Rutledge, Barnwell, Pendleton, &c., have capacity to judge of the right of such measures, as well as of their expediency?

The Missouri restriction the chief wrong of the Federal Government.

That and the tariff sustained by the South.

This Union and its Government are full of benefits unspeakable, immeasurable, to that region, its every State, as to the North, the West, and all. Most unjust, most unbecoming in the magnanimous South is it, to requite with base ingratitude, with treason and with war, the Government which has not only fulfilled, but far exceeded in its beneficence, the highest expectations of its illustrious founders.

The Federal Government full of benefits to every section.

But regardless of the past, admitting that it gave no encouragement for present and future trust in our joint Government, what was there to justify a violent destruction of it then? The success of the Republicans in the presidential contest amounted to nothing. Had any fiend incarnate been elected instead of Mr. Lincoln, what could he have done? The South Carolinians, while using the election for their purposes, boldly, frankly avow, as we shall learn, that neither the election of Mr. Lincoln, nor the nullifying of the fugitive slave law, had anything to do with this struggle. Certainly it should not, for the Supreme Court, as then constituted, was an abundant protection against any attempted oppressions by the Executive, and with a majority in the Senate opposed to the President elect, had the Southern Senators remained, that Court could not have been interfered with, at least for some years. With a Democratic Senate, too, all improper legislation was rendered impossible; and with laws as they were, what could any Executive do, however ill-disposed, to the injury of the South?

No excuse for this attack.

The Federal Government could have done the South no wrong.

Lincoln's election and anti-slavery enmity of the north no cause of Secession.

§ 14. To the South: as to the Nature of this War.

Let South Carolina fight the right Government.

Let South Carolina secede, if she chooses, and exercise her sovereign right of redressing wrongs, and thresh Massachusetts, or any erring sister-Sovereignty, if she can, to her full satisfaction; but other Sovereignties will not endure this transfer of a quarrel from a People that has given offence, to a Government, a mere Agency, that has and can have no responsibility therefor. And when the Government attacked is our own, our Federal Government, established by the united wisdom of our fathers; when in that Government lives the Union, that has been to us the means of all our advancement and happiness; that Union which the fathers of the South and of the North together fought, bled, and died to establish; be assured we shall fight for it to the death, and for the maintenance of our rights, which, if we correctly understand them, will perpetuate that Union, or rather, bring us a new one.

We will defend our Government.

This compend imperfect—

It is impossible in this compend to do more than indicate the points which we have endeavored in all candor to examine, as to the *justice* of this war. Further light no doubt will be obtained from the Southern side, possibly more, too, from the Northern; all of which shall be fairly used and presented; but applying that rule, "*The Laws of Nature and of Nature's* GOD," to the facts as understood, it seems that the South are in an *unjust* war, but under many very extenuating circumstances.

—a further examination.

The South in an *offensive* war.

But whether in a *just* or *unjust* war, there seems to be little doubt but that they are in an *offensive* war, which space will not be here taken to discuss. Lord Russell's opinion on this point will, it appears to me, be amply justified by applying that same rule to existing facts.

See p. 51.

The South misled, and think they are on the *defensive.*

The South, however, misled in part by the follies of our own Administration, wholly misconceive the nature of the conflict in which we are engaged, and also the designs and purposes of the North. An old and respected journal of the South, before quoted, has remarks upon this subject, which are introduced, not only for use here, but as corroborative of preceding views, as to the importance of examining into principles, to obtain more unanimity in the North. Division of sentiment among ourselves is no doubt the main reliance of the South, in prosecuting its plans of disunion.

Southern opinions of the Northwest.

RICHMOND ENQUIRER, *May* 24, 1863.

Signs in the Northwest.—Although it is altogether out of the question while the whole North is engaged in a war for our subjugation or extermination that we should offer terms of alliance, still less listen to any word or hint about union with them, yet it is no less true that the symptoms of disorganization which show themselves in the present Federal States are of deep interest to us, and that we ought even to do all we honorably and loyally may to give further impulse to the force which promises at some future time to break up the league of our enemies. Let us examine the exact nature and reasons of the impending quarrel.

The West to be a separate Confederacy.

The material interest of the Northwestern States, from Ohio westward, assuredly ought to impel them rather to the formation of a separate confederation, or an alliance with this Southern Confederacy, on the footing of a foreign nation, than to a Union with the East, hostile to us. It is true they ought to have thought of this before. They chose to make common cause with the Eastern Yankees against us, and rushed blindly into a war for the destruction of our rights of State sovereignty. They elected alliance with our enemies, war to the knife with us; and they, and we, must abide the issue.

A supposed mistake of the West.

Nevertheless, the material interests remain the same; the undeniable features of nature on this continent remain the same; the Northwest continues to be an agricultural and food-producing country; protective tariffs, for the profits of Eastern manufacturers, are still as oppressive to Western men as they were injurious to us in the days of the old Union. The great natural channel of traffic furnished by the Mississippi river is common to them with the Confederacy, just as the Rhine is common to France, to Germany and Holland; it is not only their natural outlet to the sea, but also their highway to the lucrative markets of the South.

§ 14. To the South: as to the Nature of this War.

A tariff for the East injurious to the West.

The Mississippi a channel to Southern markets.

All these considerations are now at last pressing themselves upon the attention of thoughtful men in the country northwest of us; and the depreciation of their staple products, combined with the enormous war debt which the cunning Down Easters induced them to incur in the vain hope of our subjugation; failure in all their attempts to command the whole stream of the Mississippi by force; the terrible prospect of increased burdens of taxation, with diminished means to bear those burdens; all these things are evidently bringing about in their minds a great change which in the future cannot fail to be wholesome for us. Not that it can produce any effect of the slightest consequence for the present. For this year, at any rate, instead of any relaxation of the atrocious war which they have undertaken, we may expect to see it prosecuted with redoubled energy, akin to desperation. The headstrong blockheads amongst them (who are the vast majority and rule in the land) still hope, by one last tremendous effort, to crush the Confederacy, to sweep the whole Mississippi clear with their fleets and armies, penetrate the heart of the cotton States, and provide, by universal plunder and confiscation, for the security of the great debt. If they fail, why then in a year, or in two years, they will offer us friendship and alliance, and the right hand of fellowship.

The West becoming considerate of the evils of present Union.

Will produce no effect for a year.

Our "blockheads" expect to crush the Confederacy. (All such expectants are properly entitled.)

Another feature in the situation must be borne in mind. The organization which used to be called the Democratic party in those Federal States, is broken up. Old issues are gone by, and the great new issue is the war, and the conduct of the war. Northeastern Democrats remember just now that they were New Yorkers or New Englanders before they were Democrats; that the interests of the Northwest, which may impel it to form a separate confederacy and seek alliance with the South, are no interests of theirs. That if the Union be finally broken forever, though the Northwest may find safety and profit in a confederacy of its own, New York, Philadelphia, and Boston are ruined at any rate. Hence we can understand the total revulsion of language and of feeling among the Democrats of New York. All their talk of amnesty or peace, all their loud assertions of State rights, all their nullification of their President and his Cabinet, and his generals, was under the delusion that we had not really seceded from them in earnest, and that we were willing to let our moral struggle pass for a Democratic Presidential campaign—a somewhat violent campaign it is true—rather more stormy than the "sour cider" one or the Know Nothing one, but still only an effort that would be amply rewarded by the spoils of office in Washington. They appear only lately to have found out that we were serious all the time, and meant what we said, to their intense disgust. They have discovered that the prize we sought, and which we thought worth the richest and reddest of our best blood, was no less than absolute independence—to be eternally clear of them and their mean politics, to ding them and all their ways, to rise out of the contaminations of their society, and begin to live our own full, strong, genial life in accord with our institutions and national character. They had been giving us credit for more practical good sense, those "Democrats;" they had thought we valued the heart's blood of our children as much as they value the Hessians they hire, and finding out their mistake they are naturally disgusted.

The Northern Democracy divided—

—particularly the East from the West.

A division of less injury to the West than East.

What has changed Eastern Democrats.

Have found the South in earnest.

Now this discovery they have made in the country north of us, both east and west, operates very differently on the Democrats of those two sections. In the eastern part it makes them drop suddenly all thoughts of conciliation, and rage and foam for war and slaughter. (See speeches of Van Buren, Brady, &c.) The very same discovery makes Western men bethink themselves that there has been too much war and slaughter already, and though they are now in for it, and must try it out, yet their

The different effects of this knowledge in the East and West.

The West to get out of the old Union.

§ 14. To the South: as to the Nature of this War.

The South have caused the disunion—their interest to encourage it.

evident policy will soon be to draw out of it, if possible, and out of the Union, and out of the debt, and out of the blunder, and bankruptcy, and philanthropy, and all the rest of it. The interests of the two sections are now separated, and it is our secession and our troops and generals that have separated them. It would be wise, undoubtedly, to encourage this break up and develop it so far as we honorably may. And the first and best way to do it is to maintain those troops and strengthen the hands of those generals.

The *Enquirer* will aid to effect Northern division.

But, as the *Enquirer* has been accused of repelling friendly advances and discouraging or preventing the course of that excellent rupture at the North, we shall try to make amends this very moment by saying the most soothing things that any Confederate properly can to help the good work. We think, then, that when the war is once over, and when the Northwestern States shall have separated themselves from the Federal Union and established a league for themselves, and taken the initiative in recognizing the independence of the Confederacy, then it is highly probable that the Confederates would enter into an alliance with that Northwestern league notwithstanding all its sins done, and would engage themselves to furnish a proportion of Confederate troops for the defence of that country, in case of the furious Yankee nation waging war to crush a second "rebellion." Further, we think the provisions of that act of our Congress, proclaiming the free navigation of the Mississippi, should be more fully made known among our Northwestern enemies, in order that they may see that the said free navigation is carefully limited to "the citizens of any of the States on its borders, or on the borders of its navigable rivers," and so exclude the Yankees proper. Further still, we believe it would be well to express to these Northwestern enemies of ours the general feeling that, so soon as they shall have ceased to be "our enemies in war," and shall have become "in peace friends," we should discriminate in all things between them and the Yankees proper, placing the latter in the category of the least favored nation, but dealing with the former on the easiest terms, because that would be for our interest, and this Confederacy will always be willing, for its own interest, to make treaties with any foreign power, whether in America or in Europe.

Desire of the West to have a league with the South will bring division.

Free navigation of the Mississippi to be more strongly assured—

—not to be allowed to other States.

The West and East to be differently treated.

"Free navigation of the Mississippi" defined.

And to prevent mistakes, here is what is meant by "free navigation of the Mississippi," as defined in the aforesaid act of Congress:—Permission to pass freely to the sea, without any duty or other hindrance, except light money, pilotage and other like charges; permission to pass freely to any port of entry on the Mississippi within Confederate limits, and to enter and load goods and freight, paying the duties thereof to the Confederate Government, and there to sell them, and to forward them, under bond or seal, as customary in such cases, with usual regulations as to warehousing and drawback. In short, on entering within the limits of the Confederacy, upon the river, a steamboat of the Northwest would be precisely in the position of a French steamer entering Prussia on the Rhine—no better, and no worse. As for the Yankee nation proper, no boat of theirs should ever enter the Mississippi at all.

Restricted to the West.

The West unreasonable not to accept this liberality—

Now here we think is an array of prospective advantages which might satisfy any reasonable people. It would not be proper for our Government to make them any further proposals, or hold out any new inducements. Our Government and Congress have already done all that consists with the dignity of an independent power; but it may not be improper for the press to reason about these matters and place them in a clear light, and make the prospect of peace as alluring as possible to one section of our enemies, which will more and more exasperate that section of our enemies against the other section of our enemies. Therefore we advise the foregoing considerations to our Northwestern enemies. If they hearken to us, well; if not (and we know they will not for this year), then let them go ahead and crush the rebellion.

—the press to use its influence alluringly—

—of no avail for a year.

Wait till next year.

In truth we do not attach much importance to all this until next year. For this reason our reliance is on our own brave army alone.

A humble protest in behalf of the West.

We cannot stop here to discuss the salient points of this article, which can best be done indirectly as the investigation proceeds; but as one of the humble Citizens of the Northwest, let me protest against any such judgment of our character and rights, or expectations of our plans and conduct.

§ 14. To the South: as to the Nature of this War.

We have not, it is true, been correct as to our *theories;* but we have been and are nearly so, as to our *practice.* Many have erroneously supposed it was necessary to subdue the "rebels," and the war has been engaged in for that purpose; and yet the effect is mainly to preserve the rights of these States. We have become confused as to the *theory* of our rights, but with the *practical* good sense of the American people, we have taken the proper course, in the main, to protect ourselves against unjust aggressions. Our President, Western man though he is, and his advisers, have done many things adverse to the judgment and feelings of the Citizens of the West; but he is our Constitutional leader, and we are with him heartily in defending our rights, notwithstanding his great wrongs. With the honored Douglas, are we "for our Government against all assailants."

The West wrong in theory, but right in practice—

—as in the war—

We are "for our Government against all assailants."

The South will find in the West apt scholars in this much-neglected science of State rights; and it is of no use to talk to us about surrendering our existing properties in the seceded States, and receiving back a part of them by treaty. *We will never part with our rights.* Even if New England were to be willing to abandon her interests therein—which she never will, I hope; could she become so thoroughly abolitionized as to determine to be wholly cut loose from any States which tolerated slavery; were she even to side with the South in this war to obtain her release and effect disunion, it would have no influence to change the course of the West. Though many have been wrong as to the *theory* of this war, believing it to be *offensive* instead of *defensive*, we shall soon get right; and we in the West, with the other Eastern States, will wage the war indefinitely for the maintenance of our rights and of the Union. Only let us become correct in *theory* as we are in *practice*, and united as we shall be through the entire North, it will not be so very difficult for us to prosecute our *defensive* war in such a manner that the South will ere long tire of it. But if any of the Eastern States are unwilling to reconfederate with slave States and should even join the South, we in the West alone can sustain a *defensive* war, till we can have our rights properly acknowledged and established by a new Confederacy. Countrymen of the Northwest! *fellow Citizens!* speak I not your sentiments to a man in declaring—We never, *never* surrender our properties in the seceded States upon compulsion?

The West taking lessons in State-rights.

New England may abandon her rights—

—will not affect the West.

The West can sustain a *defensive* war—

—till the South will give us our rights.

We never give them up to force.

All that is said in the foregoing extract as to the probability of further division, if one disunion scheme be tolerated, is freely admitted. The consideration of that very subject, as shown in the preface; alarm at the dangers which threaten us, started the investigation in 1860, which has led to the compilation of this work; for it is much less my own writing than a bringing together the wise and well-told truths and opinions of others. Month by month, as my ignorance has been enlightened by the treasures of governmental science and of history,

More disunions to follow if one be allowed.

§ 14. To the South: as to the Nature of this War.

The warning example of Greece.

Rival Confederacies, not States, divided Greece.

particularly that of the Grecian Confederacies, has the conviction been strengthened, that if we cannot preserve our Union entire, we shall be in great danger of an utter failure to sustain free institutions. The quotations that will be made in discussing the Grecian Confederacies, prove conclusively that it was not the division of those Peoples into small States that caused their dissensions and ultimate destruction, but their rival Confederacies. Aristotle's practical common-sense, taught him that Greece united in a polity of polities, could defy the world; and so could these States of ours in a league of all. But if disunited, the same rivalry between neighboring Confederacies, will be here again witnessed, that gave an opportunity to Philip of Macedon to intrigue and subvert one after another of the Grecian Unions. The monarchs of Europe can then have an excuse to interfere in our affairs, and will keep us eternally by the ears; large armies and navies vieing with each other, will be established at immense expense, and to the great danger of civil liberty; and possibly within a century or less, the free institutions we so love and cherish, will have given place to military despotisms. In the sequel we hope to show from eminent authorities, and particularly from our experience under Washington's last Administration and that of the elder Adams,[1] that a Representative system is not adapted to cope with Monarchies in the intrigues and corruption of diplomacy. Our only safety lies in strict adherence to the Monroe doctrine, keeping clear of European entanglements, which will surely be abandoned when rival Confederacies are instituted. The man is a fool, who imagines that two or more neighboring Confederacies will cherish and promote each other's interests. The jealousy and hate will be intense and well reciprocated. All the injury will be done, all the favors withheld, that are possible to neighboring enemies. The ancient animosity between England and America will be as nothing to what we shall see here; and while separation by a wide ocean has aided to remove the former, between the North and South occasions of difficulty must constantly arise, and the bitterness already engendered by this deplorable war, will grow with our growth, and strengthen with our strength.

Like results to be expected here.

Division brings foreign intrigue.

Republics not adapted to corrupt diplomacy.

Monroe doctrine to be adhered to.

Adjacent Republics rivals.

Hate between North and South.

Disunion not to be tolerated.

We cannot, must not, tolerate disunion. Sincerest friendship for the South alone, our friends there will see, should make us fight against disunion. We in the West are, and will be true friends to the South in this contest. We will fight for years to save them from the wretchedness of disunion, from the imperilling of these our glorious institutions, which their fathers and ours established. The earth was enriched by the blood of patriots shed less than a century ago, to obtain freedom and independence, that Union might here be formed to perpetuate these free institutions; let the blood of the grandsons and great-grandsons of those patriots, flow still more freely on these same ensanguined fields and many

The West true to the South.

The fathers fought for Union—

—let the descendants do so.

Gibbs' *History of Washington and Adams Administrations.*

[1] The valuable history of those Administrations by Mr. Gibbs, should be studied thoroughly by patriotic statesmen in this perilous period of dissolution, and everything that will aid to show us the danger of divisions, and the certain and great evils to result from rival Confederacies.

others, to keep from jeopardy our priceless inheritance. Talk not to the West of peace and disunion.

§ 14. To the South: as to the Nature of this War.

Occasion for the South and North to examine International Law.

Surely is there ample occasion both in the South and in the North, to study into those "*Laws of Nature and of Nature's* God," to establish the right to which for these States, our fathers jointly pledged their lives, their fortunes, and their sacred honor. Honorable men were they, and never were those "Laws" dishonored by them. If we, their sons, because of the unexampled benefits resulting to us from their faithful practice of those "Laws," have become so engaged in our individual concerns, as to have neglected our duties to the State; have lost sight of the dignity, the majesty of Sovereignty, *the Right of Command*, in the possession of free Peoples; have even become so ignorant of those "Laws" themselves, as that it is a wonder of wonders, how they have been so well practised; is it not high time we resorted to the fountain of instruction, and drew deep draughts from the "Laws of Nature and of Nature's God?" Well will it be for us both in the South and in the North, to study them thoroughly, and know our mutual rights and wrongs. Our rights, it will be easy for us to learn; let us not neglect our wrongs, which on both sides will be found grievous. Yet, having resulted chiefly from ignorance and misconception of clear, well-established principles, it will be comparatively an easy task to retrace our steps, particularly for the South. We shall return to the blissful fields of Fœderalism, in which "the stateliness of houses, the goodliness of trees," so "delighteth the eye," because resting upon "that foundation," "that root," the South have so much more correctly appreciated than the North, State Sovereignty. Honor enough is it for the South, even by war, to have saved us from the wretchedness of consolidation, we have been so earnestly seeking.

South and North to learn our mutual rights and wrongs.

To retrace our steps easy, particularly for the South—

—we return to Federalism.

May the enlightening influences of the Holy Ghost be imparted to us in rich measure, both in the South and in the North, as with our darkened understandings, we endeavor to learn what right and duty require of us as individuals and as States! Surely no obstinate determination to adhere to wrong, no malicious hate or desire to injure, will interfere with peace and reconciliation, when once an opportunity has been afforded to examine thoroughly and justly our mutual rights and wrongs, our duties to God and country. Honest, candid, honorable parties as these States have ever been, when our wise men in the South and in the North, with our true friends in Europe, shall have well considered the rights of these States, in connexion with "*the Laws of Nature and of Nature's* God," we of the North will cheerfully assent to the surrender of that to which the South is fairly entitled; and if the South finds she has claimed more than belongs to her Sovereignties by those "Laws," she will no longer insist thereon; if she finds herself in an *unjust, offensive* war, speedily will she cease that war.

An invocation, to which Christians will respond.

Evil influences will not prevent peace and reconciliation.

These States honorable.

The North will abide by International Law—so will the South.

May our God of mercy and of wisdom, teach us, His children, in both sections; show to us our duty, and give us hearts to do it.

God grant success!

§ 15. Disunion endangers State Citizenship.

§ 15.—Disunion endangers State Citizenship.

Citizens! *fellow* Citizens of the South and of the North! we little know the worth of our free institutions that are jeopardized by disunion and civil war. We are Citizens of these States, nations,—yea, these Commonwealths, known by their respective names of New York, South Carolina; Virginia, Ohio; Maine and California, and so on, numbering still four-and-thirty, for I deny that Virginia is legally divided and made into two States. Each one of these Commonwealths, by the favor of the Almighty King of nations, is a Sovereign, free and independent State, the peer of earth's mightiest empires. A high dignity, is it, too lightly estimated, to possess Citizenship in one of these free States. Let us consider in short, what it is to be a Citizen in one of these Commonwealths, to be fellow Citizens of States United and Confederated.

State Citizenship—

—what is it?

The origin of States unknown.

Of the origin of States we have no knowledge. Even the Mosaic record, the oldest concerning our race, gives no information on this interesting topic.

Nimrod's kingdom the earliest known in history.

Gen. x: 8–12.

Cush begat Nimrod: he began to be a mighty one in the earth. He was a mighty hunter before the Lord: wherefore it is said, Even as Nimrod the mighty hunter before the Lord. And the beginning of his kingdom was Babel, and Erech, and Accad, and Calneh, in the land of Shinar. Out of that land went forth Asshur, and builded Nineveh, and the city Rehoboth, and Calah, and Resen between Nineveh and Calah: the same *is* a great city.

Monarchy therefore regarded the form chosen of God.

That is a mistake.

Thus incidentally and summarily is the important fact announced of States being organized, and that Monarchs had begun to rule, for Nimrod had "his kingdom." From this it is argued that Monarchy, being the most ancient form of Government of which we are informed, was probably that originally instituted by God. However that may be, it certainly was not the form He selected for favored Israel.

No knowledge of the rise of Sovereignty.

Instruction of his creatures by Deity seems reasonable.

We have no knowledge, either, whether the Creator gave directly to any man, or any set of men, the right of exercising authority over his or their fellows. We are compelled to rely upon reason and common sense concerning this interesting question, which we have not found better discussed than by Pufendorf. It would seem reasonable that in the beginning of our race, they should have had instruction in Government, and that where all were naturally equal, the Sovereign Ruler should have deputized some of his creatures with authority to control the wayward; for though all were inclined to wrong doing, and to advance their selfish schemes, some were worse than others, and must be governed, and some were better than others and suitable for governors. Probably the beginning of this Sovereign Power—of this *Right of Command*—was by express instruction and gift from the Infinite Source of all Sovereignty

Sovereignty probably granted by God.

If not, still, of Divine origin

But if Deity did not grant Sovereignty directly from Himself, it may nevertheless be regarded, as argued by Pufendorf, of origin Divine. What is necessary to the creature from his very nature, and what that creature is permitted, encouraged and aided to do, may well be considered the work of nature's Sovereign.

A State being instituted, the Right of Command once generated,—and whether by gift from God direct, or by the concurrence of human wills with His approbation, or by both combined, is not material,—a State and its Sovereignty being once begun, it has continued in one form or another, without intermission. Amid all the fluctuations and changes of the four thousand years since the beneficent sway of Government over man by his fellow, was established or allowed by the Supreme Ruler, have States existed clothed with Supreme Power, and unaccountable to any other authority than that of God Himself.

§ 15. Disunion endangers State Citizenship.

Sovereignty granted in regular succession—

—existence perpetual, accountable only to Deity.

At times States have been divided, others have been united; some have been conquered, others created; some have had the Sovereign Power in the People, some in a Senate, some in a Monarch; yet have they ever continued to exist, deriving their right one from another, and were their histories known, each could be traced back by legitimate birth to the Father of nations. Here, at all events, is a regular succession in the State, whether there be any in the church or not. So wide-spreading, all-controlling has been the *Right of Command* of these States, that it has been over every one of our race, wherever he was born, from his cradle to his grave. Every man, woman, and child is a subject of some State, and ceasing to be a subject of one State, becomes instantaneously a subject of another. He cannot get out of an organized State, into a state of nature. He ever is and must be a subject, except the few that become Sovereigns. No man is nor can be born free.

Changes in States.

Sovereignty over everybody.

Everybody a subject.

No one can get out of a State.

No one born free.

It is further to be observed in explanation of Citizenship, that one of the prerogatives of Sovereignty is to create new bodies. As only Sovereign Power can bring into existence new objects in the realm of nature, so reason and common sense, and the highest authorities in International Law teach, that in the realm of man's dominion, only Sovereign Power can give life to new polities. Our word *body*, is in the Latin *corpus*, from which *corporate* is derived; and in part for this very purpose of creating corporations, has the Sovereign Power existence. If this power be granted to any single member of the state, it creates a *Monarchy*, either *absolute* as in Russia, or *limited* as in the United Kingdom of Great Britain and Ireland; if granted to a select few, as in ancient Venice, and some of the present Swiss States, an *Aristocracy* is created; if preserved in the People, as with us, a *Democracy* is established, which is a *simple* Democracy if People decide questions by their own votes, or *Republican* if the People elect Representatives to act for them, as in our State and Federal Governments. But in either form of Government, only the Sovereign Power speaks into being bodies corporate and politic; an idea of Pufendorf's not well considered by Congress and the Supreme Court in connexion with the United States Bank.

Only Sovereignty creates bodies politic.

The Sovereignty in *one*,

—the *few*,

—the *many*.

Simple Democracy.

Republican Democracy.

Was Pufendorf or Congress right as to the United States Bank?

The monarchs of Europe have granted charters of incorporation to many of their chief cities, the dates of some of which are lost in antiquity; others for various uses, one of the most important of which has proved to be, facilitating Colonial settlements. In the proper exercise

Cities made bodies politic:

—also Colonies.

§15. Disunion endangers State Citizenship.

of the royal prerogative, Elizabeth and succeeding Monarchs of England, granted to certain true and loyal subjects, charters to establish Colonies in their dominions in America, with powers of Government more or less extensive. The individuals participating in the Government of those cities in Europe, or in those English Colonies, as authorized by their respective charters, were Citizens of their several cities or Colonies. But only in a restricted sense can a person be entitled a *Citizen* of the State of England or of Great Britain, as at different dates the mother-land has been entitled, and hence the Colonial charters guaranteed to our fathers all the rights and immunities of free and natural *subjects;* for, though living and even born in America, we were, nevertheless, Englishmen or Britons.

Who are Citizens in those cities and Colonies.

A subject an imperfect Citizen in Britain.

The blunders in International Law that separated us from Britain.

Outrageous blunders being committed in the science of Government, even our King George III, joining with his Ministry and Parliament to put Sovereignty out of the Crown, as in the passage of the Quebec bill, led to unjust encroachments upon our rights as Britons, and our chartered privileges. We resisted the base attempt to change our form of Government from a Monarchy to an Aristocracy, and the tyrannical usurpations of Parliament; rightfully refused to be taxed by that body; assured our king repeatedly of our faithfulness as true liege subjects; had ever borne our part in making free gifts—the pride and honor of Britons—for the support of the Crown, and only shortly before had received back £200,000, that much more than our proportion having been paid by the Colonies in the French and Indian war; entreated our Monarch to stand by his rights and ours; but he, indoctrinated with the heresy that Sovereignty was in his Parliament instead of himself, turned a deaf ear to our prayers; and having, by fourteen months of war, endeavored to subject us to this usurped authority, he forfeited his claims to our allegiance, and we cast off his Sovereignty and took to ourselves the *Right of Supreme Command.* A bright and golden link of justice this, in our chain of Sovereignty, that leads back unbroken and fast to the Eternal Throne.

Our true loyalty.

Driven by war to withdraw allegiance.

Justice of our cause.

We could have become one State—

We could then have constituted ourselves a single State, with a single Sovereignty; but naturally, wisely, and emphatically Providentially, we became thirteen sovereign, free and independent States.

—became 13.

Six Colonies became States before 4th July, 1776.

The impression is generally prevalent that the Colonies were changed to States on the 4th July, 1776. That is a mistake. New Hampshire became a State on the 5th January, 1776, and has the honor of taking the lead in this important work, under the advice of the Continental Congress. South Carolina next adopted a Constitution, the 26th March; Rhode Island withdrew her allegiance from the Crown on the 4th May; Massachusetts on the 1st of May; Virginia adopted her Constitution the 29th June; and New Jersey the 2d July. The documents will be given for these important facts.

Severance conditional, except with Virginia.

All of them, however, I am happy to record, made their State organizations conditional on their being unable to arrange their differences with the mother-land, except Virginia. These Colonies were true to their King, and did not want separation, if it could be avoided. But it having become certain that reconciliation was impossible, in the judgment of the "Old Dominion," which of all the Colonies had been true to the Crown, faithful even when England herself was faithless, she made the separation unconditional and absolute. And it will be observed with interest in reading the documents, that her fundamental law having remained unaltered from the date of adoption till 1830, she continued all that intervening period in the same condition. The Commonwealth she was in 1830, she was on the 29th June, '76, possessed at both dates of the same rights and authority, that pertain to every Sovereign State, notwithstanding she and the other Sovereignties *delegated* to the Federal Agency the *exercise* of part of their Sovereign powers, first by the Constitution of 1781, and still more by the second of '89.

§ 15. Disunion endangers State Citizenship.

Virginia the same State 29th June, 1776, she was in 1830.

Another point will be observed, that has not received the attention desirable, in that New York could not vote in Congress on the 4th July, for the Declaration of Independence, her delegates not having been authorized; and that State did not pass her resolutions of Independence till the 9th July. So that while the *Old Dominion* had been a Commonwealth unconditionally for five days preceding the Continental Declaration of Independence, the Colony that is now the *Empire State*, was for five days after that event, still a part of the State of Great Britain. Such an effort has been made to make our glorious, inestimable Union, something different from what it is, a consolidation of States instead of a Union, that the reader will be glad to see the documents bearing upon the question, brought together for the first time, so that he can judge for himself as to their intent.

New York a part of the British State till 9th July, 1776—

—Virginia a sovereign State ten days earlier.

These facts correct errors as to the nature of our Union.

Although no change is or can be made in the nature of Sovereignty, and subjection can be in no degree lessened, whether existing under the form of a Monarchy, an Aristocracy, or a Democracy, yet is the *exercise* of that Sovereignty, the dignity, happiness and security of the subjects, essentially modified under these different forms. Under the first two, the people have little or no voice in appointing their rulers; in the latter, the whole power is theirs. In the former, the operatives, the machinery of the Government are the servants or agents of the Monarch or of the Senate; in the latter, they are servants or agents of the People; and in each, and all does the Sovereign Power, like the soul operating the limbs of the body, set in motion the various agencies. *To have a voice in the election of these magistrates and other officials is to be a Citizen.*

Though all are subjects to Government, yet quite a difference in forms of Government.

In free States a choice of rulers.

Those choosing rulers are the Citizens.

Nobody is a Citizen of Russia, though he may be of a city of Russia. All are subjects to the unrestricted, absolute sway of the Crown. Their Autocrat may grant rights and privileges to a certain section or city, creating the inhabitants, or a portion of them, into a body politic and corporate for purposes of Government, and with specific rights. Those to whom the power is granted to appoint the rulers of that incorporation, are the Citizens of that city.

Nobody a Citizen of Russia: —though he may be of a city of Russia.

Under the Government of our mother-land, whose admirable system

Partial citizens in Britain.

§ 15. Disunion endangers State Citizenship.

They participate in the legislation.

No taxes without their consent.

of checks and balances stands unequalled in the Monarchial form, and which, the more it is understood, will be the more admired, we see an immense advance in the privileges of Citizenship. Not only in municipal corporations, but in the entire legislation of that powerful State, known by the name of *The United Kingdom of Great Britain and Ireland*, do a large part of the male adult subjects participate. The Monarch is bound by solemn compact, to levy no taxes exept by sanction of Parliament; and by established custom, that has become a law of obligation, all bills of money-grants must originate in that branch of Parliament elected by the people. To be entitled to Citizenship, to exercise the elective franchise in that kingdom, even to this extent, is truly an high privilege. All honor to our mother-land for the great improvements she has made in the science of human Government. Her glory and renown are all our own down to 1776. And she will go on to still higher exaltation. Not yet has the sun of Britain's glory reached its zenith. Wrongs there may yet be, and doubtless are; but when her Monarch, Nobility, and People cut loose from the heresy that Parliament and not the Queen is supreme, the sound sense, good judgment, religious principle of that Christian nation, will bring forth still richer fruits. Far distant be the day when we, the daughters, shall see Britain's sun enter upon its declination.

Britain's honor and glory ours till 1776.

GOD bless and prosper her!

Citizenship had higher privileges in America than in England.

How great they were.

But the Colonial Governments, provincial, proprietary and charter, gave higher privileges of Citizenship to Englishmen in America, than at home. The privileges varied in the different Colonies; but in some, as in Connecticut and Rhode Island, the Citizens elected every officer of their Governments, even the governor and his council, who were considered the special representatives of the Sovereign. The original members, too, of those bodies politic, the Citizens, could admit whom they pleased to Citizenship, making freemen, as they were called; though how any one was made more *free* than he was before, we have not found explained. He was permitted to have a voice in the election of his rulers, an august privilege indeed, but he was none the less ruled and governed. Connecticut continued till 1818 to administer her Government under this charter, as did Rhode Island till 1842, having only made declarations transferring the *Right of Command*, the Sovereignty, from George III to themselves. This was done in Rhode Island on the 4th May, 1776, and in Connecticut in October, 1776.

Connecticut's charter continued till 1818—

—Rhode Island's till 1842: —only allegiance transferred to themselves.

The benefits of Colonial training

The training the colonists experienced, in exercising the rights of Citizenship under the liberal administration of our Sovereigns, down to George III, well prepared them to conduct their affairs independently, when, driven by misjudgment of their Monarch to take the Right of Command into their own keeping, they became Citizens of free States. Great occasion have we to revere and love our mother-land. Much pride as we have taken in our independence, foolishly, falsely as we have boasted of having ourselves effected the Revolution before the war began, when it actually took fourteen months of severe war to drive us into Revolution; we are yet in a state of probation, as present events prove; have yet to

Whether our separation from Britain is advantageous, is yet undecided.

determine, whether the blunders of George III and his Ministry and Parliament, are to be to us a lasting misfortune or a perpetual blessing.

§ 15. Disunion endangers State Citizenship.

We have a father-land as well as mother-land.

But we had not only a mother-land: a father-land is also our rich legacy; which, in some of its States, gave even still higher privileges of Citizenship than those of England. In the Netherlands, the Reformation of the 16th century was signally operative. The emperor Charles V had divided his empire, giving his son Philip II Spain and the Netherlands. Philip had sworn to maintain for the latter all their ancient rights and privileges. Resident in Spain, and a bigoted Catholic, he endeavored, in violation of his oaths, to force on the Dutch Protestants the Catholic religion and the inquisition, of which he was an energetic patron. A long and bloody war ensued, the Hollanders having for a leader the noble William, Prince of Orange, who, as a patriot, more nearly resembled our own illustrious Washington, than probably any other character in history. They cast off their subjection to their tyrant of Spain; and on the 26th July, 1581, declared themselves free and independent States. As our fathers did after them, they adhered to their chartered rights and ancient customs, each province or chartered city becoming a Sovereign State, some being Democratic, others Aristocratic.

The rise of the Netherlands.

Their oppressions by Philip II.

They become free States—

—some Aristocratic, some Democratic.

In the Democratic States, those of the inhabitants who exercised the elective franchise were perfect Citizens, which it is not possible for a man to become in a Monarchy, or in an Aristocracy, however liberal may be the grants of suffrage. If *the Right of Command* be granted to *one*, or to a select *few*, there is a limitation, a control over the suffragans, not known in a Democracy.

Full Citizenship in the Democracies.

The Netherlands remained free till 1795, when, conquered by the French, they were made to understand what "liberty, fraternity, equality" really meant, of which the Dutch, it seems, had been ignorant, notwithstanding their free institutions. Early in the seventeenth century being a land of religious freedom, even beyond that of England, our father-land furnished an asylum to pilgrims from the mother-land; and from Delft did he band sail, famous in poetry and song, to New England's shores, where

The Netherlands subjected to the French.

Their freedom.

> The breaking waves dashed high
> On a stern and rock-bound coast,

as they rolled along on a flat sand beach. The two centuries the Netherlands remained free States, witnessed the spreading of their Colonies in every quarter of the globe. The Colony of New Amsterdam, in particular, became prominent and influential; and though with all their rights in this region surrendered to England in 1674, most of their Citizens continued to reside here under the less freedom of England's Crown. As our history is studied, it becomes apparent, that the example of the States of the Netherlands in free and Federal Government, and the influence of the descendants of those Dutch Citizens among us, in leading these Colonies to become free States, and to make ourselves complete Citizens, has never been understood and appreciated.

Their Colonies.

New Amsterdam.

Conquered by England.

Influence of their example on us

Subjects of the crown of Britain, our fathers were only partial, imper-

§ 15. Disunion endangers State Citizenship.

Citizenship perfect in these States.

Not of one and the same State—

—but of our respective States.

The States separate and distinct.

How, then, are we fellow citizens?

fect Citizens of that State, though Citizens of their towns, counties and Colonies; but taking to themselves the Sovereignty, *the Right of Command*, the suffragans became perfect Citizens of these free and independent States. Such are still we, their sons, by the blessing of Almighty God, yet not of one and the same State, by any means. Most of my readers are Citizens of their respective towns or cities, counties, and States; I, of the city of Chicago, county of Cook, and State of Illinois; and our respective States are as free and independent of each other, as Russia is of France, or it would not be a State, Nation, Commonwealth as it is; and Citizenship is as distinct in our respective American States, as in the European. As merely Citizens of these States respectively, we are not *fellow* Citizens; how is it then you are rightfully addressed as my *fellow citizens?*

§ 16.—Disunion destroys Federal Citizenship.

The answer: the Netherlands are an example.

They unite in a Federal Republic.

Other examples.

Their Union gave strength.

An instructive example—

—a new history of it wanted.

To answer the above query, let us again refer to our father-land. The seven Provinces of the Netherlands, erroneously called States prior to their independence of the Sovereignty of Philip, and then again erroneously continuing to be styled the Seven United Provinces, which means a conquered country, after they became free States; these Provinces in 1579, two years prior to declaring independence, united themselves by a league into a Federal Republic. They had for examples that of the Hebrews; the Amphictyon, Achæan, Lycian, &c., of the Greeks; and for a century and a half the one existing in Switzerland. Those little States, weak, impotent by themselves individually, by their Federal Union, enabled that diminutive portion of Europe, to exercise a powerful and beneficial influence on the whole world for over two centuries. Its rise, progress and fall, about fourteen years after this Federal Republic came into being, affords an instructive lesson that remains yet to be unfolded. When American writers ascertain that the United States have the same Federal system of the Dutch, though improved; and that the great Grotius of Holland published his immortal work in 1625 to straighten out the confusion of words and of ideas with regard to Government, into which the dark ages had brought the world; some of them, instead of making confusion worse confounded, will write an intelligible history of that memorable example of Confederating.

The New England Union, 1643.

The attempt at Albany, 1754.

The influence of the Dutch not appreciated.

The Confederation of the New England Colonies in 1643, that lasted some forty years; the effort after Union at Albany in 1754, both of which will be considered, may have been consequent on our knowledge of the Netherlands, and are instructive to us as proving how well the fathers understood that, by Confederating, separate Peoples could obtain the benefits of Union, and escape the evils of consolidation. The worth of the influence of the father-land in framing our unequalled system of Federal Union, is by no means appreciated.

The Dutch Union two years before independence, ours five after.

Whereas the Dutch formed their compact, two years prior to their Declaration of Independence, ours was not concluded till almost five years after we became free States. Though the Declaration was made by the

Colonial and State delegates as "*by the Representatives of the United States of America in Congress assembled*," and though all were deeply impressed with the necessity of Union, yet must the terms be agreed on before it could be concluded. Maryland refused to give her assent till the surplus territory belonging to several of the States, should be ceded to the States unitedly. This induced Virginia and others, to authorize their delegates to form a Federal Republic with such States as might accede; but on the 2d January, 1781, Virginia passed resolutions of cession of her territory northwest of the Ohio, as New York had already done; and on the 1st March, 1781, the delegates of Maryland affixed their signatures, completing and making obligatory the first Federal compact of these States. The chief object and effect of this instrument was, to give a legal existence to a body politic that had been announced and informally instituted in the Declaration of Independence, and known by the name of *The United States of America.* Though due forms of International Law were not so closely followed as would have been desirable, and as was practised when a new Union was made in 1789; yet has it been considered legal and binding on those Sovereignties by whose joint voice, through their State Legislatures, this body politic was created.

§ 16. Disunion destroys Federal Citizenship.

The obstacles to the completion of our first Federal Union.

Completed 1st March, 1781.

It created the corporation of the United States.

The fourth of the Articles of Confederation recites:

> "The better to secure and perpetuate mutual friendship and intercourse among the people of the different States in this Union, the free inhabitants of each of these States, paupers, vagabonds, and fugitives from justice excepted, shall be entitled to all privileges and immunities of free citizens in the several States; and the people of each State shall have ingress and regress to and from any other State, and shall enjoy therein all the privileges of trade and commerce, subject to the same duties, impositions and restrictions as the inhabitants thereof respectively," &c.

Citizens of one State given equal privileges in the other States.

Articles of Confederation, 4th.

Though a little ambiguous in language, the design was, and it was regarded effective, to give Citizens of one State equal rights in any other State, with the Citizens of that other State. Thus were the privileges of Citizenship extended, and the Citizens of the several Sovereignties, became *Citizens, fellow* Citizens, of their new and duly incorporated body politic of the United States of America.

Thus made fellow citizens.

But this bond of Union proved inadequate to its purpose; and when the dangers and necessities of the Revolutionary war ended with the treaty of peace in 1783, a few years' experience convinced the States that changes must be made. They appointed delegates to a Convention, in whose deliberations for months, partook some of the best patriots, wisest statesmen, the world ever knew, and at their head was our beloved, immortal Washington. The form of new compact was sent to the Confederate Congress, with a request that it be submitted to conventions of delegates duly elected for the purpose in the several States; and experience having taught the impropriety of requiring the assent of every State in order to form the new Union; Rhode Island having been so opposed to the new scheme, that she had even refused to send delegates to the Federal Convention; Luther Martin having declared very positively that Maryland would never sanction it; Yates and Lansing hon-

The first Union insufficient.

Delegates appointed to a Convention in 1787.

Their form of compact submitted to the States.

The assent of all not required to form the new Union.

§ 16. Disunion destroys Federal Citizenship.

estly believing that the majority were bent on consolidation, the certain annihilation of individual State Sovereignty, and having withdrawn from the Convention, declaring that New York would not accede to it, and other States being more or less doubtful, particularly Massachusetts—under these circumstances, the 7th article of the new compact provided that "The Ratification of the Conventions of nine States, shall be sufficient for the Establishment of this Constitution between the States so ratifying the same."

Nine States to establish the Constitution.

Their order of accession to the new Union.

Each State then considered and decided for itself, whether to adhere to the old compact, or join the new. First Delaware broke away from the old Union, the 7th December, 1787; then Pennsylvania, New Jersey, Georgia, Connecticut, Massachusetts, Maryland and South Carolina; and on the 21st June, the new Union was made operative by the accession of New Hampshire, the ninth State. The old Union was repudiated by them, notwithstanding their agreement had been so solemnly made and declared again and again to be "*perpetual.*" Virginia the 26th June, and New York the 26th July, also joined the majority, leaving only North Carolina and Rhode Island to constitute the old body politic of the United States of America.

The old Union broken.

North Carolina and Rhode Island constituted the United States.

The rights of seceding States—of non-seceding.

It is an interesting and important question, whether if these two States, or even Rhode Island alone, had remained a party to the first compact, they or she would not have constituted the body politic of the United States. It would seem that, as in any other corporation, the sole surviving member would have been entitled to all its rights and franchises. Whether with our ideas of the Law of Nations, and the imperfections of humanity incident to the best States as well as families, Rhode Island could have held for herself the rights of the old Union, is quite another subject. Fortunately for the country then, the accession of Rhode Island to the new Union on the 29th May, 1790, saved the raising of the question. But not much longer is it to be dodged. The rights of seceding States; the rights of States in the new Union, which with GOD's blessing is to be formed; the rights of any State, that may remain in the body politic of *The United States of America*, are to be investigated and understood. No subject connected with our Government, in my humble judgment, merits equally with this, the careful consideration, the deep research, of our ablest lawyers and statesmen.

This important question to be met and decided.

The right of Secession.

Were our fathers right in thus breaking pact and faith with sister States, and leaving North Carolina and Rhode Island to shift for themselves? Most unquestionably they did right, though not precisely for all the reasons adduced by John Quincy Adams, who remarks:

J. Q. Adams' views.

ADAMS' *Address, Jubilee of the Constitution*, 1839, p. 66.

Rhode Island and North Carolina still held back. The Union and Washington marched without them. Their right to secede was not contested.[1] No unfriendly step to injure was taken; no irritating measure to provoke them was proposed. The door was left open for them to return, whenever the proud and wayward spirit of State sovereignty[2] should give way to the attractions of clearer-sighted self-interest and

[1] A decidedly cool imputation is that, on the only two States that had *not* seceded.

[2] A very naughty thing, no doubt, yet nevertheless quite essential in free States to the legitimate and necessary control of "proud and wayward" subjects, selfish and corrupt men.

kindred sympathies. In the first acts of Congress they were treated as foreigners, but with reservations to them of the power to resume the national privileges with the national character, and when within two years they did return, without invitation or repulsion, they were received with open arms.

§ 16. Disunion destroys Federal Citizenship.

The questions of secession, or of resistance under State authority, against the execution of the laws of the Union within any State, can never again be presented under circumstances so favorable to the pretensions of the separate State, as they were at the organization of the Constitution of the United States. At that time Rhode Island and North Carolina might justly have pleaded, that their sister States were bound to them by a compact into which they had voluntarily entered, with stipulations that it should undergo no alteration but by unanimous consent. That the Constitution was a confederate Union founded upon principles totally different, and to which not only they were at liberty to refuse their assent, but which all the other States combined, could not without a breach of their own faith establish among themselves, without the free consent of *all* the partners to the prior contract. That the confederation could not otherwise be dissolved, and that by adhering to it, they were only performing their own engagements with good faith, and claiming their own unquestionable rights.[1]

The opportunity in '89 favorable to consider Secession.

What Rhode Island and N. Carolina might have pleaded: —faith broken: —principles of Union changed— —entire unanimity requisite.

The justification of the people of the eleven States, which had adopted the Constitution of the United States, and of that provision of the Constitution itself, which had prescribed that the ratification of nine States should suffice to absolve them from the bonds of the old confederation, and to establish the new Government as between themselves, was found in the *principles* of the Declaration of Independence.[2] The confederation had failed to answer the purposes for which governments are instituted among men. Its powers or its impotence operated to the destruction of those ends, which it is the object of government to promote. The people, therefore—who had made it their own only by their acquiescence[3]—acting under their responsibility to the Supreme Ruler of the universe, absolved themselves from the bonds of the old confederation, and bound themselves by the new and closer ties of the Constitution. In performing

The Declaration of Independence justifies Secession.

The doctrine of *consent.*

[1] Pretty nearly correct, except, "that the Constitution was a Confederate Union, founded upon principles totally different" from that of 1781. Fundamentally, it was the same Federal Union, the chief differences being in dividing the delegated authority among three distinct Agencies, instead of committing it to a single Congressional body; and again, in extending the powers of the Agencies to commerce; and further, in allowing the Federal Agencies to operate more directly upon the individual subjects of the respective State Sovereignties, than had been the case under the first Constitution.

The present Constitution did not change our form of Government.

One would have supposed "the old man eloquent," taking this grand occasion to expatiate on the excellences of State Sovereignty, would never have termed it "the proud and wayward spirit." In exulting language, with thrilling power, he might have been expected to show the unequalled advantages of a Federal Union, composed of sovereign, free and independent States, each of which not only had the right, but was under every moral and legal obligation, to break away from a bad compact, and had the unquestionable right to make a new one, that should better promote its individual good and happiness, by forming "a more perfect Union." Had the *Right of Command* belonged to the whole People of the United States, as *some* persons have believed and affirmed, Rhode Island and North Carolina could have insisted upon preserving the first Confederacy, and a change, however necessary, would have been very difficult, if not altogether impracticable. But for the grand truth that "the proud and wayward spirit of State Sovereignty," had been and was fully possessed by each one of these States, the old Confederation could not have been thus easily and rightly dissolved. Is it not unaccountable, that this wise and excellent patriot should have neglected this opportunity to commend the great wisdom of the fathers?

An opportunity lost to extol State Sovereignty

Consolidation would have retarded the "more perfect Union.

[2] "The principles of the Declaration of Independence," notwithstanding their perversion and misconception, are true and everlasting, perfectly in accordance with International Law and the Bible, as we shall see, the only doubt being as to the intent in using the word "unalienable." We want our European friends to understand that we earnestly maintain them as Adams here well sets them forth; and that only when by impotence, or by tyranny and wrong, a Government fails to accomplish the end of its institution, may it be changed or abolished.

The Declaration of Independence accords with International Law.

[3] A distinct issue will be made on this point. The whole doctrine of acquiescence, of *consent*, has been thoroughly exploded by Dr. Lieber and other authorities. These Sovereignties instituted the first Federal Government, and subordinated their respective subjects to it; and finding it impotent to effect the objects desired, the same Supreme Powers instituted another Government, and made everybody within their respective bounds subject to its authority, whether Citizens or not. None but Citizens could give acquiescence, and they constituted but a small part of the inhabitants of any State.

This doctrine of *consent* to be contested.

§ 16. Disunion destroys Federal Citizenship.

The assent of the majority of the whole people required.

that act, they had felt the duty of obtaining the co-operation to it, of a majority of the whole people, by requiring the concurrence of majorities in nine out of the thirteen States,[1] and they had neither prepared nor proposed any measure of compulsion, to draw the people of any of the possibly dissenting States into the new partnership, against their will. They passed upon the old confederation the same sentence, which they had pronounced in dissolving their connexion with the British nation, and they pledged their faith to each other anew, to a far closer and more intimate connexion.

Rhode Island and N. Carolina could not have objected to Secession.

It is admitted, it was admitted then, that the people of Rhode Island, and of North Carolina, were free to reject the new Constitution; but not that they could justly claim the continuance of the old Confederation. The law of political necessity, expounded by the judgment of the sovereign constituent people, responsible only to God, had abolished that. The people of Rhode Island and of North Carolina, might dissent from the more perfect Union, but they must acquiesce in the necessity of the separation.[2]

A State created to have an absolute power, to promote its best good.

A State, a Nation, a Commonwealth, is created chiefly to bring into existence an authority and power, unaccountable, uncontrollable except by Deity, to promote the general good and best interests of the population within its bounds. While it has no right to trespass upon another State in any shape or manner, except for its own real defence, it is bound to use all legitimate and proper means to advance its own prosperity. Manifestly, a State has no right to make a compact that militates against its general welfare, and one so made is in its nature void or voidable at the will of any party to it, notwithstanding it may be observed. The wise and good men of the Revolution, in the stirring times of war, independence suddenly forced upon them, not having the books and knowledge requisite to frame a Confederation of free States, it is not surprising that their first effort proved a failure; and not only was it their right, but their duty also to break away from a compact so inadequate to accomplish its purposes as was the first.

The first Confederation being imperfect, the States rightfully broke it.

The new Constitution legal:

—makes *fellow* citizens.

Rightfully and legally, then, was the new Constitution ratified, granting a new charter to the body politic of the United States, which contains this clause: "The Citizens of each State shall be entitled to all Privileges and Immunities of Citizens in the several States." This, in more correct language than the first Constitution, makes the Citizens of each of these States, *fellow* Citizens of the States united.

New States admitted to fellow Citizenship.

Allusion has been made to the cession of the territory northwest of the Ohio to the States united, out of which five States have been created, and, by provision of the Federal Compact, admitted into the Federal Union; and the same rights are granted to the new, that belonged to the

---

A majority of the whole people of the U. S. not important in the Ratification.

[1] It was a merely accidental circumstance of not the least consequence, we judge, that by a small amount, the nine smallest States outnumbered the four largest States. The Sovereign Will of Delaware operated with equal power in establishing over its subjects the new Federal Authority, as did that of New York within its domain.

Adams creates a new sort of State, with different powers, from that of Grotius, &c.

[2] But for the middle sentence, unfortunately interposed, that paragraph would have been an enthymeme that would have delighted Bentham equally with any of Blackstone's. The antecedent and consequent put North Carolina and Rhode Island in an awkward fix, but "the law of political necessity" is inexorable, particularly when "expounded by the judgment of the sovereign constituent people, responsible only to God." It might, however, be asked, if reference be here intended, as is supposed, to the whole "People" of the United States, what sort of a "sovereign constituent people" that can be, of which the individual members are free to adopt or to reject its Constitution? to depart from, or to acquiesce in, a more perfect Union? That is a new organization of a People, and a different sort of Sovereignty, from any Pufendorf describes.

old States. One of these new States is Illinois, of which I have been for thirty years a resident, and for twenty-six years a Citizen. Hence, it is my privilege to enjoy the lofty honor of greeting you as my *fellow Citizens of the United States of America;* the proudest, noblest Citizenship ever known to man.

§ 16. Disunion destroys Federal Citizenship.

—Illinois one of them. We are fellow-Citizens.

§ 17.—Federalism important to protect Citizenship.

But Citizenship is to be valued, not only for the eminent honor of having a voice in the election of our rulers; its worth consists chiefly in the protection it affords. We are in a world of selfishness and wrong, manifest in State action as well as in individual men, and a man or a People that pays due regard to its interests, will make itself safe, so far as it reasonably may, against unjust aggressions from any and every quarter. It is not to give liberty, it is to create a right and power of subjection, that States are instituted; it is not to maintain equality in the social organization, but inequality, that Governments are framed; and the more perfectly is this accomplished, the less oppressed thereby is the faithful subject, the more are the State and its Government to be esteemed and sustained. It is for man fallen, selfish, depraved, that authority must be instituted; and as the authority must be administered by the same erring mortals, it becomes the important problem, as Calhoun well shows, how the *exercise* of this authority can be itself properly regulated. And probably in the sequel, it will appear that by God's kind providence, not by our own wisdom, for we have never comprehended the excellences of our Government, have we been led to frame, by union of State and Federal Agencies, the most perfect system of checks and balances the world ever had.

States are constituted to insure subjection.

Rulers liable to err, and need checks—

—Federalism gives them.

In our growing ignorance, which as thick darkness has settled upon rulers and ruled, we have lost sight of these essentials; and those in authority seem to care very little for the checks in wisdom put upon them. Paul understood this subject of Citizenship and protection, and a little circumstance in his history may well be considered. Arrested by the military authorities of the Empire, in a tumult at Jerusalem, he was given to subordinates, by the chief captain, to examine by scourging. "And as they bound him with thongs, Paul said unto the centurion that stood by, Is it lawful for thee to scourge a man that is a Roman and uncondemned?" The centurion forbears, and going to his captain, says, "Take heed what thou doest, for this man is a Roman." The captain, returning to Paul, inquires, "Art thou a Roman?" He said, "yea." "With a great sum," said the captain, "obtained I this freedom;" and Paul, with that dignity which must have pertained to the great Apostle of the Gentiles, observes, "but I was *free* born." Far off in the Roman province of Judea, the despised Christian, who enjoyed the privilege of Citizenship of Rome, was sure of the protection of its Government. The military, even in that military State, and not in the days of the Commonwealth, when the high privileges of Citizenship were far more perfectly en-

Our ignorance of them.

Paul understood Roman Citizenship.

Acts xxii, 25.

The protection Rome gave its Citizens.

§ 17. Federalism important to protect Citizenship.

Our system more perfect than Rome's—

—yet Citizenship outraged.

joyed, but after several Emperors had for half a century possessed the sovereign power, was wholly subordinate to the civil authority. With a much more perfect system of checks on a wrong exercise of power than Rome ever knew, it will not be one of the least interesting and important subjects to consider, how it is that our fellow Citizens of the United States, instead of being protected by their Federal Government, are most infamously outraged in their most sacred rights. When corrected in our *theories* as to Government and Sovereignty, such insufferable blunders and wrongs as we now patiently endure, will be neither tolerated nor committed.[1]

Habeas Corpus. President Lincoln's correspondence with the Albanians.

It is not Federalism, but its desertion that causes these blunders.

Wait a little to see the excellences of Federalism.

[1] The subject of this Section, "Federalism important to protect Citizenship," is one of the most interesting to be considered, and the appearance of the correspondence between the President and the Albanians, causes regret that more space cannot be here allotted. The lamentable occurrences, however, under the present Administration, do not at all disprove the claims made in behalf of Federalism. It is not Federalism, but its desertion, that leads to these wrongs, and the differences of opinion concerning them; and let the sufferer wait patiently till time and opportunity shall enable our Citizens to reach the deserters of Federalism through the ballot box, and through the courts of justice instituted to take cognizance of, and rectify the wrongs and injustice of any inconsiderate or base subject, who should dare to usurp the prerogatives of Sovereignty, by acting contrary to the letter of his authority, the Constitution, and we shall then be able to judge of the real worth of Federalism.

Albanians talk of "civil war," the President of "rebellion."

Habeas Corpus discussed in Part III.

The difference between Monarchy and a free State.

This correspondence shows more than ever the necessity of recurring to elementary principles. The Albanians speak of "a civil war," and the President affirms that they admit it to be "a rebellion;" and basing his argument on this mistaken hypothesis, does he go on to argue his right to suspend the writ of *habeas corpus*, &c. Though space cannot be taken to do justice to this great subject of *habeas corpus*, which will be at length considered in Part III, *Wrongs by the North*, in connection with the views of Mr. Binney, Professor Parker and others, it may be well in this compend to intimate a little of what would seem to be the result of abandoning the teachings of Locke and of Blackstone, and adopting those of Hooker, Grotius, and Vattel. It will serve, in a measure, to discover the difference between the *exercise* of Sovereignty, the *Right of Command*, by a Monarch, and by free Peoples.

In Britain the subject owes allegiance, the Monarch protection.

Grotius i, c. 3, § 20.

King above law.

Though the King does no wrong, his agents do.

Sometimes arrest improperly.

King inquires why, by *Habeas Corpus.*

Endeavors of Charles I to secure his subjects.

The subject in Britain, from the highest prince to the lowest beggar, owes allegiance to his Monarch; the Monarch owes protection to his faithful subjects. These obligations are reciprocal. The King can do no wrong, being above the law, as Grotius proves, quoting St. Hierom and St. Ambrose, who refer to David's penitential Psalm where he says, "Against Thee, Thee only, have I sinned, and done *this* evil in Thy sight." Says St. Ambrose, "David was a King, and so subject to no Laws; for Kings are free from those shackles, wherewith their subjects' crimes do entangle them; they fear no punishments, being secured by the power of the Empire." And Grotius adds: "To man therefore he sinned not, because to him he was not accountable for his actions." But though the King could do no wrong, he could not personally attend to every affair of Government, and must appoint subordinates to aid him. These might do wrong, sometimes make improper arrests, and the King, the faithful guardian of his faithful liege subjects, in order to save from unjust imprisonment, granted to all indiscriminately "the privilege of the writ of *Habeas Corpus*." The *theory* of this is, that the King, properly jealous of his subjects' rights, believing them to be innocent till they are proved guilty, issues in his own name, by his Judges appointed for the purpose, his command to bring the body of his faithful subject before a Court, to inquire wherefore his precious liberty had been infringed. If no adequate cause be found for his arrest and imprisonment, he is discharged; and in all but capital offences, admitted to bail, even if probable guilt be discovered. Charles I, in order to secure these privileges, granted to his faithful subjects the *Petition of Right;* and there being a corrupt court known as the Star Chamber, that by some adverse influences or other prevented the subjects from properly exercising "the privilege of the writ of *habeas corpus*," that was abolished by the king with the advice of Parliament.

Charles II, *Habeas Corpus Act*, 1679.

It being still found, that notwithstanding the admirable *theory*, somehow or other in *practice*, subjects did get into limbo unjustly, the Lords and Commons in Parliament assembled in 1679, prevailed upon that pattern monarch, "the King's most Excellent Majesty," Charles II, to pass that celebrated act entitled, "*An act for the better securing the Liberty of the Subject, and for the Prevention of Imprisonments beyond the Seas.*" It recites:

Statutes at Large, vol. iii, p. 374.

"Whereas great delays have been used by Sheriffs, Gaolers, and other Officers, to whose Custody any of the King's Subjects have been committed for criminal or supposed criminal Matters, in making Returns of Writs of *Habeas Corpus* to them directed, by standing out an *Alias* and *Pluries Habeas Corpus*, and sometimes more, and by other shifts to avoid their yielding Obedience to such Writs, contrary to their Duty and the known Laws of the Land, whereby many of the King's Subjects have been, and hereafter may be long detained in Prison, in such cases where by law they are Bailable, to their great Charges and Vexation:

"II. For the Prevention whereof, and the more speedy relief of all Persons imprisoned for any such criminal or supposed criminal Matters; *be it enacted by the King's most Excellent Majesty*, by and with the Advice and Consent of the Lords Spiritual and Temporal, and Commons, in this

§ 17. Federalism important to protect Citizenship.

A Citizen, too, wants strength in his State, or in its alliance offensive and defensive, to preserve it against dangers from foreign States. A trifling inducement is it for a worthy man, whether poor or rich, to become a Citizen of an insignificant Commonwealth, for the meagre honor of electing rulers, who would have no ability to defend the State and its Citizens against aggressions of other States. Selfish as are individual men, so are the States of earth, and every one of them is liable to encroachment and wrong; and no authority being constituted to judge between nations generally, it often becomes necessary to resort to the *ultima ratio regum*, the last reasoning of Kings, to maintain their rights. John

Strength in a State increases the protection of Citizens.

States liable to err.

Force sometimes required.

---

present Parliament assembled, and by the Authority thereof [and it goes on to provide that upon the writ of *habeas corpus*, a trial shall be had in three days], unless the Commitment aforesaid were for Treason or Felony, plainly and specially expressed in the warrant of Commitment, [&c. and section x. provided that if any of the rascally subjects of his excellent Majesty, Judges, Barons, &c., should dare to refuse to grant this prerogative writ], they should severally forfeit to the prisoner or party grieved the sum of £500."

Hallam states that in the reign of Charles I, five knights were arrested for refusing to submit to forced loans to the king, who sued out writs of *habeas corpus*, to which returns were made that the parties "were detained by a warrant from the privy council, informing him of no particular cause of imprisonment, but that they were committed by the special command of his majesty." "The fundamental immunity of English subjects from arbitrary detention, had never before been so fully canvassed; and it is to the discussion which arose out of the case of these five gentlemen that we owe its continued assertion by parliament, and its ultimate establishment in full practical efficacy by the statute of Charles II."

HALLAM'S account of the occasion of this act.

Constitutional History, i, 320.

Prior to that act, it appears that practice under the writ varied, but when the King graciously enacted that his judges and officers should do precisely so and so for the protection of his faithful subjects, those officials must obey; and the proceedings in the case of *habeas corpus* having at length taken the form of a statute, the King himself could not thereafter alter them or interfere with their operation, because it had become the established custom that laws should not be altered or suspended without the assent of the Lords and Commons. Hence it is that only by the concurrence of Parliament, can "the privilege of the writ of Habeas Corpus" be suspended; nor is the Sovereignty of the Crown at all impaired by this constraint, because it is supposed to be, as Vattel styles it, "an engagement into which he has very willingly entered," it being for the best good of his kingdom.

How this Act afforded security.

Laws only altered by consent of Parliament.

Now these Sovereign Peoples of ours are even more jealous of the liberties of their subjects, than ever were our English Monarchs. They have to employ officers for the protection of their own Majesties, and also for the defence of their loyal subjects; but these judges and gaolers, like those of England, may do wrong, and innocent men may get into custody. Therefore the prerogative writ of *habeas corpus*, is equally necessary here as there. "The *privilege* of the writ of *habeas corpus*," has come to be one of our natural rights as Anglo-Saxons, in the enjoyment of which our Sovereignties desired to protect us; and as in these Republican Democracies the *Right of Command* is of necessity altogether exercised by agents, it has been arranged that the mode of obtaining and administering justice by means of this great writ, should be controlled by fundamental laws, called Constitutions, and by statute laws enacted by the Legislatures. Though it be a natural right to have "the privilege" of this writ, yet the mode of its exercise depends altogether on the laws; and wherever the Legislative power resides to pass the original law, either fundamental or statute, there is to be found the authority to alter, to suspend, or to abrogate that law.

Our Sovereignties equally jealous for their subjects.

Habeas Corpus a necessary safeguard.

Its "privilege" regulated by law.

In creating the Federal Legislature, authority is given it upon various subjects, and section 8 concludes: "To make all Laws which shall be necessary and proper for carrying into Execution the foregoing Powers, and all other Powers vested by this Constitution in the Government of the United States or in any Department or Officer thereof." The writ of *habeas corpus* was of course "necessary" to any Government of Anglo-Saxons, and yet the Federal Agency being one of strictly limited powers, it might have been doubtful whether the right to issue this prerogative writ had been delegated to this Agency, but for the second clause of the ensuing section of the Constitution, which in great wisdom puts a check upon Congress in the exercise of its legislative powers enumerated in the previous section, one of which is, "The Privilege of the Writ of Habeas Corpus shall not be suspended, unless when in cases of Rebellion or Invasion the public Safety may require it." Thus negatively is the right of Congress recognized to pass laws to regulate the process of this writ, otherwise it could never have had power to "suspend;" and so properly jealous are these Sovereignties of preserving to their loyal subjects "the privilege of the writ," they declared positively that it "shall *not* be suspended, unless when in Cases of Rebellion or Invasion the public Safety may require it."

The *Federal Constitution*, Art. i, § 8,

—authorizes the control by Congress of the "privilege,"

—in cases of rebellion.

Who would ever imagine that Anglo-Saxons of talent and learned in the law, would argue, that this great safeguard of liberty, "the Privilege of the Writ of *habeas corpus*," rested upon the doubt whether a great or little "Rebellion" existed in the State or not? "In cases of Rebellion or

A quere.

§ 17. Federalism important to protect Citizenship. A strong State then desirable. Quincy Adams thought force constituted the chief element in International Law; and without doubt, with us, who so much better understand and employ *practice* than *theory*, strength will be duly estimated. When brute force is requisite, Citizenship in a powerful State or Federal Union is preëminently desirable, for the more powerful the Government, the less its liability to encroachment. The strength of Britain. What an honor, what a security, to be even an imperfect Citizen of our mother-land, in order to be protected by a "power which," in the language of New-England's great statesman, "has dotted over the surface of the whole globe, with her possessions and military posts, whose morning drum-beat, following the sun, and keeping company with the hours, circles the earth with one continuous and unbroken strain of the martial airs of England." We might have had her protection. But for the confusion of terms and ignorance of governmental principles, which are nevertheless clear as the light, and straight as an arrow, the power of these States would still have been Britain's, and we should indeed have had safety. Can we provide protection. Are we able independently to secure adequate protection? Though we have gone successfully through two wars with even Britain herself, yet was it as the United States; it remains yet to prove our capacity to keep these States united; or, if disunited, that we have ability to attack and defend.

See p. 73. Protection of Citizenship in Greece, Rome, and France. Very important in this connection are the examples, already referred to, of Greece, Rome, and France. The first exhibits the power of small States to protect each other and their individual subjects, when united in a Federal league; the two latter, strikingly exemplify the danger to which Citizenship is exposed, when protected only in a single Republic.

The "privilege" *may* be suspended, if necessary. Invasion," and when "the public Safety *may* require," then "the Privilege" *may* be suspended. That is the fair construction. In a little "rebellion" it would not be necessary, and will the wise men of this generation undertake to affirm that the fathers were such simpletons as to deprive themselves and posterity of "the privilege" of this writ in the event of a little rebellion? Their language is singular if they so intended.

Somebody must suspend it. Then if it be not "suspended," in the event of any rebellion of however small degree, *ipso jure*, by the law itself, some party must have the power of deciding when the case of rebellion or invasion reaches such degree that "the public safety *may* require" the temporary suspension of "the privilege of the writ." Only the party that can pass the law can suspend it. Some party, too, must be authorized to "suspend" "the privilege." "The privilege of the writ" is universal, regulated and controlled by public and general laws, and unless there were a provision in the law itself providing for its suspension by some authorized party, in certain emergencies, of course another law must be passed to suspend "the privilege," as well as to make any other alteration. King of Britain cannot suspend *Habeas Corpus*. This is the *theory* and the *practice* in Britain, and their security in the enjoyment of "the privilege" of this prerogative writ, rests in the fact, that they have now the right regulated by statute law, which not even the King can "suspend" without sanction of Parliament.

These Peoples have no King—meant to have none. But these free Peoples had no King to interfere with them in "the privilege of the writ of *habeas corpus*," or in any other "privilege" or right; and what is more, they took good care to guard against the possibility of being ruled by the one-man power, their special abhorrence; and in the whole Federal Constitution, is no clause that so effectually protects them against that evil, This *Habeas Corpus* writ a protection. as this negative provision concerning the *habeas corpus* writ. It is well understood, of course, that in this country, where authority is so distinctly distributed to the various Agencies, each Department is strictly confined to its own province, and here this negative provision is found in Each Department restricted. its appropriate place among the restrictions placed upon Congress. Who of the patriots of '87 to '89 could have ever imagined that, in less than a century, the whole nature and genius of our institutions would be so misunderstood and perverted, as that the President of the United States would even dare to suspend "the privilege of the writ of *habeas corpus*"? Could anything human Our ignorance of principles would, if possible, raise the dead. move the dead, Bostonians would be started out of their lethargy, by the bones of Samuel Adams, Parsons, Sumner, and the other patriots stalking about the old church in Long Lane, where they ratified the present Constitution, and then significantly changed the name of the street to FEDERAL. And so all over the land would the fathers rise from their graves in astonishment, at the degeneracy of their sons.

In Rome, the grandest, best-balanced single Republic ever instituted, was the Commonwealth overthrown by Julius Cæsar, and then by his nephew Octavius, and so entirely were the liberties of the Citizens subjected, that in less than a century, Nero was able to establish his despotism. And the obliteration of the provincial divisions of France, its complete consolidation of the separate organizations which might easily have been created into single States, and then have been united in a Federal Republic, seems unquestionably to have been the occasion of the destruction of Citizenship in that Republic. Disregarding the wisdom of their own Montesquieu, they annihilated their only safety, the provincial divisions; and their boastful title, "The Republic one and indivisible," they seem to have taken special delight to contrast, in vaunting arrogance, with the miserable division of this Republic into separate States. The wonderful wisdom of the great and good Necker, who in 1791 so correctly investigated our Federal system, and predicted the ruin of France, will strengthen our confidence in Federalism to preserve Citizenship; Lacroix will furnish us with much wise counsel, and even his errors and misconceptions will be serviceable; and the genius of De Tocqueville will supply still more valuable instruction, the result of the most thorough, philosophic examination into the genius of our institutions that has been made, and that, too, when their excellence had been tested by half a century of practice.

§ 17. Federalism important to protect Citizenship.

In Rome, easily destroyed.

Also in France.

The folly of France in disregarding Montesquieu's wisdom.

Necker, Lacroix, and De Tocqueville will teach us the value of Federalism to protect Citizenship.

When these topics shall have been well considered, particularly the example of Greece, and the wisdom of Aristotle in desiring the Union of all Greece in a polity of polities, then, and not till then, shall we be prepared to appreciate the wisdom of the fathers, in providing to admit State upon State into our Federal Union. Then can we see how wise, necessary, providential, was the Louisiana purchase, stretching from the sources of the Mississippi to its mouth, and westward to the Pacific. The annexation of Texas will have been proved judicious and Constitutional, the acquisitions from Mexico eminently desirable, all of which only foreshadow the ultimate extension of our Federal Union to the Isthmus, and to the West Indies.

A large Federal Union desirable.

Wisdom of the Louisiana purchase—

—of annexing Texas and parts of Mexico—

—further extent South.

A fair and candid examination of these topics will discover, it is believed, that not only have these States rights, in the States formed out of their common territory, not only possess the ordinary rights of Citizenship, as of free navigation, free trade, &c., but more important still, the right possessed by each and all, to the protection of Citizenship which the Union of all these States affords. Already, while the war to accomplish the first scission is at its height, do we see the attempts of a sister Confederacy to weaken its rival by division; and they will certainly be pursued and accomplished soon after the first separation is fully made. And is the South a unit? What are the threats of Texas? What mean the efforts there, to give the Lone Star again a separate existence in the political firmament? Are there no threats nor fears of further scission elsewhere?

The States have not only their common rights in these territories, but to the protection of the Union.

Attempts already to divide the North.

Will not the South be divided.

§ 17. Federalism important to protect Citizenship.

The benefits Union has given us as Citizens.

Prospering in this Union as have no other Peoples of which we have record; higher privileges of Citizenship enjoyed than any other free States ever gave; the Federal Union increased and strengthened, till it has become the equal of our strongest rivals; security afforded to our privileges of Citizenship against domestic faction, against foreign aggression, superior to any governmental system before devised; here are we, in the very height of our prosperity, endangering, many endeavoring to destroy, these priceless privileges. No longer are we fellow Citizens of Virginia, Louisiana, and the other seceded States. Not only endeavoring to deprive us of our rights in those States; the value of Citizenship in this Federal Union is largely diminished by the withdrawal of so powerful a part of these States: and division once permanently accomplished, it stops not till various rival Confederacies spring into existence, and the wars and destruction of Greece will be reënacted in America. Against these evils Providence has led us to interpose a safeguard, that may yet be found effective. If the Southeastern States have an unrestricted right of Secession, the Southwestern, it would seem, have not. They cannot withdraw from the Union without destroying invaluable rights, a destruction that the North, and especially the West, will never endure if we can help it. The privilege of being fellow Citizens of the Mississippi States below us, we shall never surrender until we are subjugated, or till the war assumes a very different aspect. Some of those States have actually seceded and joined another Confederacy without our consent. They are endeavoring to take from us our rights by war and conquest. If they have the power, we shall be despoiled; but trusting in the God of justice, we do not believe it is His will that this wrong should be done us; that this experiment in free Government, after the pattern given by Deity to His ancient People, should be jeopardized by disunion.

No longer are we fellow Citizens in all the States.

Value of Citizenship diminished.

A possible safeguard against the wrong.

Secession of Southwestern States destroys our rights—

—not willingly to be yielded.

§ 18.—Motives and Ways to Peace and a new Federal Union.

Rights jeopardized by war.

But with right on our side, and everything to encourage us in this conflict, when once we understand the theory of our rights, and the nature of this war, the issue is still uncertain. *Inter arma silent leges:* in war the laws slumber, and expose us to be despoiled of our rights. Foreign nations may interfere. Thus far the good and prudent conduct of our foreign affairs, has enabled us to preserve neutrality with other Powers, and no reason to apprehend a change is perceptible. Yet may we not rely upon the future. It is all uncertain; the changes are unknown, and we are ignorant of the period of their approach. With us in the West, foreign interference would work no change of purpose. We should still be true to the cause of justice and defence, and steadily wage the war for Union. But would it be so with the East? With their sea-ports exposed, commerce in jeopardy; with the Abolitionists seeking disunion, the peace Democrats an end of hostilities, how long could the West expect the war to be effectively prosecuted by the East?

Possibility of foreign interference.

Future uncertain.

The West would persevere.

Would the East?

We are mainly from the East, and the practical common-sense we have inherited, has not been largely diminished amid our cosmopolitan associations on the broad prairies, big rivers, and great lakes of the West. We look at things as they are, understand the imperfections of humanity, subscribe to the teachings of Pufendorf, that interest alone will govern these States. We therefore watch with painful solicitude the progress of events, and no section of the Union will hail with equal joy the first glimmering rays of honorable peace, as will the West.

§ 18. Motives and ways to Peace and a new Union.

The West desirous of honorable peace.

Brethren of the South! alien enemies that you are, yet brethren still, dear and well-beloved! when you are tired of this war, shall understand that we have taken from you practical lessons in this doctrine of State rights, that we have pluck enough to fight for these rights till you cease your endeavors to dispossess us; when tiring of "the image of the beast," the use of "force," you seek "reason" which has "more of the image of GOD,"—oh, how shall we welcome the change! We cannot speak peace to you, but most heartily shall we listen and respond to the sweet tones from you. We shall be with you, too, to form a new Union upon the Federal basis that shall not be liable to consolidation. It shall be reared firmer than ever on the solid basis of State rights.

The West cannot speak peace, but will be glad to have the South do so—

—desires a true Federal Union.

Yet speak I not by authority for the North; nay, not even for the West. In this case unquestionably "the wish is father to the thought." A humble private Citizen, I only give expression to individual hopes and expectations produced by two and a half short years of earnest, never-wearying study into the principles of Government, in their application to our country. But bringing together important documents and facts, quoting the words of wisdom from our own sages and those of other lands, there seems to be some ground of trust that this humble effort will start a series of investigations which, pursued by competent writers, will develop anew the excellences of our Federal System. When that shall be done, we shall be a united band of *Federal Republicans*, even our Abolitionists being earnest supporters of State Sovereignty, the only power we can ever hope to have, whereby what they regard as the plague-spot on humanity, is to be removed.

The writer speaks not by authority.

He only starts investigations that able men must prosecute, which will unite us as Federal Republicans.

But if over-sanguine in these hopes, if consolidation is still the desire of some, and if, on the part of others, no Union is to be formed with slaveholders, we want to know it. This can only be ascertained with precision by a Convention; and when our able statesmen and politico-economists shall have enlightened the public mind, an expression of opinion must be had as to whether we are for a reconstruction of our Union or not, and what the terms. The old compact is broken, and we shall find Webster declared a fearful truth, when he said, "A compact broken on one side, is broken on all sides." A new compact is to be made, a new Union formed, as was done in 1787 to '89. May equal wisdom, patriotism, conciliation now prevail, as then gave reunion.

The line to be drawn between Federalists and Consolidists.

A convention required.

The old Union broken—

a new one to be made.

Eminently proper is it that the old States of the East, to which the younger sisters have looked for counsel and instruction, and whose teach-

The old States to take the lead—

§ 18. Motives and ways to Peace and a new Union. —to correct their errors. Proper in Massachusetts— —New Hampshire— —Connecticut— —New York— —Pennsylvania— —Maryland— —R. Island— —N. Jersey— —Delaware.

ings have mainly led to the present condition of Federal affairs, if they find upon examination their teachings to have been wrong; very proper is it that they should lead in the effort to correct these errors. The Commonwealth of Massachusetts, that has so often and plainly affirmed her rights as a sovereign, free, and independent State; New Hampshire, that occupies the distinguished position of having first thrown off her Colonial dependence, and placed herself in the rank of sovereign nations; Connecticut, which so richly values the memories of her Johnson, Sherman, Ellsworth, and in large degree, because of their faithfulness in protecting their State Sovereignty from encroachment; New York, whose prudent and guarded form of accession, and her subsequent acts, so strongly bespeak her dread of consolidation; Pennsylvania, whose wise and judicious Wilson aided so effectually to establish Federal principles, and whose *Law Lectures* clearly demonstrate the Federal nature of our Government; Maryland, whose Luther Martin has given undying renown to the determination of that State to maintain its Sovereignty, freedom, and independence; plucky Rhode Island, which came last into the Union, when after two years' consideration she found it could be done without consolidation, and yet with most guarded resolutions to protect her Sovereignty, equally as precious to her as to the *Empire State* or the *Old Dominion;* New Jersey, which battled so manfully in the Convention of '87 for State rights; and little Delaware, the first State to ratify the present Constitution; meet is it, if these Commonwealths have the determination of the fathers, that each shall continue sovereign, free, and independent, that they take the lead in making the important declaration. The great teachers in Law and Government, coming chiefly from these Eastern States, are in conflict with the fathers, and seem to be with the old authorities also, and it is quite time to decide which is to be credited. We in the West, with due respect for our seniors, will wait reasonably for the East to take the lead.

Eastern teachers in conflict with the fathers and old authorities.

The West will not wait long.

But the East must not expect the West to lie by patiently for a long period. The statesmen of the West will soon discover whether this new line of investigation into the causes of our calamities, is worth pursuing, and whither it leads. They will not be many months in ascertaining that, if there be anything in it, the sure result is peace and reunion. When we shall have come to that conviction, the East must act quickly, if it gets the start of the West. We are very *practical* on the prairies. We are making no profit out of this war, however it may be with others. The stopping of our shipments to the South, throws upon the northern routes of transit, all the productions of the West. The owners of our railroads and of our lake vessels, mostly Eastern men, taking advantage of our necessities, have advanced prices of freight, and our farmers get a mere pittance for their produce. We have borne our grievances patiently, and shall so continue, as long as shall be found necessary. But we wish the war to end at the earliest day practicable with honor to our country, and with the preservation of our rights. If we learn that the South desire peace and reunion with us, upon the true

Is not making money by the war.

The East does.

The West will still endure war, but desires peace if consistent with honor and right.

Federal basis of our fathers, we shall not be long in giving our cordial acquiescence to both. **§ 18. Motives and ways to Peace and a new Union.**

We will not be separated from the South. We will fight them just as long as they choose to fight our Government, and endeavor to take away our rights, but with no malice or ill blood; and when they come to reason, we will be with them like brothers to reconstruct a Union indispensable to both of us. New York and Pennsylvania, New Jersey and Delaware, and Maryland, and the Pacific States, and some or all of the New England States, will go with the West and meet the South in convention to form a new Union. They can agree upon terms satisfactory to most or all, and if South Carolina shall refuse to come back, because she cannot be allowed to nullify and secede at will; if any New England State decline a Confederacy which cuts her off forever from interfering with slavery, the new Federal Republic must for a time dispense with their aid, they taking care to pay their quota of preëxisting obligations. **The West and South are not to be disjoined.** **Other States will aid to form a new Union—** **—if some refuse, they can stay out.**

The debt will be heavy, probably reaching five or six thousand millions, when all the costs and charges of this war are paid; but with reunion of most or all the States, and a tax upon exports, to which the South will now assent, having already adopted that improvement in their Constitution, the load will not be burdensome after a few years. This indebtedness will be mostly in our own hands, and with reunion, confidence will be restored; and it will be the best security in the world, in a few years, going up to 20 and 30 per cent. premium and more, and the profit be chiefly our own. When individuals can use capital to better advantage than the interest, will the bonds be sold, and by foreign investments will our cash capital be increased, ere long, two or three thousand millions. The rate of interest will be heavy till the first period of loan expires, when it will be largely reduced, and it is questionable, in view of that, and the greater ability to pay ten to twenty years hence, whether we should attempt at once by direct taxation, to meet all our interest and expenses. The danger of foreign war will have been diminished by this exhibition of our powers, and the probability of considerable expenditure for extraordinary purposes will be small, and with great propriety can the debt be made to bear no heavier upon us, than upon the next generation and those following, that will derive benefit even from this war. A sliding scale of duties that Britain has taught us, will be admirable upon our cotton, tobacco, provisions, &c., and save us considerable in taxation. And we have now a debt sufficient to satisfy the most extreme Whig for its protective excellence. That bone of contention the South itself has removed for many years, by the load of debt its war has created. When it may again be presented, the West will be the seat of empire, and its interest will be identical with the agriculture of the South; and whether it shall be expedient to look to imports or exports chiefly for our income, or to both jointly, in the twenty-five or fifty years in which all the revenues possible must be derived from both, the manufacturing interest of America will have become sufficiently established, to defy the **The debt to be heavy.** **A tax on exports.** **Indebtedness to rise in value—** **—will draw foreign capital.** **Interest large.** **Query as to paying it all by taxes.** **A tax on exports will relieve us.** **Protection of home industry is secured.** **The power of the West—its interest identical with the South.** **The South and West to rule.**

§ 18. Motives and ways to Peace and a new Union.

competition of the world. The South as hitherto, till the last three years, will plan and manage our political concerns, and the West will furnish the votes for their adoption.

The cost of this war not a dead loss.

The cost of this war is by no means a waste of funds altogether. Aside from benefits already suggested, we are taught the blessings of Union. All nations are liable to war, and for it should prudently provide.

It teaches Union.

Were we divided, the North and South being rival Republics, we should never aid each other. Jealousy and bitterness would be naturally and powerfully engendered to make us rejoice in each other's injury.

The South know the advantage of diversity of pursuits—

The South never before knew the advantages of a Union, in one section of which manufactures flourish, which in the event of war will enable us with comfort to sustain ourselves;

—also the North.

and we in the North have learned the value of Southern productions as never before understood.

European dependence ascertained.

The necessity of the great nations of Europe, too, to have our productions, has been newly demonstrated, and is to be a safeguard against wrong toward us, a strong bond to keep the peace; and the exhibition of the war power of this young and peaceful Republic, would, if united, command toward us the peace of the world.

Large demand for cotton.

The exhaustion of the markets of cotton and its manufactures, will for years insure a large demand and high prices, despite all foreign efforts to get supplies elsewhere.

The South to prosper—

The slaves in the border States will be put South to raise it, and the payments the Government is to make there for damages, will supply owners with capital to remove them, purchase land, and start plantations.

—also the Northwest and East.

They cannot afford to raise corn and provisions, for cotton and sugar will pay better, and the former the Northwest will furnish; and being exhausted of manufactures, the East will reap a harvest in their supply.

Return of kind feeling—

Many thousands of the energetic men of the North in our armies, will make their homes in the border and cotton States, not only benefiting that section by their numbers and labor, but causing a return of good feeling as the South learn, from intercourse, that they have misapprehended the North.

—and prosperity.

All the channels of commerce will feel the mighty impulse, and each section, with reunion, will have a period of prosperity never before witnessed.

The war will have taught us the excellences of Federalism.

The war, too, will give us new and lasting instruction in the principles of our Government. The confusion into which prosperity has led us, by this conflict will be dissipated, and the excellences and advantages of our State divisions and of Federalism, are to be developed as never hitherto.

Ferguson's views of War and Dissension.

FERGUSON, *History of Civil Society*, p. 32.

In this connection, we must present some views from a pious and true liberty-loving Scotchman, which also confirm the views hereinbefore advanced, as to the desirableness of Federalism; and those of Jefferson, as to the impossibility of avoiding dissension and strife. Says Ferguson, in discussing "the Principles of War and Dissension:"

SOCRATES. Some circumstances indicate amity in man, others enmity.

"THERE are some circumstances in the lot of mankind," says Socrates, "that shew them to be destined to friendship and amity: Those are, their mutual need of each other; their mutual compassion; their sense of mutual benefits; and the pleasures arising in company. There are other circumstances which prompt them to war and dissension; the admiration and the desire which they entertain for the same subjects; their opposite pretensions; and the provocations which they mutually offer in the course of their competitions."

§ 18. Motives and ways to Peace and a new Union.

WHEN we endeavour to apply the maxims of natural justice to the solution of difficult questions, we find that some cases may be supposed, and actually happen, where oppositions take place, and are lawful, prior to any provocation, or act of injustice; that where the safety and preservation of numbers are mutually inconsistent, one party may employ his right of defence, before the other has begun an attack. And when we join with such examples, the instances of mistake, and misunderstanding, to which mankind are exposed, we may be satisfied that war does not always proceed from an intention to injure; and that even the best qualities of men, their candour, as well as their resolution, may operate in the midst of their quarrels.

Difficult to apply maxims of justice, as to right of defence. (Let the North observe this.) The right of preparation for defence. War not always the consequent of malevolence.

THERE is still more to be observed on this subject. Mankind not only find in their condition the sources of variance and dissension; they appear to have in their minds the seeds of animosity, and to embrace the occasions of mutual opposition, with alacrity and pleasure. In the most pacific situation, there are few who have not their enemies, as well as their friends; and who are not pleased with opposing the proceedings of one, as much as with favouring the designs of another. Small and simple tribes, who in their domestic society have the firmest union, are in their state of opposition as separate nations, frequently animated with the most implacable hatred. Among the citizens of Rome, in the early ages of that republic, the name of a foreigner, and that of an enemy, were the same. Among the Greeks, the name of Barbarian, under which that people comprehended every nation that was of a race, and spoke a language, different from their own, became a term of indiscriminate contempt and aversion. Even where no particular claim to superiority is formed, the repugnance to union, the frequent wars, or rather the perpetual hostilities which take place among rude nations and separate clans, discover how much our species is disposed to opposition, as well as to concert.

Man's natural inclination to strife. The best have enemies. Societies naturally conflicting.

LATE discoveries have brought to our knowledge almost every situation in which mankind are placed. We have found them spread over large and extensive continents, where communications are open, and where national confederacy might be easily formed. We have found them in narrower districts, circumscribed by mountains, great rivers, and arms of the sea. They have been found in small islands, where the inhabitants might be easily assembled, and derive an advantage from their union. But in all those situations, alike, they were broke into cantons, and affected a distinction of name and community. The titles of *fellow-citizen* and *countryman*, unopposed to those of *alien* and *foreigner*, to which they refer, would fall into disuse, and lose their meaning. We love individuals on account of personal qualities; but we love our country, as it is a party in the divisions of mankind; and our zeal for its interest, is a predilection in behalf of the side we maintain.

Every situation of man known. They naturally divide.

IN the promiscuous concourse of men, it is sufficient that we have an opportunity of selecting our company. We turn away from those who do not engage us, and we fix our resort where the society is more to our mind. We are fond of distinctions; we place ourselves in opposition, and quarrel under the denominations of faction and party, without any material subject of controversy. Aversion, like affection, is fostered by a continued direction to its particular object. Separation and estrangement, as well as opposition, widen a breach which did not owe its beginnings to any offence. And it would seem, that till we have reduced mankind to the state of a family, or found some external consideration to maintain their connection in greater numbers, they will be for ever separated into bands, and form a plurality of nations.

The true doctrine of expatriation. (Contrary to Rutherforth.) A truth for North and South! Dissension not ended by division.

THE sense of a common danger, and the assaults of an enemy, have been frequently useful to nations, by uniting their members more firmly together, and by preventing the secessions and actual separations in which their civil discord might otherwise terminate. And this motive to union which is offered from abroad, may be necessary, not only in the case of large and extensive nations, where coalitions are weakened by distance, and the distinction of provincial names; but even in the narrow society of the smallest States. Rome itself was founded by a small party, which took its flight

Would not a foreign interference unite these States?

§ 18. Motives and ways to Peace and a new Union.

from Alba; her citizens were often in danger of separating; and if the villages and cantons of the Volsci had been further removed from the scene of their dissensions, the Mons Sacer might have received a new colony before the mother-country was ripe for such a discharge. She continued long to feel the quarrels of her nobles and her people; and kept open the gates of Janus, to remind those parties of the duties they owed to their country.

States naturally jealous.

SOCIETIES, as well as individuals, being charged with the care of their own preservation, and having separate interests, which give rise to jealousies and competitions, we cannot be surprised to find hostilities arise from this source. But were there no angry passions of a different sort, the animosities which attend an opposition of interest, should bear a proportion to the supposed value of the subject. "The Hottentot nations," says Kolben, "trespass on each other by thefts of cattle and of women; but such injuries are seldom committed, except with a view to exasperate their neighbours, and bring them to a war." Such depredations then, are not the foundation of a war, but the effects of a hostile intention already conceived. The nations of North America, who have no herds to preserve, nor settlements to defend, are yet engaged in almost perpetual wars, for which they can assign no reason, but the point of honour, and a desire to continue the struggle their fathers maintained. They do not regard the spoils of an enemy; and the warrior who has seized any booty, easily parts with it to the first person who comes in his way.

Hostility causes attack.

Separate societies naturally conflicting.

BUT we need not cross the Atlantic to find proofs of animosity, and to observe, in the collision of separate societies, the influence of angry passions, that do not arise from an opposition of interest. Human nature has no part of its character of which more flagrant examples are given on this side of the globe. What is it that stirs in the breasts of ordinary men when the enemies of their country are named? Whence are the prejudices that subsist between different provinces, cantons, and villages, of the same empire and territory? What is it that excites one half of the nations of Europe against the other? The statesman may explain his conduct on motives of national jealousy and caution, but the people have dislikes and antipathies, for which they cannot account. Their mutual reproaches of perfidy and injustice, like the Hottentot depredations, are but symptoms of an animosity, and the language of a hostile disposition, already conceived. The charge of cowardice and pusillanimity, qualities which the interested and cautious enemy should, of all others, like best to find in his rival, is urged with aversion, and made the ground of dislike. Hear the peasants on different sides of the Alps, and the Pyrenees, the Rhine, or the British channel, give vent to their prejudices and national passions; it is among them that we find the materials of war and dissension laid without the direction of government, and sparks ready to kindle into a flame, which the statesman is frequently disposed to extinguish. The fire will not always catch where his reasons of state would direct, nor stop where the concurrence of interest has produced an alliance. "My Father," said a Spanish peasant, "would rise from his grave, if he could foresee a war with France." What interest had he, or the bones of his father, in the quarrels of princes?

Cowardice contemned.

Contest not wholly unfavorable to man.

Contest develops noble qualities.

THESE observations seem to arraign our species, and to give an unfavourable picture of mankind; and yet the particulars we have mentioned are consistent with the most amiable qualities of our nature, and often furnish a scene for the exercise of our greatest abilities. They are sentiments of generosity and self-denial that animate the warrior in defence of his country; and they are dispositions most favourable to mankind, that become the principles of apparent hostility to men. Every animal is made to delight in the exercise of his natural talents and forces: The lion and the tyger sport with the paw; the horse delights to commit his mane to the wind, and forgets his pasture to try his speed in the field; the bull even before his brow is armed, and the lamb while yet an emblem of innocence, have a disposition to strike with the forehead, and anticipate, in play, the conflicts they are doomed to sustain. Man too is disposed to opposition, and to employ the forces of his nature against an equal antagonist; he loves to bring his reason, his eloquence, his courage, even his bodily strength to the proof. His sports are frequently an image of war; sweat and blood are freely expended in play; and fractures or death are often made to terminate the

Strife natural in animals—

—and in man.

His sports image war.

pastime of idleness and festivity. He was not made to live for ever, and even his love of amusement has opened a way to the grave.

§ 18. Motives and ways to Peace and a new Union.

Rivalry and war natural to States.

The resulting benefits.

WITHOUT the rivalship of nations, and the practice of war, civil society itself could scarcely have found an object, or a form. Mankind might have traded without any formal convention, but they cannot be safe without a national concert. The necessity of a public defence, has given rise to many departments of state, and the intellectual talents of men have found their busiest scene in wielding their national forces. To overawe, or intimidate, or, when we cannot persuade with reason, to resist with fortitude, are the occupations which give its most animating exercise, and its greatest triumphs, to a vigorous mind; and he who has never struggled with his fellow-creatures, is a stranger to half the sentiments of mankind.

Individual quarrels mean:

—not so in States.

Nobility developed in war.

A State applauded where an individual is condemned.

THE quarrels of individuals, indeed, are frequently the operations of unhappy and detestable passions, malice, hatred, and rage. If such passions alone possess the breast, the scene of dissension becomes an object of horror; but a common opposition maintained by numbers, is always allayed by passions of another sort. Sentiments of affection and friendship mix with animosity; the active and strenuous become the guardians of their society; and violence itself is, in their case, an exertion of generosity, as well as of courage. We applaud, as proceeding from a national or party spirit, what we could not endure as the effect of a private dislike; and, amidst the competitions of rival states, think we have found, for the patriot and the warrior, in the practice of violence and stratagem, the most illustrious career of human virtue. Even personal opposition here does not divide our judgment on the merits of men. The rival names of Agesilaus and Epaminondas, of Scipio and Hannibal, are repeated with equal praise; and war itself, which in one view appears so fatal, in another is the exercise of a liberal spirit; and in the very effects which we regret, is but one distemper more, by which the Author of nature has appointed our exit from human life.

The conduct of Providence in human affairs.

Our hopes at times too amiable for human nature.

Hostility natural.

Emulation desirable.

THESE reflections may open our view into the state of mankind; but they tend to reconcile us to the conduct of Providence, rather than to make us change our own: where, from a regard to the welfare of our fellow-creatures, we endeavour to pacify their animosities, and unite them by the ties of affection. In the pursuit of this amiable intention, we may hope, in some instances, to disarm the angry passions of jealousy and envy; we may hope to instil into the breasts of private men sentiments of candour towards their fellow-creatures, and a disposition to humanity and justice. But it is vain to expect that we can give to the multitude of a people a sense of union among themselves, without admitting hostility to those who oppose them. Could we at once, in the case of any nation, extinguish the emulation which is excited from abroad, we should probably break or weaken the bands of society at home, and close the busiest scenes of national occupations and virtues.

Man proposes, GOD disposes.

Phil. ii, 12, 13.

The hand of Providence in this war.

The South to have credit even for this war.

By other means than war, could the South probably have broken the spell of our enchantment, and saved us from the perils of consolidation. But while "man proposes, GOD disposes." And Paul says, "Work out your own salvation with fear and trembling. FOR it is GOD which worketh in you both to will and to do of *His* good pleasure." The same principles, the same causes, which operate in spiritual Government, concerning the affairs of eternity, direct and control in human Government, concerning the affairs of time; and the South will be found, under GOD'S providential energies, even by terrible war, to have worked out for us a salvation from a far more terrible, intolerable evil, than civil war itself; that of consolidation. A century hence, when the hidden motives and workings shall be developed, and the impartial historian shall trace out the causes and necessities of this conflict, the ignorance and confusion of the elementary principles of Government, the statesmen of the South, notwithstanding their wrongs and mistakes, will have justice done to their

§ 18. Motives and ways to Peace and a new Union.

memory, as having been in fact, though inadvertently, the saviors of their country.

War an instrument in the hand of Deity—

—to work good for His children.

The Almighty Sovereign of the universe employs war, as He does other instruments, for the accomplishment of His purposes. With our imperfect language and conceptions, we style some of these instruments good, others evil; but in the hand of Infinite Love and Wisdom, we know that they will all be made to work for the best good of our Sovereign's faithful subjects, for the highest glory of our King JEHOVAH. Even the pangs of the mother's tender heart, which cannot be comforted for the bloody death of her darling boy; the wife's deepest griefs for the most irremediable of earthly sorrows, the loss of a brave, honorable, adored husband, pangs and griefs to be counted by the hundred thousand as consequent on this conflict; even all these are to be exchanged for the voice of joy and gladness, for the shout of thanksgiving and praise, as we see, in the result, the legitimate fruits of Southern resolution and honor, coupled with their intolerant and intolerably domineering spirit, working out, under GOD's providence, the problem of free Government, given by Him to man thousands of years ago, and which, in our ignorance and folly, we were driving to destruction.

Deepest griefs— —to be changed for joy— —in the saving of our institutions.

The benefits of the war not confined to us.

Nor are the benefits of a thorough knowledge of our Governmental structure, the certain and invaluable consequence of this war, to be confined to us. Not only shall we ourselves understand better how and why it is we have so prospered, and guard effectually against future erring; but foreigners also will see the superiority of our system of Government to any the world ever enjoyed, and a new and abiding confidence will be inspired in our Federal Republic, in our Peoples, and in our free institutions. The liberty-loving will flock hither in increasing multitudes, particularly from the more elevated classes of society, and capital will seek investment in untold sums. With a new Union, this young Republic will advance as never before; and though not like Rome the mistress, yet will it be the leader of the world. And, as already intimated, an acquaintance with Federalism will protect all Peoples from despotism and tyranny. Its thorough knowledge and practice must precede the millennial day of peace and universal love.

Prosperity in a new Union.

Motives to patriotism strong.

Truly, the objects presented to the American patriot in this struggle, are sufficient to draw forth deeds of noblest heroism on the battle field; of highest wisdom in the council chamber. Ability and determination to maintain our Union and Government against any section that dares the attempt to break them up by war, are first to be demonstrated, and another half million of men will not more than suffice to do this; and the sooner they are in training, the sooner will peace return. Push on the war with might and main.

Push on the war.

Study principles of Government.

Let not the South lead us always.

While our soldiers fight, let our wise men in the North study more thoroughly into Governmental principles and apprehend them. The South are in this noble work without a doubt; let them not be always wiser than we, as has thus far been too much the case, but let us understand this grandest of all sciences, equally as well as they; and when, in a year, or two years, or three, or fifty, they are willing to try other means than force to dispossess us of our rights; let us be able to meet them in council, and discuss our rights according to "the Law of Nature and of Nature's GOD." When prepared to do us justice, which it is not in the heart of the magnanimous South to refuse, on learning that we will do justly by them, should they find, as we confidently expect, that our State rights, which they so correctly appreciate, are only to be preserved by Union; let us then so well understand the nature of Federalism, as that we can meet them in Convention, well qualified to unite our efforts with theirs, to frame a new Constitution, to form a new Union, that with the blessing of our fathers' GOD shall be enduring.

§ 18. Motives and ways to Peace and a new Union.

When they are prepared to reason, let us be ready—

—to have a new Constitution, a new Federal Union.

§ 19.—How Britain and America can be made Friends.

The examination into principles, which must be made before this war can be concluded, will bring another desirable result, a correct understanding between Britain and America, the mother and the daughters, resulting in a cordial, lasting friendship.

To understand Colonial rights, which we must investigate in order to learn the obligations and duties of the individual colonists, and of the separate Colonies, it is necessary to study into their origin, and the authority by which the Colonies were planted. We cannot understand State rights, and how we came to organize into many States instead of one, without a knowledge of these subjects. To learn our rights as Englishmen and Britons, to properly estimate our grants by charter, and our privileges established by custom, we must look into the British Constitution. This is a subject that has been investigated by their ablest statesmen, some of whom, as Lords Russell and Brougham and Mr. d'Israeli, are still living; and Hallam, De Lolme, and others have written works which have become standard authorities. The extracts to be given, choice gems from among the best of English writings, will impart a zest for this instructive reading. Lord Brougham, in particular, has written a work properly entitled "*Political Philosophy.*" All his life, long and useful and honorable, has he been qualifying himself for this important trust; and in the conclusion he remarks, that it has been "my labor for five years." He is an earnest, faithful Whig, too, ever watchful of the rights and interests of the People, and we Americans shall love and honor these our cousins and brethren, the more we understand their views. The writer will not make himself ridiculous by attempting to instruct such giant intellects, pure and faithful patriots, in the principles of their own Government; and yet there is a line of investigation that seems to have been too much overlooked.

Colonial rights to be investigated,

—to understand State rights.

The British Constitution.

Authorities concerning it.

Lord Brougham's *Political Philosophy.*

A good Whig, and friend of popular rights.

A subject yet to be investigated.

Burke and the noble band who labored so zealously against the wrongs on America, appear not to have well elucidated the why and wherefore of those wrongs. Neither have subsequent writers, that we have discov-

The Whigs did not understand Colonial wrongs.

§ 19. Britain and America to be friendly.

Locke and Blackstone's ideas confused them.

Were Parliament supreme, she could tax the Colonies.

Britain then is an Aristocracy, not a Monarchy.

ered. It would seem that our Whig friends, adopting the theory of Locke and Blackstone, that Sovereignty was in Parliament instead of the Crown, involved themselves in a maze of contradictions. If Parliament was really supreme over the British empire, never having itself engaged not to tax these Colonies, she undoubtedly had the right to adopt any measure the general good of her dominions and subjects required. But in that event, Britain, instead of being a Monarchy, must be an Aristocracy, for it is not under the rule of *one*, but of the *few*.

The documents in this First Part will elucidate this subject.

Will prove us no "rebels," but true Tories.

King agreed not to tax without consent of representatives.

Had all rights of Englishmen.

Had own Parliaments.

British Parliament had no right to tax us.

We were never subjects of Parliament.

As the documents and the facts connected with this interesting question are mostly presented in the First Part, space need not here be taken to discuss them. Their perusal, in juxtaposition, will give a new aspect to our Revolution; and when analyzed and discussed by a competent writer, they will prove our fathers, instead of having been "rebels," to have been the truest Tories in the British dominions. In asserting our Colonial rights, partly inherited as Britons, partly grants from our previous Sovereigns to faithful subjects, we properly sustained the royal prerogative against the illegal, unjust usurpations of Parliament. According to old compact with our Sovereigns, they had no power to lay taxes without the People's consent by their Representatives, the support of the Crown being wisely left to the generosity of the subjects.[1] Our fathers came here under the assurance that all our rights as Englishmen and Britons should be preserved; and further, in many charters it will be seen that the King expressly agreed we should not be taxed. We had our own Parliaments, our laws being subject to the approval of our Monarch, as were those of the Scotch Parliament when under one and the same Crown with England, and prior to the incorporation of those States into one by the name of Great Britain; and as was the case in Ireland, prior to its incorporation with Great Britain, now forming a new State under the name of The United Kingdom of Great Britain and Ireland, The English Parliament had an equal right to lay a tax on Scotland prior to union, that the British Parliament had to tax these Colonies. We were never subjects of Parliament, but of our Monarchs from Elizabeth I down to George III; and one of the most deplorable, disgraceful events in our Colonial history, was the contemptible truculence of the New England Colonies to the usurper Cromwell, and his usurping Parliament. (The documents will be given.)

Error of the fathers admitting in part the supremacy of Parliament.

We shall find from the papers of John Dickinson and others, discussing Colonial rights, that Britons here, with our countrymen at home, had become imbued with the heresy of Sovereignty in Parliament, instead

---

De Lolme, *Constitution of England*, p. 509.

The Colonies not considered wrong.

[1] De Lolme thoroughly comprehended this subject, which he discusses at length in chapter xx, added to the edition of 1781; and he perceived, that with the British theories of the supremacy of Parliament, the Colonies must not be allowed to make their benefactions to the Crown. At the same time he remarks in a foot note: "When I observe that no man who wished for the preservation of the form and spirit of the English Constitution, ought to have desired that the claim of the American Colonies might be granted them, neither do I mean to say that the American Colonies should have given up their claim. The wisdom of ministers, in regard to American affairs, ought to have been constantly employed in making the Colonies useful to this country, and at the same time in hiding their subjection from them," &c., &c.

§ 19. Britain and America to be friendly.

Dean Tucker's argument for the British.

The documents will justify our fathers.

Whig *practice* good, though *theories* were confused.

Separation from Britain may be deplored.

We are still in an experiment.

Union uncertain; the effect of disunion still more so.

of the Crown,[1] and fancying a distinction between internal and external taxes, we admitted the right to lay the latter, but denied the former. Dean Tucker's paper, which ably and fairly presents the British side, will be read with interest, and it will be a grievous disappointment, if we Americans are not able from the documents, to justify our fathers, by the British Constitution itself, in our resistance to illegal taxation and interference with our rights; and our Whig cousins of Britain, will discover new and important means for preserving the admirable checks and balances their party has labored for centuries to establish, and with such remarkable success. We shall be pleased with the excellent good sense in the *practice* of Britons here in the Colonies, and of their Whig friends at home, notwithstanding *theories* had become confused. Many of us, on both sides the water, may lament that confusion of ideas with regard to Sovereignty, plain and simple as we shall find the subject to be, should have led to the dismemberment of the British empire; an event which, with all our past prosperity, cannot yet be affirmed to have been desirable for America. We are still in an experiment, as current events prove; and though the past affords much evidence that, with Union, our free institutions can be maintained, to our own enduring benefit, to the advantage of the entire world, yet whether that Union is to be perpetuated, is now the great problem of the age; whether, if disunited, and two or several rival Republics take the place of one, they can be sustained, is still more a doubtful matter.

Many regret we have not British Government.

Growing friendship for Britain.

Not surprising is it, that in our present calamities, with the dark uncertainty of the future, well knowing the enduring foundations, the solid superstructure of the British Constitution, that thousands of our fellow countrymen should turn a wistful eye to the mother-land, and wish these chickens safe under her protecting wing. The animosities of the Revolution and of the last war have been mostly obliterated; and steadily and strongly has a natural and desirable attachment been growing, rapidly accelerated the last twenty or thirty years by tracing back our geneal-

---

BURKE'S *Speech*, March 22, 1775.

Intelligence of the Colonies in law.

Sales of Blackstone's Commentaries.

[1] Said our dear and excellent friend Burke in his speech, March 22d, 1775, on "Conciliation with America," "Permit me to add another circumstance in our Colonies, which contributes no mean part toward the growth and effect of this untractable spirit. I mean their education. In no country perhaps in the world is the law so general a study. The profession itself is numerous and powerful; and in most provinces it takes the lead. The greater number sent to the Congress were lawyers. But all who read, and most do read, endeavor to obtain some smattering of that science. I have been told by an eminent bookseller, that in no branch of this business, after tracts of popular devotion, were so many books as those on the law exported to the plantations. The Colonists have now fallen into the way of printing them for their own use. I hear that they have sold nearly as many of Blackstone's Commentaries in America as in England," &c.

Blackstone's influence, notwithstanding Bentham's and Tucker's criticisms.

We all understand, though unskilled in the law, the immense influence wielded by Blackstone in its every department, notwithstanding Bentham has exposed his fallacies connected with the British Government, and Judge Tucker, of Virginia, with reference to America. This civil war is to bring Anglo-Saxons *at home* and in America, to understand International Law as never before, and if there be those misconceptions in Blackstone and Locke, which the writer conceives, they are surely to be exploded.

Locke another eminent authority.

They teach the supremacy of Parliament.

As confirmatory of the influence of the pernicious teachings which have led us so far astray, and into this civil war, Professor Fowler and Doctor Agnew inform me that Locke was formerly one of the standard authorities in governmental science, taught in our highest collegiate institutions. The teachings of Locke and of Blackstone are one and the same on the supremacy of Parliament, and are utterly subversive of Hooker, Grotius and Vattel, or else the British Government is an Aristocracy.

§ 19. Britain and America to be friendly. Might easily be made strong.

ogies and finding our kinsfolk *at home.* Our British cousins little know how easily they could bind to them the warm hearts of America, with affection's strongest cords.

Reunion with Britain impossible. Cannot have that form of Government. The Aristocracy its safeguard, —which we cannot have till after a despotism. The check of the Aristocracy on Crown and People.

But however much we may love and revere the institutions of our mother-land, we can never again be united with her as one nation. The hand of Providence is perceptible in our severance, and reunion is an impossibility. Neither can we reasonably hope to have the form of Government of Britain. No one can examine its construction and its history, without perceiving that the Aristocracy is the safeguard, the chief bulwark of the Kingdom. No doubt an Aristocracy has its evils, as has every other branch of human Government, some of which may, and doubtless will be, alleviated; but no check on Monarchial rule has been ever devised equal to that of the British Nobility. This we can never have, till under a despotism our usurper shall find it necessary to sustain himself against the People, by creating a privileged class, who, to maintain the dignities and advantages bestowed upon them, must support the Crown. These will in time come to be a check on the Crown itself, and seek their own aggrandizement against both King and People; and then, as in the history of England, will the Crown call to its defence against the aggressions of the Nobility, the People by their Representatives.

Federalism or Despotism our only alternative. Britons wish us well.

With us the only alternative is a Democratic Federal Republic, or Despotism. After long and weary years of anarchy and tyranny, we might reach the form which it took England centuries to establish. Does Britain desire this to be our portion? Do not our friends and kinsfolk in the mother-land, as reunion with them is impracticable, wish our success in sustaining free institutions? They do; they of the Whig school especially.

Anglo-Saxons in Britain have the best Monarchial Government— —in America the best free Government. Their Citizens should have friendly sympathy. A common ancestry, —same aims in Government, —same religion and language. We should be friends.

The GOD of nations has led the People of Britain to frame the best system of Monarchial Government ever known to man. He has led us, their offspring, to establish the best system of Free Government, and after the pattern given by Him to the Hebrews of old, with improvements adapted to the advance of our race, the same original Caucasian that was made in the image of GOD. Both Constitutional Governments, each the most eminent of its kind for preserving the liberties and rights of the governed, and at the same time most effective to maintain Sovereignty, law and order, we, the Citizens under these Governments, should have a deep, strong and abiding reciprocal sympathy and attachment. United as we so largely are in a common ancestry; cherishing the same noble aims in Constitutional Government, though under antipodal forms; having the same religious principles; speaking the same language; surely, so far as rival nations can have friendship, should it be found between our mother and these her daughters. It has been well observed by Godwin:

We are not severed from our ancestry. GODWIN'S *History of the Commonwealth*, iii, 16.

Man, and generations of men, are not links broken off from the great chain of being: they are not like some of the inferior sorts of animals, having no opportunity of intercourse with those that went before them, and indebted for their systems of action only to their internal constitution and the laws of the universe, and not to imitation. Generations of men are linked and dovetailed into each other. Our modes of thinking, our predilections and aversions, our systems of judging, our habits of life, our courage or our cowardice, our elevation or our meanness, are in a great degree regulated by those of our immediate ancestors. One race of men does not pass off the stage without leaving their stamp and their ply upon those who come after them; and in this way, though generations are evanescent and fugitive, nations are, in a certain limited sense of the word, immortal."

§ 19. Britain and America to be friendly.

The Anglo-Saxon "stamp" and "ply."

We are of the "race of men" that counts among its worthies a Shakspere, Hooker, Bacon, Selden, Milton, Hale, Sidney, Somers, Goldsmith, Addison, Pope, Newton, Burke, Pitt and a host of others, a resplendent galaxy whose clear and steady light is to shine forever, and illumine every dark corner of the earth. The "stamp" of these mighty men is on us. We are true coin, no base counterfeit. Anglo-Saxon shall we be to the end of time. Let our mother have pride and confidence in her children. She is rejuvenated in these her daughters, and an empire of freemen is here to arise, which for all coming ages shall be the highest glory of England to have founded.

Our English ancestors.

Their "stamp" on us.

Britain should have pride in her children.

The mutual respect and esteem, the cordial regard, that would seem reasonable and desirable, have not existed; and in the progress of the discussion, some of the preventing causes will be intimated. In the chapter, *Dangers Past*, we shall see their efforts to divide us, and which now threaten accomplishment. But we shall before have found much cause for the jealousy of England's Nobility, which has probably been the active power at work against us, in the perversion and misrepresentation of our fundamental political principles. Indoctrinated by Locke, Rousseau and others with the idea that only consent can establish rightful authority, and that men may at will change their institutions and form of Government; all proper conceptions of Sovereignty, the *Right of Command*, perverted and confused; driven on by the infidel philosophy of France, with its false notions of liberty; believing, notwithstanding State organization, that all men are really free and equal, because their natural rights are supposed to be inalienable; very many of our leading statesmen and writers have uttered sentiments subversive of the very foundations of every Government.

Desirable regard does not exist between Britain and the United States.

Their efforts to divide these States.

The jealousy of English Nobility.

Caused by our own perversion of Governmental principles.

Our views as to liberty and equality.

Taught by our leaders.

In 1848, Illinois had a Representative in Congress, Hon. Abraham Lincoln by name. He had occasion to make a speech on the reference of the President's message, in which he said:

Right of Revolution as taught by Hon. A. LINCOLN.

Any people anywhere, being inclined and having the power, have the *right* to rise up and shake off the existing government, and form a new one that suits them better. This is a most valuable, a most sacred right—a right which, we hope and believe, is to liberate the world. Nor is this right confined to cases in which the whole people of an existing government may choose to exercise it. Any portion of such people that *can* *may* revolutionize, and make their own of so much of the territory as they inhabit. More than this, a *majority* of any portion of such people may revolutionize, putting down a *minority*, intermingled with, or near about them, who may oppose their movements. Such minority was precisely the case of the Tories of our own Revolution. It is a quality of revolutions, not to go by *old* lines, or *old* laws; but to break up both, and make new ones.

Speech, June 12, 1848, *App. Cong. Globe*, p. 94.

Any part of a People may overthrow its Government.

Old laws to be disregarded.

We cannot stop here to discuss these sentiments, or to compare them

§ 19. Britain and America to be friendly.

with the author's more matured teachings in his Inaugural Address. Between the two, is a slight difference that would be important, were "old laws" worthy of regard; but if not, not.

Difference between this and the President's Inaugural Address.

The importance of the President's opinion.

The opinion of Mr. Lincoln, M. C., was of little consequence to the world; but the opinion of Mr. Lincoln, President of the United States, is quite another affair; if, as the world might reasonably suppose, he speaks the sentiments and convictions of all these Peoples. If such be our sentiments, very well; if not, it behoves these Peoples to speak for themselves in some unmistakable manner.

He had abundant authorities for his opinions.

But Mr. Lincoln, though he did not quote authorities, could have given plenty of them taken from the speeches and writings of Americans, and of the French school of liberty. Even as good and honored a statesman as ex-President John Quincy Adams said:

J. Q. Adams' *Address, Jubilee of the Constitution*, 1839, p. 17.

Our Declaration had a different foundation from our Confederation.

One *right*, the other *power*.

> There was thus no congeniality of principle between the Declaration of Independence and the Articles of Confederation. The foundation of the former were a superintending Providence—the rights of man, and the constituent revolutionary power of the people. That of the latter was the sovereignty of organized power, and the independence of the separate or dis-united States. The fabric of the Declaration and that of the Confederation, were each consistent with its own foundation, but they could not form one consistent symmetrical edifice. They were the productions of different minds and of adverse passions—one, ascending for the foundation of human government to the laws of nature and of God, written upon the heart of man—the other, resting upon the basis of human institutions, and prescriptive law and colonial charters. The corner stone of the one was *right*—that of the other was *power*.

If there be no congeniality between right principles and these States with their Sovereignties—

—we had best cease to go by "old laws."

The same difficulty in the present, as in the first Constitution.

That is, "There was no congeniality of principle between . . . . a superintending Providence, the rights of man, and the constituent revolutionary power of the people;" and "the Sovereignty of organized power, and the independence of the separate or dis-united States." If that be really so, we are in a deplorable condition; and if such be International Law, it is quite time that we cease "to go by *old* lines, or *old* laws, but break up both and make new ones." For it will be found upon examination, that if such incompatibility existed under the first Constitution, usually called the Articles of Confederation, it continues under the present Constitution, no change having been made in the form of Government, but only in its Administration, and in the subtraction of further important powers from the State Agency, and adding them to the Federal Agency. It will appear that, from the days these several States became Sovereign, free and independent, six prior to the 4th July, six on that memorable day, and New York on the 9th July, 1776, there has not been a shadow of change in "the Sovereignty of organized power, and the independence of the separate or dis-united States," nor has the character of the Union been changed in the least, except to make it "more perfect."

No change has been made in the State Sovereignty.

A People has no right of revolution except upon necessity.

Until its Sovereignty shall have rightfully reverted to a People, either by failure of legal inheritors, or by abdication, or by forfeiture through tyranny and oppression, no People that duly regards "a superintending Providence, the rights of man, and the constituent revolutionary power of the People," can interfere to change the *Right of Command.* There is no "basis of human institutions" except "the Laws of Nature and of God," which are not as extensively "written upon the heart of man" as would be desirable. Had they been "written upon the heart" of George III and his ministry, he would never have violated our "prescriptive law and Colonial charters," which justified us in withdrawing our allegiance and in making the Declaration of Independence.

§ 19. Britain and America to be friendly.

The "Laws of Nature" the basis of all human institutions.

When our wise men succeed in finding our lost Sovereignty, a consequence will surely be to show perfect "congeniality of principle between the Declaration of Independence and the Articles of Confederation," which, it is to be hoped, has not been impaired by substituting for the latter, the present Constitution. And it seems rather desirable than otherwise, to discover that the fathers were not compelled to make a very lofty ascent to reach "the foundation of human Government." Webster thought it great absurdity in that imagined instructor of Jackson, to poise the pyramid of our institutions on the apex instead of the base; and it is scarcely credible that our wise fathers committed a greater architectural blunder, in "ascending for the foundation of human Government." They were guilty of no such impropriety as to seek the Infinite Founder "for" any other "foundation," than that already sent down to them, in the Book of Revelation and of Laws Divine, which for many centuries had been finished. Encouraged to cause their prayers to "ascend," that the Spirit's influences might descend to teach them those Laws, yet were they to "continue in the faith GROUNDED and SETTLED." They had no right to leave the solid *terra firma* of the "Law of Nature and of Nature's God," for the clouds of fancy and of vain desire; and Adams should have learned from his father and his cousin Samuel, that they never made the attempt. Our Government, Federal or State, rests upon no such "baseless fabric of a vision." They well knew that all rightful "human institutions, and prescriptive law, and Colonial charters;" yes, and the whole code of International Law, rested upon one and the same "foundation," and that none other was to be sought. Consequently, the fathers dug deep, and found "that foundation" of Hooker and Grotius, and had for their memorable Declaration, their first Constitution, and the present Constitution, and for all their institutions, but one "corner-stone," "right" or "power," *the Right of Command*, STATE SOVEREIGNTY. They really made one stone out of the two of Adams; and this "stone," although like another long "rejected," is yet, like that other glorious one, to "become the head of the corner."

Wise men will find congeniality between our Declaration and Confederation,

—not impaired by Constitution.

Ascent for a "foundation" undesirable,

—and an architectural blunder.

The fathers not guilty of seeking for a new "foundation."

Col. i, 23.

They grounded their institutions on "that foundation" of Hooker and Grotius.

—State Sovereignty, which is to "become the head of the corner."

Matt. xxi, 42; and *Pet.* ii, 7.

Though this Address contains much of similar bewildering teachings, the venerated author well shows our hatred of anarchy and revolution:

Our hatred of anarchy and revolution.

The principles proclaimed in the Declaration of Independence, as at the foundation of all lawful government, had been sapping[1] the foundations of all the governments

ADAMS, *Ib.*, p. 85.

Our Declaration did not sap European institutions, but its "substitute" did.

[1] It was not the "principles" of the Declaration, but what was "substituted" for them, that did the "sapping," as appears in the latter part of this paragraph. We are not to be held responsible for the "substitute," only for the "principles," and, as remarked by Adams in the preceding quotation, they will be found to rest upon "the Laws of Nature and of God."

§ 19. Britain and America to be friendly.

Our adverse influences.

Our sympathy with France.

French phantoms and wrongs.

founded on the unlimited sovereignty of force—the absolute monarchy of France was crumbling into ruin; a wild and ferocious anarchy, under the banners of unbridled Democracy, was taking its place, and between the furies of this frantic multitude, and the agonies of immemorial despotism, a war of desolation and destruction was sweeping over the whole continent of Europe. In this war all the sympathies of the American people were on the side of France and of freedom, but the freedom of France was not of the genuine breed. A phantom of more than gigantic form had assumed the mask and the garb of freedom, and substituted for the principles of the Declaration of Independence, anarchy within and conquest without. The revolution of the whole world was her war-cry, and the overthrow of all established governments her avowed purpose.

The French revolution and wars.

American partiality towards France.

Under the impulses of this fiend, France had plunged into war with all Europe, and murdered her king, his queen, his sister, and numberless of his subjects and partisans, with or without the forms of law, by the butchery of mock tribunals, or the daggers of a bloodthirsty rabble. In this death-struggle between inveterate abuse and hurly-burly innovation, it is perhaps impossible even now to say which party had been the first aggressor; but France had been first invaded by the combined forces of Austria and Prussia, and under banners of Liberty, Equality, Fraternity, had become an armed nation to expel them from her borders. The partialities of the American people still sympathized with France. They saw that her cause was the cause of national independence. They believed her professions of liberty, equality, and fraternity; and when the same Convention which had declared France a republic, and deposed and put to death her king, declared war against the kings of Great Britain and Spain, shocked as they were at the merciless extermination of their ancient great and good ally, they still favoured at heart the cause of France, especially when in conflict under the three-coloured banners of liberty, equality, fraternity, with their ancient common enemy of the Revolutionary war, the British king, and with their more recent, but scarcely less obnoxious foe, the king of Spain.

We have too much taught revolution,

—but not in our authoritative documents.

A bad Government a People may destroy.

Rom. xiii, 1.

Government ordained of God.

Usually without consent of subjects.

To our disgrace, our political speeches and writings contain too much of these revolutionizing, anarchical teachings; but they are not to be found in our Declaration of Independence, nor our Constitutions, as we shall endeavor to show, nor in any authoritative exposition of governmental principles. We do believe and so declare, that a Government failing to accomplish the purposes of its institution, usurping authority, violating compacts, resulting in tyranny, whether of *one*, the *few*, or the *many*, may be altered or destroyed at the will of the People. Till then, no man nor set of men have any right of resistance. "The powers that be are ordained of GOD," and till perverted from the objects of ordination by man's imperfections, equally attaching to rulers as to ruled, the subjects must submit to the authority placed over them, occasionally with their consent, but most usually without it. Do women, or infants in law, minors, give their consent? Can they give consent? Yet here are three fourths of every State made subjects; and no man, native or alien, can give his consent and become a Citizen, till he is first made subject by coming within the boundaries of that State, and being brought under its Sovereignty.

We have not taught the equality of man.

Man not now adapted to equality.

Neither have we taught the equality of man, except in a state of nature. Man may have lived in that state up to the time of Noah, which bred pollution and corruption that only the waters of the flood could wash away. We in America do not care to repeat that experiment, and expect never more to see a state of natural equality among our race, till succeeding generations, well into the millennial period, shall have had predominant selfishness uprooted from their hearts. Till that state of nature again returns, when, by the controlling power of love, civil institutions will be no longer required, we are for maintaining Government of the most effective kind, and expressly to preserve the inequality that exists most perfectly in the best form of civil State. Equality would be the aim in the natural state, could one be found, inequality is the aim in the civil State; and though Britain has given the best example of a means to preserve that inequality, we hope these daughters will in time be found to have brought another form for its maintenance, to quite as great perfection. All the equality we desire in this land of liberty, is an equal right and ability in the poor man to defend his rights, that an Astor or a Rothschild enjoys. We hope, with a little more practice, to become the equal of our mother in this noble achievement, perfection in which makes a perfect Government.

§ 19. Britain and America to be friendly.

Our object to preserve inequality.

Hope in this to equal Britain.

What kind of equality we seek.

Nor have we taught that the system of hereditary rights and superiority, was wrong *per se*. In our Bills of Rights, we refer solely to ourselves. It is not compatible with the genius of Republican Democracy, at least we have so regarded it, to perpetuate the rights of a few by primogeniture and entail. For other nations it may be best and necessary, and especially in Britain, appears indispensable to the permanence of the Nobility, which is a needful check in a Monarchy, both upon Crown and People. Should it be deemed necessary to put a limit to the accumulation of estates by entail, some of which are becoming enormous, they have wise men to decide, and make the requisite changes in the laws. The Nobility, composed mostly of gentlemen of leisure and fine mental culture, with wealth usually sufficient, often superfluous, having well stored libraries and ample means of information, and political science receiving special attention, they know quite well what is for the best good of their State; and conceding the usual quantum of selfishness to weigh in their balance of judgment, their interests as a class are too closely indentified with the general public good, to allow the adoption of measures greatly injurious to the Crown and People. If occasionally they err, wilfully or ignorantly, the counter-balances of Monarch and Commons are ample checks. The study of English and British history will convince any unprejudiced reader, that their hereditary Aristocracy has been and is indispensable, and richly worth its cost.

We have not opposed hereditary rights in other States.

Some nations require them.

The superiority of British Nobility.

Their interests identified with Crown and People.

Yet it is not deniable, that in America a strong prejudice exists against that branch of English Aristocracy, known as the Nobility, for which, as we believe, a reasonable cause exists. And it is not because they are true Aristocrats. Many American Democrats are thorough Aristocrats in their feelings, and are becoming more and more so. Common sense teaches, that to attain a high order of civil society, such as we Anglo-Saxons hope to have, we must cultivate an Aristocracy. Family and blood, and culture of manners, mind and heart, all indispensable to a genuine Aristocracy, are coming to be regarded according to their true

American prejudice against British Nobility.

What is not its cause.

We are not enemies of Aristocracy.

§ 19. Britain and America to be friendly. worth; and we should go to destruction if they were not. Without entail, or the rights of primogeniture, we shall have an Aristocracy here within a century or two, that will compare favorably with even our mother-land. We have a possible advantage of her, in that the blood of younger sons and of side-families will continually crop out, giving here to all an equal chance for elevation in society, while in England the many are overshadowed by titles and entail bestowed on the few. Blood will tell in American generations as in British, whether in man or horse, and titles and primogeniture have precious little to do with results.

We shall have a high one,

—more numerous than in Britain.

Blood will tell.

Still Britain's Aristocracy superior as yet to ours.

Notwithstanding this seeming advantage in America as to multiplying Aristocrats, the workings in practice, and in particular the effect upon the State, the most important of all considerations, have not thus far demonstrated our superiority. The chief good of an Aristocracy is to supply well qualified persons to administer the authority of the State, whether proceeding from a Sovereign, who has received from his People, or inherited, the *Right of Command*, or from a People which has kept to itself its Sovereignty. In England the Aristocracy has for centuries furnished a class, the superior of which to conduct affairs of State, and continuing for an equal length of time, can scarcely be found. The administration may be changed, Whigs put in and Tories out, but men, who for many years have devoted themselves to the science of Government, have gained intimate acquaintance with public affairs home and foreign, and know every spar and sail and line and all the workings of the ship, are brought to the helm and to other official positions; and though the course of the ship of State may be more or less veered, she sails splendidly under the command of officers ever qualified for their high calling. No ship can make a long and successful voyage except under such conduct. The storms of passion, the tornadoes of popular fury, must be encountered; sometimes driven on a lee-shore of clashing interests with rival nations, only the most skilful pilotage will save her from wreck and destruction; the crooked, intricate channels of diplomacy must be well known, or great injury results if not ruin, when the ship's company think they are about to reach a haven of peace and prosperity. Unquestionably is it owing, in large measure, to Britain's Aristocracy, and particularly that part called the Nobility, that her voyage has been so prosperous as to entitle her to the proud appellation of *the Mistress of the Ocean.*

An Aristocracy wanted for Government.

Benefits of this in England.

Change of parties makes no difference.

Ship of State well managed.

Skill required to conduct these ships.

Skill has made Britain mistress of the Ocean.

Americans undervalue skill.

We Americans are very liable to misjudge as to this important topic. Crazy with our success, not perceiving that it has been owing mainly to our natural advantages, and our isolation, we think our ships can sail themselves; at least we often require very little nautical skill in our officers. When one studies into the mysteries of governmental science, as little even as has the writer, he will see what preeminent knowledge and ability are requisite to conduct affairs of State. Have we generally regarded this? In choosing our rulers have we inquired, Is he honest, is he capable, is he a true Aristocrat? Or have we supported our candidate because of the advantage to our party, and to secure to ourselves or

Government requires skill.

We have not taken Aristocrats to sail our ships.

friends the spoils of office? Has the good of the State been our lofty aim? or mean, selfish, filthy lucre?

§ 19. Britain and America to be friendly

The superiority of British Aristocracy.

It must be admitted that thus far the British system, granting exclusive privileges to a few of their Aristocracy, has produced superior results to our American free system; for it will be evident in the sequel, that we have not prospered because of good management, but from peculiar circumstances attending the settlement of a new country of immense area, and with unequalled advantages. One needs only to look into our unwieldy, confused, contradictory mass of statutes that every State and every lawyer, even from Philadelphia, is perplexed with, and scrutinize the views of our leading statesmen as presented by Professor Fowler, in his *Sectional Controversy*, and glance at the mistakes and wrongs of our present Administration, to discover that our success is not to be attributed to Aristocratic skill employed in sailing our ships of State. New ships will bear a deal of maltreatment and abuse, that would founder an old one; and were we old States like Britain, with such management continued, as has been ours, we should soon be in the deep ocean buried.

Our success not occasioned by skill, but fortuitous circumstances.

New ships bear more than old.

We must change or we shall founder.

We must have a more perfect Aristocracy, and make of it a better use. A pure Democracy is our special abhorrence. We are *Republican*-Democrats, having a much more perfect Republican basis, than any Democracy of which we have knowledge. We shall adhere to Republicanism if we are to prosper and preserve our liberties; and in choosing our Executives, Legislators, Judges and other officials, our aim is to be, must be, more and more to put forward into public life our best men, our Aristocrats.

More Aristocracy necessary.

Aristocrats must be our rulers.

Our chief difficulty has been, that hitherto proper regard has not been paid to this important point. Yet had we done pretty well in the main, till that pernicious principle came into vogue, "to the victors belong the spoils;" since which, the strife has been both by electors and elected, less with reference to qualifications for office, less to the plans of Government, State or Federal, less to the protection of faithful subjects, and the advancement of the glory of these Sovereignties; than to the profits to be made out of the office by the recipient, and the patronage to be bestowed on his followers. We must discover and apply an effective remedy to this evil, or we go to destruction.

This has been neglected.

"To the victors belong the spoils," pernicious.

Must be remedied.

And here again may it be observed in passing, we see the beneficial influence of Federalism over a wide country. These evils have been felt much more in the North than in the South. Had we in the North been by ourselves, the consequences would doubtless have been more injurious; but the South have continued in the main to give to the Federal service their best men, their Aristocrats, as from the beginning, and there is no measuring the value of Southern influence in directing our Federal concerns. The North will in time reciprocate these benefits, if they have not already. We cannot dispense with the checks and balances of North and South, East and West.

The excellence of Federalism proved in our escape from these evils.

The South have given us more Aristocrats.

Checks of North and South indispensable.

We shall make rapid progress in building up an Aristocracy as we come to understand the nature of our Government, the study of which

We shall build up an Aristocracy.

§ 19. Britain and America to be friendly.

this war has forced upon us. A *mixture* of it is quite as essential to our Democracies as to Britain's Monarchy. We have laid a proper groundwork for its development, particularly in the North, in our system of free schools, which enables a poor man's son to look forward with equal probability of becoming an Aristocrat, as if his father were a millionaire. Some of the best bloods of England, as of America, fall into reduced circumstances; but it is far more difficult to recover there than here. Great wealth is not requisite to a proper Aristocracy, but a competency is, which may easily be acquired in this country, with a small portion of a man's time properly bestowed on business, leaving the larger portion to be employed in qualifying himself to be an Aristocrat. Space must not here be taken to discuss this interesting topic; but we shall endeavor hereafter to prove, that we shall surely establish an Aristocracy in these Democratic States, equal if possible, perhaps even superior, to that of Britain.

Our free school system favors it.

We shall have an Aristocracy equal to Britain.

Strife between Britain and America as to hereditary and free Aristocracy.

An interesting feature in the friendly struggle for supremacy in Aristocracy is to be, the ascertaining whether the hereditary system of Britain, securing privileges to a part, is equal or superior to the free system of America. Of paramount importance is the subject to us, for the whole problem of maintaining popular Governments, rests upon this one question. If we cannot have and perpetuate a high grade of Aristocracy, from which our rulers shall be almost uniformly elected, we can never sustain free Governments. Revolutions and anarchy must be our fate, till we find relief in Despotism; and then, fortunate shall we be, if by establishing an hereditary Aristocracy, with all its burdens, we shall reach as free a condition as Britons enjoy.

A high Aristocracy necessary to us.

We shall earnestly maintain it.

Our inhabitants, too, of every grade will earnestly maintain Aristocracy. We live and labor for our children, are more regardful of the interests of posterity than of this generation; and the more cultivated we are, the more strongly this sentiment will possess and actuate us. Even in the humbler walks of life, among those making no pretension to Aristocracy, though often better entitled to rank among Aristocrats than many who look down upon them with contempt; among the sons of poverty and toil, do men understand that their little boys may rise to eminence and power, and become the leading Aristocrats of the land. They have stronger inducements, even, than the rich man, to preserve the present order of the State, which, more than any other, gives to true merit a liberal chance for promotion. In these States emphatically, "Worth makes the man, want of it the fellow."

Our humble Citizens friends to Aristocracy.

Aristocracy not understood by us.

Soon will be.

These things have not been well understood; and we in middle life and on the decline, may never fully comprehend them; yet with the practical good sense of Americans, most will soon discover that they are no patrons of the pernicious doctrines of equality so much in vogue, to help greedy politicians to places of power, that they might plunder the public coffers. The plain People want our institutions perpetuated, which can only be done by changing our system, and electing true Aristocrats to office. Most of our Citizens, thank GOD, are farmers, and know that

Our farmers understand this thing of blood.

occasionally a mare drops a foal that, without a pedigree, gives indication of superiority, which care and training render famous. Good blood is there, and no one doubts it; though it may be several generations back, and untraceable. So will many a son, with parentage unknown to fame, in this land of true equality—equality of right to qualify for the highest grade of Aristocracy, and to obtain it—rise to places of eminence and power. Sherman came from the shoemaker's bench; Burritt and Corwin from the anvil; Douglas from the cabinet wareroom; Webster from the farm; and a host of others could be named, all from the plain common people; and no one doubts their having good blood from some ancestor. Thousands more such instances are to be seen, if our institutions are preserved, of unknown blood cropping out to the glory of the family, and State, and Union; to the good of the world. What a stimulus has the humble Citizen, or even the humblest subject, who never aspires to the high dignity of Citizenship for himself, to labor to preserve our Aristocracy, and bring it into power, that his descendants may enjoy this inestimable privilege of Citizenship, and have an equal chance of preferment to the highest ranks of Aristocracy! And the next and succeeding generations, are to be much better instructed on this subject than are we.

§ 19. Britain and America to be friendly.

Their sons at least equal to a horse.

Examples.

Blood will tell.

The interest of the humble citizen or subject to preserve our institutions.

Succeeding generations will understand this.

Though we in the North are far in advance of the South in laying a solid basis of Aristocracy in our educational plans, which must continue, too, owing to the large plantation system of the latter; their Aristocracy is now more prominent, and has been of much more service to themselves and to our whole country, than ours. Living on their estates, with well chosen libraries of the best authors ancient and modern, their solid thoughts not all frittered away with newspapers and magazines (which in moderation have also their right place) and with "yellow-covered literature," they study more thoroughly into subjects than most do in the North. Then, too, those genuine Aristocrats are better treated than are ours. The science of Government, the noblest of all, receiving their special attention, they are qualified to become political leaders, and term after term they fill the same office, or are promoted. This training and advancing are the means of making eminent statesmen; but in the North, when a cub has sucked long enough in the opinion of his partisans, he is choked off the teat; and usually, after a single official term, when he begins to be a little qualified to serve his constituents and his country, he gives way to a successor. Ever after the spoils, and without regard to qualifications, as a general thing, we devote our efforts and votes to that candidate who can give us and our party most probable success; and the measure of success, is the amount of public plunder secured. The true Aristocrat of the North, the wise and good Citizen, who has leisure to give to study, and has qualified himself to fill with honor the highest places of power, is seldom brought forward into the political arena; but the brawling partisan, contemptible pot-house politician, carries all before him, and the country may go to—one place or another. This difference between the two sections, accounts for the control the South have had

The North seem to have the advantage, yet the South lead in Aristocracy.

And why?

Minds more thoroughly cultivated.

Are better treated.

They study politics, and are kept in office.

Different in the North.

Frequent changes.

Our object the spoils.

Our Aristocrats have no chance.

—only brawling partisans elected.

This enables the South to rule.

§ 19. Britain and America to be friendly. in our public affairs, to which they are fairly entitled by the superiority, in both political knowledge and experience, of the statesmen they put forward. And it is because a change must be a gradual work of many years, that the remark has been previously made, that we in the West will look to the South to devise measures of Government, and will give the votes to put them in operation. *We will not be separated from the South*, and all we ask is, that they shall plan as well in the future as in the past, and almost their every project shall have success. We should have been worse situated than we are now, but for the South.

A sudden change not expected,

—therefore the West desire a new Union with the South.

A change will be made.

In time, we shall find some means in the North of guarding ourselves from these harpies of office seekers and public plunderers. Then will the Aristocracy have rule, and by improved practice, we shall develop much further the excellence of our compound system of free Governments. Let every reader study into the science of Government in particular, and set his children at the same work, for an high Aristocracy cannot be otherwise attained. We have no cause of discouragement, not in the least. Considering our circumstances, the short period we have had to accomplish what can only be done by persevering efforts of generations, and also the erroneous ideas as to freedom and equality generally prevalent among us, notwithstanding our correct enunciation of principles in our Declaration of Independence and our Bills of Rights; it is quite remarkable that we have made so much progress in true Republican, anti-Democratic, institutions. We subscribe to the observation of Dugald Stewart: "I before took notice of that natural Aristocracy, which we find in every community, arising from the original differences among men, in respect of intellectual and moral qualities. That these were intended to lay a foundation for civil Government, no man can doubt who does not reject altogether the inferences which are drawn from the appearances of design in the human constitution."

Aristocracy to rule.

Study Government to become an Aristocrat.

No cause of discouragement.

Former adverse influences.

Our progress remarkable.

DUGALD STEWART on natural Aristocracy. *Works*, ix. 417.

A mixture of *Administration*, necessary—not of Sovereignty.

We must have the *mixture of Administration*—not of Sovereignty, the *Right of Command*, which, being one and indivisible, is incapable of mixture with anything—the mixture of the *exercise* of Sovereignty, which has worked so admirably for centuries in the mother-land, for almost a century with us their offspring; and at the same time study sufficiently into the *theory* of Government to learn, that, while we have an Aristocracy, we are still Democracies, though Republican, our Sovereignty being in these several Peoples; as Britain, with her Aristocracy, is still a Monarchy, though Limited, her *Right of Command* being in her excellent Majesty, the Queen.

Examples in Britain and America.

Mixture not a new idea.

This idea of mixture, and yet preserving Sovereignty one and entire, is no modern invention to gull the People, or deceive Monarchs. "*James Howell*, Esquire, one of the Clerks of his *Majesties* Most Honourable *Privy Council*," wrote in the time of the Long Parliament (the date is 1644) an interesting paper on "The Preheminence and Pedigree of Parlement," which we find in that invaluable collection, *Lord Somers' Tracts*, from which we shall draw several treasures. Says Howell:

JAMES HOWELL, 1644.

. . . . So I may say to have cause to rejoyce that I was born a Vassal to the Crowne of *England;* that I was borne under so well moulded and tempered a Government, which endowes the Subject with such Liberties and Infranchisements, that beare up his naturall Courage, and keep him still in Heart, that free and secure him eternally from the Gripes and Tallons of *Tyranny:* And all this may be imputed to the authority and Wisdome of the High Court of *Parlement*, wherein there is such a rare Co-ordination of Power, (though the Soveraignty remaine still entire, and untransferrable in the Prince) there is such a wholsome Mixture 'twixt *Monarchy*, *Optimacy*, and *Democracy;* 'twixt Prince, Peers and Communalty, during the time of Consultation, that of so many distinct Parts, by a rare Co-operation and Unanimity, they make but one *Body-Politicke*, (like that Sheafe of Arrows in the Emblem) one entire concentricall Peece, and the Results of their Deliberations, but as so many harmonious Diapasons arising from different Strings.

§ 19. Britain and America to be friendly.

Rejoices he is under so good a Government.

Free of tyranny.

Because power is divided, —while Sovereignty is entire.

The different *parts* united in one body politic.

And we shall learn, I think, that at the settlement of the Crown on William and Mary, great care was used not to change the ancient Constitution. The documents and debates, which have been examined and will be quoted, seem to prove that Sovereignty was granted as of yore, so that William and Mary could rightfully grant their faithful subjects in Massachusetts the charter with such privileges and powers, as enabled those Colonists, when forsaken by the King's representatives, the Governor and Lieutenant-Governor, as they were, to appoint those officers for themselves.

No change in 1688.

William and Mary full sovereigns.

Could grant Massachusetts a charter.

Let the Nobility of Britain understand, that they have in us earnest coadjutors to maintain Aristocracy; and if they choose to make a part of theirs hereditary, not only do we freely admit that it is none of our concern, that we have no right in any shape or form to interfere; but further, we see clearly, that it is the best means of establishing a permanent and reliable check upon Monarch and People, indispensable in that form of Government. While we cannot have their form, most probably ours is not adapted to them, at least they think so; and the British People have not only ability to judge for themselves, but a long experience of the benefits of their Government, should make them slow to change essentially, while with due inquisition they ascertain abuses, if any there be, and make such improvements as may be in their power. We need desire no more success than that attained and attaining, in Britain's progress past and present. We Anglo-Saxons glory in our mother-land. God bless and prosper her for many centuries to come, as in centuries past; and when we shall have attained her present age, may we be able to show as honorable a record.

We will maintain Aristocracy.

We will not interfere with Britain's hereditary Aristocracy.

They can judge what is best.

Should be slow to change.

To equal them would satisfy us.

Prosperity on the mother-land!

The time has come for Anglo-Saxons of Britain and of these States, to have a better understanding. Two of the leading powers of earth, neither acknowledging any superior; being the two best examples of the opposite forms of Government, Monarchy and Democracy, one or the other of which every nation will, probably, in time imitate; we seem at first glance to be rivals, between whom concord is doubtful. Let us see.

Anglo-Saxons should have friendship.

Possibility of disagreement.

The competition in commerce and manufactures should give no occasion of difficulty beyond what arbitration can remove, already several times successfully employed; and when our Supreme Court shall be

As to commerce and manufactures.

§ 19. Britain and America to be friendly.

Difficulties easily settled,

—if we understand International Law.

remodelled in our new Constitution, and put upon a proper, enduring basis, beyond the possibility of interference with it either by the Executive or Congress, it will be a tribunal to which British Citizens, or even the British and other Governments, will resort with confidence that justice will be administered, according to true principles of International Law. Let British and American Citizens understand the Law of Nations, and seldom will its provisions be violated; and when difficulties arise, they can be adjusted in their own Courts, or the British Courts, or by arbitration. Seldom will any occasion of difficulty arise between these nations that cannot be thus settled.

No danger of rivalry as to our diverse forms of Government.

We are not to plant Colonies.

No danger of collision if allowed to manage our own affairs.

The probable extent of our Republic.

No territory will be unfairly obtained.

Our revolutionizing sentiments to be corrected.

The next most serious ground of rivalry may be, as to the spread of our respective forms of Government. But in that is no danger. We are never to engage in planting Colonies, not even for the Negro, having land enough of our own for the present, and more than we can speedily settle; and when we want more, we shall buy it or annex independent States in Mexico or the West Indies. We have land enough in our own and contiguous territory, without going abroad to plant Colonies. So that, supposing Britain will allow us to manage our affairs as we please, in our own neighborhood, Canada, Jamaica, &c. excepted, there appears to be no danger of collision. If she be not resolved on this course, she had best by all means attempt now to interrupt our destiny, which is probably to embrace in one Federal Union the Islands and the Continent to the Isthmus of Panama. She will let us go on our way rejoicing in America, as will she in the East. Neither shall we ever obtain Cuba or Jamaica, or any other territory, by any *fillibustering* means or other wrong conduct. We shall bide our time, and take our chances, faithfully living up to the Law of Nations; and though some of our people attempted once to interfere with Canada, and others with Cuba, we shall know our duties better in future. The revolutionizing sentiments of man's freedom and right to overthrow Government at will, are never again to have support in this land of true liberty. Licentiousness and wrong, our Sovereignties will control and punish. What even Rousseau condemns, we shall not practise nor permit, when we better understand principles of Government.[1]

Rousseau's *Discourse on Inequality.* *Dedic'n*, p. vii.

Man under a "yoke,"

—subject to laws.

No man exempt.

Two heads in a State cannot be obeyed.

Agrees with our Saviour's teaching.

A new Republic disliked for fear of change.

[1] Rousseau observes in his dedication to the Republic of Geneva, of "*A discourse upon the Origin and Foundation of the Inequality among Mankind:*"

"I should have chose to live and die free, that is to say, subject to the Laws in such a manner, t. at neither I, nor any other Member of the same Society, should be able to shake off their honourable Yoke; this wholesome and pleasant Yoke, which the proudest necks carry with so much the greater Docility, as they are not made for carrying any other.

"I should therefore have desired, that no Member of the State should be able to boast of his being superior to its Laws, nor the State have any Reason to fear its being obliged to receive Laws from any other. For, let the Constitution of a Government be what it will, if there is but one man in it exempt from the Laws, all the other Members must necessarily be at his Discretion; And when there are two Heads, one National, and the other Foreign, let them divide the sovereign Authority in the best manner it can be divided, it is impossible that should be well obeyed and the Government properly administered."

Thus does this infidel corroborate the immaculate teachings of our blessed Saviour, that a man cannot serve two masters, and that therefore Sovereignty over man must be one and indivisible, however its *exercise* may be distributed. A further quotation must be made from this distinguished teacher of *freedom* and *equality*.

"I should not have liked to belong to a Republic lately formed, whatever good Laws it might be blessed with; for as the Government of it might possibly be otherwise framed than present

Nor is there danger of collision elsewhere, in disseminating governmental principles. We have no right to interfere with any other State, to induce a change in its form, nor would interest prompt us to the attempt. Believing we have the best system of Government ever devised, provided it possess seeds of perpetuity, it is not for our advantage to have a similar and powerful one in Europe or elsewhere. As philanthropic individuals, we might rejoice in the spread of free institutions; but with all the rest of the world, owing to the imperfections of humanity, we have been compelled to unite ourselves into these States; those greatest moral persons, that are without heart or conscience, and who are created for the very purpose of advancing their own individual good. These States of ours need, most of all, population for themselves and for the vacant territories they own in common. The worse the Governments of Europe, the more will their people flock hither.

§ 19. Britain and America to be friendly.

We are not to be political apostles.

Neither right nor interest prompts us to interference.

As individuals we rejoice in the spread of free institutions, not as States.

The worse other Governments are, the better for us.

As nations we should even deprecate the adoption by other nations of Britain's improvements in the science of Monarchial Government, much more our own in Republican Government. France, for instance, we hope, will forever adhere to its determination to be "one and indivisible." It is a sure safeguard against her becoming a permanent Republic; and we want the liberty-loving Frenchmen here. More admixture of that sprightly blood is quite desirable. The commingling of blood from the various families of the Caucasian race, no doubt accounts for the superiority of American character, and Powers in statuary, and Morphy in chess, are only specimens of what will be often witnessed in every department of the arts and sciences. We desire more and more of the best blood of Europe, and shall have it, if we can only maintain our Union, and thereby give confidence in the perpetuity of our institutions. And we as a nation of nacions, however it may be with individuals, do not care to see improvements made in European Governments adapted to keep their Citizens at home.

These States do not want other States to improve.

We want their inhabitants.

Benefits of mixing blood.

We discover no cause to apprehend difficulties between Britain and these States united, except the natural jealousy of rival nations. This should not have usual strength between us. We the daughters should have none of it, especially if these States can be once again united; for with Union we shall as certainly lead her as that the wheel of time revolves. We have not been, we shall not be jealous of Britain, and,

No cause of difficulty except national jealousy.

We have no jealousy of Britain.

Exigencies required, I could not promise myself that it would not be shaken and destroyed, almost at its Birth, either because the new Administration did not suit the Subjects, or the Subjects the new Administration. It is with Liberty as with those solid and succulent Aliments or generous Wines, which, tho' fit to nourish and strengthen the robust Constitutions that have been accustomed to them, can only serve to oppress, to disorder and destroy such weak and delicate Frames as had never before made use of them. Men, once accustomed to Masters, can never afterwards do without them. The more they bestir themselves to get rid of their fetters, the farther they stray from the Paths of Liberty, inasmuch as, by mistaking it for an unbounded Licence which is the very reverse of Liberty, they almost always become in the end, the Slaves of Impostors, who, instead of lightening their Chains, make them a great deal heavier than they before ever were," &c.

True ideas of liberty.

Men accustomed to masters cannot dispense with them.

It would be agreeable to quote further the testimony which this anti-Christian, God-despising, Sovereignty-hating miscreant had to bear in favor of the right, the necessity of Government; utterly subverting, even in the dedication, one of the most detestable, revolutionizing attempts ever made by a wretched, fallen creature, to overthrow the Heaven-ordained bulwark of humanity, *the Right of Command.*

Rousseau corrects his own wrong teachings.

§ 19. Britain and America to be friendly. patiently biding our time, will rejoice in the prosperity that may be showered upon our worthy mother, which, however great, must here be surpassed. We are true Anglo-Saxons, and rivalry on our part shall be, by virtuous deeds, peerless achievements, to prove ourselves not unworthy of our ancestry of England, more faithful supporters of its glory, than even the sons at home. We feel our debt of gratitude for the wisdom of our Monarchs, which led to the liberal grants of self-government, that qualified the Colonies to become free and independent States; and had George III as properly asserted the royal prerogatives, as faithfully sustained the British Constitution with its ancient Monarchial form of Government, as did his predecessors, he would never have mourned the loss of these jewels from his Crown. We know not yet whether to sorrow or to rejoice at the egregious blunders in the science of Government that led to our separation. But reunion being impossible, we would next have warm and constant friendship with our cousins; and let the two branches vie in manly, loving strife, which shall do most for the honor of our common lineage. We glory in being of that true liberty-loving stock; in speaking the language of England, which we will aid to spread with all its accompanying blessings to every continent, to all the islands of the seas. In the beautiful thoughts and words of our distinguished historian do we say with all our hearts:

Will rejoice in her prosperity. Will try to prove ourselves worthy sons. Our indebtedness for liberal grants. Had George III been faithful as our earlier Kings, we had not been separated. Reunion being impossible, let our strife be to most honor our common lineage.

> Go forth, then, language of Milton and Hampden, language of my country, take possession of the North American continent! Gladden the waste places with every tone that has been rightly struck on the English lyre, with every English word that has been spoken well for liberty and for man! Give an echo to the now silent and solitary mountains; gush out with the fountains that as yet sing their anthems all day long without response; fill the valleys with the voices of love in its purity, the pledges of friendship in its faithfulness; and as the morning sun drinks the dewdrops from the flowers all the way from the dreary Atlantic to the Peaceful Ocean, meet him with the joyous hum of the early industry of freemen! Utter boldly and spread widely through the world the thoughts of the coming apostles of the people's liberty, till the sound that cheers the desert shall thrill through the heart of humanity, and the lips of the messenger of the people's power, as he stands in beauty upon the mountains, shall proclaim the renovating tidings of equal freedom for the race!

An apostrophe to the English language.

BANCROFT, *History of the Revolution*, ii. 450.

Nor should our mother be jealous of the rising glory of her daughters. The noblest, farthest-reaching work of modern centuries, was the planting of England's Colonies in America; a work worthy of the great Queen Elizabeth and her illustrious Raleigh. Had the same clear ideas of Sovereignty and its rights been perpetuated, which Sir Walter gave, and will be found in this first volume, we had to-day probably been with her. It would be in vain to speculate upon results that might have been witnessed, but for the confusion with regard to the *theories* of Government, which led our King and his Ministry, Tories as they were, to put Sovereignty out of the Crown into Parliament. A magnificent kingdom would it have been when, in time, the American portion, largely outstripping the European, it would have become wise and necessary to transfer the court to this side of the Atlantic. Ignorance and confusion prevailed, dismem-

Britain should not be jealous of her offspring. Separation caused by errors. Vain to speculate on what might have been. A magnificent kingdom ruptured.

berment was accomplished, and the wrongs cannot be righted. We have to deal with facts as they are, not as they might have been.

§ 19. Britain and America to be friendly.

The separation no cause of enmity.

Nor should any grudge be borne us on account of the separation. We were never rebels. We stood by prerogatives of our Sovereign, our rights as Britons, and our chartered privileges, and resisted the base endeavors to destroy the ancient Constitution of England and of Britain, and by transferring the Supreme Power from the King to Parliament, to change the Government from a Monarchy, limited with great wisdom, to an unlimited Aristocracy. We had those who sought revolution; but the documents will prove how strongly we affirmed our allegiance to our King, and how earnestly we desired to continue a part of the British State; and though bewildered by Locke and Blackstone in our *theories*, we were about right in *practice*. An extract of a letter from Jefferson to Wirt, confirms this, and we shall have more of the same sort:

Had not the King violated the British Constitution, it would not have occurred.

We opposed *separation*.

JEFFERSON, *to Wirt*, Aug. 14, 1814. *Works*, vi. 368.

. . . The Address of 1764 was drawn by Peyton Randolph. Who drew the memorial to the Lords, I do not recollect, but Mr. Wythe drew that to the Commons. It was done with so much freedom, that, as he has told me himself, his colleagues of the Committee shrank from it as bearing the aspect of treason, and smoothed its features to its present form. He was, indeed, one of the very few, (for I can barely speak of them in the plural number,) of either character, who, from the commencement of the contest, *hung our connection with Great Britain on its true hook, that of a common king*. His unassuming character, however, made him appear as a follower, while his sound judgment kept him in a line with the freest spirit. By these resolutions, Mr. Henry took the lead out of the hands of those who had heretofore guided the proceedings of the House, that is to say, of Pendleton, Wythe, Bland, Randolph, Nicholas. These were honest and able men, had begun the opposition on the same grounds, but with a moderation more adapted to their age and experience. Subsequent events favored the bolder spirits of Henry, the Lees, Pages, Mason, &c., with whom I went in all points. Sensible, however, of the importance of unanimity among our constituents, although we often wished to have gone faster, we slackened our pace, that our less ardent colleagues might keep up with us; and they, on their part, differing nothing from us in principle, quickened their gait somewhat beyond that which their prudence might of itself have advised, and thus consolidated the phalanx which breasted the power of Britain. By this harmony of the bold with the cautious, we advanced with our constituents in undivided mass, and with fewer examples of separation than, perhaps, existed in any other part of the Union.

Being subject to the King was our tie to Britain.

Moderation of the leaders.

Young men wanted to go faster.

Waited for the elder ones.

Harmony of the Revolution.

The Colonists will be found to have been the only true Tories in the British dominions, faithful subjects in maintaining the royal prerogative, even against the faithless Tory King and Ministry themselves. And our noble Whig friends, Burke, Fox, Chatham, &c., having been joined in this bewildering fashion by their opponents, seem never to have comprehended their position, or how to extricate themselves, from their difficulties. The Tories, adopting for the time the Whig notions of the supremacy of the Legislature, as in the Quebec Bill, if the Whigs were right, Parliament must have the power to pass any and all laws to promote the general good of the kingdom, in America as elsewhere. Lord Mansfield's argument is perfectly unanswerable. This the sound practical sense of the Whigs, caused them to resist, notwithstanding their theories were confused; and they were obliged to take the strange position, that a

We were true Tories.

Whigs were confused by the Tories acknowledging the supremacy of Parliament.

Whig sense governed in *practice*, but contradicted *theories*.

§ 19. Britain and America to be friendly.

We fought for the British Constitution.

No chance for compromise.

power supreme in all its dominions, had no authority or right to make and enforce certain laws in particular sections of the State. Our cousins will find that instead of our being *rebels*, we fought hard for fourteen months in defence of our Constitution and ancient rights, as Britons; and finding it of no use, that even the Tories were determined to change our system from a Monarchy into an Aristocracy, our Sovereign thereby forfeiting all claim to our allegiance by these violations of his oaths, we cast off his *Right of Command*, taking it to ourselves. We would have disgraced our parentage had we done differently. Compromise was out of the question. The sensible Dean Tucker said:

DEAN TUCKER, *Pleas of the Mother Country and of the Colonies, Tract* 5, p. 11.

> The misfortune is, that in the present case, any scheme for a *Compromise* is absolutely impracticable. And the reason is, because in all compromising schemes, it is believed, and taken for granted by both parties, that what they give up for the sake of peace, doth not invalidate their right and title to that, which they choose to retain. But this is by no means the present case: For the claim of right on either side must be universal, or there must be no claim at all: And neither party have it in their power to recede a tittle from their pretensions, without subverting the very foundation of their claim to all the rest.

Division of right impossible.

Right to lay one tax gave right to all taxes.

We opposed change in our Government.

That was precisely the case. If Parliament had any right to legislate for us, she had the whole right. If she could lay an external tax, she could an internal; and if allowed to levy three-pence on tea, she could go at her own option to twenty shillings in the pound. No limit can be assigned to a Supreme Legislature. We had never acknowledged the supremacy of Parliament; were never its subjects. Without well understanding the *theory*, we had too much good *practical* sense to consent, that our Monarchial Government should be changed into that most miserable of all forms, an Aristocracy. Had George III only been as good a Tory as were our fathers, the noble fellow, for he was a splendid Monarch, would never have endured the mortification of acknowledging the independence of these States.

Providence directed the change.

Republicanism incompatible with Monarchy.

Division was anticipated.

Probably it was a kind Providence that brought about the separation then, when its cost of blood and treasure was less than it could have been at any time since. The growth of Republicanism in the Colonies, was incongruous with the British form of Government, which was not foreseen in the early stages of settlement, and even had it been anticipated, could scarcely have been guarded against. In time this must have generated dissension and strife, and probably ultimate division. Her wise statesmen have foreseen this. Lord Kames wrote only three years before the separation:

LORD KAMES, *History of Man*, ii, 94.

Rapid growth of the Colonies.

Will become independent and Democratic.

> Our North American colonies are in a prosperous condition, increasing rapidly in population and in opulence. The colonists have the spirit of a free people, and are inflamed with patriotism. Their population will equal that of Britain and Ireland in less than a century; and they will then be a match for the mother-country, if they choose to be independent: every advantage will be on their side, as the attack must be by sea from a very great distance. Being thus delivered from a foreign yoke, their first care will be the choice of a proper government; and it is not difficult to foresee what government will be chosen. A people animated with the new blessings of liberty and independence, will not incline to a kingly government. The Swiss cantons joined

in a federal union, for protection against the potent house of Austria; and the Dutch embraced the like union, for protection against the more potent King of Spain. But our colonies will never join in such a union; because they have no potent neighbour, and because they have an aversion to each other:[1] We may pronounce with assurance, that each colony will choose for itself a republican government. And their present constitution prepares them for it: they have a senate; and they have an assembly representing the people. No change will be necessary, but to drop the Governor who represents the King of Britain. And thus a part of a great State will be converted into many small States.

§ 19. Britain and America to be friendly.

Can never have Federal Union.

Each Colony will be independent.

Small change in their Governments.

Reunion is neither possible nor desirable. Nor can we have Britain's excellent form of Government, unless through anarchy, long despotism, and seas of blood, we should be able to find rest under the conservative influence of an hereditary Aristocracy like that of hers, the growth of centuries. Our kinsfolk desire for us no such fate, at least till we have tried longer whether Anglo-Saxon stock has not capacity to rule under another form of Government than Monarchy. We believe it will be found capable of doing anything Caucasians have ever done; and our cousins should have pride in us and earnestly aid our efforts to maintain the God-given form instituted in the early stages of our race. These two most Christian nations, happy and joyous in the benevolent and philanthropic efforts of each other's Citizens to improve man's condition wherever found, whether of our race or of those inferior; efficient co-laborers in the harvest of the world, with what strong cords of affection should the hearts of these great and good Peoples be bound together! It will be so, if we can only be brought rightly to understand each other; and present circumstances afford an opportunity that centuries to come may never give.

Reunion with Britain, or their form of Government, impossible.

Anglo-Saxons should aid us to maintain Government.

Britain and America should be friends.

Any animosity of late years on our part against Britain, has been caused by the belief that her Nobility are inimical to us, and have persistently sought our division. It is not a thing susceptible of positive proof, though we have corroborative evidence, which will be given in the sequel, and which the British have been aware of and could have disproven, had they deemed it best. Without the counter-evidence, we have been more and more strengthened in our convictions of their enmity. If it has existed, we see we have given too much occasion, in the inflammatory teachings, by our stump-orators and ignorant, selfish politicians, of equality and the right of revolution; and this fault on our part it is hoped we shall well correct. Doing this frankly and thoroughly, we hope to have full evidence, either that we have misjudged their Aristocracy, or

We are inimical to Britain, because her Nobility seek our division.

We have given cause for their dislike in our erroneous teachings of equality.

We will correct this, and they will correct their wrongs.

---

[1] Lord Kames remarks in another place: "The English colonies in North America, though they retain some affection for their mother-country, have contracted an aversion to each other. And happy for them is such aversion, if it prevent their uniting in order to acquire independence: wars without end would be the inevitable consequence, as among small States in close neighbourhood."

Lord Kames, *Ib.* 33.

Colonies averse to each other.

This is not the only testimony we shall have as to ancient hostility between these Colonies. Union probably would never have been formed but for the necessities of the war. That Union, imperfect as it was, proved too advantageous to allow of its being given up, and a more perfect one was made. Under its beneficent influences and growing intercourse, ancient aversion and hatred had nearly died out, till within the last thirty years the slavery question arose, and owing to misconceptions of our Federal Union, has engendered more bitter feelings than ever. Only by a return to true Federalism can we ever again become friends; and an immense Federal Union, seems to be the truest safeguard against petty jealousy and enmity.

Further testimony.

Union compelled by war had wrought friendship, till the slavery question brought dissension.

§ 19. Britain and America to be friendly.

that our wrongs being corrected, they will desist from their purposes of weakening us by division.

The present a favorable opportunity.

We are in confusion as to Governmental principles.

Slavery could not have brought this war but for ignorance of International Law.

Our Sovereignty lost.

Various ideas of its whereabouts.

Britons will aid to find it.

Such aid as Mr. Spence's not wanted.

LORD BROUGHAM on Supreme Power in America.

The present affords a remarkable opportunity to convince us of their sincerity. We are all in confusion as to principles of Government. Slavery has been made the ostensible and exciting question, in the discussion of which, Britain seems to have powerfully stimulated our variance and animosity, in order to effect division even with civil war. But slavery is only an incidental evil at most; and could never have worked great injury, had we properly understood International Law, particularly the rights of Sovereign States united by a Federal League. We have become perplexed and cannot agree as to where our Supreme Power is, which regulates States and their every interest, slavery included. Some of our great statesmen affirm that our Sovereignty is in the United States, some in the people of the United States, some in the Government of the United States, some in State Governments, some that it is divided, part to the United States or their Government, and part to the States or their Governments; and here and there a man is found with the strange hallucination, that it is in the People—the People by States. Now we want the aid of Lord Brougham, Lord Russell, Mr. Disraeli, Mr. Mill and others, who write as though they understood this question of Government, to aid us in discovering where our Sovereignty—our *Right of Command*—is located. We do not desire further assistance like that of Mr. Spence, for its tendency is strongly toward disunion; and we believe, if we can only know positively where we have our Supreme Power, we can arrange our differences and be saved from disunion. Our English friends themselves do not appear to have well studied into our system, for Lord Brougham in his able work remarks:

Political Philosophy, iii. 335.

Because the Legislature is bound, we have no Supreme Power.

We have now seen that this Constitution professes to lay down certain fundamental laws, which are binding not merely on the subject but upon the Congress itself, and upon all the State Legislatures. Hence arises this anomaly, that the supreme power is fettered: there is not, properly speaking, a supreme power; Congress is tied up: that is done by the American Constitution, which in ours is held impossible; the hands of the Legislature are bound; a law has been made which is binding on all future Parliaments.

This an effect of Federacy.

State independence.

(Interpolations to suit existing facts.)

The Constitution a Treaty, for the benefit of each State,

—altered only by general consent.

Federal Union not a refinement.

When we at first contemplate this state of things, it appears to be sufficiently anomalous; and yet a little reflection will show us that it is, at least to a certain extent, the necessary consequence of the Proper or Perfect Federal Union. There is not, as with us, a government only and its subjects to be regarded; but a number of Governments, of States having each a separate and substantive, and even independent existence, originally thirteen, now six and twenty [now thirty-four], and each having a legislature of its own, with laws differing from those of the other States. It is plainly impossible to consider the Constitution [now Constitutions] which professes to govern this whole Union [profess to govern these whole Unions], this Federacy [these Federacies] of States, as anything other than a Treaty [Treaties], of which the conditions are to be executed for them all [for the States respectively forming each Confederacy]; and hence there must be certain things laid down, certain rights conferred, certain provisions made, which cannot be altered without universal consent, or a consent so general as to be deemed equivalent for all practical purposes to the consent of the whole. It is not at all a refinement, as we have already remarked, that a Federal Union should be formed; this is the natural result of men's joint operations in a very rude state of society. But the regulation of such a Union upon pre-established principles—the formation of a system of government and legislation in which the different subjects shall be not individuals but States—the application of legislative principles to such a body of States—and the devising means for keeping its integrity as a Federacy, while the rights and powers of the individual States are maintained entire—is the very greatest refinement in social policy to which any state of circumstances has ever given rise, or to which any age has ever given birth.*

§ 19. Britain and America to be friendly.

Such a system as this of ours, —the greatest refinement in social policy.

It is believed that this examination, in the sequel, will be found to justify the strong language as to our having made "the very greatest refinement in social policy, to which any state of circumstances has ever given rise, or to which any age has ever given birth." And this "refinement" was attained by Anglo-Saxons, in only twelve years from the time we ceased to be Britons. Have our cousins *at home* any cause to be ashamed of us, for neglecting and not practising the principles of liberty and of true Government, established by centuries of English experience? Are we not true coin? bear we not "the stamp" of a long and noble line of Anglo-Saxon ancestry, whose blood has brought this "refinement"? Indeed have Anglo-Saxons in Britain and America abundant occasion for mutual congratulation; for reciprocal respect, esteem, and love.

Our Confederacy "the very greatest refinement."

This done by Anglo-Saxons.

Let not our cousins be ashamed of us.

Yet, while taking proper pride in our achievements, encouraged by our wonderful success to mightier efforts to "work out [our] own salvation" for time as well as for eternity, let not these Christian Peoples forget the Power that works within us or be unthankful for it. Hardly had the Hebrews of old more occasion to recognize the hand of Providence in their affairs of State, than have Britain and America. Most applicable to us is the message of the angel to the prophet:

We must not forget GOD'S providence in our affairs.

This is the word of the LORD unto Zerubbabel, saying, Not by might, nor by power, but by my Spirit, saith the LORD of hosts. Who *art* thou, O great mountain? before Zerubbabel *thou shalt become* a plain: and he shall bring forth the headstone *thereof with* shoutings, *crying*, Grace, grace unto it. Moreover the word of the LORD came unto me, saying, The hands of Zerubbabel have laid the foundation of this house; his hands shall also finish it; and thou shalt know that the LORD of hosts hath sent me unto you. For who hath despised the day of small things? for they shall rejoice, and shall see the plummet in the hand of Zerubbabel *with* those seven; they *are* the eyes of the LORD, which run to and fro through the whole earth.

Zech. iv, 6-10.

Man performs what GOD directs.

And in all our glorying, let us heed the word of GOD by another prophet:

Let us glory in GOD.

Thus saith the LORD, Let not the wise *man* glory in his wisdom, neither let the mighty *man* glory in his might, let not the rich *man* glory in his riches: But let him that glorieth glory in this, that he understandeth and knoweth me, that I *am* the LORD which exercise loving-kindness, judgment, and righteousness, in the earth: for in these *things* I delight, saith the LORD.

Jer. ix, 23.

We need to look no farther than this work of Lord Brougham's to discover, that it is not by earthly "might" and "wisdom" that the excellent institutions of Britain and America have been established and preserved. This *Political Philosophy* is one of the very best works on Government of the past century. Hon. Charles Francis Adams remarks

Our own might and wisdom have not established our institutions in Britain or America.

* The power of Congress in America extends not only over the different States, but over the inhabitants of each.

§ 19. Britain and America to be friendly.

in editing the works of his grandfather; a duty, by the way, admirably discharged, and well deserving the commendation bestowed by Mr. Trescott in his *Diplomatic History of the Administrations of Washington and Adams:*

C. F. ADAMS, *John Adams' Works*, iv. 277.

Lord Brougham's "philosophical examination."

> Whether owing to this cause or not, the fact is certain, that no leading political man, since his [John Adams'] day, has been known to express a serious doubt of the immaculate nature of the government established by the majority. The science has become reduced in America to a eulogy of the Constitution of the United States; and we are compelled to look abroad, to Sismondi, De Tocqueville, Lord Brougham, and other writers, who have studied on a broader scale, for the only philosophical examinations that are free from a bias seriously affecting their permanent value.

Lord Brougham will not contend that Government can exist without Sovereignty.

He sees the Federal Government is not supreme—

—yet the Constitution, &c., is "the Supreme Law."

Having no supreme Legislature, he thinks we have no supreme power.

The philosophic Lord Brougham, good Whig as he is—GOD bless all such—will never contend that a Government,—the machinery to control a People,—can be rightfully instituted, that does not rest upon Sovereignty, the *Right of Command.* Without that, the would-be authority is a usurpation, which English Whigs of all men can never tolerate. He rightly judges that the Federal Government cannot be supreme, because it is subject to a Constitutional Law; and he knows there is a power above it to alter that Law. Yet, while recognizing the subjection of this power, he also discovers a clause in the Constitution declaring itself and the laws and treaties made under it, "the Supreme Law of the Land," so that all the other Legislatures—those of the States—are subjected to this Federal Authority, which is also itself subject. We have no other Legislature, and he having clear convictions, according to the Whig school, that Sovereignty is in the Legislature if anywhere, and properly understanding that it could not possibly be divided,[1] so that these various Legislatures could each have a part, he comes to the inevitable conclusion that "there is not, properly speaking, a supreme power."

We do not believe our Governments are without Sovereignty.

Troubled to find it.

Want help.

English Whigs will be pleased with the discovery.

We have made great blunders in our expositions of Government; but not a single writer in America has been discovered who thinks we have Governments without any *Right of Command.* All are very sure we have it somewhere, but the trouble is to find it. And we want Lord Brougham and other good friends of the Whig school, not objecting either to good Tories, like Mr. Disraeli, to aid us in searching for our runaway Sovereignty. They can find it if they try; and it seems probable that they will not only be rewarded with the hearty thanks rendered by us their cousins, but the Whigs will be delighted to discover how correct was the *practice* of their old-time partisans, in resisting the Tory efforts to tax the Colonies and dismember the British kingdom, though

Addendum, p. 72, on Mr. Freeman's views.

He divides Sovereignty.

That is not Federal doctrine.

[1] In the haste to send the printer the interpolated remarks on Mr. Freeman's views, one of the most important differences between him and the old authorities escaped notice. Will the reader please consider the following an *addendum* to the first paragraph on p. 72, ending, "and other parts of their bodies politic:"

Yet is there not at all "This complete division of sovereignty," which this learned writer says "we may look upon as essential to the absolute perfection of the Federal idea." It is a base imputation on "the Federal idea," that it should be guilty of attempting to destroy the very essence of the *Right of Command*, its oneness and indivisibility. Mr. Freeman must study more into the "History of Federal Governments." There is no such nonsense as that in them. The truth is, "that ideal is one so very refined and artificial, that it seems not to have been" altogether comprehended by Mr. Freeman.

a little wrong as to the *theory*. The Tories, too, will be pleased to find that their chief wrong has been in deserting Tory principles, and allowing in any degree the supremacy of Parliament. They will be stronger Tories than ever.

§ 19. Britain and America to be friendly.

The Tories, too.

We love our Whig friends, and are happy that Lord Russell in particular is in power. He will aid his distinguished friend and others, who may join in the search for our Sovereignty; and when the discovery is made, which is sure as the sun in the heavens, it is believed it will be found thoroughly intrenched in the separate Peoples constituting these several States. As a consequence of its existence there, it will be found that, like Britain herself, or any other free and independent nation, each one of these States had the power to withdraw itself from a compact which it deemed injurious, though no doubt good faith required it should first have fairly employed the means provided in the Compact to protect its rights and interests. But having withdrawn, and no treaty obligations preventing, it had the right to make any sort of compact it pleased with other Sovereign States. Some of these States, formerly in our Federal Union, have withdrawn (without due regard, it is true, to the rights of States with which they had been united, and the settlement of which rights is still in abeyance, yet nevertheless withdrawn), and have formed another Union by the name of *The Confederate States of America*. They improperly and unnecessarily began a war upon us their former Confederates, soon after forming their Union; but they have conducted their affairs with remarkable skill, having organized their Confederate Government in the midst of war. We did the same thing before, it is true, when we resisted the Tory wrongs and Whig mistakes that caused our Revolution; but that war was a trifle to this. They have nobly sustained themselves; have far better and more correctly conducted their Government, new as it is, than have the North; are better able to-day to continue the contest than when they began it,—we are happy in his Lordship's assurance that they did begin it—and have proven themselves worthy branches of the Anglo-Saxon stock. Should not such a power be recognized by sister-nations as having an existence? We have recognized her *practically* in various ways, notwithstanding our conceited ignorance of *theories;* and though a dread of Fort Lafayette would deter the writer from even suggesting, that the British might follow our example; yet, if they should themselves think of it, and deem it advisable, it would be very grateful to that courageous young Republic. Their heart and soul is in this struggle for existence, and of all things do they desire to be recognized by sister-Sovereigns as an established power in the earth. Most grateful will it be to them to have the mother-land take the lead in Europe, and more than aught else she could do, would it attach to her the generous hearts of the South. And thousands of us in the North will rejoice that Britain so properly maintains the doctrine of State-rights. It must be done before these States can be again united. We glory in the pluck of our Southern friends, alien enemies though they be; and while

When our Sovereignty is found, it will be in the People of each State.

A Sovereign State can withdraw from a compact.

Having withdrawn, can form another.

Some of these States withdrew.

Have formed a new Confederacy.

They began war, but have managed skilfully.

Have proven true Anglo-Saxons.

Should they not be recognized?

We have done so.

The British might think of this.

The South would be gratified to have Britain recognize them.

§ 19. Britain and America to be friendly.

we are determined to have justice ourselves, we also want justice done to them. True Anglo-Saxon Americans are they; let them possess and enjoy due honor and respect.

The British will also find points in International Law favorable to the North.

But we hope, on examining further the Law of Nations, the wise men of Britain will also discover points that work in favor of the North. We in the Northwest especially wish to learn, whether we are not correct in our opinion, that these Sovereign States, in becoming joint owners in their common territory, have become possessed of properties and franchises with which we have never parted, and of which war cannot rightfully dispossess us. We are impressed with the words of wisdom which Jefferson penned to our excellent friend La Fayette: "I think with others, that nations are to be governed with regard to their own interests, but I am convinced that it is their interest in the long run, to be grateful, faithful to their engagements, even in the worst of circumstances, and honorable and generous always. If I had not known that the head of our Government was in these sentiments, and that his national and private ethics were the same, I would never have been where I am."

These States have rights in their common territory.

JEFFERSON, *Letter to Lafayette*, April 2, 1790. *Works*, iii, 132.

States to be honorable and faithful to engagements.

Those were Washington's sentiments.

That "head of our Government" was our beloved WASHINGTON. "These sentiments" of being "faithful to their engagements, even in the worst of circumstances, and honorable and generous always," were indeed preëminent in the Father of his country. His countrymen of the South will never desert the principles of Washington, Jefferson, the Pinckneys, Mason and the host of patriots, whose memory is a common and rich inheritance to all these Peoples. They *will* be "faithful to their engagements, even in the worst of circumstances;" *never* can the South belie themselves, and be other than "honorable and generous always." If they find they are mistaken as to principles of International Law, and that faith and pact are unjustly, unnecessarily violated by some of the States seceding, those States will retrace their steps and endeavor to frame a new and proper Federal Union, in which all these States can enjoy their common rights and franchises.

Never will the South desert his principles.

If mistaken as to International Law, they will correct their errors.

The North will not be less faithful.

Nor will we in the North be less "faithful to our engagements," less "honorable and generous always," than our sisters of the sunny South. The declaration has been made that we will not give up our *rights* in the seceded States, and we never will be dispossessed by force of arms. But if we are wrong as to the Law of Nations, learn either that these States never had rights beyond their own boundaries, or have rightfully and completely parted with their rights to each new State, as it has been admitted into the Federal Union "on an equal footing with the original States;" if we have no rights in States seceded from the Union, in others which may and will secede; if the Union cannot be restored, let us know it, and we shall not longer fight for them. We shall only continue the war begun upon us till the South are satisfied, and make propositions to conclude it, when we shall frankly and heartily say, "Wayward sisters, go in peace."

We will not be dispossessed by force of rights, yet if in error, will resign them.

Whichever way this question of our rights, according to the Law of

Nations, may be decided by competent authority, it surely brings peace, for we are no "beasts." We white folks, both in the South and in the North, belong to that race which was made "in the image of GOD." "Reason" not "force" will govern us, when we can learn what is "reason." We cannot, as States, be governed by "force," either in the North or in the South.

§ 19. Britain and America to be friendly.

According to International Law, is this question between North and South to be decided.

Our kindred and friends of the mother-land almost as earnestly as do we, desire peace. In our strife and excitement, we are not competent judges of these nice questions of International Law; and the authors of the Code of Nations do not seem themselves to harmonize on all points as perfectly as would be desirable, and we must have counsel and instruction. To our muddled intellects there is an apparent difference of considerable moment, between the teachings of Grotius, Pufendorf, Vattel, &c., and those of Locke, Blackstone, and the Whig school of England. If Sovereignty be in the Legislature, according to the latter, then Pufendorf and the others are quite in error as to the Legislature being only one of the "*parts*" of Sovereignty, and that a perfect *Right of Command* must not only have a power to make laws, but also a power, another "part," to judge concerning those laws, called a Judiciary; a power to execute, called an Executive; a power to tax, to create corporations, the right of eminent domain, &c. To decide whether there be any difference between these authorities, and what it is, would seem to be the first question to examine, though there probably is not much in it, for Locke and Blackstone can hardly be wrong; and had Grotius and his followers so entirely disagreed with the others, the differences and errors would long ago have been discovered. If our friends can determine these points for us, if there be anything in them, we shall then be able to find our long-lost Sovereignties, and as faithful subjects will we return to our allegiance.

Britain desires our peace.

Excitement renders us improper judges of right.

Difference between authorities as to Sovereignty.

To decide is the first point,

—if our friends aid to find it, we return to our allegiance.

Having found and properly located our Sovereignties, we can then learn the rights and wrongs of these States, concerning which we also need advice. Seldom is it, not once in centuries, that the statesmen of Britain can have an equal opportunity to perform a kindness, and gladly will they avail themselves of it beyond a doubt; with usual British honesty and sincerity and justice, will the work be done.

Deciding as to Sovereignty, will decide rights and wrongs of States.

British opportunity.

It will take some little time to make the examination, and meanwhile the war goes on. And though it was impolitic and imprudent to intimate how the British Government could please the South by recognition; yet as a "faithful liege subject of the Federal Government," as our wise statesmen use the words, we may declare openly a means of securing Northern confidence and friendship. Our good Whig friend, Lord Russell, remarked, as before quoted, that "the South have made war on the Government of Abraham Lincoln." His lordship knows that the "necessity" the Law of Nations requires, did not exist to justify the South in beginning this war; that notwithstanding many circumstances greatly extenuate, they scarcely justify, and therefore they are in an "unjust,

During examination, war goes on.

Chance to secure Northern friendship.

The South made war—

—is *unjust, offensive.*

§ 19. Britain and America to be friendly.

This Britain cannot aid.

Yet her captains dodge her regulations.

More English than French do this.

No complaint by us,—

—as our captains may dodge us.

offensive war," which no Christian nation can aid or abet, and they are bound by every principle of *Jus Gentium*, and of honor, to prevent their subjects from aiding our enemies, especially in articles contraband of war. Some captains will be smart and dodge the authorities, get out of port, cross the ocean, run the blockade, and sometimes by accident they carry arms, ammunition, &c. We observe that many more vessels, somehow or other, run away from Britain than from France; but we do not complain of this, because the British coast is extensive, and we shall no doubt sooner or later be neutral to a nation or nations at war, when we shall understand how difficult it will be to watch so long a coast and prevent contraband trade. It will be almost impossible to keep our smart Yankee captains from trying to make a little more profit, even with a good deal of risk. So we do not now complain of our friends' want of care, and we shall by and by know how to sympathize with them, in the inability of Government to control these smart captains.

The Alabama a bad example—

—our builders may imitate.

But it is very naughty in our cousins to allow such things as that Alabama to be built, freighted, and manned in their ports, and receive supplies in others, to prey upon our commerce. It is a bad example for our mother to set her daughters, one which they may be so unwise as to imitate. When there is occasion, our shipyards will very likely be building just such things for the Cantons of Switzerland, San Marino, and all the other great maritime nations; and when they put to sea and find it difficult to sail direct to those States, they may cruise elsewhere.

If Britain desires Northern friendship, she has a chance to secure it.

Must change her course.

If Britain desires the friendship of these Northern States, she can have it; and probably no like opportunity as the present, will soon recur to gain it. She must, however, somewhat shift her course, to be successful; yet only in uniformity with the rules and the demands of friendship. Britain knows us. She believes this Anglo-Saxon stock will always stand by a friend, punish a foe when it is right and opportune. We shall take good care that her confidence is not misplaced.

These States deeply interested in International Law.

Britain next.

Importance of commerce.

Importance to them of International Law to regulate it.

Must know where their Sovereignty is.

Of all States, these of America have deepest concern in thorough knowledge of the Law of Nations, the rule of conduct between them. Next to us, Britain probably is most interested. Kent, Story, and Wheaton agree, as we have seen, and their judgment is confirmed by Hume, Bentham, Ferguson, Mackintosh and other authorities, that commerce in good part has created the necessity for the modern International Code, and caused its rise. Commerce between these States and that of Britain is unsurpassed by that of any other nations. So that, aside from questions of our own reunion, and of war and peace, present and future, a clear determination of what is that Law to regulate that commerce, is of much consequence. Also is it of fundamental importance, that these Peoples, and their several individual members, know perfectly in whom their Sovereignty, their *Right of Command*, is to be found, in order to know whence comes the authority to enforce that Law.

Britain's Colonies.

Britain, though a single State, has important Colonies widely spread, which have rights dependent on the Law of Nations. The commerce of that State and her Colonies, is the greatest of all the world. She needs to well understand the International Code; and we should suppose that, if Whigs and Tories could come to an understanding, whether their *Right of Command* were really in her Majesty, though limited by fundamental laws, as it was in Saul and David; or in Parliament, creating an Aristocracy, it would tend to promote good understanding and correct management, and save other ruptures like that of ours in '76.

§ 19. Britain and America to be friendly.

To understand where is her Sovereignty, desirable.

While still adhering to the determination not to commit the folly of attempting to instruct the wise men of Britain as to their Government, it may not be improper to suggest some points in the early history of our common country and its Government, which are hardly questionable.

Some points in British history.

England was conquered by William the Norman, in 1066; and though this is denied by some English writers, yet his bearing the title, by common acceptation, of THE CONQUEROR, and the acts recorded of him, prove the fact incontestably. Says Ormerod in his History of Chester:

The Norman conquest.

> The general confiscation which may be presumed to have followed [the attack of the Normans on the Saxons], and the murder of the earl of Mercia in the year following [1070], prepared the way for the establishment of the NORMAN EARLDOM OF CHESTER, first granted to *Gherbod*, a noble Fleming, and then conferred on Hugh d'Avranches, the king's kinsman. To constitute an efficient counterpoise to the neighbouring Welshmen, the vast privileges of the ancient palatinate were annexed to the grant, making the earl a sovereign prince within his limits, owing fealty indeed to the greater empire of England, but holding the whole (in the words of the grant) as freely by the SWORD, as the king held his realm by the CROWN, as "a dignity inherent in the sword, as purchased by it, and to be kept by it also."
>
> This grant included the entire lands of the palatinate, with the exception of those held by the bishop, and nearly all the Saxon proprietors appear to have been ejected. This deprivation, and the subsequent distribution of lands to his Norman followers, was finished before the year 1086, &c.

ORMEROD'S *History of Chester, Introduction*, xxvii.

Division of lands by the Conqueror to his followers.

Thus was the British Monarchy instituted, and the Conqueror distributed his lands to his subjects; and though various grades of honors and privileges were established, the recipients were still subjects of their King. To get their contributions, the early Kings after William called the Nobles together, and their assent has been supposed to have always been given to the laws. When the People, by their representatives, first began to join in making their grants and giving assent to laws, is unknown; but in 1322 an act of Edward II declares that "the matters to be established for the estate of the king and of his heirs, and for the estate of the realm and of the people, should be treated, accorded and established in Parliament, by the king, and by the assent of the prelates, earls and barons, and the commonalty of the realm, as had been before accustomed." It seems unquestionable, that the English Government was a Monarchy down to the usurpation of the Sovereignty by the Long Parliament, and the murder of Charles I. It was then an Aristocracy, the State being under the rule of the *few*, till Charles II was able to assume the *Right of Command* which he had inherited, and which was actually his, from the day of his father's death. His brother, James II, inherited the crown, which by his tyranny and violation of his oath he doubtless

British Monarchy instituted.

Kings convened nobles—

—then People's Representatives.

England a Monarchy til Cromwell's usurpation.

Crown inherited by Charles II—

—then by James II—

§ 19. Britain and America to be friendly.

—by him forfeited.

No change made in grant of crown to William and Mary.

forfeited, and the Commons seem to have been right, as appears from their *Journal*, in insisting upon their resolution, that James II had "abdicated the Government, and that the throne [was] thereby vacant," to which the Lords reluctantly assented. In settling the crown on William and Mary, both Lords and Commons were very particular to make no change in their form of Government; and though the Commons desired to grant the crown conditionally upon their Majesties making farther concessions, they receded, and the joint Declaration reads:

Journal of the House of Lords, p. 100.

Assert ancient rights—

—which are undoubted.

Declaration of Prince of Orange.

Confidence in him.

William and Mary declared King and Queen.

William to be King.

The descent of Crown.

Oath of allegiance.

> And thereupon the said Lords Spiritual and Temporal and Commons, pursuant to their respective Letters and Elections, being now assembled in a full and free Representative of this Nation, taking into their most serious consideration the best means for attaining the ends aforesaid, do in the First Place (as their Ancestors in like Case have usually done) for the vindicating and asserting their ancient Rights and Liberties Declare, [then follow thirteen declarations, to be given in the fuller recital, adding] And they do claim, demand and insist upon, all and singular the Premises, as their undoubted Rights and Liberties; and that no Declarations, Judgments, Doings or Proceedings, to the Prejudice of the People in any of the said Premises, ought in any Wise to be drawn hereafter into Consequence or example. To all which Demand of their Rights they are particularly encouraged, by the Declaration of His Highness the Prince of *Orange*, as being the only Means for obtaining a full Redress and Remedy therein. Having therefore an entire Confidence that His said Highness the Prince of *Orange* will perfect the Deliverance so far advanced by him, and will still preserve them from the Violation of their Rights which they have here asserted, and from all other Attempts upon their Religion, Rights, and Liberties: The said Lords Spiritual and Temporal, and Commons, assembled at *Westminster*, do Resolve, That *William* and *Mary*, Prince and Princess of *Orange*, be, and be declared, King and Queen of *England*, *France* and *Ireland*, and the Dominions thereunto belonging; to hold the Crown and Royal Dignity of the said Kingdoms and Dominions, to them the said Prince and Princess, during their Lives, and the Life of the Survivor of them; and that the sole and full Exercise of the Regal Power, be only in, and executed by, the said Prince of *Orange*, in the Names of the said Prince and Princess, during their joint Lives; and after their Deceases, the said Crown and Royal Dignity of the said Kingdoms and Dominions to be to the Heirs of the Body of the said Princess; and for Default of such Issue, to the Princess *Anne* of *Denmarke* [who became Queen], and the heirs of her Body; and for Default of such Issue, to the Heirs of the Body of the said Prince of Orange. And the said Lords Spiritual and Temporal and Commons do pray the said Prince and Princess of *Orange* to accept the same accordingly. And that the Oaths hereafter mentioned be taken by all Persons, of whom the Oaths of Allegiance and Supremacy might be required by Law, instead of them; and that the said Oaths of Allegiance and Supremacy be abrogated: I, *A. B.* do sincerely promise and swear, That I will be faithful, and bear true Allegiance, to their Majesties King William and Queen Mary. So help me God, &c.

William and Mary proclaimed King and Queen.

The above was adopted the 12th February, 1688. The next day the Lords and Commons waited upon the Prince and Princess, and made to them in person their Declaration, which, with the crown, was graciously accepted in a short speech, after which the Lords and Commons proceeded to Whitehall gate, and publicly proclaimed the Prince and Princess of Orange, King and Queen, followed by three similar proclamations by the same parties in other parts of the city.

Form of Government unchanged.

Some acts were passed, which received their vitality from the assent of the King, strengthening the rights of the People, as had been desired by the Commons; but no important change is perceptible in the form of Government. If it was ever a Monarchy, it is one yet. The Scottish Parliament made a similar declaration and settlement of rights, and granted their Sovereignty also to William and Mary; and under Anne, in 1707, the two kingdoms were consolidated, taking to the new State their ancient name of *Britain;* and upon the consolidation with Ireland, the name was again changed to *The United Kingdom of Great Britain and Ireland.*

§ 19. Britain and America to be friendly.

Change of name of State.

There seems to be reasonable ground to believe, that the generous aid of friends *at home*, in the pursuit after our lost Sovereignties, will not be without benefit to themselves, in obtaining more definite knowledge as to the location of their own *Right of Command.* It is all in *theory*, to be sure, but it would perhaps aid in *practice*, to have the point determined whether the People and the Nobles are subjects of the Queen, or whether Queen, Lords, and Commons are subjects of Parliament. Her Majesty is either subject or Sovereign; she cannot be both; and it seems quite as essential for Britons to know whether their *Right of Command* is in Queen or Parliament, as it is for Citizens of these States, rulers and ruled, to know whether their Sovereignty is in the People by States, or in the whole People of the United States, or in their Federal or State Governments. Correctness in *theory* on these topics is quite essential to correctness in *practice.*

An examination to be of benefit to Britain, —to learn where their Sovereignty is, —equally as for these States.

At the same time, this theorizing is easily over-done; and, however feeble may be the writer's powers of apprehension, he has read too much of the able discussions of the English in the seventeenth century, not to know to what treatment these views expose the holder, not the authors.

Theorizing may be overdone.

Says Milton in his "*Defence of the People of England: in answer to Salmasius's Defence of the King:*"

MILTON'S *Defence of the People of England. Works*, i, 141.

Aristotle likewise in the third book of his Politics: "Of all kingdoms," says he, "that are governed by laws, that of the Lacedemonians seems to be most truly and properly so." And he says, all forms of kingly governments are according to settled and established laws; but one which he calls, παμβασιλεια, or Absolute Monarchy, which he does not mention ever to have obtained in any nation. So that Aristotle thought such a kingdom as that of the Lacedemonians was to be and deserve the name of a kingdom more properly than any other; and consequently that a king, tho' subordinate to his own people, was nevertheless actually a king, and properly so called. Now since so many and so great authors assert, that a kingly government both in name and thing may very well subsist even where the people, tho' they do not ordinarily exercise the supreme power, yet have it actually residing in them, and exercise it upon occasion; be not you of so mean a soul as to fear the downfall of grammar, and the confusion of the signification of words to that degree, as to betray the liberty of mankind and the state, rather than your glossary should not hold water. And know for the future, that words must be conformable to things, not things to words. By this means you will have more wit, and not run on in infinitum, which now you are afraid of. "It was to no purpose then for Seneca," you say, "to describe those three forms of government, as he has done." Let Seneca do a thing to no purpose, so we enjoy our liberty. And if I mistake us not, we are other sort of men, than to be enslaved by Seneca's flowers. And yet Seneca, tho' he says, that the sovereign power in a kingly government resides in a single person, says withal, that

ARISTOTLE on Spartan Kingdom, —favored a limited Monarchy— —which was yet a kingdom.

A rap at *theory.*

Things, more important than words.

Three forms of Government.

The power of the King belongs to the People.

§ 19. Britain and America to be friendly.

"the power is the people's," and by them committed to the king for the welfare of the whole, not for their ruin and destruction; and that the people has not given him a propriety in it, but the use of it.

Sparta was a true kingdom, but limited.

An absolute Monarchy merely theoretical.

Writers treat of three forms of Government.

Their difference consists in the location of Sovereignty.

The above extract serves further to elucidate the confusion of ideas. Lacedæmon, or Sparta, was undoubtedly a true kingdom, as treated by Aristotle, as we shall hereafter see, yet one of the most strictly limited of which we have knowledge. Of Aristotle's παμβασιλεια, *kingly power over all*, Absolute Monarchy, he presents no example, and it is merely treated theoretically, as being the most perverted specimen of a true and proper Kingdom. It is generally supposed that Aristotle was nobody's fool; and he, as did Polybius, Tacitus, Seneca, Cicero, &c., whose views we shall have occasion to examine, treated of Government under the three forms, Monarchy, Aristocracy, and Democracy. Now, the whole difference between these three forms consists solely in the location of the Sovereignty, the *Right of Command*, as it shall be lodged respectively in the *one*, the *few*, or the *many*. It is one and indivisible, and cannot be lodged partly in the *one*, partly in the *many*.

Milton and Locke do not properly classify.

The Hebrews granted Sovereignty to Saul—

—it reverted,

—was granted to David.

Milton seems to confound, as Locke did after him, the occasional reverting to the People of their *Right of Command*, with its permanent continuance in a true Commonwealth or free People. Before the Hebrews had Saul for a king, their Sovereignty was in the possession of their several Peoples, Tribes, or States. They granted this away, *lodged* it in Saul, and he by his crimes forfeited his propriety in it, and it reverted to the Peoples, when they had the power to keep its possession, or again to grant it. All the States, however, but Judah, adhered to the house of Saul for seven years and a half. The People of Judah soon granted their *Right of Command* to David; and seven years and a half after, all the States granted to him their Sovereignty.

God teaches that Sovereignty may be granted.

It may be inherited.

It may be united by marriage of Sovereigns.

If granted conditionally, may be forfeited.

The Almighty Sovereign, it will be admitted, ought to know something about Sovereignty, however it may be with ignorant mortals such as Aristotle; and He has too unmistakably pointed out the difference between retaining and granting the *Right of Command*, to question the fact that the latter can be, and has been, done. And in some States is the *Right of Command* so effectually granted to and possessed by the King, that he can grant it to others as he pleases, as David did to Solomon, and as was done by Charles V to his brother Ferdinand and his son Philip. In other States is the possession so complete, that the possessors by their marriage unite their States, as Aragon and Castile were consolidated by the marriage of King Ferdinand with Queen Isabella, creating a new State that became Spain, though the consolidation seems to have been imperfect till their two crowns came to be inherited by their grandson Charles I. But it is worthy of note that, while the "*propriety* in it" is actually, completely conveyed away, absolutely parted with, and not barely "the *use* of it," yet, like any other right, this of Sovereignty may be granted upon conditions, and the grantee disregarding or violating the conditions of the grant, the right reverts to the grantors.

§ 19. Britain and America to be friendly

Hobbes' division of the *rights* of Sovereignty.

The next year after Milton published his answer to Salmasius, Hobbes published his *Leviathan* (1651), in which he divides up the *rights* of Sovereignty, very much as Pufendorf does after him, as the right of judging of what shall be crime, of judging what is necessary for the peace and defence of his subjects, of judging what doctrines shall be taught, the right of making laws, the right of judging and deciding controversies, the right of making war and peace, the right of choosing counsellors and ministers, the right of rewarding and punishing, the right of establishing the honor and order of the subjects. Following the presentation of these rights, Hobbes remarks:

Leviathan, *Works*, iii, 167–169.

The location of Sovereignty.

Rights may be transferred.

If one right is gone, all the rest of no effect.

These are the rights which make the essence of sovereignty; and which are the marks, whereby a man may discern in what man, or assembly of men, the sovereign power is placed and resideth. For these are incommunicable and inseparable. The power to coin money; to dispose of the estates and persons of infant heirs; to have præemption in markets; and all other statute prerogatives, may be transferred by the sovereign; and yet the power to protect his subjects be retained. But if he transfer the *militia*, he retains the judicature in vain, for want of execution of the laws: or if he grant away the powers of raising money; the militia is in vain; or if he give away the government of doctrines, men will be frighted into rebellion with the fear of spirites. And so if we consider any one of the said rights, we shall presently see, that the holding of all the rest will produce no effect, in the conservatism of peace and justice, the end for which all commonwealths are instituted.[1] And this division is it, whereof it is said, *a kingdom divided in itself cannot stand:* for unless this division precede, division into opposite armies can never happen. *If there had not first been an opinion received of the greatest part of England, that these powers were divided between the King and the Lords and the House of Commons, the people had never been divided and fallen into this civil war;*[2] first between those that disagreed in politics; and after between the dissenters about the liberty of religion; which have so instructed men in this point of sovereign right, that there be few now in England that do not see that these rights are inseparable, and will be so generally acknowledged at the next return of peace; and so continue, till these miseries are forgotten; and no longer, except the vulgar be better taught than they have hitherto been.[3]

A division destroys a kingdom.

The controversy then about the location of Sovereignty.

The English then right.

Will not so continue unless better taught.

No matter about appearance if Sovereignty be retained.

And because they are essential and inseparable rights, it follows necessarily, that in whatsoever words any of them seem to be granted away, yet if the sovereign power itself be not in direct terms renounced, and the name of sovereign no more given by the grantees to him that grants them, the grant is void: for when he has granted all he can, if we grant back the sovereignty, all is restored, as inseparably annexed thereunto.[4]

Sovereignty indivisible.

This great authority being indivisible, and inseparably annexed to the sovereignty, there is little ground for the opinion of them, that say of sovereign Kings, tho' they be *singulis majores*, of greater power than every one of their subjects, yet they be

---

Rights may be delegated, yet belong to the Sovereign.

[1] That is, "the holding of all the rest [of the rights] will produce no effect," if "any one of the said rights" be wanting in the Sovereign. They must all belong to the Sovereign to be used when required, to effect "the end for which all Commonwealths are instituted." But it is no division of *Sovereignty* to divide the *exercise* of its powers; the soul is still one and indivisible operating through different agencies, the feet, the hand, the eye, &c.

Our war about the location of Sovereignty.

[2] Neither had we "been divided and fallen into this [more terrible] civil war," but for the absurd attempt to divide up the Sovereignty of these States to subordinate agents, as the Federal Government, Congress, the President, the State Governments, &c.

[3] Precisely applicable to our case, are these observations made over two hundred years ago.

These States have preserved their Sovereignty.

[4] This great writer fully confirms the view herein advocated, as to a sovereign State recalling its grants or its delegations. Not the first syllable can be shown of any State having granted away its Sovereignty, and of necessity it retains it, and with it all the rights and powers "as inseparably annexed thereunto."

§ 19. Britain and America to be friendly.

A King must have the whole power of the People.

universis minores, of less power than them all together. For if by *all together*, they mean not the collective body as one person, then *all together*, and *every one*, signify the same; and the speech is absurd. But if by *all together*, they understand them as one person, which person the sovereign bears, then the power of all together, is the same with the sovereign's power; and so again the speech is absurd: which absurdity they see well enough, when the sovereignty is in an assembly of the people; but in a monarch they see it not; and yet the power of sovereignty is the same in whomsoever it be placed.

Hobbes confutes Milton.

Herein agrees with Hooker, Grotius, &c.

The last paragraph appears to confute Milton's idea, that the people never part with Sovereignty; and though Hobbes had some detestable sentiments, yet on this question of Sovereignty he is mainly coincident with Hooker, Grotius, Pufendorf, and Vattel; the chief difference being that he considered the King could never forfeit his rights. On this important point, one crediting the Bible, as Hobbes did not, finds an ample precedent in the case of Saul.

Deceit of James I, styling his kingdom a Commonwealth—

—as did Roman emperors.

Locke follows the example.

Locke's Constitution for North Carolina.

In the age of Milton, the science of Government, the *theories* concerning it, had not become settled. The Kings did not want the subject understood; and hence James I, one of the most thorough asserters of prerogative, gulled his subjects by styling his domain a Commonwealth, just as the Emperors of Rome continued to speak of the *civitas* or Commonwealth, after they had usurped the *Right of Command*, and changed the Roman Republic into an Empire, a free State into a despotism. The son and grandsons imitated the shrewd conceit of that great king; and Locke, in his work on Government, says: "I crave leave to use the word Commonwealth in that sense, in which I find it used by King James the first; and I take it to be its genuine signification; which, if anybody dislike, I consent with him to change it for a better." We shall soon have, too, another specimen of Locke's wisdom in *practice* as well as *theory*, in the Constitution of Government formed by him for North Carolina.

Writers on International Law.

Genius of Vattel.

He first styles Sovereignty *Right of Command.*

His preliminaries are axioms.

Following the lead of Aristotle, Cicero, Polybius, Tacitus, Hooker, Ridley, Grotius, Usher, and Hobbes, have Pufendorf, Cumberland, Filmer, Locke (correct in part), Sidney, Barbeyrac, Burlamaqui, Montesquieu, Wolf, Rutherforth, Vattel, and others, aided to develop political science, till in the latter we see its culmination. Vattel was a wonderful genius, fully the equal of Montesquieu, and with a happier faculty of bringing his thoughts within the comprehension of ordinary intellects. He seems to have more thoroughly mastered his subject than his predecessors, for though agreeing in the main concerning Sovereignty, he first appears to have styled it what all in effect regarded it, *the Right of Command, le Droit de commander* (quoted from the original edition). The chief fault to be found with his immortal work is, that having so thoroughly mastered the science he was about to treat, the truths and their reasons appear to have been so self-evident to his apprehension, he did not deem it necessary to discuss and establish his Preliminaries. With only a small part of the knowledge of previous writers which he possessed, it will be found these Preliminaries are truly axioms, the results

§ 19. Britain and America to be friendly.

His work superior to all others.

of the profound reasonings of his predecessors, and an admirable epitome of the fundamental truths in governmental science. Upon the solid basis they had laid, is his "elegant" superstructure reared; his *Law of Nations* being the most perfect and thorough application of eternal principles to the Government of these greatest moral persons, Sovereign States, that has been written. The previous works are more thorough in establishing principles; his more complete in their application.

Locke has been followed instead of Vattel.

The authority of writers of the Vattel school to be further presented.

Since Vattel, with the exception of Martens, writers on Government seem to have followed Locke instead of the other school; at all events, notwithstanding pretty diligent search, modern teachings of the school of Vattel are very scarce. Hence it is, that some effort has been made in the beginning of this Compend, to establish the authority of the writers coincident with Vattel; and this interesting and important branch of the subject will be further prosecuted, till any reasonable man shall be made willing to admit, that if there be any such thing in existence as International Law, or if there be any likelihood of ever having such a science, the writers of the Vattel school are the founders.

Anglo-Saxons interested.

Hobbes, 1651, proves the confusion then as to Sovereignty.

Our Revolution from same cause,

—also this civil war.

And of all Peoples, nations, and languages, should Anglo-Saxons desire to have this subject investigated and decided. Barbeyrac styles Hobbes "one of the most penetrating geniuses of his age," and his judgment is substantiated in the remarkable discovery Hobbes made in 1651, that the whole confusion of that stormy period arose from the misplacement of Sovereignty, putting it into Parliament, instead of the King; and we shall prove, if we prove anything—and not by our reasoning, but by the documents and these principles of International Law, if they can be established as Law—that civil war was again caused in Britain by this same infernal heresy Hobbes had exploded, ending in Revolution and our dismemberment from the British Kingdom, not Commonwealth; and then, in Part IV, when this civil war comes to be considered, it will very likely appear, that the same bewildering, absurd, ridiculous—all the adjectives in the language, and curses thrown in, are indequate to express the idea—these same teachings of Locke and of Blackstone, have caused our differences and this most terrible of modern wars.

How long before Anglo-Saxons will understand this subject of Sovereignty?

How many more civil wars, how many more dismemberments, are requisite to make Anglo-Saxons, who pride themselves, and with great propriety, in being the most intelligent, most Christian nations, most regardful of International Law, and of our rights under it; how many times must these calamities be repeated, to cause us to study sufficiently to obtain clear conceptions of, at least, one idea of the science, and that the most fundamental—what and where is *the Right of Command*, Sovereignty?

Locke and Blackstone have been followed too long.

British and American success,

We have long enough groped in the bewildering labyrinths of Locke and Blackstone; have suffered enough evils from their poisonous heresies, to be willing to try some other field of exploration, to test the efficacy of other medicaments, for bodies politic. We see in the mother-land, in these young Republics, the highest adornment of our landscapes; and

§ 19. Britain and America to be friendly.

—for which be thankful.

Seek Divine aid to find Hooker's "foundation."

"the stateliness of houses, the goodliness of trees, when we behold them, delighteth the eye." With hearts overflowing with thanksgiving to the Infinite Author of all this "stateliness," and "goodliness," who has showered His mercies upon us, in spite of our ignorance and folly; let us humbly seek His aid to enable us to search diligently for "that foundation which beareth up the one, that root which ministereth unto the other nourishment and life." And when discovered, we shall find there, too, the fountain of life and health; the use of which, though it will not exempt these bodies politic from the ailments and sorrows incident to this state of imperfection and of trial, will yet afford the best antidote, the surest relief.

Authority of the Vattel school to be established, and their chief teachings quoted.

It is proposed to prove, by competent authorities, that the school of Vattel has established a Code of International Law, and then bring together in a plain, intelligible way, their chief teachings, which any schoolboy can understand sufficiently, not completely; for, no doubt, truths are yet to be developed, which even Aristotle, or Montesquieu, or Vattel, neither apprehended nor comprehended. Having established the authority of these founders, and quoted their leading principles, these principles must then be applied to the documents and facts in English and British history antecedent to our separation; and then to the documents and facts connected with our own independent State organizations, and the creation of our State and Federal Governments. The concord will be found remarkable and perfect; and even plain business-men, like myself, can see there have been somewhere outrageous wrong and blundering, to cause lucid subjects like these to become so dark and incomprehensible.

Their principles to be applied to our history and the documents.

Concord will be found perfect.

Wise men will examine,

Then, when our cousins, Lords Brougham and Russell, Messrs. Disraeli, Mill, and others; and Doctors Lieber, Hopkins, and McGuffey, Professors Bledsoe and Bowen, Messrs. Rives, Everett, Hunter, Benjamin, Curtis, and others, set to work jointly and thoroughly to investigate the causes of Anglo-Saxon departure from these admirable *theories*, we shall understand this science of Government as never before; and both branches of this Anglo-Saxon family are to have a confidence and pride in each other, hitherto unknown. In new and more striking light will be exhibited, how admirably these antipodal forms of Government have been arranged to fulfil Biblical instructions, both in letter and spirit, as for instance those through St. Peter, who says:

—and teach us governmental science.

Perfect subjection inculcated.

1 *Peter* ii, 13–15.

> Submit yourselves to every ordinance of man for the Lord's sake: whether it be to the king, as supreme; or unto governors, as unto them that are sent by him for the punishment of evil doers, and for the praise of them that do well. For so is the will of God, that with well doing ye may put to silence the ignorance of foolish men: As free, and not using *your* liberty for a cloak of maliciousness, but as the servants of God. Honour all *men*. Love the brotherhood. Fear God. Honour the king.

Object of Government chiefly to punish.

While Government is truly "for the praise of them that do well," it is mainly established "for the punishment of evil-doers;" and whether the submission be "to the king as supreme, or unto governors that are sent by him," as is the case in Britain, "or unto governors that are sent by" the supreme power in free States, as with us, the submission must be absolute; not so absolute as to justify the authority in being unjust and tyrannical, for that is beyond the Sovereignty of Deity, yet nevertheless absolute, even though the *Right of Command* be in the possession of a Nero, as it was when Peter wrote. And these great men will show us how our English ancestors contrived, notwithstanding this *Right of Command* must exist in every State unaccountable, uncontrollable by any human authority, to limit, chain down its *exercise*, the means of which are well elucidated by Pufendorf, so as to protect the subjects from injustice and oppression more perfectly than was ever before done under a Monarchy.

§ 19. Britain and America to be friendly.

Sovereignty must be absolute,

—yet not justify wrong.

How England controls the exercise of her Sovereignty

Then these wise and good men will show how these Anglo-Saxon Colonies in America, being obliged to take Democracy, the antipodal form of Government to that we had in the State of Great Britain, contrived to limit, to chain down the *exercise* of our *Rights of Command.* Calhoun will have taught us the difficulties of doing this, and that Sovereignty, *the Right of Command*, being even more arbitrary and despotic in a Democracy than under any arrangement of Monarchy, the control of its *exercise*, while less easy, is the more essential; and then we shall learn how well this was effected, by grafting the Republican principle on "that root" of Democracy. They will show, too, how in a single Republic like that of Rome (the importance of which example justifies us in again referring to it), a genius like Julius Cæsar will be able, with favoring circumstances, to usurp the *Right of Command*, which, though it returned to the People, and was for a while exercised by a triumvirate, &c., was again usurped by his nephew Octavius, after which the Roman Commonwealth had no existence, being transformed into an Empire.

How these States control the exercise of their Sovereignty.

Democracy despotic.

Sovereignty may be usurped in a single Republic.

They will show how a wise Providence brought good out of the jealousies and animosities that existed between these Colonies, and prevented their consolidation into a single State, causing their division into thirteen States, now increased to thirty-four. Then the war of the Revolution[1] compelled these States to unite and create a Federal Agency, to which they could jointly delegate a part of the exercise of Sovereignty belonging to each State. The first attempt was a failure; and finding that it was best to delegate the exercise of important powers, as the control of commerce and of taxation in part, and having learned by practice in the Colonial and State Governments the wisdom of dividing up the *exercise* of authority to separate and independent agencies, which, we shall find, John Adams best explained; instead of the single Federal

Providential division of the Colonies.

War caused Union.

First a failure.

Improvements in the second Union.

[1] As we review our history, we can see distinctly the hand of Providence in using war as the means of bringing together those hostile Colonies. He had allowed the natural traits of man to operate and cause alienation and even enmity, in order to prevent our consolidation into a single State; and then He employs war to force us, against our inclinations, into a proper Union, which, though imperfect at first, not only became "more perfect," but the most perfect Federal Union ever formed.

And it will not be another century, before the historic Christian statesman will point to this war as having been the means employed by that same GOD of our fathers, to bring us their children back to the knowledge and practice of the true principles of Federal Union. Oh, how should these Peoples love, and serve, and trust their GOD!

Providence by war united the Colonies,

—by this war brings us back to Federalism.

§ 19. Britain and America to be friendly.

body, we organized a Senate and House of Representatives for the Legislative Department, and created Judicial and Executive Departments.[1] Each one of these States having, in like manner, divided up, in its individual Government, the *exercise* of its Sovereignty upon all subjects except those delegated to the Federal Agency, we have secured in these Democracies, that are naturally most terrible despotisms, the most perfect system of checks upon the wrong exercise of authority, of which we have any recorded example. No Cæsar can ever usurp the Sovereignty of all; for he will have these thirty-four organized Governments (or so many as there may be in the new Union) to resist him. No one State, nor a few States, can be subverted; for our Constitutions, Federal and Confederate, guaranty protection against any form of Government other than Republican, and so will the new Constitution. The Federal Agency has, in this respect, the right of coercion, which will be exercised whenever necessary. And, whereas Democracies have been proverbially turbulent and disorderly, so that wise and good men like Jefferson and Legaré have considered tumult and sedition inseparable concomitants, we have had little of them, much less than was to be expected in the first beginnings to establish free Government, and especially when we consider the adverse and erroneous teachings of liberty and equality, with which the world was flooded when these States began their independent existence. And we shall have less and less.

—the most perfect checks in Government yet discovered.

Usurpation impossible.

These Democracies free of tumult.

Examination into errors will be candid.

Nor is there any vain conceit, as before intimated, to interfere in the slightest measure with a candid and thorough examination into the nature of past teachings, whatever errors and misconceptions may be discovered. The occasion allows an exhibition of true Anglo-Saxon sense, magnanimity, nobility of soul, that every writer who has been named, and many others, will rejoice they have lived to see. If the misconceptions and contradictions herein imagined have no existence, they can show it. If they exist, and shall have impregnated any of the productions of these wise men, they will not hesitate to perform their duty, though to remove the evils should destroy their choicest, most cherished works. They will rejoice in any sacrifice, however great, that inures to the benefit and glory of all these Anglo-Saxon Peoples; to the advantage and permanent good of the entire world. And the casual circumstance that an inexperienced person happens to suggest something of the line of investigation, will not deter from its pursuit, if those capable of judging find the subject worthy of attention. No unusual circumstance is it that an inferior intellect, coming freshly to examine a subject, not schooled to a particular set of views, should discover some mistakes even in great men; and while a fool can tear down and destroy, it takes wise men to build up. So that, while the writer has considerable confidence that his compilation of documents and facts will supply to the masses the information every Amer-

No hesitancy to correct mistakes.

Immaterial who happens to first suggest the errors.

A hope that this compilation will be serviceable.

[1] These ideas, it is true, have been presented as probable consequences of this examination itself, and we hope to make good the expectation; but if not, these wise men will have better success. These important excellences of Federalism cannot be too often presented to the consideration of American Citizens.

ican Citizen needs, and that the truths from the school of Vattel will overthrow those of the Locke school, yet is there to be a great work done to set Anglo-Saxons right in Britain and in America, in the knowledge and in the practice of their Governments. This can only their wise and pious intellects achieve.

§ 19. Britain and America to be friendly.

The People of Britain, the Peoples of these States, will with impatience wait for the unfolding anew of the principles of Government, or rather their new application to our practice. Let us speedily have the knowledge; and respect and confidence, esteem and affection, will be rapidly and powerfully engendered between these closely allied Anglo-Saxons, these Christian Peoples. Not that we shall resort to any entangling alliances, or seek to give each other undue advantages over other nations. We wish strictly to observe equality and neutrality between nations, living up closely to the rules of International Law. That will result, not only in the best good and happiness of each, but of all the families of man, not only of our own Caucasian race, but of all inferior races, whether Indian, Mongolian, Malayan, or even Negro; and henceforth till time shall be no longer.

Impatience for the views of wise men.

Anglo-Saxons to become strong friends, —yet not entangled.

§ 20.—Friendly aid from other European States.

To our ancient ally, *la belle France*, may we also appeal with confidence that we shall have her kind aid to straighten out our entanglements. Her Montesquieu is an oracle; and the wisdom of her Necker, Lacroix, and De Tocqueville, already noticed, will be made profitable in this examination, and much more so when handled by our wise men. Several other important works by their deceased authors, will also be carefully studied in order to select such parts of their wisdom as will be appropriate to the sequel of this compilation. French intellect has worked upon the science of Government with great effect, and to the good of the world, notwithstanding the calamitous perversion of the principles of liberty witnessed in the last century.

France will lend aid.

Value of former teachings.

Nor is the wisdom of France all in the grave. The good, the excellent Guizot is yet spared, and had we none other of his many and excellent works than his *History of Representative Government*, the loss would have been severe, though unknown, had he never lived. But it is to be hoped that in joining in the search for our lost Sovereignty, he will find that in Vattel's *Right of Command* is a true and solid foundation for the temple of Representation he has so handsomely erected. Then they have MM. Hautefeuille, Laboulaye and others, abundantly competent to examine the science of Government to its very foundation; and the writer has constantly feared that some of them would publish their views, properly developing the nature of our Government and Union, before we should have started the investigation.[1]

Living writers: Guizot.

Other eminent authorities.

[1] Neither of M. Gasparin's works, the *Uprising of a great People*, or *America before Europe*, is at all satisfactory. The first thing for him to have done in rendering the aid he desired, with great goodness of heart, was to search after our lost Sovereignty, which he, with some of our own authors, imagined had gotten into the United States.

Gasparin's new works not what is wanted.

§ 20. Friendly aid from other European States.

France will learn how she failed as a single Republic,

—how to save herself from tyranny, by means of Federalism.

French authors will have much satisfaction in again examining these interesting topics, and finding precisely how and why it was France failed as a Republic; why and how it is we have had such good promise of success; and alarmed at the danger to liberty of having this experiment prove a failure, will they aid us in examining the causes of our difficulties and in rescuing us from peril. The wisdom of Montesquieu will be more radiant than ever, and they will make the subject so well understood by Frenchmen, that whenever again their People shall be cursed with a tyrant's sway, they will cast him off, take their Sovereignty, *Right of Command*, into their own keeping, subdivide France into its ancient provinces, and make each one a State, and unite them in a Federal Republic.

France specially interested in International Law.

Her right to grant Sovereignty to whom she pleases.

Napoleon the peer of Sovereigns.

The nation insulted in the refusal of his alliance by marriage.

The French, it appears to me, should take particular interest in studying, and aiding still more perfectly to establish, International Law. It is the privilege of every State to choose its own form of Government, to keep in its People, or grant to whom it pleases, the *Right of Command;* and if granted, to fix the terms of its descent or transfer. Whether right or wrong to displace the Bourbons, and by gradual steps transfer the Sovereignty to Napoleon, is nobody's business outside of France. When he became Emperor, he was the peer of Sovereigns, whether of the house of Hapsburg or of Hanover; and if, as has been said, a matrimonial alliance with a princess was refused because he was not of royal lineage, it was an insult that gallant nation should have washed out with blood. The French want the rights of States, of their Emperor, of their young prince, better understood; and a fresh overhauling of cardinal principles of the Law of Nations, will bring the knowledge.

France has a good Government.

Napoleon loves France,

—wants her well ruled,

—yet she is liable to tyranny.

France is now blessed with an excellent Government. On the throne, or on the war-horse, in the council-chamber or battle-field, Napoleon has proved himself master of his situation. He will reign over that People to their great benefit and happiness to the day of his death, unless he change immensely for the worse. He loves France with his whole heart, and will do anything to promote her prosperity and glory. He hopes his son will fill, and worthily, the father's throne. But does he know it? Has his boy a guaranty of life? Is his future character known, and whether his birth will prove to the weal or woe of France? If premature death remove him and other heirs, what is to be the fate of that careless and joyous People? With even good Monarchs for generations, the time may come when insupportable tyranny may rule, and there shall be no patriot with power and influence to lead the People to safety.

Napoleon may be studying Federalism,

—may divide France into its ancient provinces, and unite them in a Federal Republic.

Napoleon has an intellect to grasp these subjects; a heart to do for his country what duty and prudence would dictate. Already he may have considered and formed his plans; and if the wise patriots of France enlighten the People on this important question of Federal Republicanism, they may prepare the way for Napoleon to accomplish his great and benevolent purposes. To divide France into its ancient provinces and make of them States, and unite them in a Federal Republic, would establish her on a sure and solid foundation; and Napoleon, a second Washington, would be elected President and reëlected, till the Government had become well ordered and sure. And when the petty States adjoining could find excuses and means to rid themselves of their expensive Governments, and become free States, they would almost surely join the French Republic, and no Bourbon would ever again ascend the throne of France, for there would be no throne. Thus, in a legitimate, philanthropic, honorable manner, would he repay the jealous Monarchs about him for their affront to him as Emperor. It is an object to achieve, worthy of his great name. Eclipsing the dazzling brightness of his uncle, Napoleon III would become another *pater patriæ;* and, alongside of our Washington, would his name be forever emblazoned on the scroll of fame.

§ 20. Friendly aid from other European States.

Small German States might join.

A just way to punish his enemies.

Make himself a *pater patriæ*

Whether such a change should now be deemed practicable and expedient by the Emperor or not, is immaterial as to the necessity of studying thoroughly into Federalism. Nothing will be more effectual to control Monarchs, and prevent them from attempting arbitrary sway, than to have the People well informed in the science of Government. Then, if tyranny is attempted, the People, knowing that the Monarch has forfeited their allegiance, will take the *Right of Command* into their own keeping; and whenever France is compelled to do this, she must be divided into small States and united in a Federal Republic.

If this be not done, still study Federalism,

—to prevent tyranny.

More than any other Monarchy of Europe, does she give promise of having that system; and though, as States, it would not be for our interest, yet as individual men would we rejoice to see liberty well established in the powerful Federal Republic of France. No other important State but Britain would be suited to the Republican form at present, and she does not want it. Her Government is too good to tamper with any experiments, however promising; and could France, and all Europe, work gradually into her system of checks and balances, it would probably be best for them and for the world. Unless they do, the several States will constantly be liable to misrule and revolution. No continental State would be as likely again to try Democracy, as France. Under a good leader, with favoring circumstances, she might succeed, if attempted under the Republican, Federal Republican, form; not otherwise.

France most likely to become a Federal Republic.

Britain does not want a change.

Her Government best form for Europe.

Federalism might succeed in France.

We may reasonably expect the aid of learned statesmen in Belgium, Holland, and all the German States, whose interest it is to have this Federal Union maintained in all its plenitude and strength, in order to have an independent power in the earth, far removed from them, and without danger of being involved in their dissensions and strifes, able to protect its every right under the Law of Nations, to which the States, especially the weaker ones, could look for legitimate supplies in the event of war and of necessity, and whose flag would be a protection to commerce, which, without it, must be interrupted or suspended. Spain desires we should thoroughly understand International Law and practise it; lest through some inadvertence, we should start filibustering expeditions after Cuba. Her statesmen had best be aiding us to discover where our *Right*

The German States will aid in the examination.

Their interest in our Union being preserved.

Spain interested.

§ 20. Friendly aid from other European States.

Every European State,

—Russia, even.

of Command abides, that we may properly control and punish our refractory subjects who should dare to infringe upon the rights of the Sovereignty of Spain. Every State in Europe has a direct interest with us in developing more perfectly this important science of the Law of Nations. Not even our staunch, fast friend, the Russian Bear, is an exception. The Czar, and all his faithful subjects, never desire to see this power in the earth shorn of its strength, by division into rival Confederacies.

These States to have dignity among the nations.

We do not teach right of Revolution, except in extreme cases.

States have no right to interfere with each other.

Teachings of our *Declaration.*

We shall not interfere in Europe.

The examination of our wise men, and the bold, high stand these free Peoples will surely take upon the solid foundation of International Law, will, in large measure, relieve us of European jealousy, and dread of our example, and of direct interference in their concerns. According to the Laws of Nature and of Nature's GOD, no People has a right to change its Government, so long as it is well administered. Both Kings and Nobles have become possessed of legitimate rights, of which no People may dispossess them, until by misrule, unjust and illegal oppression, their vested rights shall have been forfeited. And other States, near or remote, have no right in any shape or manner to interfere. Every People is to be its own independent judge of its every right and wrong; and while we believe in the everlasting truths of our Declaration of Independence, "that, whenever any form of government becomes destructive of [its] ends, it is the right of the people to alter or to abolish it, and to institute a new government, laying its foundation on such principles, and organizing its powers in such form, as to them shall seem most likely to effect their safety and happiness;" and while we would sympathize deeply with any oppressed People in their resistance of tyranny, the Law of Nations we must live up to, and that allows of no interference directly or indirectly, where we are not personally concerned.[1]

What sort of Revolution we deem right.

Our *Declaration of Independence.*

As we have taught in that grand Declaration, which is replete with true principles of International Law, "Prudence, indeed, will dictate that Governments long established, should not be changed for light and transient causes; and, accordingly, all experience hath shown, that mankind are more disposed to suffer, while evils are sufferable, than to right themselves by abolishing the forms to which they are accustomed. But when a long train of abuses and usurpations, pursuing invariably the same object, evinces a design to reduce them under absolute despotism, it is their right, it is their duty, to throw off such Government, and to provide

---

The Poles: partition accomplished, —must be abided by.

We will not interfere.

Oppressed subjects may come here.

But we will enforce Monroe doctrine against Europe.

[1] The Polish question is a case directly in point. The partition of Poland, whether right or wrong, is a *fait accompli*, and is to be so regarded by all nations, equally as the conquest of England by the Normans. The Czar, the Emperor of Austria, the King of Prussia, may grind their poor subjects into the very dust, if they please, and it is none of our concern. We have naught to do with the affairs of other States, near or remote, except as they affect ourselves. States know no sentiment except to care for themselves; and if the Poles, or Irish, or French do not like their Governments, and cannot effect a change, they must bear their oppressions or remove into another State. This land of liberty is open to them. Our sentiments as Peoples upon this subject, Mr. Seward has no doubt well expressed in his despatch to the Russian Minister in May last, and which was so satisfactory to our friend the Czar. But when it comes to the conquest of a North American State by one of the States of Europe, we have a right to interfere for our own protection, and we will interfere when necessary, whether against France or any other power. She may compel from Mexico her rights, the payment of her just dues; no more. The Monroe doctrine will be maintained, if we have power sufficient.

new guards for their future security." Look at the long catalogue of abuses that these Colonies for many years patiently endured; consider that it took fourteen months of cruel, unrelenting war, on the part of our King, in his endeavors to change completely our form of Government, and to subject us to an authority most of us had never acknowledged, that of Parliament; and little will be found in our example to justify Revolutions, except in extreme cases.

§ 20. Friendly aid from other European States.

See our endurance before we risked Revolution.

Nor are we to intermeddle in any way with the affairs of Europe. One of the most dangerous attempts to drag us into foreign interference, was that of France, so well portrayed by Mr. Gibbs in his *History of Washington's and Adams' Administrations*, though it was not to bring about interference with a State in managing its own concerns, but to involve us in war with Britain. A more disgraceful, infamous effort was that of Kossuth in behalf of Hungary. Never will another such base attempt be tolerated in this land of liberty, not licentiousness; in this land of double nationality, doubly resting on the eternal principle, of the Law of Nations. The cause of freedom, of sound Constitutional Government throughout the world, is to be most effectually promoted, by these States united, setting a bright example of strict adherence to the letter and to the spirit of the International Code. Let us know that Law;[1] and let our Federal Governments, and especially the new one to be instituted, to which as to the present ones, all authority in the premises will be properly intrusted, attend to its rigid enforcement. Such is the will of these Sovereignties; let no recreant, perfidious subject, whether of high or low degree, interfere with the behest of his Sovereign State.

Efforts to entangle us with Europe,

—in Washington's and Adams' times.

The Kossuth attempt.

We must live up to International Law.

We must know it, and our Federal Agency enforce it.

These Nations united, depend so entirely on correct knowledge, complete observance of the Law of Nations, that we should be patterns to the world in our judgment and practice of its edicts. The decisions, in our Supreme Court, of questions arising under it, should and will, with reunion, have a weight of authority unsurpassed by any in Christendom. We can and should have this Court so established, so far removed from extraneous influences, political or otherwise, as not only to possess the unbounded confidence of these Peoples and their individual Citizens, but of all nations; and removed, as are we, from the rest of the world, more disinterested than it is possible for other States to be, we might expect in time, that our Supreme Court would become the tribunal to which all great questions, arising between other nations under the International Code, would be submitted for arbitrament. Let us, Citizens, be considering, studying into these great subjects, so that when the time comes for a Convention of all these States to frame a new Federal Compact, the members will be prepared to give an expression of our real sentiments upon the Laws of Nature and of Nature's God, correcting the errors which party and misconceptions have led our orators and writers to

These States should be patterns in its practice.

Our Supreme Court,

—should be independent.

Its dignity abroad,

—umpire of nations.

Let us obtain the high respect of other nations.

[1] Let us only know the Law of Nations, and we shall see no more such blunders, as in the McLeod affair, when Gov. Seward was such a courageous, but erroneous asserter of State rights, interfering in a matter wholly committed by his Sovereignty, to the Federal Agency.

Gov. Seward in the McLeod affair.

§ 20. Friendly aid from other European States.

express, and thereby to secure to ourselves the respect and regard of the law-abiding of other nations, to which much of our past teachings and conduct have not entitled us.

A People must be prepared for freedom.

To examine the application of principles to the practice of nations, and the progress of States, in the science of Government, will develop yet another important point, that a People must first become qualified for liberty, before it can successfully administer a free Government. With all the knowledge Anglo-Saxons possessed, with the unequalled advantages afforded by a century and more of Colonial training, we barely escaped shipwreck; and that we did, was not owing to our own wisdom, but to Providential care and favoring circumstances; and that wreck may yet be witnessed. The views of Rousseau, a Citizen of one of the Swiss Republics, on this important topic accord with Aristotle, and are no doubt correct.

Our narrow escape from ruin.

Rousseau's views. *See* p. 154.

Changes in Europe difficult,

—increased because Federalism is indispensable.

For any European State to change its form of Government, surrounded on all sides by Monarchies, would be quite difficult; and the difficulty will appear the greater, as Federalism comes to be regarded as an indispensable concomitant. It was probably not without due consideration, that Infinite Wisdom applied the Federal principle to the first free Governments of antiquity; it was not without wisdom that the sages of Greece united their States by Confederating; Switzerland has shown for four centuries, what can be done by Federalism, in even the imperfect freedom of Aristocratic States; and the Netherlands for two centuries afforded another bright example in favor of Federalism; and the more the subject is investigated, the more hearty will be the approval of Montesquieu's wisdom, in judging that free States must be of moderate extent, and are to provide for their safety by Federal Union. So that not till a number of small States shall be able beforehand to agree to form a Confederacy, or not till some large State can be divided into small States for the purpose, will a successful effort be made in Europe to establish Democracy in any form.

Democracy in Europe improbable without Federalism.

A Nobility incompatible with a free State,

Nor can an hereditary Nobility exist in a proper Commonwealth, or free State. The Roman Republic was, for this reason, imperfect; though the very imperfection, the Patrician and Plebeian division, was, no doubt, an advantage to that immense consolidated State, creating necessary checks that for a long period preserved it from usurpation and tyranny. But in a true *civitas* or *Common*wealth, all the privileges and honors must be open to the competition of every one who is admitted to the dignity of Citizenship. To merely destroy the Monarchy, and to leave the Nobility in power, even with Representatives of the People, as in the Long Parliament, would be merely changing from a Monarchy to an Aristocracy; the worst possible form of Government, because responsibility is so much divided.

—in which all honors must be free.

Aristocracy as well as Monarchy, then, to be overthrown in a free State.

Not only, then, has the Monarchy to be overthrown, but the Aristocracy also; and the attempt in almost any European State would more likely result in greater tyranny, than in an increase of liberty. As

European States approximate to British liberty, will they improve; and if Continental Monarchs and Nobility are faithful to their trusts, it is probably the highest advance that will be made for centuries. And not till our experiment shall have been much longer tested, are we able to decide, whether Anglo-Saxons in the mother-land have not made the highest attainments in the science of Government, of which our Caucasian race is susceptible. § 20. Friendly aid from other European States.

Nor is the important point to be overlooked, that every State of Europe, except the Swiss Cantons, has a deep and abiding hostility to the successful establishment of Democracy, of the Federal or any other form. Those States have a right, according to the Law of Nations, to provide for their safety; and the same principle which will justify us in enforcing the Monroe doctrine, and keeping North America clear of Monarchy, will justify them in keeping Democracy out of Europe. And the immense advantage, before alluded to, that Monarchies have over free States, in the intrigues and corruption of diplomacy, will be of itself nearly all-sufficient to prevent a permanent success in a Democratic experiment. General hate of Democracy. States may provide for their safety. They may exclude Democracy, as we may Monarchy.

§ 21.—Ultimate Reliance, however, must be on ourselves.

No doubt we shall have considerable and influential aid in studying and determining questions of International Law, a knowledge of which is necessary to peace, indispensable to reunion. But, after all, we have mostly to do the work for ourselves. Our own judgments are to be convinced as to our rights and wrongs as individual Citizens, as Sovereign States; so thoroughly convinced as to control every feeling, and make us willing, in the North and in the South, to submit to whatever the "Laws of Nature and of Nature's God" require. Those "Laws" were on full record before that noble band of patriots in Independence Hall in Philadelphia, in 1776, affirmed their title to them; by those same "Laws" our rights and wrongs are to be adjudged. No *ex post facto* legislation is sought, or would be tolerated. We only need to study and to know what those "Laws" require of us, and as honest, legitimate sons of noble sires, will our duties be performed at all hazards, at any sacrifice. Though we may have aid, the work of examination to be done by ourselves. Must know the Laws of Nations. Laws unchanged since '76. *Ex post facto* laws not wanted.

As already observed, the great men of the South are, no doubt, thoroughly investigating this all-important subject; and if we in the North are not wiser in future than in the past, do not show less greed for the almighty dollar, and more for sound political knowledge, the South will continue, as hitherto, to have the advantage of us in the science and practice of Government. The North may still be led by the South.

Fortunately, there are a few in the North who give themselves to scientific pursuits. High-minded, noble patriots, genuine Aristocrats, they live and labor for their country. First and foremost among them is Hon. Edward Everett. He, of course, is giving his strong powers, cultivated intellect, large experience, matured judgment, to a reinvestigation of Governmental principles, to ascertain the causes of our difficulties, and to apply the remedies. As might be expected, this eminent statesman is The North has some Aristocrats. Mr. Everett. He is studying for a work on the Law of Nations.

§ 21. Ultimate reliance on ourselves.

Its publication delayed.

engaged in preparing a new work on International Law; and the writer is not a whit astonished, that the papers inform us, that "Edward Everett's new work on 'The Law of Nations' is not likely to be published for some time. The research and labor involved in it will occupy a much longer period than was originally contemplated."

And why? Having followed erroneous ideas about our Government,

No doubt of it. Mr. Everett has received for truth the common idea that we had somehow or other conjured up a nondescript, mongrel sort of Government, to which the antiquated principles of Governmental science could never apply. The writer has had occasion to examine, with some care, the eloquent Oration delivered by Mr. Everett, on the 4th July, 1861, various parts of which will be quoted and examined in the progress of this compilation; and it is not surprising, if, when the author's strong powers were applied to the Law of Nations, he should have discovered some little discrepancy between it and his own teachings. This, too, has possibly caused him to think a little harder on the Constitution of Massachusetts, in which the 4th Article of the Bill of Rights declares:

—finds his teachings do not accord with the Law of Nations.

Is studying the *Constitution of Massachusetts.*

—which declares herself a "free, sovereign and independent State."

The People of this Commonwealth have the sole and exclusive right of governing themselves, as a *free, sovereign and independent State:* and do, and forever hereafter shall, exercise and enjoy every power, jurisdiction and right, which is not, or may not hereafter be by them expressly delegated to the United States of America, in Congress assembled.

Compact of the People, forming the COMMONWEALTH OF MASSACHUSETTS.

And further, the following compact is introduced at the head of Part II:

The People inhabiting the territory formerly called the Province of Massachusetts Bay, do hereby solemnly and mutually agree with each other to form themselves into a free, sovereign and independent body politic or State, by the name of—THE COMMONWEALTH OF MASSACHUSETTS.

Adams took these ideas from Pufendorf.

Now these ideas must have been taken by John Adams, who drew the Constitution, right straight from Pufendorf, as we shall see; and Theophilus Parsons, and the other learned men, who aided to frame that Constitution, knew perfectly well, that the "Laws of Nature and of Nature's GOD" fully authorized that People to become a SOVEREIGN, FREE, AND INDEPENDENT COMMONWEALTH; and, as a protection against the base recusancy of any traitorous subject, who might dare to deny the august truth of that being a Sovereign State, they required every official to take that long and tremendous oath which begins:

The People were right.

To protect against traitors,

—required a strong oath.

I, A. B., do truly and sincerely acknowledge, profess, testify, and declare, that the Commonwealth of Massachusetts is, and of right ought to be, a free, sovereign and independent State; and I do swear that I will bear true faith and allegiance to the said Commonwealth, and that I will defend the same against traitorous conspiracies, and all hostile attempts whatsoever, &c., &c.

Did Mr. Everett ever take it?

Did Mr. Everett ever take that oath? The answer depends upon whether he held an office prior to 1821, when, in altering the Constitution, the oath was exchanged for a shorter one, of similar import:

Another form of oath.

I, A. B., do solemnly swear, that I will bear true faith and allegiance to the Commonwealth of Massachusetts, and will support the Constitution thereof. So help me GOD.

The last oath he has taken repeatedly, as he has been called to fill all sorts of offices, even to the very highest, that of Governor; and yet so far does the Aristocracy of his nature, the dignity of his character, outrank any official honor, that he is seldom styled Governor, but the more eminent title of MISTER EVERETT is his proud cognomen. Fortunately for that great State, grand and noble still, notwithstanding her sinking into the foul cesspool of Abolitionism; fortunately for Massachusetts, she has repeatedly availed herself of the aristocratic services of her distinguished son and subject, and every time he has taken office, has he solemnly sworn to "bear *true faith and allegiance to the Commonwealth of Massachusetts.*"

§ 21. Ultimate reliance on ourselves.

This Mr. Everett has taken repeatedly.

Mr. Everett's dignity not enhanced by office.

No limit is to be found anywhere, to the Sovereignty of Massachusetts, any more than to that of Russia or of Britain, yet in that 4th of July oration Mr. Everett remarks:

No limit to the Sovereignty of Massachusetts.

Certainly the States are clothed with Sovereignty for local purposes; but it is doubtful whether they ever possessed it in any other sense; and if they had, it is certain that they ceded it to the General Government, in adopting the Constitution.

MR. EVERETT denies positively that Massachusetts is Sovereign. *Address*, p. 11.

Space cannot here be taken to prove whether the People of Massachusetts best understood their *Right of Command*, or Mr. Everett; but enjoying the proud distinction of being a son of the old Bay State, it shall be my pleasant task, if life and health are spared, to vindicate the honor of my mother against an assault from any one, however distinguished and honorable. GOD SAVE THE COMMONWEALTH OF MASSACHUSETTS.

These points will be attended to hereafter.

Beyond peradventure, Mr. Everett's examination has led him to discover more or less the discrepancy between our prevalent *theories* and those of the old authorities, and his matured wisdom leads him to coincide with Kent, that "In cases where the principal jurists agree, the presumption will be very great in favor of the solidity of their maxims; and no civilized nation, that does not arrogantly set all ordinary law and justice at defiance, will venture to disregard the uniform sense of the established writers on International Law."

Mr. Everett has discovered his errors, and coincides with KENT.

See p. 32.

Then, too, he is a true-hearted son of our honored and honorable old Commonwealth, and he is trying to discover whether, after all, the fathers were not right in *practice*, notwithstanding a little confusion in *theory*, and both of our systems of Government, State and Federal, in strict accordance with "the uniform sense of the established writers on International Law." No confusion of right and duty is made in the oaths of the respective Constitutions. That of the State properly requires the official to "bear true faith and allegiance to the Commonwealth of Massachusetts, and support the Constitution thereof;" that of the Federal Agency, merely declares that an official "shall be bound by Oath or Affirmation, to support this Constitution." If the subject "bear true faith and allegiance" to his Commonwealth, he must obey the Federal Government his Sovereignty has placed over him, in all measures which that Agency adopts pursuant to its Constitution. And so, on every

He is a true son of the old Bay State.

No conflict in his State and Federal oaths of office.

Concord between our Constitutions and the Law of Nations, perfect.

§ 21. Ultimate reliance on ourselves.

single point all the way through, will there be found the most perfect harmony between all our documents and most of our *practice* and the principles of International Law, notwithstanding our confusion of *theories*.

Mr. Everett will find our errors to be chiefly in *theory*,

Mr. Everett has probably discovered, ere this, that our errors and difficulties have resulted more from mistakes in *theory* than in *practice;* and no one will, with more hearty satisfaction, join to correct these theoretic errors, no one will more cheerfully, magnanimously acknowledge his share in them, than will Hon. Edward Everett.

—will correct his share.

Mr. Curtis' *History of the Constitution*,

We have other able teachers, excellent Aristocrats, who have not to correct so much what they have taught, as to connect their instructions with principles of International Law. Mr. Curtis' valuable *History of the Constitution* is a case in point. One little alteration, it is to be hoped, he will be able to make, in order to harmonize our Governments with our Saviour's teachings. He thought a man could not serve two masters; and if, instead of subjecting every individual to a State Sovereignty and a Federal Sovereignty, Mr. Curtis should discover from Pufendorf, and Vattel, and our history, that, after all, we have only one Sovereignty —the People of each State—it will be decidedly agreeable. We Christians do not like to put our Saviour in the wrong; and it probably is not necessary to the proper understanding and operating of our Governmental machinery. Each individual, whether a Citizen or merely a subject, is obligated to bear true faith and allegiance to his Sovereign Commonwealth. He owes, and can owe, none to any other. The chief means of discharging our obligations of faith and allegiance, are found in obedience to the Laws and Governors placed over us. Each of these our Sovereignties has delegated the *exercise* of *parts* of its *Right of Command*, to various Agencies in the State, as the Governor, Legislature and Judiciary, and these again have power to sub-delegate parts to subordinate official agents, county, town, &c. Then, too, these Sovereignties have joined with each other and delegated the *exercise* of certain other very important *parts* of the *Right of Command* to various Federal Agencies, as the President, Congress, Judiciary, &c., who again have power in certain specified cases to re-delegate to other subordinate officials. To put an independent *Right of Command* in each one of these Agencies—and it must be given equally to one as to the other—would subject a man not to two, but to an indefinite number of masters. It seems very probable that, on further consideration, Mr. Curtis will prefer the theory of Pufendorf and Vattel, which our noble old Commonwealth of Massachusetts has so well practised, to that of a double Sovereignty. Then each subject can easily comprehend how true faith and allegiance to the *Right of Command* in his Commonwealth, require him to render strict obedience to the laws and rulers his Sovereignty has placed over him. This little change is the chief one he needs to make in his most valuable work. But he will not with that cease his efforts. His Fourth of July Address, and a more recent one, prove that he realizes the danger of consolidation, and he will be one of the most efficient co-laborers with his friend Mr. Everett, in

—only wants a little change as to Sovereignty, to agree with our Saviour.

Matt. vi, 24.

Everybody a subject of his Sovereignty.

Owes only to that allegiance.

The Sovereignty has delegated authority to State Agents,

—also to Federal Agents, which the subjects must obey.

Were these Agents Sovereign, a subject would have an indefinite number of masters.

Mr. Curtis will take Vattel's *theory* as did our native State.

That will simplify this double Sovereignty theory.

Will further prosecute examinations, and aid in bringing a new Union.

correcting our theoretical errors and bringing back our wandering steps to the paths of Federalism, with the attendant blessings of peace and a new Union.

§ 21. Ultimate reliance on ourselves.

Mr. Motley, and his letter to the *London Times.*

Then there is another Massachusetts man, Mr. John Lothrop Motley, who has made himself famous by his truly interesting Histories of the Netherlands; but he will become more notorious in consequence of his remarkable letter to the *London Times.* We shall be relieved from the disagreeable task of attending much to his case, as Mr. Henry B. Dawson has a rod in pickle, that will be sufficient to whip him into the traces, whether he can be made to draw in the paths of Federalism or not. We do not despair even of Mr. Motley, and trust he is yet to become a genuine aristocrat and aid to restore our native State to former glory and renown.

Mr. Dawson will attend to him.

President Hopkins, his aid desirable.

Massachusetts, too, has other noble sons to labor in her high and holy cause, of whom, further mention will only be made of President Hopkins. Could his clear head, cultivated taste, warm heart, abundant knowledge be given to this great subject, he would produce the crowning work of his long and useful life; and with what heartfelt delight would his affectionate pupils and many loving friends listen to his matured judgment.

Dr. Lieber.

It is not necessary to particularize the wise and good men of other States, who will bestow their labors upon this important investigation, and space will be taken to refer to only one, of high reputation in the South and in the North, who is probably the leading authority in political science on this continent, Doctor Francis Lieber. Knowing the reputation of his works, they have been among the last examined, for considerable acquaintance with the subject seemed desirable to comprehend his deeply grounded philosophy. An earlier study of them might have been better, but it has been quite satisfactory, and strengthened confidence in my views and plan to find (I trust it is not altogether vain conceit) that they so generally harmonize with those of this eminently *practical*, as well as correctly *theoretical* writer. The chief point of difference is as to Sovereignty, which is fundamental, it is true; and yet is perhaps more fancied than real. The learned author believes in Hooker's Sovereignty, which is good enough for me, and seems to be of the same sort as that of Grotius and Pufendorf, and as the *Right of Command* of Vattel; and it seems, that he only needs to drop his excellent work a hair's breadth, and it rests securely on "that foundation" of Hooker.

Is the chief authority in political science.

We only differ as to Sovereignty.

The difference perhaps only in fancy.

His upsetting of the theory of *consent*, held by Locke and others, is the best performance of that important work which has been noticed; and upon other points the excellence of his views will be apparent in this compilation, particularly in discussing the doctrine of instructions.[1]

His correct views of *consent*, and of the doctrine of Instructions.

[1] The *theory* of Hooker and Vattel would, indeed, furnish Doctor Lieber with even another point in his able argument against the propriety and right of a Representative being instructed by his constituents, particularly in these free States, somewhat after this fashion:

The Doctrine of Instructions.

In all Governments, but especially in a large Democracy, is it necessary to employ the well known legal maxim, *qui facit per alium, facit per se,* What he does by another he does by himself. Upon this principle, is authority *delegated* by a free People to its faithful subjects and

The delegation of authority to Agents.

§ 21. Ultimate reliance on ourselves.

The Judiciary should aid in the examination.

Beside the examinations to be made by our wise and good men, in private life, we have other and most suitable machinery to bring light out of darkness, in our Supreme Court of the United States, in the Supreme Court of the Confederate States. What else is the chief province of these Courts, except to examine and to decide precisely such legal questions as those between these Sovereign States? The real parties are still States, though operating their governmental machinery in part through their Confederate and Federal Agencies. Suits should at once be instituted in both Courts, involving all the important questions at issue, and very probably the same results would be attained in each. And could the two Courts be in some way united, and our statesmen and lawyers be pitted against each other in a fight of "reason," there would be much more of both "force" and "reason" in that measure, than in arraying these armies of soldiers by the hundred thousand against each other. Only to think that Christian brethren, in this nineteenth century, can find no other means of adjudicating their mutual rights and wrongs, except by devastation and slaughter! How much of these damnable means are required

Suits should be brought to test the questions at issue in both sections.

A union of the two courts more sensible than war, to decide the questions at issue.

A free People never grants authority.

subordinate agents, but is never *granted*. The entire *Right of Command*, all authority in a free State, belongs to, and is under the control of that People.

A People establishes its Constitution.

Usually the first step in properly organizing a Government in a free State, is for the sovereign People, in some proper manner, to elect and send delegates to a Convention, to frame what is called a Constitution, which is to be the fundamental law of that People, and regulate the powers and acts of its chief officials. Commonly the precaution is adopted to declare in the Constitution, that the object of instituting their Government, is to promote the general good and happiness of that People, and not the particular advantage of individuals, or of certain localities; and all officials are required to take an oath to be faithful and impartial in the performance of their trusts, and to follow strictly the Constitution.

The object to be the general good, —not special.

Other laws requisite.

But the Sovereign People needs to have other laws passed to regulate the duties of its faithful subjects and protect their rights from the aggression of wicked subjects, and it defines, in its Constitution, what sort of a subject may be chosen a legislator, and who are to be his electors, who are always endowed with the august privilege of Citizenship. In order to have all of the Citizen subjects fairly represented in the legislature, the State is divided into districts, each of which chooses one or more as the Sovereignty has ordained. But each delegate, while he is called a Senator or Representative *from* such a county or town, is nevertheless the Senator or Representative *of* his State, and he is sworn to impartially and faithfully discharge his duties as legislator, and to support the Constitution.

Who a legislator, who electors.

A legislator *of* his State.

Oath and Constitution to be regarded, not instructions.

Now, suppose a question arise in which the constituents of a certain Senator are deeply interested, are they true and faithful liege subjects to their Sovereign State, if they seek unfairly or otherwise to promote their own good at the general cost? Have they any right to require the Senator chosen by them to do anything, but what in his best judgment shall best promote the general good? Is the Senator to regard his oath, or the instructions of his constituents? Is he to be required to resign, and the sovereign People be deprived of the services of one of its most faithful subjects and legislators, because a fraction of the People desire unfairly, unjustly to attain selfish ends? Who is sovereign in that State, the constituents of a Senator, or the People?

Who is Sovereign?

More absurd to instruct Federal Senators.

Still more apparent is the absurdity of instructing Representatives in the Federal Agency. Here, equally as in the State Government, the sole object is to promote the general good, and for that, are Senators and other officials appointed. The several State Sovereignties had to provide a means of appointing these Senators, and with great wisdom was that important trust committed to the State Legislatures. When the Senator is elected, the duty of the Legislature to its Sovereignty in that regard ends, and that of the party elect begins. His Sovereignty has required him to swear to support the Federal Constitution; and in the discharge of his trust arises a question of vital importance to the entire Confederate States, as in the Maine boundary, the whole charge of which has been committed by that sovereign State to the Federal Agency, in delegating to it the treaty-making power; yet here the Legislature of the State of Maine steps in impertinently between the Sovereign State and the Senator, and requires him to vote so and so! Shall the Senator obey the commands of his Sovereign State and his oath, or this mere State Agency, that has no right or authority in the premises? Shall the State and the Union lose the services of its able Senator, because the Maine Legislature differs with the Senate of the United States and the President, as to what is best and expedient?

Maine boundary. Legislature wrong.

A little study into principles will straighten out a good many of these crooked, knotty questions.

to conclude the case? When will the verdict be rendered, and what will it be?

§ 22. The Conclusion.

§ 22.—The Conclusion.

This compend not so perfect in its order as would be desirable.

Quite time is it that this long compend, extended more than half beyond the size intended, should come to a close. In some respects quite unsatisfactory to the writer, it may reasonably be expected to prove more so to the reader. "Order is Heaven's first Law;" and a work, pretending to aid the searcher into the Law of Nature and of Nations, should possess "order" in a high degree. But this was not planned for an analytic synopsis, which would have been dry and uninviting, and, to have had any value, would have required the space of a volume. The subject is too comprehensive, has too many ramifications to be analyzed in an introduction, and the desire has only been to call attention to a few of the important topics the people need to investigate. To methodize these and allow one thought to follow another in due order, can only be accomplished in the work itself. The object has also been, less to prove what was right, than to establish the existence of fundamental errors; or if not to fully establish them, which is by no means claimed to have been done generally, at least to show the possibility of grave errors existing, which may need examination and correction. It is designed more for popular than scientific readers; although, with a liberal exercise of charity, it is hoped even the skilful can endure its perusal.

Not designed for an analytic synopsis.

The object not to prove the right, but the existence of errors.

Is more popular than scientific.

Having for more than two years devoted himself with unceasing industry, and an interest deeper by far than in any other subject he ever investigated, and deepening month by month as he has advanced, the writer has gathered a large amount of materials that seem to him of special interest to every Citizen in this period of our beloved country's calamities and perils. To trace the progress of his investigations, and the steps whereby particular results were attained, may interest some few, of which an account is more suitable in the preface.

Studies have been prosecuted over two years.

Though many of the views are novel in this age, they were not so a century and more ago; and the whole of our disagreements, and even this civil war, seem to have resulted from ignorance or misconception, and the perversion of the clearest and most important principles of International Law. And though fully realizing that he is but on the threshold of investigation, deeply sensible of his imperfect qualifications to judge of truths touching these weighty matters of Government; he feels, notwithstanding, that he would be grossly derelict in faith and duty to his fellow Citizens, did he not call their attention to the line of investigation which the hand of Providence seems to have cast in his way.

If the views are novel, they were not so last century.

Very much of his reading has been in works that are scarce, and inaccessible to the masses; yet with parts of which, at least, every CITIZEN should be perfectly familiar. And so far from the thoughts being abstruse and metaphysical, unsuited to the common reader, they are perfectly within the comprehension of a lad of ordinary intelligence. Are the ex-

The knowledge important to Citizens,

—is easily comprehended,

§ 22. The Conclusion.

tracts already made from Hooker, Grotius, &c., hard to understand? The others will be no more so; and if Cumberland be to any an exception, he will probably be the sole one; and even the extracts from him, which must be given, being the best that have been observed to meet Calhoun's views, seem very clear and plain. And not only will the quotations be understandable and profitable, they will also be deeply interesting. Many a business man will be surprised that he never happened to meet such agreeable, as well as instructive reading.

—and interesting.

The compilation is for business men.

Having been from boyhood an active man of business, the writer should know what business men want; and this compilation will be made chiefly for them; and under the judicious counsel, and careful revision of Doctor Agnew, it is hoped no great blunders will be committed. Having obtained, not merely the aid, but the most hearty coöperation of this distinguished scholar, makes the hastening of the publication more suitable than it would be, relying altogether on my own judgment. Doctor Agnew has thoroughly examined my copies of Grotius, Pufendorf, Vattel, Montesquieu, the Federalist, Madison Debates, Curtis's History of the Constitution, etc., etc., in connection with my extended notes, this Introductory Compend, and other parts of my writings, and he thereby well understands the substance and the drift of my views, and we agree in the main on every important point. Other persons, properly qualified to judge, have considered the views more or less, and if not in full accord, they admit that the subject is newly presented and eminently worthy of consideration. From some of these, the writer hopes to have testimonials commending the work to public consideration, when they shall have been able fairly to judge of its merits.

Dr. Agnew's aid.

His examination of my views,

—and approbation.

Others also.

This justifies their presentation to the public.

It seems, therefore, not improper that the compiler should begin to present to his fellow Citizens some of these extracts from the wisdom of the past, which will aid to bring us to reflection, both in the North and in the South. As the compilation will necessarily extend to four or five volumes, which it will take six or eight weeks each to print, it seemed desirable to present something of an indication of the objects aimed at. To effect that, led to the preparation of this Compend, which, at the instance of Doctor Agnew, has been somewhat altered in order to make it suitable for circulation by itself. No pretence is made herein to having discussed any important point, not even that of Sovereignty, or of *Habeas Corpus.* They cannot be discussed till the principles of International Law, the documents that have secured our rights, and other historical facts, are presented to the reader. He can then judge for himself, and the point will need no elaborate argument. So that while it has been necessary to present subjects for consideration in our own language in this Compend, the reader will have much less of it in the ensuing pages. The ideas will be submitted in the words of others, whose authority will be unquestioned; the compilers merely stringing the thoughts together as on a thread, and by foot notes connecting important ideas and facts with other extracts, and adding such comments as seem desirable.

Their extent required a Compend to be prepared.

Subjects not discussed in it.

The work itself will have little of the writer's own language—a compilation of wisdom of old writers.

§ 22. The Conclusion.

It shall have system,—a complete index.

If the work possess no other merit, it shall at least have system, however deficient in that characteristic may be the Compend. The heads of the Part, Chapter and Section, will clearly indicate the subject treated; the marginal notes will call attention to the leading thought; and a very full and thorough index in the conclusion, whereby the reader can instantly refer to any important document, or person, or thought, or fact, will, it is believed, enable any lad of ordinary capacity, to understand his Governments, the rights he hopes to enjoy of Citizenship, his duty as a liege subject of his Sovereign State; and if in doubt on any point, he shall at least have the authorities to solve it indicated; and with the Divine blessing upon a candid, honest purpose, that shall be pursued to its conclusion with unflagging resolution and industry, we trust it will be admitted in the sequel, that the title is not inappropriate to the work—OUR FŒDERAL UNION: STATE RIGHTS AND WRONGS.

A lad can understand it.

It shall be appropriate to its title.

While the writer feels the most perfect assurance that he is starting a line of investigation which will take us again into the paths of peace and reunion, and that nothing else can be devised that will do it; he is too well aware of the prevalence of opposing views, the strength of fixed habits of thought and of action, to expect immediate results. We Americans—that is a detestable word that we have to use, and in changing our name for the new Union that is to be made, can we not select one appropriate to this part of America?—we Americans think quickly, decide quickly, act quickly, and we shall move with at least ordinary speed on this path of investigation. Yet, let our wise men do their best to instruct us in the truth; let their magnanimity be more than human in acknowledging and correcting their errors, if such shall be discovered: many long months must elapse ere the North shall be convinced of its wrongs and perversion of governmental principles, and be willing to return to pure Federalism. Until that wished-for period arrive, the war goes on; and oh, the horrid waste of precious lives in this fratricidal strife! The money sunk, the property destroyed by the thousand millions, is a mere baubee, in comparison with the heart's blood of our beloved kindred and friends, which is being shed in this unnatural, inhuman conflict. But the bloody tide ceaseth not to flow, until principles are reinvestigated, and the rights and wrongs of these Sovereign States are understood. And with all its horrors and atrocities, not a century will have elapsed before the two hundred millions and more, who will then enjoy the blessings of freedom in this "ocean-bound Republic" (the canal being made across the Isthmus), and liberty-loving Christians throughout the world, will thank GOD for this war, as having been one of the most productive agencies of good for ourselves, for the entire Caucasian race, for all inferior races, by which the Infinite Sovereign accomplishes His eternal purposes for man's Government. May Almighty GOD continue to us His protecting favor, and allow this war to go on, until we shall be made to know and practise the principles of Government, which He, in His infinite love and wisdom, gave our race thousands of years ago!

The work not to effect immediate results.

Cannot our name *Americans*, be changed for a better?

Months requisite to change the opinions of the North.

Meanwhile the war goes on—the horrid sacrifice!

To examine principles will alone stop the flow of blood.

We shall bless GOD even for this war.

May it continue till we learn governmental principles!

§ 22. The Conclusion.

The examination may bring more division in the North. Some opposed to State Sovereignty. Have eminent examples. To examine may change their views, —will be interesting and exciting, —will bring firm resolution. All to be in the conflict.

Possibly, too, the examination into principles, instead of bringing Union in the North, which we hope and confidently expect, will breed still more dissension among ourselves. Many excellent men and pure patriots consider this doctrine of State Sovereignty the bane and ruin of our body politic, this "nation" of the United States. They only follow in the footsteps of some of our wisest, ablest statesmen, as Jay, Hamilton, Morrises, King, &c., in considering Democracy, even of the Republican type, to be untrustworthy, unstable; and as did those good and great men, they look for a change, and desire a stronger Government. It is hoped that a candid examination, particularly into our errors and wrongs, the results not of Federalism, but of its desertion, will change the sentiments of many and give a new and stronger confidence in this Heaven-sanctioned form. The examination is to be profoundly interesting, and, whatever be the result, is to stir the intellect and heart of these Peoples in the South and in the North, as even this war has yet failed to do. It is to bring men to conviction as to their rights and duties, to realize the worth of our imperilled institutions; and in every breast will be formed the stern resolve to do and die, if necessary, for the defence of our priceless heritage. Everybody, from the most lordly aristocrat to the lowliest peasant, is to have his heart and his hand in this controversy.

The struggle in 1800 to be now far exceeded. Then differences were fancied, now real.

The struggle in the days of Adams and Jefferson, was nothing to what this is to be. Then the distinctions were in the main more fancied than real. While a few of the Federalists, under the lead of Hamilton, sought consolidation, and what they deemed a stronger Government, the masses were nearly all true to their party name, and differing little from their opponents, the Republicans, in fundamental views. A few of the latter, too, held extreme Democratic opinions, in favor of the absolute freedom of man, and the right of revolution at all times; but there was no sectional issue, no fanatical question, to stir the heart of man to its very depths, as now.

Sincere Abolitionists not easily to change. To reason with them is idle. They abhor Federalism.

Many of the old-fashioned Abolitionists, sincerely conscientious haters of slavery, believe the time for which they have prayed and worked has at last come, and that the detested institution totters to its fall. Not easily are they to be made to acquiesce in means and measures that evidently must give it an indefinite existence, probably establish it more permanently than ever, and very possibly for all time. It is idle to reason with them, that this grand principle of Federal Union gives them no responsibility; for that very reason do they hate Federalism. They want responsibility, and would glory in following John Brown to the gallows, for the honor of having a part in destroying slavery. Federalism do they abhor equally with slavery.

Their numbers few, but have coöperators, —in Republicans.

But men of this type are very few in number; and though strong in will and energy, could effect little if left to themselves. But unfortunately, there is another class of large numbers, who zealously coöperate with them. Disapproving of slavery, though not with abolition hate, they would have kept it within present bounds, and hope earnestly for its

§ 22. The Conclusion.

speedy extinction. But now that civil war has come, and because the South have taken decided action to perpetuate the institution, they look upon it as the prime cause of our differences, and the war is really believed by them to be the "slaveholders' rebellion." They suppose that, if slavery could be extinguished, "rebellion" would end, and that we can only be safe against the poisonous influences, by destroying the upas tree at the root; that we shall never be safe against "rebellion," till slavery is extinct. They are intelligent, have given much thought to the subject, are earnest in their convictions, properly understand that the South began the war; but, while designing to be fair, by no means discover the immense provocations given the South; and believing Providence has permitted the slaveholder to bring on this war, in order to accomplish the Divine purpose of extinguishing slavery from this land of freedom, they joyfully lend themselves as willing instruments, and heartily coöperate with the extremest Abolitionists; though the latter by no means give their coadjutors the credit that is their due.

They consider slavery the cause of "Rebellion."

They are intelligent,

—believe Providence designs to destroy slavery, and they aid willingly.

Yet even this union of forces would not render the task of reformation very difficult, at least by no means desperate, were it not that, as the war has progressed, many of the strongest conservatives, Democrats as they are called, loving the Union, properly appreciating our institutions, and willing to make any sacrifice for their preservation, as their hopes of conquering a peace are long deferred by the skill and indomitable resolution of our worthy foe, are becoming willing to adopt any measures to save our free institutions from the perils of disunion. They would coöperate even with Abolitionists to wage the war for Union, and not properly regardful of means and appliances, they are willing that slavery, or anything else, should be destroyed to save the Union.

These forces are strengthened by Democrats,

—whose object is purely Union.

Not till we see the effect of the approaching examination into principles of Government upon this class of Democrats, so called; upon this class of conservative Republicans, so called, can we form any judgment of the issue. Indeed does the occasion make us feel our ignorance of the future. The Christian Citizen never had more occasion to put his trust in the God of our fathers, who has so blessed and prospered us hitherto; to seek His guidance and strength to enable each one of us to do our duty, and to trust our never-failing God for the result.

We must know the effect of the examination upon Republicans and Democrats to judge of results.

We must trust in God.

He that dwelleth in the secret place of the Most High, shall abide under the shadow of the Almighty. I will say of the Lord, *He is* my refuge and my fortress: my God, in him will I trust.

Psalms, xci. 1.

Dear reader, turn to that and the preceding psalm of Moses, and let our hearts be strengthened in the God of Israel, our fathers' God and our God. He will deliver us, even in these sore calamities, if we put our trust in Him, and manfully, heroically, as becomes beings made "in the image" of Jehovah, go forth to the discharge of every duty.

God will deliver if we trust in Him.

Should the examination into principles result as we hope, and confidently expect, then the great majority of the North will conclude, that, while it was not at all singular, not in the least unpatriotic, in the great

Not singular that Hamilton and other patriots were not earnest Federalists.

§ 22. The Conclusion.

They rightfully reprobated Democratic errors.

Yet the examination will establish the wisdom and prudence of the other fathers.

and wise Hamilton—who with his coadjutors had the genius to divine the excellences and superiority of the British Government, rightfully reprobated and despised Democracy as then taught in the French school, in which Jefferson was an acknowledged leader, and the effects of which in less than half a dozen years were witnessed in anarchy, and in the torrent of the richest blood of France—to have had no confidence in a Federal Union, of which that of the Netherlands with its incongruous mixture of Aristocratic and Democratic States, furnished the best example of many ages;—while it will not be deemed unwise under the circumstances, that a few of even our ablest and best statesmen of that day desired something else than Federal Republican Democracy, yet we believe, as the examination progresses, that confidence will strengthen in the prudence and discretion of the fathers, if not in their wisdom, as, yielding themselves to the guiding hand of Providence, they went on step by step to the adoption of the most perfect of all Federal Unions.

Federalism was a little understood by the fathers, also Democracy, —not Republicanism.

This the grand principle, *qui facit*, &c.

Something of Federalism, the Union of States for certain purposes, was comprehended; as was also something of Democracy, the keeping of authority in the People; but the grand connecting and enlivening principle, that of Republicanism, was little apprehended, not at all comprehended. That principle is, *qui facit per alium, facit per se*, WHAT HE DOES BY ANOTHER, HE DOES BY HIMSELF. This it is, and this only, which enables a great and free People, even counting by millions as do New York, Ohio, Pennsylvania, and Virginia, to keep in itself its Sovereignty, its *Right of Command;* and by subordinate Agencies, to rule with most despotic sway its faithful liege subjects. This is the glorious principle, so little understood, that enables these Sovereign States to provide against all emergencies, to protect effectually against foes within and foes without, by establishing two completely distinct and independent sets of Agents, one State and one Federal.

John Adams did not understand this, though he drew the Constitution of Massachusetts,

—also his *Defence of the American Constitutions.*

In 1789 he affirmed we were consolidated.

So surely as our wise men examine, will they teach us—and if they fail through disinclination or other cause, the writer feels himself competent for that little task of instruction—that John Adams, though he framed the Constitution of Massachusetts, the most perfect embodiment of the whole theory of Representation that is to be found in any of our Constitutions except that of New Hampshire, which is mainly a copy of the former; that John Adams, though he then went immediately abroad, and while there published his work in three volumes defending the American Constitutions against Turgot's attack, and which one would suppose must have led that strong, clear intellect to thoroughly comprehend *qui facit*, &c.;—we shall find from two letters of this very patriot, John Adams, written in '89 to General Lincoln, soon after his return home, consequent upon his election as Vice-President, that he so little understood the A, B, C of this fundamental principle of the Constitution he had drawn for Massachusetts, so little that of the Federal Union, that he then took the ground that these States were consolidated and Sovereignty transferred to the Federal Government. And yet, at the same

§ 22. The Conclusion.

time, his good *practical* common sense led him against his *theory* to coöperate with Jefferson rather than Hamilton, as their correspondence proves. With his erroneous *theory* on this point, and Jefferson's erroneous *theory*, that every man was a sovereign instead of a subject, it is no wonder that party strife ran high in 1800 about mere shadows, and almost to civil war.

Though so wrong in *theory*, nearly right in *practice*.

Jefferson's error as to natural freedom.

The examination that must be no longer postponed, will satisfy Anglo-Saxons, who have shown such remarkable correctness in the main in *practice*, the importance of getting well grounded in *theory*. And while the contest in 1800 was upon imaginary distinctions chiefly, it is now to be upon solid, fundamental differences. Still, so tenaciously were opinions then adhered to, so high ran party spirit, so bitter the animosity engendered, that the strife almost came to blows and blood.

We must get right in *theory*.

The contest, imaginary in 1800, is now to be real.

The contest then alarming, is now to be tremendous, most terrific. Well will it be if the conflict can be restrained to words. Only by exercising the utmost prudence and forbearance, will civil war among ourselves in the North be prevented. What an opportunity have these free Peoples to exhibit to the world, the worth and superiority of free Governments, and our adaptation to such Governments! Oh, let us seek strength and wisdom from Deity to enable us to improve this golden opportunity of many centuries! Let reason and the ballot box, not the sword, decide the important issues!

The contest, then alarming, is now to be terrific.

Our opportunity to show the excellence of Republicanism.

Reason, not sword, should decide.

Yet will it not be the most improbable of circumstances, if the Federal Republican Citizens of the North should be joined with the armies of the South, to reëstablish the Federal institutions of our fathers against the efforts of Consolidists and Abolitionists. May God save us from such an horrid catastrophe; yet, if it must come in order to save our institutions, Amen! Our system is now unquestionably Federal, and if bloody strife instead of reason and argument shall be employed to effect a change, the responsibility rests upon the revolters, the rebels,—rebels against their Sovereignties, which the Citizens of the seceded States are not. The Captain of our salvation will never desert the true soldier of the Cross, fighting to maintain the very form of Government He gave Himself to his favorite family of our race. The result of such a conflict cannot be uncertain. "Woe unto him that striveth with his Maker."

Federal Republicans of the North and South may be united to restore Federalism.

Responsibility of conflict will be on the rebels.

God will aid us.

Isaiah xlv, 9.

Probably many a Christian reader, whether agreeing with the views of the writer or not, struck with the manifest conflict of opinion between wise and honest men upon these important and interesting subjects, has felt that more than human wisdom was requisite to understand the "Laws of Nature and of Nature's God." He has realized the necessity of Divine illumination, and repeatedly has he invoked it. In the language of the Monarch Psalmist, does he say:

Divine aid is required.

> Teach me, O Lord, the way of thy statutes; and I shall keep it *unto* the end. Give me understanding, and I shall keep thy law; yea, I shall observe it with *my* whole heart. Make me to go in the path of thy commandments; for therein do I delight. Incline my heart unto thy testimonies, and not to covetousness. Turn away mine eyes from beholding vanity; *and* quicken thou me in thy way.

Psalms, cxix, 33–37.

§ 22. The Conclusion.

Individuals will realize their necessities.

Also these States.

Have we always had these sentiments?

The whole of that interesting psalm would be most apposite in this connection; and the reader should peruse it. As individuals, deeply sensible of our own imperfections and weakness, we shall resort to the Infinite Fountain of knowledge for direction, and shall draw large supplies. But we are not there to stop. As Peoples, as Sovereign States, must we seek unto our KING, for wisdom to direct us, for grace to perform our every duty. Usually we have recognized our obligations to Deity for our many and unequalled blessings, and it is supposed that on every important occasion we have sought Divine aid. Bishop Hopkins published a valuable work, *The American Citizen*, in which he dwells with wisdom and emphasis on Christian duty, and every Citizen should study it. The Bishop observes:

Bishop Hopkins' views.

American Citizen, pp. 28, 29,

Prayer in the Convention of 1787.

> But we have the best evidence of their Christian feeling in the well known fact, that at the first assembling of the convention in 1787, when the spirit of dissension threatened to run high, Benjamin Franklin proposed the introduction of prayer, as the only mode of securing the Divine guidance and blessing on their discussions. The motion was adopted unanimously. The Rev. Dr. Duché, an Episcopal minister of Philadelphia, was invited to attend; and that service of Christian prayer, which has since been so well depicted by the pencil of an American Artist, produced the happiest effect on the subsequent proceedings, until they finally closed in the adoption of the Constitution.

This conflicts with Madison.

Dr. Duché not in the country.

Bishop White's Memoirs, pp. 63, 65.

The mistake not in the name of the clergyman.

Bishop White not the person. *Ib.* p. 117.

This statement by such eminent authority, seemed so in conflict with Madison's account, which, with Franklin's interesting and pious speech, will be presented in Part II, that the point has been somewhat examined. In Bishop White's memoirs, it appears Dr. Duché wrote him from England the 2d April, '83; and it is further stated that Dr. Duché postponed his return from England till '92. He therefore could not have been in Philadelphia in '87. Nor does it appear probable that the mistake is merely in the name of the clergyman. Dr. White had been the chaplain of Congress, and in '86 was elected Bishop of Pennsylvania, and went to England for consecration. He arrived in New York on the 7th April, '87; and though he was chaplain of Congress, yet all the month of June (Franklin's motion was on the 29th), and early in July, there was no quorum in attendance, as the Journals show, and he could therefore have officiated in the Convention, and would almost certainly have been the person chosen, and so interesting an event would scarcely have escaped record in his memoirs. Perhaps Bishop Hopkins refers to Matteson's picture representing the Continental Congress in its first prayer, in 1774.

Was Matteson's picture referred to?

MADISON'S testimony,

Besides this negative evidence, Madison records that,

—*Papers*, ii, 986.

> After several unsuccessful attempts for silently postponing this matter [Franklin's motion for prayers] by adjourning, the adjournment was at length carried, without any vote on the motion.

Madison has no further reference to the subject, and Mr. Sparks appends this note to Franklin's speech:

SPARKS, v, 155. *Franklin's Works.*

> *Note by Dr. Franklin.*—"The convention, except three or four persons, thought prayers unnecessary!"

§ 22. The Conclusion.

Astonishing the fathers should have omitted prayers.

The great and venerated Franklin, esteemed by some heretic and infidel, puts an exclamation point after his record; and to have added them by the million, would not have sufficed for the astounding declaration, that in such a Convention, only "three or four persons thought prayers necessary!" It seems incredible that a few years of peace and prosperity, should have wrought such a change. Prayers were, perhaps, kept up in Congress from habit; at all events, the Convention of '87, many of the members no doubt tinctured with the then fashionable doctrines of the French school of infidelity, considered themselves wise enough to dispense with Divine aid in planning their Constitution. And in this horrid war, do we see the results!

They trusted themselves, and we see the results.

Our prosperity under the first Confederation.

It has been supposed that, prior to the adoption of the present Constitution, we were almost in anarchy; to use the words of the elegant Mr. Motley, "in chaos." Mr. Dawson will soon publish a reply to Mr. Motley's famous letter to the London *Times*, to which the reader's attention is earnestly bespoken, wherein he demonstrates our immense prosperity at that time, and beyond doubt, it could have been said of us as Moses sang of the Hebrews:

Answer to Mr. Motley.

Our self-confidence.

But Jeshurun waxed fat and kicked: thou art waxen fat, thou art grown thick, thou art covered *with fatness:* then he forsook God *which* made him, and lightly esteemed the Rock of his salvation.

Deut. xxxii, 15.

Not only self-sufficient, but refused to recognize Deity.

Read the whole of that remarkable song, and see how exactly it suits our case. And not only were the fathers so self-sufficient, that they needed not to seek Divine aid in the accomplishment of their plans, but they even dared to omit all recognition of Deity in the instrument itself! From beginning to end of that august instrument, is there no recognition of the infinitely more august Majesty of Heaven! Read the account of God's dealings with the house of Eli, where He says by the prophet:

God will be honored.

Wherefore the Lord God of Israel saith, I said indeed *that* thy house, and the house of thy father, should walk before me forever: but now the Lord saith, Be it far from me; for them that honour me I will honour, and they that despise me shall be lightly esteemed.

1 *Sam.* ii, 30.

Propriety of our recognizing Jehovah.

Was it not eminently proper for these Christian States, which had so recently, so signally been blessed of God; whose mighty Hand those very fathers themselves had repeatedly acknowledged in His special interpositions in their behalf—special to them, not to the Infinite, who can know no change of purpose; was it not little enough for them, in exercising the highest privilege of Citizenship, the gift of their Heavenly Father, in framing "a more perfect Union" between these Sovereign States; was it not to have been expected, that in their league of Union, their Infinite Protector would at least have been so far "honored," as that His favors should have been acknowledged, and His name most surely inscribed in the instrument? Was this done? Not from beginning to end of that compact is even the name of Deity mentioned; not the slightest allusion, in any manner, to an overruling Providence. "They that despise me shall be lightly esteemed," says our God; and as our fathers thought, "We,

It was not done.

The consequence of the neglect.

§ 22. The Conclusion.

the People of the United States," could of themselves "form a more perfect Union," did not need Divine assistance to "ordain and establish this CONSTITUTION for the United States of America;" we see already how strikingly the declaration is verified in our confusion and disgrace. The very first three words—"WE THE PEOPLE,"—of that instrument, drawn without a public invocation of Divine wisdom, with no recognition of the Sovereign of the universe, have been the prime, almost the sole cause, of leading these Peoples astray, and into this civil war. And the sons have sinned equally with the fathers, in that for over seventy years we have enjoyed the fruits of our beneficent Ruler's care, have made repeated additions to our Constitution, and yet have failed to correct this most important omission.

The first three words of the Constitution led us astray.

The sons have not corrected the error.

Not honoring JEHOVAH, the Constitution is accursed.

"They that despise me, SHALL BE lightly esteemed," says the Sovereign Majesty of Heaven; and who is the impious subject that shall dare to gainsay JEHOVAH'S declaration? Accursed be the instrument, no matter what loved and honored names are attached to it, that thus dishonors the Monarch of all Peoples. Tear it to shreds, trample it in the dust, damn it to everlasting infamy, that it thus ignores, dishonors our KING, JEHOVAH. "Them that honor Me, I will honor; and they that despise Me, shall be lightly esteemed." Let it be our wisdom to follow the example of Nebuchadnezzar, after his punishment, as we have chosen to imitate his vain conceit and pride, which brought GOD'S judgments upon him:

Destroy it.

Let us humble ourselves for our sin.

Dan. iv, 34, 35.

And at the end of the days I Nebuchadnezzar lifted up mine eyes unto heaven, and mine understanding returned unto me, and I blessed the most High, and I praised and honoured him that liveth forever, whose dominion *is* an everlasting dominion, and his kingdom *is* from generation to generation: and all the inhabitants of the earth *are* reputed as nothing: and he doeth according to his will in the army of heaven, and *among* the inhabitants of the earth: and none can stay his hand, or say unto him, What doest thou?

GOD rules.

Duty to show mercy to Caucasians as well as Negroes.

Read the context; it is full of appropriate instruction. May the same glorious result be ours; and some readers will please bear in mind, that "by showing mercy to the poor," the Father of the Caucasian race had probably no design to have it excluded altogether from the "mercy" of white folks, for the benefit of the Negro.

Proper to study the past, not the future.

Most becoming is it for weak, finite man to tread softly in the vestibules of JEHOVAH'S presence, as we seek to learn His teachings. It seems unwise, impious to pry into futurity, as some do with regard to the prophecies, but duty to study the past. Luke records an instruction to the disciples after our Saviour's resurrection:

Acts i, 6, 7.

When they therefore were come together, they asked of him, saying, Lord, wilt thou at this time restore again the kingdom to Israel? And he said unto them, It is not for you to know the times or the seasons, which the Father hath put in his own power.

Prophecy an evidence of GOD'S controlling power.

Nobody has yet been able, as we have discovered, to prove our Saviour false. Prophecy of the future seems sealed to our vision, and designed only to be a perpetual memento to us of the truth of our GOD, as the scroll of time's events unrolls, and they are found to accord with predictions made ages ago, as in the miraculous preservation of the Hebrew race, and of the Arabs with their characteristics; and to afford us proof incontestable, that the Infinite Author must have known

§ 22. The Conclusion.

. . . the end from the beginning, and from ancient times *the things* that are not *yet* done, saying, My counsel shall stand, and I will do all my pleasure.

Isaiah xlvi, 10.

But while we may not pry into hidden mysteries, we are advised and required to study into the past, to consider well the present, and perform faithfully its duties; and the Bible is replete with historic illustrations for the one, with positive commands for the other. Nor are we as Peoples, any more than as individuals, to be able by quibbles and false reasoning to dodge our responsibility. We know not, GOD has not seen fit to explain to our feeble comprehension, how man's freedom, individually or collectively, is to be reconciled with Infinite pre-ordination. We cannot understand how the Creator,

Study of the past—present practice.

Our responsibility for our conduct as States.

Free agency incomprehensible.

. binding nature fast in Fate,
Left free the human will.

POPE'S *Universal Prayer.*

But that we can neither comprehend nor apprehend a truth, is not the slightest evidence against it, "for now we see through a glass darkly." It seems a direct contradiction that we are free, and yet that GOD completely rules our every action. But we know it is so, for He so declares; and "yea, let GOD be true, but every man a liar." We are perfectly conscious, too, that we have the free exercise of every power and faculty with which we are endowed. The weak tool, strong in his powers and will, stronger still in his own conceit, knows that according as he chooses to arise from his couch, and take the steps to get his breakfast, he will have it; and if not, he goes breakfastless, notwithstanding his every step and motion must have been pre-ordained from eternity.

1 *Cor.* xiii, 12.

We are free, yet GOD rules us, as He declares.

Rom. iii, 4.

Our consciousness of this.

What shall we say then? *Is there* unrighteousness with God? God forbid. For he saith to Moses, I will have mercy on whom I will have mercy, and I will have compassion on whom I will have compassion. So then *it is* not of him that willeth, nor of him that runneth, but of God that showeth mercy. For the scripture saith unto Pharoah, Even for this same purpose have I raised thee up, that I might show my power in thee, and that my name might be declared throughout all the earth. Therefore hath he mercy on whom he will *have mercy*, and whom he will he hardeneth. Thou wilt say then unto me, Why doth he yet find fault? For who hath resisted his will? Nay but, O man, who art thou that repliest against God? Shall the thing formed say to him that formed *it*, Why hast thou made me thus?

It is right GOD should rule.

Rom. viii, 14-20.

We know little of anything, and the more we investigate a subject, the more certain are we of our ignorance of it; the more we see there is to be learned. Even in physical sciences is this true; much more so in the spiritual. And as the senses appeal most strongly to us, GOD'S system of providences is specially adapted to our nature in this respect, or we to it. Had the Creator etablished everything in nature by laws facile and systematic to our comprehension, we might have come to infer that the universe needed no Sovereign to regulate it; which erroneous idea Paul counteracted so beautifully when the heathen Lycaonians would

Man's limited knowledge.

GOD teaches us by His providences.

§ 22. The Conclusion.

worship him and Barnabas for curing a lame man; and stopping their idolatry, he preached to them of the true GOD:

Acts xiv, 17.

Nevertheless he left not himself without witness, in that he did good, and gave us rain from heaven, and fruitful seasons, filling our hearts with food and gladness.

GOD'S goodness in His providences.

As opportunities occur, casual to us, the providence of GOD seems to interpose for our benefit; and in the direction of the weather, the most uncertain of all things to our senses; and in the particular character of the different seasons, so varying from year to year, do we see unmistakably that some beneficent power must govern.

Infinite control of events by Deity.

If a single event is controlled by Deity, every event must be likewise. What are to us great affairs, are often traceable to what we term trifling incidents. Said our Saviour:

Matt. x, 29-33.

Are not two sparrows sold for a farthing? and one of them shall not fall on the ground without your Father. But the very hairs of your head are all numbered. Fear ye not therefore, ye are of more value than many sparrows. Whosoever therefore shall confess me before men, him will I confess also before my Father which is in heaven. But whosoever shall deny me before men, him will I also deny before my Father which is in heaven.

How these thoughts should impress us.

How vast, how unutterable the thoughts these simple and beautiful words unfold! To think of a Being who from eternity must have known the dropping of every sparrow; must have established the starting and the stopping place of every breeze, as it bears along its course a solitary hair that had been ours!

How little we can conceive of GOD.

What can we conceive of such a Being, either of His existence, of His nature, of His attributes, even of His works, palpable as they are to our sense? Shall man attempt to pry into such mysteries? Because he cannot comprehend them, will he pronounce the Divine existence a lie? Rather let him bow in profoundest humility, worship and adore.

GOD'S condescension.

Yet even this glorious Being condescends to be our GOD. By His Son, the second person in the incomprehensible Trinity, has been given the above most precious promise; and oh, consider the alternative! Fellow sinner! are you confessing or denying the LORD who bought you?[1]

Numb. xxiii, 19.

God *is* not a man, that he should lie; neither the son of man, that he should repent: hath he said and shall he not do *it?* or hath he spoken, and shall he not make it good?

The dignity of man in that he can honor JEHOVAH.

Not one of the least incomprehensible of Divine truths, if it be proper to use the comparative in infinity, is the fact that such insignificant creatures as we seem to be in the scale of creation, should be able to honor

---

Religious toleration our glory.

[1] The boast of our country, is its toleration in religion. We are divided into various sects, and Protestants think Catholics have strange errors as to the Virgin Mary and transubstantiation; some Trinitarians think no Unitarian can truly love our Saviour; and some Baptists think a faithful Christian must be immersed. Yet the members of our various denominations, and many attendants upon their worship, consider themselves Christians, and we all adore the same GOD, believe in the same Bible, however much we fail to practise its precepts.

Our dependence on GOD in our present exigencies.

Never has there been an occasion in our history, when Christians of every denomination should so realize their dependence on the Almighty arm, as now; and the writer has believed ever since he began this work, and the sentiment has constantly grown upon him, that if our country is to be saved, it is to be through the influence of RELIGION.

Duty to GOD to govern us.

Nothing but a true sense of our duty to our GOD and Saviour, our KING JEHOVAH, will govern these excited, erring individuals, which

JEHOVAH. Yet has He most graciously declared and with a precious promise, in the passage already quoted, "Them that honour me, I will honour." Surely is there a character, a worth, an excellence in humanity, of which we have little conception.

§ 22. The Conclusion.

1 *Sam.* ii, 30.

And God said, Let us make man in our image, after our likeness: and let them have dominion over the fish of the sea, and over the fowl of the air, and over the cattle, and over all the earth, and over every creeping thing that creepeth upon the earth. So God created man in his *own* image, in the image of God created he him; male and female created he them.

Man made in GOD'S image.

Gen. i, 26, 27.

Is it supposable that, with all our imperfections, we are able, in the slightest degree, to appreciate the august truth that we live, the very "image" of the Infinite Creator? Such is the solemn fact, and so important is it that man should comprehend something of his nature, that in this succinct account of the majestic work of creation, is it thrice declared that man is "the image" of GOD. Again does GOD repeat it to Noah after leaving the ark. In these mortal bodies in which we are clothed as a punishment for our transgression of our Sovereign's righteous Law, we can little realize what we are, what we are to become; and yet, wretched, fallen creatures that we are, let us endeavor to conceive something of the dignity of our existence "in the image" of the immaculate JEHOVAH; of being heirs, coheirs with the Son of GOD to the throne of the universe. For,

Man unable to appreciate his dignity.

Thrice declared to be "in the image of GOD,"

—and again repeated.

Heirs of God, joint heirs with Christ.

The Spirit itself beareth witness with our spirit, that we are the children of God: And if children, then heirs; heirs of God, and joint heirs with Christ.

Rom. viii, 16, 17.

And while we debased our immaculate "image" in the fall, it has not been destroyed. This is proved by GOD's reason given to Noah, the second father of this Caucasian race, for the infliction of capital punishment:

Our "image" not destroyed by the fall.

Whoso sheddeth man's blood, by man shall his blood be shed: for in the image of God made he man.

Gen. ix, 6.

---

constitute these States. And though decided in his own belief, he would grasp as affectionately the hand of a colaboring Catholic or Universalist, as of a Presbyterian. All are, or should be, equally zealous to preserve our free institutions, whose highest glory is religious toleration. And the toleration should not be in words, in form merely; but in the spirit, in the heart.

All Christians to be colaborers,

The writer being known to many in the West as a Presbyterian, and his main object having been to inculcate the necessity of correct *theories*, which is even more essential in religion than in politics, it might be inferred that he only addressed those as Christians, who are usually denominated orthodox.

—of all denominations.

To a considerable degree, the writer appreciates the importance of correctness in *theory;* and that, as Peter enjoins, every Christian should be "ready always to *give* an answer to every man that asketh [him] a reason of the hope that is in [him] with meekness and fear." And as men will differ about religion as about politics, divisions in the Church militant are quite as essential to peace and tranquillity, as in the political world; and seem alike approbated by Deity. The members of these rival churches, too, appear to be equally sincere in their piety and patriotism. Therefore is this appeal designed for every one, of whatever name, who has living faith in Christ as his Saviour. All such, in the writer's estimation, are Christians, whether Church members or not, and are cordially, earnestly solicited as brethren dear and well beloved, to join their prayers and their efforts, in saving our imperilled institutions. And it is a lamentable illustration of the imperfections of humanity, that so many who really love their Saviour, should fail to acknowledge Him before men. Brother! could not you with propriety connect *yourself* immediately with one of the divisions of the army of our Heavenly King, and pray earnestly, fight manfully to maintain toleration, by perpetuating this Federal Republic?

A correct *theory* important.

1 *Peter* iii, 15.

Men will differ in religion as in politics,

—are yet sincere.

Who are addressed as Christians.

Neglect to profess religion.

§ 22. The Conclusion.

Man's disregard of God's command to use proper means to defend God's "image."

And yet against this most positive command, that has never been in the slightest degree changed, do impious wretches dare to set up their appeals for the pardon of the murderer; more impious still, are those baser rulers that dare to listen to their fellow mortals, instead of the Sovereign of the universe; arrogating to themselves to be better judges of what is best, more perfect philanthropists, than our God, who gave His Son to die to save the guilty murderer; not from temporal, but eternal death. What is the use of having laws, and courts, and jails, and gallows, with such contemners of justice, of the God of justice, as are some in Executive chairs, who might with propriety be named?

Man superior to the angels.

Man's superiority, even over the angelic host, is evident from Paul:

Heb. i, 14. 1 *Cor.* vi, 3.

> Are they not all ministering spirits, sent forth to minister for them who shall be heirs of salvation? . . . Know ye not that we shall judge angels?

Christ's death the highest proof of man's worth.

But no truth in any degree illustrates God's estimate of our worth—and He alone can comprehend it—which is at all comparable with the death of Christ upon Calvary's hill. Paul observes:

Rom. v. 8, 9.

> But God commendeth his love toward us, in that, while we were yet sinners, Christ died for us. Much more then, being now justified by his blood, we shall be saved
> viii, 31, 32. from wrath through him . . . What shall we then say to these things? If God *be* for us, who *can be* against us? He that spared not his own Son, but delivered him up for us all, how shall he not with him also freely give us all things?

And, oh, with what majesty, befitting the exalted theme, does the great Apostle to us Gentiles, pursue his argument! an argument which seems to have no equal in written language.

God never made an unwise sacrifice.

The God of infinite love and wisdom never made a sacrifice without a benefit most abundantly compensatory. As with everything else, this subject is entirely incomprehensible, that beings of such dignity should have been created and then allowed to fall. Yet even we can see, that it was a greater achievement to have formed a creature with a free will, than a mere automatic machine, governed altogether by the will of his Creator. As a consequence, however, these lofty characters fell from their high estate to a low degree of infamy, and God in His eternal counsels, revealed to us more through Paul's writings than any others, provided a way of redemption for these beings made "in his image." So exalted were they, so enormous was the guilt of such characters in revolting against the Sovereign Majesty of Heaven, that nothing less than a Divine atonement would suffice to restore the dignity of God's broken Law. And it seems quite probable, that for nothing else than man's salvation, was it necessary for God to divide up the *exercise* of His Sovereignty. And Paul seems to teach, that when the work of redemption is complete, and death destroyed, the distribution of office in the Godhead is to cease.

The grandeur of creating a free will.

Man's fall, and God's plan to save him.

The atonement must be infinite.

To accomplish it may have been the cause of God's division of the *exercise* of Sovereignty.

The division may cease when redemption is accomplished.
1 Cor. xv, 24–28.

> Then *cometh* the end, when he shall have delivered up the kingdom to God even the Father. . . . And when all things shall be subdued unto him, then shall the Son also himself be subject unto him that put all things under him, that God may be all in all.

However it may be, as to the division of the *exercise* of God's Sovereignty of which we shall learn ere long, we do know from the foregoing passages and others, which we shall have occasion to quote in treating of Sovereignty, that the *exercise* of the *Right of Command* in Heaven was divided up, the Son, the second person of the Godhead, assuming that of Mediator between God the Father and His rebellious children. The Son came to earth, assumed our nature, and by His death upon the cross, made such atonement for man's guilt, that the Father could pardon; and the Holy Spirit, the third person in the Trinity, operates upon the hearts of these rebellious children to bring them back to love and to obedience. Do we need aught else to teach us our worth, than the story of Calvary's sacrifice? the crucifixion of God's holy Son, that we might be saved?

§ 22. The Conclusion.

The division of the *exercise* of Sovereignty to Father, Son, and Holy Ghost.

The Son Mediator between us and the Father.

The Spirit influences us.

And what is required of these offenders to avail themselves of this infinite atonement?

What must we do to be saved?

Then Peter said unto them, Repent, and be baptized every one of you in the name of Jesus Christ for the remission of sins, and ye shall receive the gift of the Holy Ghost. For the promise is unto you, and to your children, and to all that are afar off, *even* as many as the Lord our God shall call.

Acts ii, 38, 39.

Surely might it be expected that every man whose guilt had made the infinite Sacrifice necessary, would accept the atonement; that no one would fail to reciprocate the Saviour's love, but with unfeigned repentance, would return to his allegiance to the Majesty of Heaven. Yet so depraved are many of these wretched creatures, that they not only reject this salvation with contempt, but dare to defy the omnipotence of Jehovah, and constantly employ the life and health He gives them, in rebellion against His high and holy laws; and they would endeavor to prevent all men from loving and serving God, and make a very hell of earth. To control this wickedness in some degree, is the chief object of Government by man over his fellow, for which God has given us so much instruction in His holy Word.

Will not all men accept mercy?

Some are too depraved,

—bid defiance to Jehovah,

—would make a hell of earth.

These must be governed.

This is man's probationary state, as most of us Christians believe; and whatever is to be effected to restore fallen, depraved man to the pristine glory of his creation, when innocent and holy he stood forth a perfect man, "in the image of God;" whatever results are to be obtained for the benefit of our race from the infinite atonement of our blessed Saviour, must all be done here in this short hand's-breadth space of time. If the guilty sinner fail to accept here the offers of salvation, he sinks to eternal woe. And such is the proneness of man to sin, so easily is he led into the paths of folly, that it becomes of the highest consequence to remove as much as possible all corrupting influences. This should, equally with punishing crime, be the object of Government, and the writer is confident, as of his existence, that God's providence has led us to adopt the very best system for this purpose that was ever devised. As Christians shall study into this subject, realize anew that we and our children are here to prepare for a never-ending eternity, consider the worth of the toleration

This is man's probation.

Man, failing to repent in time, is lost forever.

Man easily led astray.

Object of Government to remove temptation.

For this our Federal system best.

§ 22. The Conclusion.

Christians should not consent to jeopardize it by disunion.

which our Governments afford, and investigate the improvements of which our compound system allows; will they never, in the South or in the North, consent to have our institutions jeopardized by permanent disunion.

God has broken our compact.

But Almighty God having waited on us, for seventy years, to correct our error and acknowledge Him in our Federal Compact, He, by His providence, has allowed it to be broken, to be annulled forever. Each of these States is now at liberty to form another compact, being obliged, however, to provide its portion to meet existing obligations incurred in the old Union. Until they shall have seceded, are they liable for their proportion of all Federal engagements. Each State is at liberty, even, to join the Confederate States, with their consent, which, as chief among several improvements in their Constitution, recognize in the preamble their dependence on Almighty God. But for us to go to them, is no more to be expected under the circumstances, than for the South to return to the old Union.

Each State at liberty to frame another,

—might join the Confederate States, who recognize God, but probably will not.

A Convention to be held.

A Convention must be held of delegates from such States as please to send, as in '87. Various important changes will be considered,[1]

Probable changes in the new Union.

Impossible here to discuss them.

Changes must be moderate.

[1] It has been the design of the writer, under a sectional head, *Improvements to be made*, to suggest the propriety of various changes, and the reasons for them, which this Providential rupture of our Union gives occasion to consider. But this Compend is already too long, and considerable space would be requisite. Indeed, all the facts and documents and views that will be presented in this entire compilation, and many others, need to be well understood to discuss the subject of changes. There is one point, however, that will no doubt deeply impress the reader, as it already has the writer, as he pursues the investigation, and sees more and more the excellences of the system we now have, which is, that we must be slow to make alterations. "*Let well enough alone*," must be our firm resolve; and we shall have a great deal of wise counsel to be prudent in fundamental changes in Government.

Taxing exports.

The Judiciary.

This great balance wheel must be made secure.

Its dignity.

The taxing of exports has already been suggested; also a change in the Judiciary. This great balance-wheel of our system is to be more properly appreciated, and placed beyond the reach of political influence. The Constitution might provide for dividing the country into ten or twenty districts, each with its Judge to be appointed as now, with liberal salaries, to constitute the Supreme Court, and not perform circuit duties. Inferior Courts and Judges to be established. Let no Judge of a Federal Court be ever eligible to any other office of trust or emolument of a State or of the United States, except promotion to a higher station on the bench. With careful safeguards against injustice to the Judges in occupancy, provide that each twenty years or so, the Districts should be rearranged according to population, perhaps somewhat increased in number. We can have such a tribunal, as that every Citizen, every State, will be perfectly sure of justice being done, and it will soon become the most eminent Court of Christendom. What an honor to be a Judge of the Supreme Court of the ——— States, according as the new Union shall be entitled!

Equality of votes in the Senate.

A change, though right, may be inexpedient.

The West can rule the whole country.

The enmity of the South to New England.

Changes not to be made to gratify spite.

The question, too, is again to arise, as to the equality of votes in the Senate, in which the small States will not be able to govern the large ones against all justice, as they did before. But there are important considerations as to expediency, as well as to right and justice; and though the writer as a western Citizen was naturally inclined to favor the equalizing of votes in the Senate, as in the House; yet as the investigation has proceeded, he has become more and more doubtful concerning it. Not that he deems it important to give the large and small States each the same power in one branch of Congress, to guard against consolidation, as did Luther Martin, Patterson, Yates, and Lansing and others; this subject of State rights, State Sovereignty, will never again be misunderstood as it has been, and there will be no danger of consolidation. But the West is soon to have the power, and will almost rule the whole country. It surely would, if the States are allowed votes in the Senate according to population. We shall have power enough in the West, in any event, for our own good, for the good of the country; so that while it is reasonable and just that the Senatorial representation should be equalized, its expediency seems a doubtful question. The South would no doubt like at this time to strike down the power of New England; and to many of their Citizens, it would remove one of their strongest objections to reconfederating with the North, to alter the Senatorial representation. But the changes must not be made to gratify present enmities and spite, but with broad statesman-like views, arranged for a Union that shall be Continental. We in the West love power as well as any body, and the South know that on the chief subject of our Federal Union, that of taxation, we shall be with them, and they may be glad some of which may be distasteful to particular States, and all may not at once come into the new Union. But it is believed the chief States, both in the South and in the North, can agree upon a Constitution; and if any choose to try an independent existence for a while, it will probably prove no detriment to the permanency of the Union, when ultimately they may return. And no State will be allowed to shirk its quota of existing obligations, whether of the Confederate or of the United States. There will be strength enough in the new Union, if one be practicable, to protect against any such injustice.

§ 22. The Conclusion.

Changes to be made.

Chief States can form a new Union.

States may join or not, but cannot shirk their responsibilities.

And in conclusion, we have a proposition to make to Christians in the South and in the North, which the writer would premise by remarking that the last sermon he heard from his pastor, was upon the efficacy of prayer. Mr. Patterson remarked that Christians, both in the South and in the North, were earnestly invoking the Divine blessing upon their respective causes. Both parties praying with faith, both must be graciously answered; yet to give victory to the armies of one, was to bring defeat to the armies of the other. How then was it that GOD could be faithful to His promises, and answer the prayers of these inimical children?

A proposition to Christians.

A sermon alluded to upon the efficacy of prayer.

How can GOD answer the prayers of North and South?

Said Mr. Patterson, in substance, while the sincere Christian prays for particular blessings, which seem to him desirable for himself, his country, the world, he yet appreciates his fallibility; and he addresses the Being who knows precisely what is for the best; One who has the will and power to accomplish whatever is desirable, and in the best possible manner. So that the true prayer of the righteous man is strongest in the desire, that even his most cherished wishes may be over-ruled, if GOD sees it to be best; and the substance of his prayer is, that the Sovereign of the universe will accomplish such purposes, and in such ways, as He shall judge will best promote the greatest happiness of man, the highest glory of GOD. In this way, whether victory come to the armies North or South; whether Union or Disunion triumph, will the Christian's prayer be answered by our never-failing JEHOVAH.

The true Christian prays that GOD will accomplish His purposes in the best way.

Such prayers will be answered, whether North or South are victorious.

---

to give us the control. But there are other questions to arise, in which it will be important for the other sections united, to be able to overpower the giant West. Inland, little interested directly in losses on the ocean, we may be headstrong and aggressive on other nations, in order to have war. The South, the Pacific States, the Eastern, should unitedly have always strength enough, at least in the Senate, to outvote the West. But we cannot here discuss this great question.

The other sections should be able to control the West.

Whether it be proper to inquire into the status of any subject within a State, in apportioning representation and taxation, is to be another point not to be dodged. To make a whole negro in Kentucky, count only three fifths of one in Indiana and Illinois, seems to be an anomaly and injustice; and it may be best in the new Constitution to ignore the negro question completely. A general provision recognizing the principles of International Law, and providing that, if a dog or horse or other property escape or be carried for a time into another State, the rights of property shall be protected, according to the laws of the State of which the proprietor shall continue to be a Citizen, would seem to cover the whole ground, and enable our Southern cousins and brothers to visit us and our watering places, with considerable more comfort and satisfaction than hitherto.

The status of subjects, and slave representation.

International Law to be recognized.

A good many changes are to result from the Providential breaking of this present Compact, which must yet have its continuance by sufferance for a time longer. Hard will some of them be to bear, yet must they be cheerfully endured to bring a new and cordial Union. Even the Star-spangled Banner may have to give way to another emblem, that shall not speak of blood and woe to the hearts of our Confederates.

The Star-spangled Banner may have to be given up.

§ 22. The Conclusion.

The views were too reasonable, too practical, as are all the sermons of that excellent and beloved pastor, not to have made an abiding impression, and the entire two years and more intervening have they influenced the writer. Never has a day been appointed for fasting and prayer, either in the North or in the South, which has not been hailed with delight. Yet we do not witness results on either side which give evidence that we have offered, "the effectual fervent prayer of a righteous man [which] availeth much." Evidently, we have not had true faith in our GOD, which He has a right to expect of us above all others of the creatures that have existence "in His image," because of His unexampled goodness toward us, all our lives through. Instead of trusting the Almighty Arm, we must have relied upon our poor selves to work out our deliverance. Instead of being willing to take and to pursue GOD's plans, we have been trying to make the Sovereign of the universe adopt our methods to advance His glory, to promote our best good. Many of us in the North are determined, at all hazards, to raise to an equality with this our race, which exists "in the image of GOD," the very lowest race in the scale of humanity; and many in the South are determined, that at all hazards they will be forever separated from such detestable wretches. These are the extremes, no doubt, and few are they, who with such base hatred in their hearts, have dared to approach the throne of Love with their accursed supplications. But between these extremes have nearly all of us erred more or less. We have not put our full confidence in the GOD of our salvation, but have wanted our own particular measures adopted, that we as individuals, as States, as rival Confederacies, might have the glory.

Days of fasting and prayer have been appointed in both nations. We do not have answers. *James* vi, 16. Have not trusted God. The North require GOD to destroy slavery. The South require to be separated from such wretches. We have all sought our own glory.

The fault must be ours.

The fault must be in ourselves, for GOD has explicitly declared with regard to his faithful children, that

GOD's promise to hear prayer instantly.

> They shall not build, and another inhabit: they shall not plant, and another eat: for as the days of a tree *are* the days of my people, and mine elect shall long enjoy the work of their hands. They shall not labour in vain, nor bring forth for trouble; for they *are* the seed of the blessed of the LORD and their offspring with them. And it shall come to pass, that before they call, I will answer; and while they are yet speaking, I will hear. The wolf and the lamb shall feed together, and the lion shall eat straw like the bullock: and dust *shall be* the serpent's meat. They shall not hurt nor destroy in all my holy mountain, saith the LORD.

Isaiah lxv, 22–25.

Prayer—how can it have efficacy?

Here is another phenomenon in religion, which, like the many in nature on all sides surrounding us, we have not faculties to comprehend. How is it possible that the supplications of a fallen, depraved creature, should have efficacy with the infinite JEHOVAH? When GOD's decrees have established unalterably, and from eternity, every circumstance connected with every creature in His dominions, how is it possible that any change could be made by prayer, whoever may be the offerer, whoever the Intercessor? As we know not how the sun shines, yet are sensible of its genial influences, so does the Christian feel the rays of the Sun of Righteousness; and that these beings in GOD's image may have a part in obtaining the blessings ordained to them from eternity, our Father has

GOD's favor in allowing us to ask for blessings.

graciously declared, in connection with His rich promises to His People of old, "I will yet *for* this be inquired of by the house of Israel, to do *it* for them." The Bible is filled with encouragements to prayer, and we too little appreciate our high privilege of being thus made co-workers with GOD in the accomplishment of His eternal purposes. Bespeaks not this our dignity? And whereas the New Testament truths are chiefly addressed to man individually, the Old are applied more to man collectively. As Peoples, as States, must we worship and pray to our King, JEHOVAH, and as States shall we be blessed.

> § 22. The Conclusion.
>
> *Ezek.* xxxvi, 37.
>
> Privilege of being co-workers with GOD.
>
> States to be religious.

The context of the above passage is so full of instruction to these Peoples, that a part must be quoted, and the reader should study and ponder well the whole of it. Our King is jealous of His honor; He will have "pity for [His] holy name." How debased is man, associated man, that he neglects to avail himself of the high dignity accorded to him, of honoring JEHOVAH! And if GOD could reasonably complain of His People of old for not honoring Him, how much greater the wrong done by us in failing to recognize Him in our Federal Constitution, when possessed of so much more knowledge of Deity and of our duty imparted by the later revelations, and when the claims to our allegiance have been strengthened by the highest privileges ever bestowed on our race. Says our King JEHOVAH:

> GOD jealous of His honor.
>
> Man's guilt in not honoring Him.
>
> Ours exceeds the Hebrews'.

But I had pity for mine holy name, which the house of Israel had profaned among the heathen, whither they went. Therefore say unto the house of Israel, Thus saith the Lord GOD, I do not *this* for your sakes, O house of Israel, but for mine holy name's sake, which ye have profaned among the heathen, whither ye went. And I will sanctify my great name, which was profaned among the heathen, which ye have profaned in the midst of them; and the heathen shall know that I *am* the LORD, saith the Lord GOD, when I shall be sanctified in you before their eyes. For I will take you from among the heathen, and gather you out of all countries, and will bring you into your own land. Then will I sprinkle clean water upon you, and ye shall be clean: from all your filthiness, and from all your idols, will I cleanse you. A new heart also will I give you, and a new spirit will I put within you: and I will take away the stony heart out of your flesh, and I will give you an heart of flesh. And I will put my spirit within you, and cause you to walk in my statutes, and ye shall keep my judgments, and do them. And ye shall dwell in the land that I gave to your fathers, and ye shall be my people, and I will be your God. I will also save you from all your uncleannesses: and I will call for the corn, and will increase it, and lay no famine upon you. And I will multiply the fruit of the tree and the increase of the field, that ye shall receive no more reproach of famine among the heathen. Then shall ye remember your own evil ways, and your doings that *were* not good, and shall lothe yourselves in your own sight for your iniquities and for your abominations. Not for your sakes do I *this*, saith the Lord GOD, be it known unto you: be ashamed and confounded for your own ways, O house of Israel. Thus saith the Lord GOD, In the day that I shall have cleansed you from all your iniquities, I will also cause *you* to dwell in the cities, and the wastes shall be builded. And the desolate land shall be tilled, whereas it lay desolate in the sight of all that passed by. And they shall say, This land which was desolate is become like the garden of Eden; and the waste and desolate and ruined cities *are become* fenced, *and* are inhabited. Then the heathen that are left round about you shall know that I the LORD build the ruined *places, and* plant that that was desolate; I the LORD have spoken *it*, and I will do *it*. Thus saith the Lord GOD, I will yet *for* this be inquired of by the house of Israel, to do *it* for them; I will increase them with men

> GOD's pity for His holy name.
>
> *Ezek.* xxxvi, 21-38.
>
> God operates for His own honor,
>
> —which man dishonors.
>
> His People distinguished.
>
> To have a new heart.
>
> GOD's promise to the sanctifiers of His name.
>
> Their great prosperity.
>
> The People to be humble for their sins.
>
> GOD performs not for man, but for His own name's sake.
>
> The rebuilding of cities and waste places.
>
> To be like the garden of Eden.
>
> The heathen shall know the LORD,
>
> —yet is man to inquire of GOD for these blessings.

§ 22. The Conclusion.

Great prosperity to ensue.

like a flock. As the holy flock, as the flock of Jerusalem in the solemn feasts; so shall the waste cities be filled with flocks of men: and they shall know that I am the LORD.

We must have trusted to ourselves, have sought to carry our own purposes.

Surely as that "GOD *is* not a man that He should lie; neither the Son of Man, that He should repent," must the fault be ours, that we have had to fight and pray, and pray and fight, for over two years, in order to obtain what we on both sides believe to be our just rights. We have fought in our own strength, have prayed Almighty GOD to accomplish our own selfish purposes, not His; and how long must these Christian Peoples pursue this course? How many more hundred thousands of our dear relations and friends, must be consigned to bloody graves—and many of us have them who are falling on both sides; often their spirits hurried from this world of probation to stand before the judgment bar of GOD, with their sins unrepented, no interest in the atonement purchased with our Saviour's blood! Oh, in GOD's name, how long before these Christian Peoples will consider their ways, and return to reason and to duty!

How many more victims must be sacrificed before we will change?

Having tried the efficacy of prayers separately, let us now try them together.

We have tried pretty effectually this plan of praying separately, and we are very likely to be restricted in our faith, to our own peculiar views of what is right and expedient. Let us now try another way and see what will be the effect; and this is the proposition we desire to make, after having consulted several Christians in the North: it is, that when the brethren in the South shall deem it advisable, they shall name a day, some two or three months in advance, to be observed as a day of fasting and prayer, for GOD's enlightening influences, to enable us to know our mutual rights and wrongs; to strengthen us to do our whole duty at any sacrifice; to give us hearts to make all atonement within our power; and to preserve us from like guilt in future.

The South to appoint a day of fasting and prayer.

The North will observe it, and probably Christians throughout the world.

We in the North will observe it for like holy objects; and we might reasonably expect Christians of the mother-land and on the Continent, to join their prayers with ours, that if consistent with GOD's holy purposes, this grandest experiment in free Government should not be jeopardized by disunion; and yet fervently will they and we in the North add, in the memorable words of our beloved Saviour, in His darkest hour, "nevertheless not my will, but Thine be done." We can, we will trust the GOD of Israel and of our fathers, for every good, whether for time or for eternity.

The Hebrews will also observe it.

The Hebrews, too, will unite with Christians in earnest prayer to the GOD of Abraham, Isaac and Jacob; to the Infinite Author of our system of Government, for the preservation of this example of the form which was given by Him to His chosen family of our race, their fathers, thousands of years ago.

Let our united supplication be, GOD DEFEND THE RIGHT.

MOB RULE AND STATE SOVEREIGNTY.

These two species of authority are totally incompatible. One or the other must be master. And of all men, the honest poor man is most deeply concerned in putting down the former, in exalting and establishing the latter.

It is the misfortune of Cities to have an undue proportion of ignorant population. They are also the chief resorts of knaves and villains of every description. A large part of the honest and ignorant, as well as of the knaves, are foreign born, and have come hither with vague ideas of liberty, deeming it their privilege and right to do whatever they please. Nor do native-born, intelligent American citizens properly instruct themselves or foreigners in their rights and duties. Recently, a leading conservative paper, discussing the topic of *allegiance*, affirmed the word had no significance in this country; that we were not *subjects*, but were all *Citizen-sovereigns.*

Because of this entire ignorance of the plainest and most important principles of our Government, do we witness such lamentable occurrences as the mobs in New York City from the 13th to the 20th July. The thieves and robbers, taking advantage of such teachings, and availing themselves of popular prejudices, as against the conscript act, work upon a few of the lowest and most ignorant of the population and incite them to riot, that the real instigators may rob and plunder. How can it be expected that the ignorant can have proper knowledge of duty and be submissive, when taught they are no subjects, but actual sovereigns?

No one is a sovereign in this land of equal rights. Sovereignty, the *Right of Command*, is in the possession of the People, the body of the Citizens of each State. To that Sovereignty does every individual within the boundaries of that State owe allegiance. Should one of these States grant away its *Right of Command* to a select *few*, an Aristocracy, as in some of the Swiss States, allegiance would be due to them; should it convey it to *one*, as in Britain, or Russia, allegiance would be due to the Monarch. Every individual in these States, from the President to the pauper or convict, is a subject of the State Sovereignty where he resides, and to it owes his allegiance.

These Sovereignties have created their State Agencies, by which they *exercise* their *Right of Command* in most affairs of Government. They have also joined together to create a Federal Agency for certain defined purposes of Government, and they wisely permitted this Agency to operate directly upon their respective subjects. This feature is, indeed, one of the most notable, important improvements in Federalism which we have made, and does *not*, in any degree, "nationalize" the system, as Madison imagined. To be able to protect against aggression, the Federal Agency must, in periods of emergency, have the control of the militia, and with cautious safeguards in the appointment of officers, was it granted. Congress has the power, and very properly, to compel from each State its quota, and the officials of the State Agency would violate their allegiance to their Sovereignty, did they in any way interfere, so long as the Federal Agency duly observes the restrictions of the Constitution.

Because Congress has wisely or unwisely incorporated unpopular provisions in the conscript act, as in the $300 clause, affords not the least excuse for resistance to the law; and if there be in the law essential wrongs, we have courts provided expressly to remedy them. In this land of law and order, never should forcible resistance to the laws be tolerated in the least. If any of these subjects, enjoying the protection and high privileges which these free States afford, can be so base as to resist lawful authority by mob violence, force alone should be used to quell it. A liberal use of powder and ball, with well-directed aim—fire blank cartridges after the mob is dispersed—is the only proper antidote. We are to have immense Cities in this country, whither are congregating the vile and wicked from all quarters of the globe. They must be taught effectually what they are to expect if they dare to insult the august majesty of any of these free Peoples' Sovereignty.

When principles of Government are once understood in this land of liberty, not licentiousness, we shall have few mobs; and the more summarily, the more severely are they quelled, the less the likelihood of repetition. The truest mercy, is the most extreme severity.

It has been the good fortune of the writer, to have witnessed the rise of a City. The hundred or two of souls that in 1832 lived about Fort Dearborn, have increased to 140,000, and possess a fair character as the City of Chicago. She has many circumstances to which she can refer with pride, but none equals the proud day of her triumph over passion, when her excitable, mercurial population, so nobly stood by law and order, and resisted the temptations and provocations to violence, consequent upon the outrages, by misjudging military officials, of sacred rights and Constitutional guarantees, in attempting to destroy the freedom of speech and of the press. And may our worthy Citizens never permit the glory of that day to be dimmed by any outburst of popular fury. Let Chicago, every City of the West, resolve through all this trying ordeal, to stand by law and order. Let there be no violent resistance of any tyrannical act, under any circumstances, unless attempts be made by military usurpers to interfere, in some way or other, with the expression of the sovereign will of these Peoples, through the ballot box. In that event, which may God forefend, let every Citizen defend his sacred rights to the death.

But fortunately for the future of our country, the political power is not now, is not hereafter to be, in Cities, which are most liable to mob rule. In the rural population, the little towns and hamlets, are the votes to be given that will direct the affairs of these existing Federal Republics, of the new one which, with God's blessing, is in time to be organized. The strongest ground of trust in the permanency of our institutions, under Providence, lies in the fact, that so large a part of the Citizens of the Federal Republic that is to be, are Farmers in New York, Pennsylvania, the South, and swarming in the West. And although immense Cities are speedily to arise here, within a half-century or so outstripping any on the sea-board, they will have little power against the dense population yet to occupy a country of such unsurpassed fertility, extent, and resources. It will not be denied, that the future power of this Continent, lies in the great Northwest; nor will it be questioned, that it is a precious boon of Providence, securing in the best possible manner the safety of all sections in the exercise of that power, that agriculture is, and must be indefinitely, the predominating interest of the West. Can any section, however highly favored and prosperous, find it advantageous and desirable to be separated from the West?

Let us all through the West feel the measure of our responsibilities in this trying, eventful period. Immense are our obligations to the old States, particularly to the South. Let the young West avail itself of this grand opportunity to repay its debt of gratitude.

www.ingramcontent.com/pod-product-compliance
Lightning Source LLC
LaVergne TN
LVHW011202110826
845150LV00006B/1295

* 9 7 8 1 4 2 5 5 1 8 6 8 4 *